Goodwill Impairment

BOCHUMER BEITRÄGE ZUR UNTERNEHMUNGSFÜHRUNG UND UNTERNEHMENSFORSCHUNG

Band 70

PETER LANG
Frankfurt am Main · Berlin · Bern · Bruxelles · New York · Oxford · Wien

Thorsten Sellhorn

Goodwill Impairment

An Empirical Investigation
of Write-Offs under SFAS 142

Mit deutscher Zusammenfassung

PETER LANG
Europäischer Verlag der Wissenschaften

Bibliographic Information published by Die Deutsche Bibliothek
Die Deutsche Bibliothek lists this publication in the Deutsche Nationalbibliografie; detailed bibliographic data is available in the internet at <http://dnb.ddb.de>.

Zugl.: Bochum, Univ., Diss., 2004

D 294
ISSN 0175-7105
ISBN 3-631-52707-1
US-ISBN 0-8204-7317-0

To my parents,
Dorothea & Dieter Sellhorn,
who are always there.

– Thank you.

Preface

Accounting for goodwill, the premium paid in business combinations over the value of the purchased identifiable net assets of the acquired business, is one of the most controversial issues in financial reporting. Generations of accounting academics and standard setters have struggled with the challenge of developing a theoretically consistent accounting treatment for goodwill. In the quest to promulgate high-quality accounting standards that generate relevant and reliable information for investors' decision-making needs, the U. S. Financial Accounting Standards Board (FASB) and the European International Accounting Standards Board (IASB) have recently adopted a dramatic change of policy: Goodwill is no longer amortized over its useful life. Rather, goodwill is carried on the books at historical cost until an impairment test indicates that its carrying value is no longer supported by the fair value of the business units to which it has been allocated.

This shift to an impairment-only approach has triggered heated debates for various reasons. Anecdotal evidence suggests that it has been shaped by the lobbying efforts from financial statement preparers as much as by conceptual considerations. Due to the late-1990s merger wave, goodwill is currently one of the most significant items in many firms' balance sheets. Critics argue that the impairment treatment brings unprecedented discretionary freedom to the process of measuring accounting income. At the same time, the increasing frequency in recent years of publicly disclosed accounting manipulations suggests that investors' faith in managers using their financial reporting discretion to paint accurate pictures of their companies' financial condition is at an all-time low. Preceding the adoption of the new standards on goodwill accounting in fiscal 2002, market participants were curious to see how firms would how firms would apply these standards once they were in effect.

Against this background, Thorsten Sellhorn empirically analyzes the factors associated with publicly traded U. S. firms' write-off behavior. Based on a conceptual review of the debate surrounding goodwill, he first analyzes in detail the empirical literature on goodwill and acquisition accounting in order to ascertain how managers and capital market participants perceive different aspects of accounting for business combinations. Under the assumption that goodwill impairment charges taken under SFAS 142 are discretionary asset write-offs, Thorsten Sellhorn then investigates what can be learned from prior research relating to such events. In this context, he systemizes the theoretical underpinnings of different financial reporting incentives, on which a wealth of empirical research on earnings management is based. This systematic literature review extends far beyond the boundaries of the discretionary write-off literature and is a self-contained scientific achievement on its own. Since financial reporting incentives can only manifest themselves where accounting standards involve choices, estimates, or judgment, Thorsten Sellhorn then carries out a comprehensive, in-depth analysis of SFAS 142 with regard to such discretionary parameters. He confirms the priors of most academics and other interested parties regarding the impairment-only approach: Management is unconstrained in determining the existence and amount of a goodwill write-off and thereby can produce accounting results that promote their own interests.

Based hereon, Thorsten Sellhorn carries out cross-sectional tests of a number of hypotheses about how U. S. publicly traded firms make the transition to SFAS 142 in the adoption year 2002. His findings might come as a reassurance to standard-setters, including the IASB: On average, write-off behavior appears to be driven by sample firms' economic developments rather than by managers' financial reporting incentives. However, closer inspection reveals that a certain portion of the sample, specifically the large, high-profile firms apparently use the goodwill write-off decision to manage their earnings.

Thorsten Sellhorn's thesis contributes to the accounting literature in several ways. First, his analyses of the goodwill and discretionary write-off literatures represent systematic and concise summaries of two diverse and complex areas of research. Second, his investigation of SFAS 142 provides a much-needed confirmation for the popular notion that this new approach to goodwill accounting is fraught with discretion and might therefore produce potentially unreliable results. Third, his empirical findings give important insights into management behavior not only with regard to goodwill accounting, but also relating to the adoption of a mandatory accounting change, the effect of which is recorded "below the line" as a change in accounting principle. His findings also show how conflicting incentives influence financial reporting behavior.

With the year 2005 approaching, many European firms are preparing to apply the IASB's International Financial Reporting Standards for the first time. The recently adopted IFRS 3 prescribes a goodwill accounting treatment essentially similar to that required by SFAS 142. It will be interesting to investigate whether Thorsten Sellhorn's results regarding U. S. firms' goodwill write-off behavior generalize to the European setting and how any deviations might be explained.

Bochum, June 2004 Bernhard Pellens

Foreword

This thesis was accepted in February 2004 as a doctoral dissertation by the school of business and economics (Fakultät für Wirtschaftswissenschaft) of the Ruhr-Universität Bochum, Germany. It emerged during my first four years as a research and teaching assistant at the Chair for International Accounting. My doctoral advisor, Prof. Dr. Bernhard Pellens, successfully aroused my interest in goodwill accounting with basically the first assignment that he gave me. I thank him for taking an active interest in my pursuits, for being an interested, encouraging, and extremely competent discussant, and for regularly excelling at being a great "Cheffe" in all respects.

I am also indebted to Prof. Dr. Hannes Streim, who served as a second examiner of my thesis and, in doing so, taught me to look at my chosen topic from a different perspective. In addition, I thank Prof. Dr. Dr. h. c. mult. Walther Busse von Colbe, Prof. Dr. Jochen Hundsdoerfer, Prof. Dr. Wim Kösters, and Prof. Dr. Stephan Paul for conducting my oral doctoral examinations.

Usually in forewords, companions from the professional environment and private friends are acknowledged in separate paragraphs. During recent years, I have been in the enviable position of seeing the line between these categories become indistinct. From among my great colleagues, I find it difficult to single anyone out. However, I feel I have to do so nonetheless: Dr. Rolf Uwe Fülbier and Dr. Joachim Gassen, true friends, have contributed critically to making these last five years a time that I will always treasure. Already "old hands" when I came along, they saw me through all phases, painful and otherwise, of my dissertation project. They could not even be deterred from proofreading the manuscript and contributing valuable, and some invaluable, suggestions and comments. Special thanks go to Joachim, first, for calling my attention to the fact that something like "empirical accounting research" exists and is actually pretty interesting, second, for helping me find out how it might be conducted, and, third, for rapping me on the knuckles when I was about to go astray.

I am also indebted to Dr. Franca Ruhwedel, my officemate in our beginning years, who tolerated my quirks with warm cordiality. She was also my fellow sufferer until she decided, long before I was able to, that she needed to stop whining and just write up the darn thing. Marc Richard, always helpful, cheerful, and sometimes refreshingly tongue-in-cheek, Kerstin Basche, fellow lunchtime runner, and Stefan Neuhaus, self-proclaimed "Snowboardgott", also helped my dissertation along by relieving me of some burdens in the sweltering summer of 2003, when cool air and time became very precious commodities. I also thank my other (former) fellow assistants, Dr. Andreas Bonse, Dr. Nils Crasselt, Karsten Detert, Dirk und Ralf Jödicke, Uwe Nölte, Dr. Ralf Schremper, Dr. Claude Tomaszewski, and Markus Weinreis, for helping me in ways they might not even be aware of. Our secretaries, Beate Preuß and Steffi Horten, who have always ensured that our potentially unorganized lot remained functional, and our student assistants, too numerous over the years to be listed in full, who procured huge stacks of literature as well as an aesthetic and very imaginative doctoral cap, are equally acknowledged.

In 2002, I had the opportunity of presenting an embryonic outline of my dissertation project at the PricewaterhouseCoopers doctoral colloquium of the European Accounting Association in Kalundborg, Denmark. I thank the workshop faculty, professors Philip Brown, Christian Leuz, Jan Mouritsen, and Peter Pope, for their comments and suggestions. I also acknowledge the contributions of my fellow student participants in the financial accounting section. Further, I thank the directors of the Institut für Unternehmungsführung und Unternehmensforschung and its executive secretary, Dr. Martin Seidler, as well as Peter Lang Publishing Group, impersonated by editor Dr. Hermann Ühlein, for admitting my dissertation into this series.

There are, of course, friends and loved ones beyond the workplace. Among them, I thank Maurizio Agresti, Andree Elsner, and those who would almost be Marcus[3] for providing much-needed perspective and tons of downright, plain fun!

However, my greatest debts I owe to my family, especially to my fiancée Melania and to my parents, who were always there for me, took pride in my endeavors (some more than others), and supported me in every way possible. I have small hope of being able to pay it all back – but I will try.

Bochum, June 2004 Thorsten Sellhorn

Zusammenfassung in deutscher Sprache

Goodwill-Wertberichtigung
– Eine empirische Untersuchung außerplanmäßiger Abschreibungen nach SFAS 142 –

SFAS 142, Goodwill and Other Intangible Assets, wurde im Juni 2001 vom Financial Accounting Standards Board (FASB) veröffentlicht. Der Standard bildet den vorläufigen Abschluss einer Jahrzehnte währenden Debatte über die angemessene Bilanzierungsweise für den erworbenen (derivativen) Geschäfts- oder Firmenwert (Goodwill). Das US-amerikanische Rechnungslegungsgremium vollzog damit eine Abkehr von der bis dato international üblichen Vorgehensweise, den Goodwill planmäßig über seine voraussichtliche Nutzungsdauer zu amortisieren. Nach dem nunmehr stattdessen geltenden Impairment-only Approach ist der Firmenwert regelmäßig einem Niederstwerttest zu unterziehen und bei Vorliegen einer Wertminderung außerplanmäßig abzuschreiben.

Diese Reform der Goodwill-Bilanzierung stieß auf ein überwiegend skeptisches Echo bei Bilanzadressaten und anderen Interessengruppen. Während die theoretisch-konzeptionelle Zweckmäßigkeit der neuen Vorgehensweise kaum bezweifelt wird, beklagen Kritiker das enorme Ausmaß bilanzpolitischer Ermessensspielräume, welches der Goodwill-Niederstwerttest dem Bilanzierenden eröffnet. Die ebenfalls ermessensbehaftete Vorgängerregel SFAS 121, Accounting for the Impairment of Long-Lived Assets and for Long-Lived Assets to Be Disposed Of, wurde immerhin durch die planmäßige Abschreibungspflicht des Goodwills entschärft, welche sicherstellte, dass dieser dubiose Bilanzposten über einen prognostizierbaren, wenn auch willkürlichen Zeitraum ergebniswirksam aufzulösen war. SFAS 142 indes bietet die Möglichkeit, den Goodwill unter Umständen auf unbestimmte Zeit in der Bilanz zu führen.

US-GAAP-Anwender hatten den neuen Standard im Geschäftsjahr 2002 erstmals zu befolgen. Auf Grund der speziell bei Erstanwendung sich bietenden erheblichen Ermessensspielräume sowie der abwartenden Haltung, mit der viele Bilanzadressaten der Neuregelung begegnen, bot sich den Unternehmen die einmalige Gelegenheit, ihr Wertberichtigungsverhalten mit ihren bilanzpolitischen Anreizen und Zielvorstellungen abzustimmen. In diesem Kontext wird in der vorliegenden Studie analysiert, wie die Manager einer umfangreichen Stichprobe börsennotierter US-Konzerne dieses bilanzpolitische Potenzial nutzen und zu welchem Grade die Wertberichtigungsentscheidung tatsächlich ökonomische Gegebenheiten widerspiegelt.

Zwecks Herleitung von Hypothesen über das erwartete Wertberichtigungsverhalten werden in der vorliegenden Arbeit zwei unterschiedliche Forschungsbereiche analysiert: In **Kapitel 2** zeigt eine Auswertung empirischer Befunde zur Goodwill-Debatte, dass Manager insbesondere die ergebnismindernden Konsequenzen der Goodwill-Bilanzierung fürchten und daher entsprechende Aufwendungen zu vermeiden und/oder zeitlich aufzuschieben suchen. Diesem Verhalten liegt offenbar die Annahme zu Grunde, Kapitalmarktteilnehmer beurteilten die Vorteilhaftigkeit von Transaktionen primär anhand der mit ihnen verbundenen bilanziellen Auswirkungen und seien außer Stande, entsprechende realökonomische Implikationen zu durchschauen. Kapitalmarktstudien zeichnen indes ein anderes Bild: Investoren durchschauen offenbar derart „kosmetische“ Bilanzpolitik und ziehen für ihre Erwartungsbildung vielfältige, über den veröffentlichten Abschluss hinaus gehende Informationsquellen heran.

In **Kapitel 3** wird die erstmalige Goodwill-Wertberichtigung beim Übergang auf SFAS 142 als Musterbeispiel einer ermessensbehafteten außerplanmäßigen Abschreibung (discretionary asset write-off) charakterisiert. Diese Gruppe von bilanziellen Vorgängen ist durch hohe und im Zeitablauf steigende ökonomische Signifikanz gekennzeichnet und basiert auf Rechnungslegungsregeln, die in hohem Maße auf Einschätzungen und Erwartungen des Managements zurückgreifen und daher bilanzpolitisch gestaltbar erscheinen. Sie sind nicht zuletzt auf Grund ihres hervorgehobenen Ausweises in den Rechenwerken zum Gegenstand umfangreicher empirischer Analysen geworden. Beruhend auf der Annahme, dass die Wertberichtigungsentscheidung weitgehend ins Ermessen des Managements gestellt ist, wurden primär die Bestimmungsgründe sowie die Kapitalmarkteinschätzung des Wertberichtigungsverhaltens empirisch überprüft. Durch eine kritische Analyse dieser Untersuchungen sollen die Implikationen des in der Vergangenheit beobachteten Wertberichtigungsverhaltens für die erstmalige Anwendung von SFAS 142 herausgearbeitet sowie ein theoretisches Fundament für die Hypothesenbildung gelegt werden. Die Ergebnisse zeigen, dass außerplanmäßige Wertberichtigungen vielfach ökonomische Wertminderungen reflektieren, häufig jedoch in höherem Maße durch die bilanzpolitischen Anreize des Managements erklärbar sind. Diese Anreize werden in zwei Gruppen unterteilt: Zum einen versuchen Manager, rechnungswesenbasierte Vertragsfolgen (erfolgsabhängige Entlohnungskomponenten, restriktive Klauseln in Kreditvereinbarungen) zu steuern; zum anderen ist ihnen an der Beeinflussung des Investorenpublikums gelegen. Als vielleicht beständigstes Forschungsergebnis erweist sich, dass ermessensbehaftete außerplanmäßige Abschreibungen vielfach im Anschluss an Wechsel in der Unternehmensspitze erfolgen, möglicherweise um Investoren die Beendigung verlustbringender Engagements und damit eine bevorstehende Trendwende zu signalisieren. Kapitalmarktuntersuchungen zeigen, dass derartige Wertberichtigungen vielfach antizipiert werden, und dass Ausmaß und Richtung einer Aktienkursreaktion entscheidend von der Art der vermittelten Informationen abhängt.

Die Erwartung, die erstmalige Anwendung von SFAS 142 werde durch bilanzpolitisches Verhalten geprägt sein, beruht auf der Annahme, dass der neue Standard tatsächlich in hohem Maße schwer objektivierbare Ermessensentscheidungen erfordert. Zu diesem Zwecke ist **Kapitel 4** der eingehenden Analyse des Impairment-only Approach gewidmet, um die Vielzahl der bilanzpolitisch nutzbaren Parameter aufzuzeigen. Die Untersuchung zeigt, dass nahezu alle Ebenen der Wertberichtigungsentscheidung auf schwer nachprüfbaren Einschätzungen und Erwartungen des Managements fußen. Dies gilt insbesondere im Geschäftsjahr der erstmaligen Anwendung, in welchem zentrale Weichenstellungen hinsichtlich Methodik und Bewertungsparametern erfolgen.

Kapitel 5 schließlich ist einer empirischen Untersuchung der erstmaligen Wertberichtigungsentscheidung bei einer umfangreichen Stichprobe börsennotierter US-Konzerne, die einen Goodwill ausweisen, gewidmet. Aus den im zweiten und dritten Kapitel vorgestellten theoretischen und empirischen Befunden werden zunächst Hypothesen über die Bestimmungsgründe des Wertberichtigungsverhaltens abgeleitet. Diese lassen sich in drei Kategorien unterteilen: Erstens hat der in SFAS 142 geforderte Niederstwerttest die Aufgabe, ökonomischen Wertverfall des Goodwills zu diagnostizieren. Aus diesem Grunde wird erwartet, dass die wirtschaftliche Entwicklung der Unternehmen, ausgedrückt in Kennzahlen der bilanziellen und aktienkursbasierten Performance, einen Zusammenhang mit der Wertberichtigungsentscheidung aufweist. Zweitens ist anzunehmen, dass sich das Management bei der Wertberichtigungsentscheidung von erwarteten, aus einer etwaigen Abschreibung resultierenden Vertragsfolgen leiten lässt. Folglich liegt die Vermutung nahe, dass zwischen dem Wertberichtigungsverhalten und Variablen, die derartige Vertragsfolgen repräsentieren, eine Relation besteht. Drittens, sofern Manager qua Wertberichtigungsentscheidung auf die Erwartungen des Kapitalmarktpublikums Einfluss nehmen wollen, ist davon auszugehen, dass Kenngrößen für entsprechende Anreize in einer Wechselbeziehung zum Wertberichtigungsverhalten stehen.

Die Ergebnisse deskriptiver Untersuchungen, univariater Vergleichstests sowie von Probit- und Tobit-Regressionen legen den Schluss nahe, dass die erstmalige SFAS 142-Wertberichtigungsentscheidung dem Grunde sowie der Höhe nach primär ökonomischen Wertverfall widerspiegelt, welcher sich bis zu zwei Jahre im Voraus dokumentieren lässt. Abschreibende Unternehmen sind zudem größer und höher verschuldet als diejenigen, deren Management sich gegen eine Wertberichtigung entscheidet. Diese Resultate sind auch bei Abwandlung der Testmethodik und bei Verwendung alternativer Variablendefinitionen stabil.

Eine Vertragsfolgen-basierte Motivation der Wertberichtigungsentscheidung lässt sich nicht nachzuweisen, was möglicherweise darin begründet ist, dass wegen fehlender Datenverfügbarkeit auf ungenaue Stellvertretervariablen zurückgegriffen werden musste. Ferner fehlen substanzielle Hinweise darauf, dass Unternehmen, die ihre Ergebnisziele übertreffen, ihr Wertberichtigungsverhalten an dem überschießenden Betrag orientieren.

Speziell bei der Untersuchung von Untergruppen der Stichprobe zeigt sich, dass bestimmte kapitalmarktbasierte Anreize das Wertberichtigungsverhalten zumindest teilweise beeinflusst zu haben scheinen. Dies dokumentiert sich darin, dass insbesondere großen Unternehmen offenbar daran gelegen ist, den Ausweis eines Jahresfehlbetrages zu vermeiden und, wo dies nicht gelingt, künftige Perioden durch Vorwegnahme drohenden Abschreibungspotenzials zu schonen. Offenbar sind diese Unternehmen daran interessiert, künftige Jahresergebnisse und Managementvergütungen vor drohenden Wertberichtigungen zu bewahren.

Zusammenfassend ist zu konstatieren, dass der in SFAS 142 kodifizierte Impairment-only Approach offenbar erfolgreich Wertminderungen feststellt, die möglicherweise unter der Vorgängerregel verborgen geblieben waren. Sofern darüber hinaus bilanzpolitische Motive die Wertberichtigungsentscheidung entscheidend geprägt haben, ist dies auf der Grundlage der hier gewählten Hypothesen und der angewandten Methodik nur eingeschränkt und lediglich für bestimmte Untergruppen der Stichprobe festzustellen.

In künftigen Forschungsarbeiten auf diesem Gebiet könnten insbesondere die Marktreaktionen auf erstmalige SFAS 142-Wertberichtigungen einer Untersuchung unterzogen werden. Auch wäre zu prüfen, ob und inwieweit sich die Bestimmungsgründe künftiger Wertberichtigungsentscheidungen von den bei der erstmaligen Anwendung vorherrschenden Determinanten unterscheiden. Ferner könnte ein diesbezüglicher Vergleich von SFAS 142 und der Vorgängerregel SFAS 121 Aufschlüsse darüber geben, ob das FASB die angestrebte Qualitätsverbesserung der Rechnungslegungsregeln in diesem Punkte erreichen konnte.

Table of Contents

List of abbreviations

adj.	adjusted
AktG	Aktiengesetz
ANOVA	Analysis of variance
APB	Accounting Principles Board
ASB	Accounting Standards Board (U. K.)
AT&T	American Telephone and Telegraph Company
BV	Book value
CEO	Chief executive officer
CFROI	Cash-flow return on investment
DCF	Discounted cash flow
DRSC	Deutsches Rechnungslegungs Standards Committee
DTE	Debt-to-equity
e.g.	exempli gratia
EBIT	Earnings before interest and taxes
EBITDA	Earnings before interest, taxes, depreciation, and amortization
ED	Exposure draft
EITF	Emerging Issues Task Force
EMH	Efficient market hypothesis
EPS	Earnings per share
esp.	especially
et al.	et alii
etc.	et cetera
EU	European Union
EVA	Economic value added
FASB	Financial Accounting Standards Board
FCF	Free cash flow
FIFO	First in, first out (method of inventory valuation)
FIN	FASB Interpretation
fn.	footnote
FRS	Financial Reporting Standard (issued by the APB)
FTE	Flow to equity

GAAP	Generally Accepted Accounting Principles
GAS	German Accounting Standard(s)
GASC	German Accounting Standards Committee
GDP	Gross domestic product
GW	Goodwill
HGB	Handelsgesetzbuch (the German Commercial Code)
I/B/E/S	Institutional Brokers Estimate System
i.e.	id est (that is)
IAS	International Accounting Standard(s)
IASB	International Accounting Standards Board
IBEI	Income before extraordinary items
IDW	Institut der Wirtschaftsprüfer (German Institute of Auditors)
IFRS	International Financial Reporting Standard(s)
IOA	Impairment-only approach
IOS	Investment opportunity set
IPO	Initial public offering
LIFO	Last in, first out (method of inventory valuation)
lit.	litera
LR	Likelihood ratio
M&A	Merger(s) and acquisition(s)
max	maximum
MBO	Management buyout
med	median
min	minimum
misc.	Miscellaneous
ML	Maximum likelihood
MTB	Market-to-book
MU	Monetary unit
MV	Market value
N	Number of firms
NA	not applicable
NCR	National Cash Register Company
NGW	Non-goodwill
NI	Net income

NWO	Non-write-off
NYSE	New York Stock exchange
OLS	Ordinary least squares
p.	page
P/E	Price-to-earnings
par.	paragraph(s)
pct	percentile
Ph.D.	Philosophiae Doctor (Doctor of Philosophy)
PP&E	Property, plant and equipment
pp.	pages
qrt	quartile
R&D	Research and development
ROA	Return on assets
ROE	Return on equity
RU	Reporting unit
S&P	Standard & Poor's
SAB	Staff Accounting Bulletin
SEC	Securities and Exchange Commission
SFAC	Statement of Financial Accounting Concepts
SFAS	Statement of Financial Accounting Standards
SIC	Standard Industrial Classification
SSAP	Statement of Standard Accounting Practice
SSRN	Social Science Research Network
StDev	Standard deviation
U. K.	United Kingdom
U. S. (A.)	United States (of America)
vol.	volume
WACC	Weighted-average cost of capital
WO	Write-off

List of symbols

(For more detail, refer to Table 6 in the text.)

α	intercept term
β	slope coefficient
ΔCEO	Dichotomous variable: 1 where a change in the CEO position occurred during 2001 or 2002; 0 otherwise
ΔPWOROA	Change in pre-write-off ROA in 2002 over regular ROA in 2001
ΔROA	Percentage point change in ROA between the fiscal years 2000 and 2001
ε	error term, disturbance term
AIP	Mean of assets-in-place, measured as the relation of PP&E (net of accumulated depreciation) to total market value, at the end of 2001 and 2002
DIF _PP	Difference between annual pre-write-off net income and the prior year's level, deflated by prior-period total assets, in 2002
DIF _Z	Difference between annual pre-write-off net income and zero, deflated by prior-period total assets, in 2002
DTE	Mean of the differences between the DTE ratio and the median DTE ratio in the two-digit SIC industry, at the end of 2001 and 2002
EQ	Pre-write-off common equity, deflated by pre-write-off total assets, at the end of 2002
FYR	Dichotomous variable: 1 where the fiscal year-end in 2001 is December 31; 0 otherwise
GW	Goodwill book value, deflated by total assets, measured at the end of 2001
H_A^{EC}	Economic factors hypothesis about the transitional SFAS 142 goodwill write-off amount
H_D^{EC}	Economic factors hypothesis about the transitional SFAS 142 goodwill write-off decision
H_A^{FR}	Financial reporting incentives hypothesis about the transitional SFAS 142 goodwill write-off amount
H_D^{FR}	Financial reporting incentives hypothesis about the transitional SFAS 142 goodwill write-off decision
HERF	Mean of the Herfindahl indexes of the two-digit SIC industry, measured as the sum of the squares of the market shares of each firm in the industry, at the end of 2001 and 2002
i	index variable for number of firms

MSH	Mean of the market shares, measured as the relation of firm sales to two-digit SIC industry sales, at the end of 2001 and 2002
MTB	MTB ratio, measured at the end of 2001
PME	Pre-managed earnings
R	Reserves available for earnings management
RATING	Long-term domestic issuer credit rating in 2001
RESTR	Restructuring cost (pre-tax), deflated by total assets, measured at the end of 2002
RET	Cumulative stock performance, measured over the fiscal years 2000 and 2001
SIZE	Size, measured by the mean of market values of equity at the end of 2001 and 2002
SIZE_LOG	Natural logarithm of SIZE
SPEC	Special items and write-downs (pre-tax), deflated by total assets, measured at the end of 2002
t	index variable for number of time periods
T	Target earnings figure
TARGET_PP	Dichotomous variable: 1 where annual pre-write-off net income is above the prior year's level in 2002; 0 otherwise
TARGET_Z	Dichotomous variable: 1 where annual pre-write-off net income is above zero in 2002; 0 otherwise
TGWO_A	Amount of *transitional* SFAS 142 goodwill write-off, deflated by prior-period total assets, measured at the end of the first fiscal quarter 2002
TGWO_D	Dichotomous variable: 1 where a *transitional* SFAS 142 goodwill write-off is recorded; 0 otherwise
WO_A	Write-off amount
WO_D	Dichotomous variable: 1 where a write-off is recorded; 0 otherwise
y	dependent variable
y*	latent dependent variable

List of figures

List of tables

"No one returns with good-will to the place
which has done him a mischief."

Phaedrus (1st century A.D.),
Fables, Book i, Fable 18, 1.

1 Introduction

1.1 Problem

In the first quarter of 2002, media giant AOL Time Warner shocked the financial world by announcing a $54 billion write-off of goodwill. Due to a fourth-quarter goodwill charge of another $45.5 billion, the company ended up posting the largest one-year loss in U. S. corporate history – a $100 billion deficit roughly equal to the GDP of Hungary.[1]

Deutsche Telekom AG, the German telecommunications group, soon followed suit: In November of 2002, it announced a three-quarter loss of €24.5 billion, unprecedented in Germany after World War II. Much of this deficit was due to goodwill write-offs related to the firm's acquisition of U. S. mobile telecommunications firms VoiceStream and Powertel in 2001. These charges were announced immediately after a new CEO had taken office. In the preceding months, financial analysts had repeatedly urged management to write off the inflated goodwill on Deutsche Telekom's books. The stock price dropped on the announcement day of the write-off but bounced back up the day after. Commentators suggest that the write-offs allowed the new CEO to start with a "clean slate". The firm finished the year with a net loss of €24.6 billion.[2]

Both firms' write-offs were recorded in the adoption year of new accounting rules: Statement of Financial Accounting Standards (SFAS) 142, *Goodwill and Other Intangible Assets,* introduced in June 2001, requires that firms no longer amortize goodwill over its useful life but review it for impairment at least annually.[3] The standard took effect for fiscal years beginning on or after December 15, 2001.[4] Firms were given a full year to

1 These events were covered in the business press; for example, see Kort (2003) and Taub (2003).

2 Refer to Deutsche Telekom AG's consolidated U. S. GAAP financial statements for the period ending on December 31, 2002, filed with the SEC on form 20-F.

3 Under previous rules, goodwill was amortized over a useful life not to exceed 40 years. See Accounting Principles Board (APB) Opinion 17, *Intangible Assets,* par. 29. It is important to note that impairment tests for goodwill had also been required *before* SFAS 142. See Henning, Shaw and Stock (2002, p. 3). However, these tests only had to be conducted when indicators of a decline in value were present. Pre-SFAS 142 accounting rules for goodwill are explained in greater detail in section 2.3.2.2.1 below.

4 At the same time, SFAS 141, *Business Combinations,* became applicable. Among other provisions, it eliminated the popular pooling-of-interests method of accounting for business combinations.

apply its provisions to the goodwill balances on their books. Any write-offs resulting from this transitional test were disclosed as the effect of a change in accounting principle.

According to the Financial Accounting Standards Board,[5] this "impairment-only approach" provides financial information that more faithfully reflects the economic impact of acquired goodwill on firm value than does the previously prevalent goodwill amortization. The goodwill impairment test prescribed by SFAS 142 is expected to adequately capture goodwill impairment.[6] Apparently, this reasoning and its desire to converge its standards with U. S. GAAP convinced the International Accounting Standards Board[7] to prescribe widely similar rules in its International Financial Reporting Standard (IFRS) 3, *Business Combinations*, in March 2004.[8]

The outcome of a five-year standard-setting process, SFAS 142 was the subject of heated discussion, both before and after its final publication.[9] The standard setter's long-standing determination to ban the much-abused and conceptually flawed pooling-of-interests method collided with firms' desire to circumvent the earnings strain associated with goodwill amortization.[10] Amongst an academic dispute regarding the economic substance of the goodwill asset,[11] the FASB ultimately concluded that an impairment-only approach was theoretically superior to amortizing goodwill over some arbitrary estimate of useful life.[12] However, in the mind of some, that decision merely represented the result

---

5 The Financial Accounting Standards Board (FASB) is the private-sector organization responsible for developing financial reporting standards for firms required to file financial statements with the U. S. Securities and Exchange Commission (SEC). For details, refer to Miller, Redding and Bahnson (1998). See also Pellens (2001, pp. 102-13).

6 See SFAS 142.B99.

7 The International Accounting Standards Board (FASB), based in London, is a private-sector standard-setting body. Recent European Union (EU) regulation requires that, from 2005, its pronouncements be applied in the consolidated financial statements of most firms listed on capital markets within the EU. For a detailed description of these requirements, refer to Kahle (2003) and Kirsch (2003).

8 Along with IFRS 3, amendments to IAS 36, *Impairment of Assets*, and IAS 38, *Intangible Assets*, were adopted. Interestingly, several of the IASB members passing IFRS 3, including *James J. Leisenring* and *Anthony T. Cope*, formerly served with the FASB when it issued SFAS 141 and 142.

9 For a detailed summary of that debate and a historical perspective on goodwill accounting, refer to section 2.3 below.

10 Under the pooling-of-interests method, no goodwill is recorded. A comparison of the financial statement effects of the pooling-of-interests method and the purchase method is presented in section 2.3.1.

11 In Germany, much of the debate surrounding goodwill accounting focused on the question whether goodwill was a "Vermögensgegenstand" (the German asset concept) at all. Refer to section 2.2 below.

12 One of the FASB's main arguments for abandoning amortization was that "at least part of goodwill may be a nonwasting asset and thus may have an indefinite life" (SFAS 142.B71).

of political horse-trading.[13] Nonetheless, it is widely accepted that SFAS 142 represents one more step towards a fair value-based accounting model.[14]

In the aftermath, attention turned to the details of SFAS 142. It was frequently argued that, while conceptually sound,[15] the standard provided firms with almost unprecedented discretion regarding the decision whether and how much of goodwill to write off.[16] Given SEC Chairman Levitt's (1998) harangue against financial statement manipulation, most commentators were concerned that managers would use this discretion to engage in earnings management to achieve their financial reporting objectives, thwarting the FASB's effort to promote financial statement reliability.[17] However, the analyst community greeted SFAS 142 with downright indifference,[18] although goodwill charges are likely to become less predictable and, as a consequence, bottom-line earnings more volatile, which might impair earnings (and forecast) quality.

In Germany, considerable debate surrounded the issue of whether consolidated U. S. GAAP financial statements established under SFAS 142 fulfill the requirements of section 292a par. 2 Handelsgesetzbuch[19], which would relieve firms from the obligation of establishing additional German GAAP consolidated accounts. Among other criteria, such foreign-GAAP statements would have to be established according to "internationally accepted accounting principles", e.g. U. S. GAAP, and be consistent with EU financial reporting directives, which, as was maintained by some, require goodwill amortization.[20]

---

13 See, for example, Beresford (2001), Busse von Colbe (2001a), and Pellens and Sellhorn (2001b, p. 713).

14 See, for example, Hitz and Kuhner (2002, pp. 279-81).

15 Conceptual criticism that did occur focused mainly on the commingling of purchased and internally generated goodwill, the argument that the useful life of goodwill is indefinite, and the decision not to allow goodwill to be written up to fair value. See Pellens and Sellhorn (2001a, pp. 1685-6).

16 See, for example, Hommel (2001b, p. 1944) and Teitler-Feinberg (2001, p. 336).

17 See, for example, Hitz and Kuhner (2002, p. 285) and the literature cited there.

18 According to Alich (2001), some analysts view goodwill as irrelevant to firm valuation, recommending that investors focus on earnings numbers that exclude goodwill charges, such as earnings before interest, taxes, depreciation, and amortization (EBITDA).

19 The Handelsgesetzbuch (HGB) is the German Commercial Code. It contains, among other regulations, the accounting rules applicable to German firms' individual and consolidated financial statements.

20 The German Accounting Standards Committee (GASC) assumed an affirmative stance on this issue when it adopted its German Accounting Standard (GAS) 1a, *Exempting Consolidated Financial Statements in accordance with § 292a of the Commercial Code*, in January of 2002. Altenburger (2002), Arbeitsgruppe "Normierung der Rechnungslegung" (2002), Busse von Colbe (2001c), Kleindiek (2001), Pellens and Sellhorn (2001a, pp. 1686-8), and others contribute to the related discussion.

1.2 Research question and contribution

As of January 1, 2002,[21] publicly traded U. S. firms carried on their books goodwill balances in excess of $1.4 trillion.[22] In this dissertation, concerns about earnings management potential inherent in SFAS 142 are investigated by a detailed analysis of its discretionary parameters. An empirical analysis of the factors associated with the transitional SFAS 142 goodwill write-off behavior exhibited by publicly traded U. S. firms is conducted in order to assess whether firms used the new rules to manage their earnings.[23] It is hypothesized that a firm's write-off behavior is influenced by economic determinants (i.e. goodwill impairment) as well as two groups of financial reporting incentives.[24] The first group stems from positive accounting theory, according to which managers have incentive to influence reported accounting numbers because economic consequences arise from firms' accounting-based contracts with third parties. These contracts include compensation agreements as well as debt covenants. The second cluster of incentives rests on the notion that managers attempt to influence the perceptions of capital market participants, including investors and rating agencies, about their firms' future prospects.

The initial application of this standard represents a unique setting to investigate the financial reporting behavior of managers with regard to a variety of fundamental accounting issues. First, the analysis contributes to a large body of literature concerned with the determinants of discretionary financial reporting decisions in general.[25] However, much of this literature relies on potentially noisy aggregate measures to detect earnings man-

---

21 SFAS 142 was adopted as of this date by calendar-year firms.

22 These data pertain to 22,078 firms included in the Compustat Industrial Annual tape. Jennings, LeClere and Thompson (2001, p. 22) point out that goodwill is likely to be even more relevant in the future since most of the large acquisitions in the past had been accounted for as poolings of interests. Had the purchase method been used, substantial goodwill amounts would have been recognized.

23 Goodwill write-off behavior under previous accounting standards is not investigated here because the SFAS 142 adoption setting is fundamentally different in several respects from prior years. For example, prior goodwill write-offs were recorded in addition to annual amortization charges, biasing their potential amounts downwards. In addition, incentives are different when pre-SFAS 142 impairment charges are reported "above the line" versus "below the line" as an accounting change. For a comparison of the two accounting regimes, refer to Segal (2003). See also Henning, Shaw and Stock (2002).

24 These determinants are discussed in detail in section 3.3.2 below.

25 This research is referred to as the "earnings management" literature. Beside the determinants of earnings management behavior, researchers in this area are also interested in capital market responses to that behavior. Comprehensive reviews include Beneish (2001), Dechow and Skinner (2000), Fields, Lys and Vincent (2001), Healy and Wahlen (1999), and Schipper (1989). Refer to section 3.3.1.2.

agement.[26] Studies of specific accounts appear to be more promising tests of discretionary financial reporting behavior.[27]

Second, a distinct subset of the research focuses on the determinants and consequences of discretionary asset write-offs.[28] Researchers find this area interesting largely because of, first, the economic significance of the write-offs and their resulting effect on firms' financial statements,[29] second, the flexibility in (or, in some cases, even the absence of) applicable accounting guidance,[30] and, third, the recent issuance of new accounting pronouncements.[31] The present study adds to this field by focusing on write-off behavior that not only relates to a balance sheet item of outstanding economic magnitude, but that is furthermore guided by discretionary accounting rules only recently introduced.[32]

Third, choosing the adoption year of a new accounting standard provides the opportunity to study the strategic nature of financial reporting decisions. It is argued that the requirement of consistency implies that firms' choice of parameters for the transitional impairment test limits their ability to modify these parameters in the future to accommodate changing financial reporting incentives.[33]

Fourth, the initial application of SFAS 142 yields fresh insights into the age-old debate on accounting for business combinations and the residual intangible item known as "goodwill". Bottom-line income of acquisitive firms, ceteris paribus, will be either boosted by the absence of goodwill amortization or slashed by a goodwill write-off.

---

26 Models of total accruals, originally used by Healy (1985) and DeAngelo (1986), as well as models of discretionary accruals, introduced by Jones (1991), are widely used in the research. These models are frequently criticized with respect to their lack of power and reliability to measure the extent of earnings management. McNichols (2000) provides an excellent discussion. See also section 3.3.2.2 below.

27 See, for example, Beneish (2001, p. 11), Bernard and Skinner (1996, p. 324), and McNichols (2000, pp. 333-5).

28 Alciatore et al. (1998) and Wilson (1996) review of the related literature. Refer to section 3.3 below.

29 See Francis, Hanna and Vincent (1996, p. 121) and Riedl (2002, p. 2).

30 See Alciatore et al. (1998, pp. 1-2).

31 See Alciatore et al. (1998, pp. 1-2). For essentially the same reasons, Healy and Wahlen (1999, S. 372) argue that charges such as loan loss provisions of banks and claim loss reserves of insurance companies are interesting objects of study.

32 SFAS 142 requires that the implied fair value of goodwill be assessed. According to Wilson (1996, p. 173), goodwill is inherently difficult to value since it cannot be measured directly or even observed in an active market. With specific regard to SFAS 142, Riedl (2002, p. 4) argues that write-offs of goodwill generated under this standard, perhaps even more than other asset write-offs, are subject to management discretion, which makes them ideal earnings management instruments.

33 An important criterion in the FASB's Conceptual Framework, consistency stands for "[c]onformity from period to period with unchanging policies and procedures." See SFAC 2, *Qualitative Characteristics of Accounting Information*, Glossary of Terms.

Firms' perspectives on goodwill accounting and the purchase/pooling controversy have the potential to yield predictions as to their exercise of discretion in applying SFAS 142.

Finally, since any transitional impairment is reported as the effect of a change in accounting principle,[34] issues regarding the use of non-recurring items to manage financial reports also arise in this setting.[35] It has been maintained that such transitory items are less costly to manage than other, more persistent accounts.[36]

1.3 Outline

This dissertation proceeds as delineated in Figure 1.

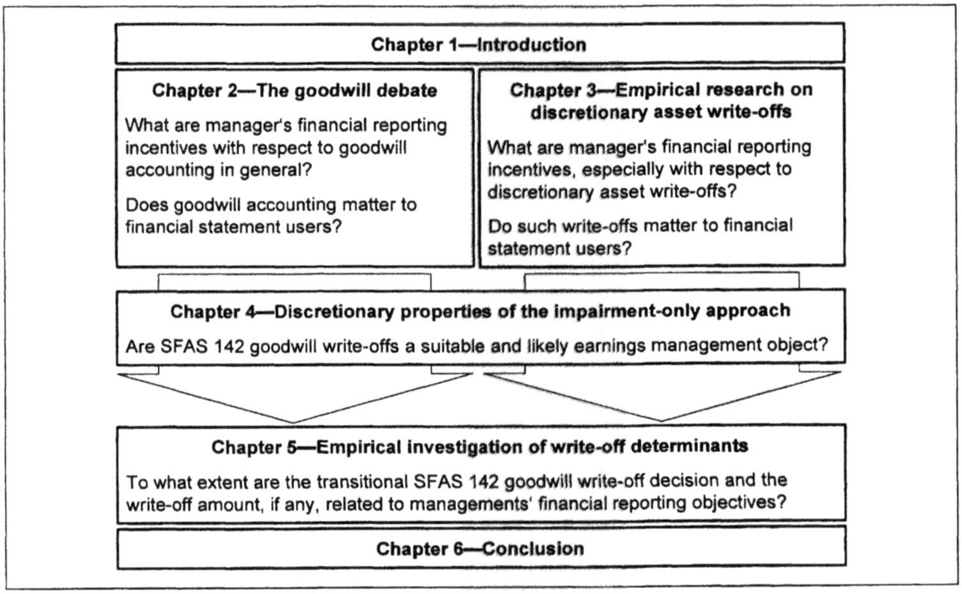

Figure 1: Structure of the analysis

34 The charge appears in the income statement between the captions "extraordinary items" and "net income". While any goodwill impairment had to be measured as of January 1, 2002, it might not have been disclosed until far into 2003, as a restatement of the first-quarter report of the adoption year. See SFAS 142.55-6. Therefore, this information might have been ignored by capital market participants as "old news", a fact that might have made management less reluctant to disclose it.

35 It has been alleged that firms use labels such as "non-recurring" and "unusual" to mask items that reduce reported income. This behavior is sometimes referred to as "classificatory smoothing". For example, refer to Barnea, Ronen and Sadan (1976) and section 3.3.2.4.4. Under U. S. GAAP, the generic term "non-recurring items" comprises unusual/infrequent items, extraordinary items, discontinued operations, and accounting changes. See White, Sondhi and Fried (2003, pp. 52-61).

36 See Bartov (1993, p. 840) and Marquardt and Wiedman (2002, p. 5). For a discussion of this notion, refer to 3.3.2.4.8 below.

In **chapter 2**, the enduring debate about goodwill and the related controversy surrounding the purchase and pooling-of-interests methods of accounting for business combinations are summarized. The reflections are intended to establish why goodwill is viewed as a material and controversial item, the accounting treatment of which might affect management's utility, e.g. by influencing how financial statement users perceive firm performance. Much of the chapter is dedicated to reviewing the research in this area and to drawing conclusions from the findings.

The main purpose of **chapter 3** is to establish a theoretical basis for hypothesis development and to highlight the contribution of this study. For this purpose, a broad body of research on discretionary asset write-offs and certain related one-time charges is reviewed. The first branch of this literature focuses on the determinants of these high-profile accounting events, attempting to discriminate between economic explanations (impairment) and factors that indicate earnings management. The second research program, complementary to the first, analyzes how capital market participants respond to discretionary asset write-offs. For both aspects, the respective motivations and research questions are outlined, followed by analyses of the theoretical underpinnings and hypotheses. A discussion of the findings and their implications concludes the chapter.

In **chapter 4**, the main provisions of SFAS 142 are analyzed. Much of this dissertation rests on the notion that write-off behavior is influenced by financial reporting incentives. Therefore, it is critical to show that a transitional goodwill write-off recorded under SFAS 142 can be characterized as a discretionary write-off with respect to its existence, amount, and timing. Consequently, the bulk of the chapter focuses on an in-depth analysis of SFAS 142, isolating the parameters involving estimates, judgment, and other areas of managerial discretion.

The discretionary nature of the impairment-only approach exposed, an empirical investigation of firms' initial application of the goodwill impairment test under SFAS 142 is presented in **chapter 5**. Hypotheses are developed to predict the occurrence and, if any, magnitude of goodwill write-offs, depending on economic factors and firm characteristics that represent various financial reporting incentives. Sample selection and data are discussed next. After that, descriptive statistics, univariate comparisons, and multivariate regression results are presented and certain econometric issues and other limitations are addressed.

In **chapter 6**, the findings of the study are summarized and suggestions for further research are discussed.

2 The goodwill debate

2.1 Chapter overview

As noted above, goodwill accounts for a massive portion of total assets in many firms. The accounting for this balance sheet item, affecting a firm's financial position as well as earnings performance, is controversial today and has been for many years. Until recently, accounting standards in most jurisdictions, including the U. S., allowed certain acquisitions to be accounted for using the pooling-of-interests method,[37] under which goodwill does not arise. Today, the purchase method is widely established internationally as the only method of accounting for business combinations.[38] Ayers, Lefanowicz and Robinson (2000b) document that using the pooling method generates enormous amounts of unrecognized assets. Recording and amortizing these assets, as required under the purchase method, would produce significant balance sheet and income statement effects.[39] From the viewpoint of most firms, these effects are undesirable.[40]

In this chapter, the issues central to the enduring controversy related to the accounting for business combinations and any resulting goodwill are presented.[41] With regard to the research question outlined in section 1.2 above, this chapter contributes evidence on managers' financial reporting incentives as well as investors' views pertaining to this specific accounting issue. The chapter is organized as follows: In section 2.2, the concept of goodwill and possible viewpoints regarding its economic characteristics are introduced. Section 2.3 contains a summary of the main arguments brought forth by various contributors to the debate on accounting for goodwill and the purchase/pooling choice. First, the financial statement effects of the purchase and pooling methods of accounting for business combinations and goodwill are illustrated. Second, accounting alternatives for goodwill are derived conceptually from its economic attributes. Third, the historical development and present status of relevant accounting rules in selected jurisdictions is presented and, where possible, links between the goodwill debate and contemporary

---

37 For ease of exposition, this method is hereafter referred to as the "pooling method".

38 Despite mounting criticism, the pooling method is still permitted under German GAAP.

39 For a simple simulation of these effects, refer to section 2.3.1 below.

40 Ayers, Lefanowicz and Robinson (2000b, pp. 12-16) analyze 269 pooling acquisitions made during the period 1992-1997. They document that key ratios (ROE, EPS, and MTB ratio) of the acquirer deteriorate significantly when calculated "as if" the purchase method had been used. See also Pellens and Sellhorn (1999).

41 This controversy is hereafter referred to as the "goodwill debate" and its subject, accounting for business combinations and goodwill, as "goodwill accounting".

standard-setting decisions are established.[42] Fourth, financial statement preparers' stance on the goodwill debate is reviewed. Finally, a theoretical perspective, taking users' behavior into account, on preparers' arguments is developed. Section 2.4 contains a review of empirical evidence relevant to two aspects of the goodwill debate: First, evidence on managers' financial reporting incentives surrounding goodwill and the purchase/pooling choice is analyzed. Second, investors' views regarding these accounting issues are inferred from empirical findings. The assumption underlying this literature review is that managers' and investors' standpoints in the goodwill debate are informative about managers' expected behavior upon transition to the impairment-only approach under SFAS 142. Finally, in section 2.5, the implications from this chapter are summarized.

2.2 The concept of goodwill

The concept of goodwill is central to this dissertation. Therefore, a brief review of terminological and conceptual issues seems warranted.[43] According to some, the "term 'goodwill' defies precise definition"[44] and is "neither 'fowl nor fish'".[45] Depending on the context, it is used in at least three different ways that are not without overlap and lack clear-cut separating lines.

First, goodwill is an accounting concept. It is a technical residual that results when the value of a firm's net assets (assets less liabilities) is subtracted from firm value as a whole.[46] The two components of this difference are defined in terms of the recognition and measurement rules of a given financial reporting system. Whenever goodwill arises from the acquisition of one entity or business by another, the term "purchased" or "acquired" goodwill denotes the goodwill inherent in the acquired entity.[47] Absent an acquisition, the term "internally generated" goodwill is used. Since internally generated good-

---

42 A strictly positivistic approach is adopted, i.e. the emphasis is on explanation, as opposed to normative prescription, of accounting practice. The term "accounting practice" is used here to comprise firms' actual financial reporting and lobbying behavior as well as standard-setters' decision processes.

43 For a detailed, historical and linguistic review of the term "goodwill" and its synonyms, refer to Gräber (1981, pp. 5-17).

44 Gomes (1988, p. 23). See also Huijgen (1996, p. 54).

45 Falk and Gordon (1977, p. 443).

46 See Hoyle, Schaefer and Doupnik (1998, p. 52): "Traditionally, the term goodwill has referred to a computationally derived excess payment". Kieso, Weygandt and Warfield (2001, p. 608) introduce labels such as "plug" or "gap filler" to highlight these characteristics. See also Lüdenbach and Frowein (2003, p. 217).

47 The term "acquisition" is used here in a non-technical way and refers to a wide variety of instances in which an entity purchases another entity's shares (share deal), assets (asset deal), or another group of assets that constitutes a business.

will is not recorded under most accounting regimes, this dissertation focuses on purchased goodwill.[48]

Definitions of purchased goodwill are widely similar across major accounting regimes.[49] The relevant pronouncements of selected financial reporting standard-setters include the following:[50]

> "The excess of the cost of an acquired entity over the net of the amounts assigned to assets acquired and liabilities assumed shall be recognized as an asset referred to as goodwill" (SFAS 141.43).[51]
>
> "Any excess of the cost of the acquisition over the acquirer's interest in the fair value of the identifiable assets and liabilities acquired as at the date of the exchange transaction should be described as goodwill and recognized as an asset" (IAS 22.41).[52]

---

48 Measuring a firm's internally generated goodwill involves a great deal of subjectivity, which casts doubt on the reliability of such information. See also Brunovs and Kirsch (1991, p. 139) and Kieso, Weygandt and Warfield (2001, p. 608). In the words of Chauvin and Hirschey (1994, p. 161), internally generated goodwill is not capitalized because "opponents refer to internally-generated goodwill numbers as soft and not based upon independent, arm's length transactions."

49 Brunovs and Kirsch (1991, p. 139) note this fact for the standards in English-speaking countries.

50 The prevalent German term is "Geschäfts- oder Firmenwert".

51 Under the predecessor standards, goodwill was defined very similarly: "[T]he excess of the cost of the acquired company over the sum of the amounts assigned to identifiable assets acquired less liabilities assumed should be recorded as goodwill" (APB Opinion 16, *Business Combinations*, par. 87). „[T]he excess of the cost of an acquired company over the sum of identifiable net assets" (APB Opinion 17.1).

52 In its December 2002 Exposure Draft (ED) 3, *Business Combinations*, the IASB refers to the cost of goodwill as "the excess of the cost of the business combination over the acquirer's interest in the net fair value of the identifiable assets, liabilities and contingent liabilities [...]" (ED 3.50). This definition was carried over into the final standard; see IFRS 3.51 (b).

The German standard setters' definitions are largely equivalent: For asset deals accounted for in a firm's separate financial statements, section 255 par. 4 HGB states: „Als Geschäfts- oder Firmenwert darf der Unterschiedsbetrag angesetzt werden, um den die für die Übernahme eines Unternehmens bewirkte Gegenleistung den Wert der einzelnen Vermögensgegenstände des Unternehmens abzüglich der Schulden im Zeitpunkt der Übernahme übersteigt".

The following definition applies to acquisitions effected by share deals and accounted for in consolidated financial statements: „Ein bei der Verrechnung nach Absatz 1 Satz 2 Nr. 2 entstehender oder ein nach Zuschreibung oder Verrechnung nach Absatz 1 Satz 3 verbleibender Unterschiedsbetrag ist in der Konzernbilanz, wenn er auf der Aktivseite entsteht, als Geschäfts- oder Firmenwert ... auszuweisen" (section 301 par. 3 HGB).

The German private-sector standard setter, the German Accounting Standards Committee (GASC), defines goodwill in par. 27 of its German Accounting Standard (GAS) 4, *Purchase Accounting*, as follows: „When the cost of acquisition exceeds the interest of the acquirer in the net amount of the fair values of the assets and liabilities acquired, the excess should be recognised as goodwill in the consolidated balance sheet".

Consistent with this "technical" view, in these definitions provided in standard setters' pronouncements no attempt is made to specify the factors influencing the acquirer's decision to incur such an excess payment or to characterize its economic nature, probably because "the conditions that can influence a purchase price are virtually unlimited".[53]

Recognizing the shadowy existence of internally generated goodwill, standard textbook definitions also center on purchased goodwill.

> "The excess of acquisition cost over the parent's equity in the fair value of the identifiable net assets of the subsidiary on the date of acquisition".[54]
>
> "Whenever the price paid in a purchase exceeds total fair market value, all of the subsidiary's assets and liabilities are consolidated at fair market value with the additional payment allocated to the intangible asset goodwill".[55]
>
> "[T]he excess of cost over fair value of the identifiable net assets acquired."[56]

Note that goodwill is consistently based on the acquirer's share in the net assets of the acquiree and on the purchase price paid for that share. Only recently, the IASB proposed to deviate from that concept when it re-introduced the notion of "full goodwill".[57] Under this approach goodwill would be calculated as the excess of the acquiree's total value over the fair value of all of its net assets, even where less than 100% of the acquiree is purchased. In effect, goodwill would be assigned to minority interests in equity.[58]

Second, goodwill can be interpreted from a valuation perspective. It denotes the difference between the values generated by two conceptually different valuation methods, an earning-capacity value and a net asset value.[59] In this respect, it is structurally similar to the accounting concept of purchased goodwill introduced above.[60] However, it abstracts

---

53 See Hoyle, Schaefer and Doupnik (1998, p. 52). One notable exception is IFRS 3.52, which states that goodwill "represents a payment made by the acquirer in anticipation of future economic benefits from assets that are not capable of being individually identified and separately recognized."

54 Jeter and Chaney (2001, p. 936).

55 Hoyle, Schaefer and Doupnik (1998, p. 52).

56 Kieso, Weygandt and Warfield (2001, p. 608).

57 That concept had been briefly discussed in Europe in the late 1980s when the European Community's financial reporting directives were transformed into national laws. For example, refer to Kommission Rechnungswesen (1985, p. 273). Busse von Colbe and Ordelheide (1993, p. 245) also briefly mention this "reine Neubewertungsmethode".

58 Refer to Pellens, Basche and Sellhorn (2003) for a description, historical overview and criticism of this concept. See also Grünberger and Grünberger (2003).

59 The German terms are "Ertragswert" and "Substanzwert", respectively. For example, refer to Ballwieser (1998, p. 283) and, in the specific goodwill context, Möhrle (1999, pp. 22-31).

60 See also Holthausen and Watts (2001, p. 54).

from concrete, prescribed definitions of firm value and the value of net assets.[61] Under a valuation approach, goodwill represents the present value of a firm's future earnings in excess of a normal rate of return.[62] This excess earning capacity cannot be separated from the business as a whole. It stems from imperfect markets, since all firms would earn a normal rate of return in the absence of market imperfections.[63]

With the introduction of SFAS 142 and the IASB's IFRS 3, this valuation notion of goodwill has attained greater significance in accounting, because firms are required to test goodwill associated with their reporting units[64] for impairment. In that process, reporting units must be valued as a whole unless quoted market prices are observable.[65]

Third, goodwill is a broader management concept. When the economic characteristics of goodwill, i.e. the reasons behind the existence of this technical accounting residual, are analyzed, several factors are usually cited. These factors represent sources of future excess earnings that can be exploited by management.[66] These include, in no particular order, a loyal customer base,[67] potential for restructuring,[68] synergies between the acquirer's and the acquiree's operations,[69] real options,[70] the creative ability of a research group,[71] specific market conditions that surrounded the acquisition,[72] a favorable location,[73] a premium paid to acquire control,[74] and several others.[75]

---

61 In that sense, it corresponds to the accounting concept of internally generated goodwill.

62 See, for example, Baker, Lembke and King (1996, pp. 11, 14), Beams, Brozovsky and Shoulders (2000, p. 18), Chauvin and Hirschey (1994, p. 162), Choi and Lee (1991, p. 226), Gomes (1988, p. 24), Hendriksen and van Breda (2001, pp. 640-2), Hoyle, Schaefer and Doupnik (1998, p. 52), and Jensen et al. (1994, p. 15).

63 See Falk and Gordon (1977, p. 448).

64 The IASB's term is "cash-generating units".

65 Refer to section 4.5.1 for details.

66 This is the point made by Gynther (1969, p. 247), who stresses that goodwill is *not* the discounted value of projected excess earnings, but a summary label for the *reasons behind* such excess earning capacity. See also Lee (1971, p. 324).

67 This notion is among the oldest concepts of goodwill. See Catlett and Olson (1968, p. 9). See also Gomes (1988, p. 23).

68 See, for example, Johnson and Petrone (1998).

69 See, for example, Johnson and Petrone (1998).

70 Refer to Sellhorn (2000, p. 890).

71 See Chauvin and Hirschey (1994, p. 162) and Hoyle, Schaefer and Doupnik (1998, p. 52).

72 See Hoyle, Schaefer and Doupnik (1998, p. 52).

73 See Gomes (1988, p. 23).

74 See Baker, Lembke and King (1996, p. 11).

Perhaps the most influential attempt at systematically decomposing goodwill was made by Johnson and Petrone (1998), who identified six elements:[76] (1) Excess of the fair values over the book values of the acquiree's recognized net assets, (2) fair values of other net assets not recognized by the acquiree, (3) fair value of the "going concern" element of the acquiree's existing business, (4) fair value of synergies from combining the acquirer's and acquiree's businesses and net assets, (5) overvaluation of the consideration paid by the acquirer, and (6) overpayment (or underpayment) by the acquirer.[77]

This decomposition perhaps highlights the differences between the three concepts of goodwill (see Figure 2): The first and second components are no part of goodwill from an accounting standpoint, but potentially from a valuation perspective, depending on how net asset value is measured. The third and fourth components, in aggregate referred to as "core goodwill" by Johnson and Petrone (1998), are part of goodwill under each of the concepts. Finally, the fifth and sixth components belong to goodwill from an accounting viewpoint, but not from the perspective of the other two concepts.

Valuation concept of goodwill					
Excess of fair value over book value	Fair value of unrecognized net assets	Going concern element	Synergy element	Overvaluation of consideration paid	Overpayment by acquirer
			Accounting concept of goodwill		

Figure 2: Concepts and components of goodwill

German academics have for a long time debated the "accounting characteristics" of goodwill.[78] At the heart of this controversy is the normative question whether goodwill

75 According to Colley and Volkan (1988, p. 36), Falk and Gordon (1977) have compiled the "most comprehensive list of empirically identifiable factors as well as elements (characteristics) of goodwill ... in the literature." Refer to Falk and Gordon (1977, p. 453) in particular. For a review of work on the constituting factors of goodwill, see also Davis (1997, pp. 333, 336). Perhaps one of the earliest systematic overviews of goodwill components that is based on pertinent jurisdiction is provided by Preinreich (1936).

76 Refer to Johnson and Petrone (1998, pp. 294-6). Sellhorn (2000) expands on this approach. See also Alvarez and Biberacher (2002) and Busse von Colbe et al. (2003, p. 236).

77 This concept has been integrated into SFAS 141.B102-6. For a similar concept, refer to Wöhe (1980).

78 See, for example, Baetge, Kirsch and Thiele (2002a, pp. 238-9), Breidert (1994, pp. 166-71), Döring (1993), Doralt (1976), Gräber (1981), Kinne (1989, pp. 166-73), Krämling (1998, pp. 63-9), Küting (1995a, 1995b, 1997, 2000), Möhrle (1999, pp. 17-20), Moxter (1993), Müller-Dahl (1981), Ordelheide (1997, 1998), Söffing (1988), Streim (1988, pp. 72-4), Weber and Zündorf (1989), Wöhe (1980), and Zielke (1995). Refer to Arnold (1997, pp. 103-22), Ludz (1997, pp. 68-89) and Sauthoff (1996, pp. 168-75) for summaries of the pertinent arguments and the related literature.

represents a "Vermögensgegenstand", the German asset concept, at all. Alternatively, goodwill is viewed as an accrued item ("Rechnungsabgrenzungsposten"), as some form of accounting "aide memoire" ("Bilanzierungshilfe"), as an equity adjustment, or, resigning, as a one-of-a-kind "idiosyncratic item" ("Wert eigener Art") or "aliud".[79] At present, this theoretical debate seems unresolved.[80] In Anglo-American accounting regimes, an equally fruitless and ongoing discussion has been conducted for decades.[81]

2.3 Main issues

In this section, the main issues surrounding the goodwill debate are introduced. To provide a basic understanding of the controversial financial statement repercussions of goodwill accounting and the directly related coexistence of the purchase and pooling methods, a simple numerical example is presented first. Second, the arguments put forward by participants in the discussion are summarized. Third, these arguments are evaluated from a theoretical perspective.

2.3.1 Pooling and purchase methods illustrated

Under the purchase method, "the assets and liabilities of the acquired firm are valued at fair market values, including the recording of goodwill implied by any excess of purchase price over the net fair value". Under the pooling method, "the assets and liabilities of the combining firm are carried forward at their historical book values. This method, which requires the use of stock as the medium of exchange, is sometimes justified as the uniting of two groups of shareholders into a single 'pooled' entity, with no group being dominant".[82]

The following simplified example illustrates the APB's point that the "accounting treatment of a combination may affect significantly the reported financial position and net income of the combined corporation for prior, current, and future periods":[83] Firm A and Firm B are combined in a stock-for-stock transaction. Table 1 shows their respective in-

---

79 Refer to the extensive literature reviews by Baetge, Kirsch and Thiele (2002a, pp. 260-4), Baetge, Kirsch and Thiele (2002b, pp. 238-9), and Krolak (2000, pp. 8-16).

80 See Busse von Colbe (2001b, par. 5) and Weber and Zündorf (1989, pp. 333-4).

81 See, for example, Brunovs and Kirsch (1991), Colley and Volkan (1988), Falk and Gordon (1977), Gynther (1969), Hodgson, Okunev and Willett (1993), Huijgen (1996), Krolak (2000, pp. 16-9), Lee (1971), Ma and Hopkins (1988), McCarthy and Schneider (1995, pp. 70-72), Miller (1973), Mujkanovic (2001, pp. 814-6). Most of these authors provide further, partially historical references.

82 Jeter and Chaney (2001, p. 939 [both quotes]). The pooling method is discussed by Rammert (1999).

83 APB Opinion 16.2.

dividual balance sheets, in monetary units (MU), after the transaction has taken place at the end of year t.[84]

	Firm A	Firm B		Firm A	Firm B
Assets	800	700	Equity	1,200	350
Investment in Firm B	800		Debt	400	350
Total	**1,600**	**700**	**Total**	**1,600**	**700**

Table 1: Individual balance sheets for Firm A and Firm B subsequent to the business combination

Under the assumption that the fair values of Firm B's assets exceed their respective carrying values by the amount of 150 MU, accounting for the business combination using the pooling and purchase methods yields the consolidated balance sheets displayed in Table 2.

	Pooling	Purchase		Pooling	Purchase
Assets	1,500	1,650	Equity	750	1,200
Goodwill	0	300	Debt	750	750
Total	**1,500**	**1,950**	**Total**	**1,500**	**1,950**

Table 2: Balance sheets for the combined firm under the pooling and purchase methods

The example shows that total assets and equity of the combined firm are lower when the pooling method is used to account for the business combination. The difference can be explained by the amount of the fair value adjustments (150 MU) and of goodwill (300 MU) that are recorded under the purchase method.

Three further assumptions are made to illustrate the effect on earnings in later periods: The goodwill asset is amortized over its expected 5-year useful life. The combined firm's earnings before goodwill amortization are 100 MU in each of the five years following the business combination. Half of annual earnings (after goodwill amortization) are distributed as dividends each year. Table 3 shows the balance sheet and income statement effects of the business combination, depending on whether pooling or purchase treatment was adopted.

84 The example draws on Pellens and Sellhorn (1999, pp. 2126-30). See also Ayers, Lefanowicz and Robinson (2000b), Davis (1996, pp. 52-3), Desai et al. (2001, pp. 6-7), Hopkins, Houston and Peters (2000, p. 258, 260), Huijgen (1996, pp. 87-93), Telkamp and Bruns (2000, p. 745), and Vater (2001, pp. 1843-4).

Pooling-of-interests method	t	t+1	t+2	t+3	t+4	t+5
Equity	750	800	850	900	950	1.000
Total assets	1,500	1,550	1,600	1,650	1,700	1,750
Goodwill	0	0	0	0	0	0
Earnings before goodwill amortization	100	100	100	100	100	100
Goodwill amortization	0	0	0	0	0	0
Earnings	100	100	100	100	100	100
Dividend	50	50	50	50	50	50
Debt-to-equity ratio	1.00	0.94	0.88	0.83	0.79	0.75
Return on equity (earnings / equity)	13.3%	12.5%	11.8%	11.1%	10.5%	10.0%

Purchase method	t	t+1	t+2	t+3	t+4	t+5
Equity	1,200	1,220	1,240	1,260	1,280	1,300
Total assets	1,950	1,970	1,990	2,010	2,030	2,050
Goodwill	300	240	180	120	60	0
Earnings before goodwill amortization	100	100	100	100	100	100
Goodwill amortization	60	60	60	60	60	60
Earnings	40	40	40	40	40	40
Dividend	20	20	20	20	20	20
Debt-to-equity ratio	0.63	0.61	0.60	0.60	0.59	0.58
Return on equity (earnings / equity)	3.3%	3.3%	3.2%	3.2%	3.1%	3.1%

Table 3: Financial statement effects of the pooling and purchase methods

Two key financial ratios are observed: While the purchase method has a favorable effect on the combined firm's debt-to-equity (DTE) ratio, which is low and declines steadily, the pooling method generates a much higher ROE. The latter finding results from two effects: First, the combined firm's equity is comparably low because no fair value adjustments were made and no goodwill was recognized. Since equity is the denominator in the ROE formula, ROE is higher. Second, the numerator in the ROE formula, earnings, is undiminished by any goodwill amortization and, not explicitly considered here, by any additional depreciation resulting from fair value adjustments to depreciable assets. Depending on the amount of the difference between the acquired firm's book value of net assets and the purchase price (called the acquisition premium),[85] pooling accounting can make a business combination look much more profitable than it would appear in case of the purchase method. However, from a balance sheet perspective, purchase firms appear to be more solid due to lower financial leverage.

2.3.2 Arguments raised in the discussion

In the U. S. and other countries, the accounting methods applicable to business combinations and the related issue of accounting for goodwill have been the subject of a "century-

---

[85] See Davis (1996, p. 50).

old controversy".[86] While much of this debate centers on conceptual issues rooted in accounting theory, financial statement preparers have also been concerned from a practical standpoint about the financial statement effects of alternative methods of accounting for goodwill. Since issues addressed in the former portion of the discussion are largely normative in nature, little information can be derived from them regarding the incentives of managers with respect to goodwill accounting. Therefore, this section focuses largely on the practical aspects of the debate and the relevant assertions of the preparers of financial statements. However, the conceptual issues are briefly reviewed first in order to establish a common ground from which the practical aspects can be understood and discussed.[87]

2.3.2.1 Conceptual issues

The discussion focuses on purchased goodwill, the accounting concept, as defined in section 2.2 above. There are different ways to account for goodwill acquired in a business combination (see Figure 3).

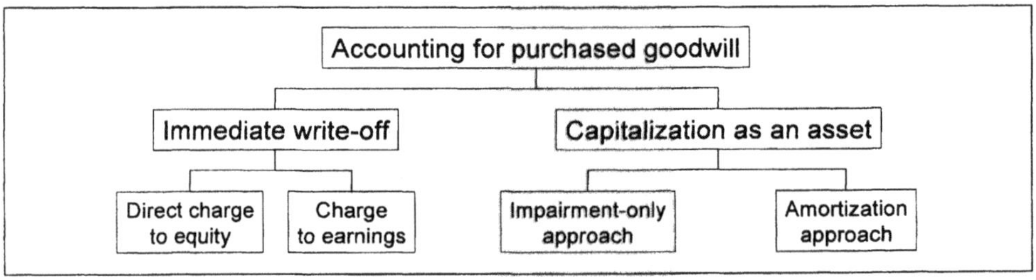

Figure 3: Methods of accounting for goodwill acquired in a business combination

Common to all of them is the fundamental problem of initial measurement of this technical residual, which involves a comparison of two components: The purchase price and the fair value of net identifiable assets acquired. Measuring purchase price might be controversial in a stock-for-stock acquisition and/or when it is unclear whether incidental expenses, such as accounting and legal fees, should be included.

Once measured, the subsequent treatment of goodwill conceptually depends on its economic characteristics.[88] Purchased goodwill can be written off[89] immediately or capital-

---

86 Colley and Volkan (1988, p. 35). Hopkins, Houston and Peters (2000, p. 258) observe a "decades-old controversy". Brunovs and Kirsch (1991, p. 137) cite evidence according to which references to goodwill were made as early as 1417.

87 For a summary of these issues, refer to Brunovs and Kirsch (1991, pp. 137-55) and Davis (1992, pp. 78-83).

88 Refer to section 2.2 above.

89 In this context, "write off" is a neutral term that does not necessarily imply a charge against earnings.

ized as an asset on the balance sheet.[90] Under the first alternative, goodwill could be either charged directly against equity, bypassing the income statement, or deducted from earnings, reducing current income by the excess purchase price paid in the business combination. The popular pooling method is a variant of the direct write-off to equity.[91] The direct write-off of goodwill avoids goodwill-related earnings charges in future periods. While the write-off to earnings generates such charges in the acquisition year, both the direct write-off to equity and the pooling method permanently circumvent any goodwill-related earnings effects of the business combination.[92]

When goodwill is capitalized, the issue of its subsequent accounting treatment arises. In principle, goodwill could be either carried indefinitely as a permanent asset (similar, for example, to land) or reduced gradually via amortization. At the heart of this decision is the conceptual question whether goodwill is subject to "wear and tear", i.e. whether it has a finite useful life or is valuable into infinity.[93] When the useful life of goodwill either is assumed to last permanently (*infinite* useful life) or cannot be estimated (*indefinite* useful life), goodwill is subjected to recurring impairment tests in order to detect any extraordinary deterioration in value.

On the other hand, an amortization approach assumes that the useful life of goodwill is both finite and reasonably estimable. Again, much flexibility is involved in this process, and any estimate of useful life must be regarded as more or less arbitrary. In addition, the appropriate method of amortization must be determined. The widely used straight-line method of amortization would suggest that goodwill not only declines in value over its useful life, but that it does so in an unchanging, predictable way. While management has

---

90 It has been mentioned briefly in section 2.2 above that, in Germany, it is a much-disputed issue whether goodwill fulfills the criteria of the German asset concept. Although relatively little disagreement exists in the U. S. regarding the asset nature of goodwill, this question used to be subject to considerable debate. For a summary, refer to Catlett and Olson (1968, ch. 2). See also Davis (1997, pp. 334-5).

91 Refer to the example in section 2.3.1 above. The main difference between the pooling method and the direct charge of goodwill to reserves (see, for example, section 301 par. 1 HGB) is that, under pooling, the assets and liabilities of the acquiree are carried over at book value and *not* remeasured to fair value. Any difference between purchase price and the acquiree's stated capital is charged completely to the combined entity's reserves.

92 As an added benefit, the pooling method creates "instant earnings" because it allows the combining entities' earnings to be aggregated as of the beginning of the reporting period in which the business combination occurred. See Jeter and Chaney (2001, p. 29). It must be noted that, in contrast to the pooling method, the direct write-off to equity does not prevent future earnings charges resulting from amortization of any acquired intangible assets or depreciation of any fair value adjustments.

93 See, for example, Duvall et al. (1992, p. 1).

no way of avoiding goodwill-related earnings charges under this approach, the yearly amount of these charges can be controlled by selecting an appropriate useful life.[94]

2.3.2.2 Status quo of accounting rules

Depending on conceptual preferences and lobbyism in the standard-setting process, standard setters select from among the available accounting alternatives for goodwill. In this section, the development of the relevant rules applicable in the U. S. and selected other jurisdictions are described briefly.[95]

2.3.2.2.1 United States

Prior to the issuance of SFAS 141 and 142, accounting for business combinations and goodwill was governed by APB Opinions 16, *Business Combinations*, and 17, *Intangible Assets*, both issued in August 1970. Based on conceptual groundwork by Wyatt (1963) and Catlett and Olson (1968), the APB argued that goodwill is an asset that should be recorded by the combined entity. However, where the ownership interests of two or more relatively equal companies are combined by exchange of equity securities, firms should be permitted to carry over their assets and liabilities at book value under the pooling method, provided that 12 criteria are met.[96] The pooling method was used frequently[97] during a wave of mergers and acquisitions in the 1960s. Since concerns arose that the method was inappropriately applied to business combinations that did not, in fact, represent poolings of interests, the APB decided to install stricter criteria.[98]

---

94 See, for example, Duvall et al. (1992, p. 2).

95 See, for example, Hommel (2001a), Klein (2000), Krolak (2000), Küting and Wirth (2003, pp. 480-4), Küting and Harth (1999a, 1999b), Lachnit et al. (1999), Lopatta (2000), and Sellhorn (2000). Comparative textbook representations are given in Baetge, Kirsch and Thiele (2002b, pp. 238-45), Coenenberg (2003, ch. 9), Pellens (2001, pp. 292-304, 310-20, 495-9), and Schildbach (2001, ch. G). While IAS/IFRS and German standards are reviewed in some detail, a brief reference to U. K. accounting rules is given in fn. 129 below.

96 These criteria are contained in APB Opinion 16.45-8. In essence, they restrict certain financing and investing opportunities, such as share repurchases, and provide target firms with additional bargaining power in the negotiations. They are usually grouped into three categories: (1) Characteristics of the combining companies, (2) specifics of the stock-for-stock transaction, and (3) restrictions on post-combination activities. For details, refer to Böcking, Klein and Lopatta (2001, p. 20), Desai et al. (2001, pp. 7-8), Rammert (1999, p. 622), Vincent (1997, p. 5), and Weber (2000). Lys and Vincent (1995, pp. 365-8) document in a case study setting that satisfying these criteria can be costly.

97 According to some, the use was excessive. See, for example, Davis (1997, p. 332).

98 For a detailed description of the development of the purchase and pooling methods, refer to Wyatt (1963) and Catlett and Olson (1968). Watts and Zimmerman (1986, p. 232) document that the pooling method was introduced in 1943 to prevent utility firms from incorporating asset revaluations and goodwill (representing "monopoly rents") into their asset bases used to calculate allowable profits.

Goodwill arising from business combinations accounted for using the purchase method was subjected to an amortization approach, owing to the APB's belief that "the value of intangible assets at any one date eventually disappears and that the recorded costs of intangible assets should be amortized by systematic charges to income over the periods estimated to be benefited."[99] The amortization period was arbitrarily[100] restricted to 40 years,[101] and amortization was required to follow the straight-line method unless it could be demonstrated that another method was more appropriate.[102] In addition to continual reviews of the amortization period, APB Opinion 17.31 states that an "[e]stimation of value and future benefits of an intangible asset may indicate that the unamortized cost should be reduced significantly by a deduction in determining net income". However, no guidance was provided on how this impairment test should be conducted.[103]

In March 1995, the FASB added to these provisions by issuing SFAS 121, *Accounting for the Impairment of Long-Lived Assets and for Long-Lived Assets to Be Disposed Of.* That statement required that (a portion of) goodwill be tested for impairment along with assets or asset groups with which it was associated.[104] Notably, goodwill impairment was avoided when the first test step indicated that the sum of the expected *undiscounted* cash flows generated by an asset or asset group exceeded their carrying value (including goodwill).[105] Once impaired, goodwill was not allowed to be written back up to avoid a blending of purchased and internally generated goodwill.[106]

APB Opinions 16 and 17 were extremely controversial for two reasons:[107] First, the strict pooling criteria made it costly for firms to structure business combinations in a way that

---

99 See APB Opinion 17.27. Therefore, "[a]llocating the cost of goodwill ... over time is necessary because the value almost inevitably becomes zero at some future date" (APB Opinion 17.23).

100 "Since the date at which the value becomes zero is indeterminate, the end of the useful life must necessarily be set arbitrarily at some point or within some range of time for accounting purposes" (APB Opinion 17.23).

101 See APB Opinion 17.29. Additional, shorter limit were imposed by the SEC on certain industries.

102 See APB Opinion 17.30.

103 See also Küting, Brakensiek and Wirth (2000) and Segal (2003, p. 8). Henning, Shaw and Stock (2002, p. 3) conclude that the test had to be applied at the enterprise level. They note that "[t]hree methodologies evolved in practice: a market value method, undiscounted cash flow methods, and discounted cash flow methods."

104 See SFAS 121.12. SFAS 121.4-5 specified certain impairment indicators, i.e. "events or changes in circumstances [that] indicate that the carrying amount of an asset may not be recoverable."

105 See SFAS 121.6. However, in such circumstances a review of the amortization period might nonetheless be in order.

106 See SFAS 121.11.

107 See, for example, Davis (1997, p. 332) and Vincent (1997, p. 5).

allowed them to qualify for this desired accounting treatment. Second, the upper limit on the amortization period forced firms "stuck" with the purchase method to incur relatively large periodic goodwill charges against earnings. Commentators suggest that these disputed rules eventually led to the demise of the APB, which was replaced in 1973 by the FASB.[108]

However, the FASB itself did not change these provisions until 2001, when it issued SFAS 141 and 142 after a five-year standard-setting process and intense discussions with constituents.[109] These standards not only introduce an impairment-only approach to goodwill but also prohibit use of the pooling method entirely. The SEC, in August 1996, had urged the FASB to reconsider the accounting treatment of business combinations,[110] primarily due to an increase in merger and acquisition activity and the resulting awareness that economically similar transactions could be accounted for using different methods that generated dramatically different financial statement results.[111] Taken together, SFAS 141 and 142 alleviate some of firms' formerly voiced concerns about the accounting treatment of goodwill.[112] While the pooling method is no longer allowed, depriving firms of the option to avoid recording goodwill,[113] amortization is also no longer mandatory. The impairment-only approach causes goodwill charges to no longer be an annual

---

108 See Vincent (1997, p. 5).

109 These standards are the subject of chapter 4 below. SFAS 142.B2-B15 gives an overview of the project history that eventually resulted in the issuance of SFAS 141 and 142. Jennings, LeClere and Thompson (2001, pp. 21-2) note that this process involved two exposure drafts, numerous public hearings and several field visits. Schoderbek and Slaubaugh's (2001) instructional assignment provides students with an opportunity to study contextual factors influencing the standard-setting process preceding SFAS 142.

110 See Vincent (1997, p. 5).

111 See SFAS 142.B5.

112 These concerns are described in more detail in section 2.3.2.3 below.

113 However, it is interesting to note that firms' ability to immediately write off certain acquired R&D in process activities is not restricted under the new rules. SFAS 141.42 carries over "the requirement in paragraph 5 of FASB Interpretation (FIN) No. 4, *Applicability of FASB Statement No. 2 to Business Combinations Accounted for by the Purchase Method,* that the amounts assigned to tangible and intangible assets to be used in a particular research and development project that *have no alternative future use* shall be charged to expense at the acquisition date" (emphasis in original). However, the FASB recently announced its intention to revoke FIN 4 in order to achieve convergence with IFRS. Deng and Lev (1998, p. 17) argue that "the accounting procedure of immediately expensing acquired R&D-in-process ... allows firms to use purchase accounting while approaching in substance the consequences of pooling." This statement is true with the exception that, while the immediate write-off of R&D reduces income in the acquisition year, the pooling method does not. Consistent with this argument, Hopkins, Houston and Peters (2000, pp. 263-4, 268) document that, for purchase business combinations in which any premiums are written off as in-process R&D, test persons' stock price assessments do not differ statistically from those for pooling business combinations.

burden on earnings but a more or less discretionary item.[114] This fact has led commentators to suggest that SFAS 141 and 142 represented a mere concession to lobbyists.[115]

2.3.2.2.2 International Accounting Standards

The International Accounting Standards Board (IASB) addresses the accounting for business combinations in IAS 22, *Business Combinations*.[116] Under that standard, business combinations that are acquisitions are accounted for using the purchase method. However, in unusual circumstances, when an acquirer cannot be identified in a transaction of equally sized parties (uniting of interests), the pooling method is required.[117] Goodwill arising in a purchase acquisition is capitalized as an asset,[118] amortized over its useful life and tested for impairment according to IAS 36, *Impairment of Assets*.[119] IAS 36 requires that goodwill be reviewed for impairment whenever indicators suggest that the fair value of a cash-generating unit with which goodwill is associated is not recoverable.[120] An impairment loss must be recognized in the amount by which the carrying amount of the cash-generating unit (including goodwill) exceeds its recoverable amount.[121] A rebuttable presumption exists that the useful life of goodwill does not exceed 20 years.[122] The straight-line method is required unless persuasive evidence suggests that another method reflects the pattern of value decline more appropriately.[123] In contrast to U. S. GAAP, IAS 36 requires that a goodwill impairment loss be reversed if it

---

114 In chapter 4 below, the discretionary nature of the impairment-only approach to goodwill is explored in more detail. Jennings et al. (1996, p. 513) provide evidence that this approach was recommended as early as 1991. See also Wang (1995, p. 46).

115 See, for example, Beresford's (2001) powerful account of political involvement in the standard-setting process preceding SFAS 142. See also Busse von Colbe (2001a), Pellens and Sellhorn (2001b, p. 713).

116 IAS 22 was revised in July 1998 and became effective for annual financial statements covering periods beginning on or after 1 July 1999. It was issued by the IASB's predecessor, the International Accounting Standards Committee (IASC), which reconstituted itself in 2001 and was renamed IASB. For an overview of that process, refer to Mandler (2003).

117 See IAS 22.8, 13-6, 77-83. See also Böcking, Klein and Lopatta (2001, pp. 19-20) and Vater (2001, pp. 1841-2).

118 Mujkanovic (2001, pp. 814-6) takes issue with this notion, arguing that goodwill lacks the characteristics of an asset.

119 See IAS 22.41-58.

120 See IAS 36.79-83. For an introduction to IAS 36, refer to Küting, Dawo and Wirth (2003).

121 See IAS 36.8. The recoverable amount is the higher of the cash-generating unit's net selling price and its value in use.

122 See IAS 22.44. Where a longer amortization period is used, goodwill must be tested for impairment at least annually, in addition to the requirements of IAS 36.

123 See IAS 22.45.

was caused by a specific, exceptional external event, the effect of which has been subsequently overturned.[124]

In July 2001, the IASB initiated a project to revise the provisions of IAS 22 and align them with U. S. GAAP. This process resulted in Exposure Draft (ED) 3, *Business Combinations*, published in December 2002.[125] The final standard, IFRS 3, was issued in March 2004, entering into effect by fiscal 2005.[126] IFRS 3 essentially mirrors the provisions of SFAS 141 and 142 in that it eliminates the pooling method and proposes an impairment-only approach to goodwill. The impairment test procedure itself, regulated in IAS 36, remained essentially unchanged. IAS 36 prescribes a one-step test, which deviates from the two-step procedure required in SFAS 142.

2.3.2.2.3 Germany

In Germany, accounting for goodwill has traditionally been characterized by an abundance of accounting choices. The German Commercial Code, while requiring the purchase method in most cases, allows firms to opt for the pooling method when at least 90% of the acquiree's net assets are purchased in a stock-for-stock business combination with no significant cash adjustment.[127] Goodwill arising in consolidated financial statements can be treated in accordance with most of the alternatives discussed in section 2.3.2.1 above.[128] According to section 309 par. 1 HGB, goodwill can be written off di-

---

124 See IAS 36.109-12.

125 Along with ED 3, accompanying amendments of IAS 36, *Impairment of Assets*, and IAS 38, *Intangible Assets*, were proposed.

126 Amendments of IAS 36 and IAS 38 were adopted at the same time. Articles reviewing ED 3 include Bieker and Esser (2003), Brücks and Wiederhold (2003), Fladt and Feige (2003), Grünberger and Grünberger (2002), IDW (2003), Pellens and Sellhorn (2003), Streim, Bieker and Esser (2004), and Wüstemann and Duhr (2003). The American Accounting Association's (AAA) Financial Accounting Standards Committee has authored a commentary on the proposal. See AAA Financial Accounting Standards Committee (2003). For summaries and critiques of the final standard, see Bieker and Esser (2004), Küting and Wirth (2004), and Brücks and Wiederhold (2004).

127 See sections 301-2 HGB. See also Adler, Düring and Schmaltz (1995/2000, section 302 HGB), Böcking, Klein and Lopatta (2001, p. 19), Busse von Colbe et al. (2003, pp. 346-52), Küting, Dusemond and Nardmann (1994, pp. 4-5), Mujkanovic (1999), and Vater (2001, p. 1841).

128 In this respect, the German legislator carried over most of the choices provided in section 30 of the European "Consolidated accounts" directive (83/349/EWG). Küting (2000), Küting, Dusemond and Nardmann (1994) and Rammert and Wilhelm (1991a, 1991b) review the methods used by selected German firms. However, as will be discussed shortly, an impairment-only approach to goodwill accounting was not commonly considered to be consistent with the directive.

rectly to reserves,[129] amortized over its useful life or charged to earnings over a period not to exceed four years.[130] An impairment loss must be recorded when a permanent decline in goodwill value occurs.[131] Considerable debate surrounds the issue whether goodwill write-offs can be reversed.[132]

In August 2000, the German private-sector standard setter, the German Accounting Standards Board (GASB), issued German Accounting Standard (GAS) 4, *Acquisition Accounting in Consolidated Financial Statements.*[133] According to GAS 4.8, acquisitions are accounted for under the purchase method.[134] The accounting procedures prescribed with respect to goodwill are widely similar to those of IAS 22 and 36, one notable exception being that a disaggregation of the firm into cash-generating units or other subunits is not required, but only recommended.[135] Similar to IAS 36, subsequent write-ups are required under certain restrictive criteria.[136]

---

129 Apparently, this option is behind the fact that the pooling method never gained much popularity in Germany. See Böcking, Klein and Lopatta (2001, p. 17 fn. 3). The benefits of avoiding goodwill charges are less costly for firms to attain under this alternative than when the pooling criteria must be satisfied. Interestingly, the U. K. was among the few countries that also used to permit firms to use this accounting treatment for goodwill. Higson (1998, p. 141) notes that "UK companies clearly enjoyed [this] netting option, since they have almost invariably chosen it." Lee (1973, 1974) provides early evidence on this phenomenon. Exposure Draft (ED) 47, in which the U. K. Accounting Standards Board (ASB) proposed to abandon this option in 1990, met with strong opposition. Nobes (1992, pp. 155-7) and Warnock (1999) document the political influence exercised in this standard-setting process. See also Huijgen (1996, p. 62).

130 The direct write-off to equity is not available to goodwill recorded in a firm's individual financial statements. See section 255 par. 4 HGB.

131 See sections 298 par. 1, 253 par. 2 HGB. No impairment testing procedure is specified. The write-off is optional when the decline in value is deemed to be other than permanent. See also Adler, Düring and Schmaltz (1995/2000, par. 24 on section 309 HGB), Arnold (1997, pp. 165-8), Breidert (1994, pp. 176-8), Busse von Colbe (2001b, par. 19), Busse von Colbe et al. (2003, p. 247), Dörschell and Schulte (2002, pp. 1669-75), IDW (2000), Kraft (2002, par. 33), Krolak (2000, pp. 105-8, 120-4), Ludz (1997, pp. 326-7), and Weber and Zündorf (1989, p. 336). Förschle and Hoffmann (2003, par. 17-8) suggest a testing procedure similar to that required by IAS 22 and 36. See also Weber and Zündorf (1998, par. 29-31).

132 See Förschle and Hoffmann (2003, par. 19) and the literature cited there. See also Arnold (1997, pp. 168-9), Breidert (1994, pp. 177-8), Busse von Colbe et al. (2003, pp. 251-2), Kraft (2002, par. 35), and Ludz (1997, pp. 327-9).

133 The standard was published in December 2000 by the Federal Ministry of Justice and is therefore regarded as an authoritative pronouncement. It (or the proposal preceding its issuance) is reviewed by Böcking, Klein and Lopatta (2000), Fülbier (2000), and Moxter (2001).

134 Since the standard only applies to acquisitions, it does not address the question whether the pooling method should be permitted to account for business combinations that are not acquisitions. See also Böcking, Klein and Lopatta (2001, p. 25).

135 See GAS 4.35.

136 See GAS 4.37.

2.3.2.3 Practical issues

As explained above, pre-SFAS 142 U. S. GAAP and most other accounting regimes, including IAS, required that goodwill be amortized over its useful life. Therefore, much of the debate has centered on the issue that purchased goodwill must be charged against earnings in the years subsequent to acquisitions accounted for using the purchase method.

Beams, Brozovsky and Shoulders (2000) have neatly summarized the problem that preparers of financial statements have with goodwill amortization:[137]

> "Once goodwill is on the books of a company, it can become a nuisance and a serious drag on earnings".[138]

Firms domiciled in countries where this accounting treatment is mandatory claim that competitive disadvantages arise from the resulting earnings dilution. The primary concern is an adverse stock price effect due to the earnings effect of goodwill amortization.[139] Similarly, acquirers using the purchase method feel discriminated against in relation to those using the pooling method[140] and to foreign firms that are subject to less strict accounting rules.[141] For example, it has been claimed that U. K. firms can afford to outbid U. S. firms in offers for mergers and acquisitions because U. K. standards at the time allowed the direct write-off of goodwill to equity.[142] This suggestion implies that U. K. firms will incur higher marginal costs in acquisitions, allegedly because they believe that these costs are offset by benefits resulting from a favorable accounting treatment.[143]

---

137 Consequently, the following arguments are referred to as the "preparer's perspective" by Duvall et al. (1992, p. 2).

138 Beams, Brozovsky and Shoulders (2000, p. 18). In the words of Ellis (2001, p. 112), "there is a continued obsession with pooling-of-interests and EPS accretion, rather than price paid, value received, and the economic implications of future growth."

139 Desai et al. (2001, p. 1) maintain that the FASB eliminated goodwill amortization "at least partially in response to concerns that goodwill amortization adversely affects share prices of acquirers." See also Blackburn Norris and Ayres (2000, p. 79), Brown, Tucker and Pfeiffer (1999, p. 13), Clinch (1997, p. 346), Davis (1996, pp. 50, 54), and Duvall et al. (1992, p. 2). Hopkins, Houston and Peters (2000, p. 258) cite additional references.

140 FASB (1976) reports that 66% of 122 firms responding to a survey agreed with the statement that many business combinations accounted for by the pooling method would not have been consummated if the purchase method would have had to be applied to them. Hong, Kaplan and Mandelker (1978, pp. 33-4) cite several early articles expressing the view that "companies using pooling-of-interests accounting would have higher stock prices than were justified." Rammert (1999, p. 628) interprets the pooling method as an instrument for "window dressing".

141 See, for example, Davis (1997, p. 338).

142 This choice was provided by Statement of Standard Accounting Practice (SSAP) 22. It was abandoned when Financial Reporting Standard (FRS) 10, *Goodwill and Intangible Assets*, was issued in 1997.

143 For empirical evidence on this suggestion, refer to sections 2.4.3.3.1 and 2.4.3.4.2 below.

Apparently, these perceived drawbacks of goodwill amortization make firms reluctant to disclose this specific charge even when required to do so by the SEC.[144]

Likewise, the financial press claims that managers are indeed concerned about having to take goodwill write-offs.[145] Explaining the mechanics of the goodwill impairment test under SFAS 142, the author concludes that, if company B's likelihood of having to record a goodwill impairment loss pertaining to a contemplated acquisition in the near future is higher than company A's, "it would be less likely to offer a large premium than company A."

Consequently, firms have argued in favor of the pooling method, allegedly because this method allows them to avoid this goodwill-related "drag on earnings".[146] As explained above, the pooling method allows firms to avoid recording goodwill in an acquisition, even when the purchase price paid exceeds the fair values of the net assets acquired. As a result, acquiring firms' earnings subsequent to the business combination remain undiminished by the fact that a premium over the acquiree's book value has been paid.

2.3.3 Theoretical analysis of arguments raised

While managers are apparently worried about how goodwill accounting affects their financial statements, some academics have been unwilling to acknowledge the validity of these concerns, arguing that users of financial statements do not behave as suggested by financial statement preparers' arguments.[147] When firm value is a function of expected future cash flows, a combined firm's market value of equity should not depend on the method applied to account for the transaction, provided that the accounting method chosen will not affect the expected future cash flows of the combined entity. Accounting choices or changes that have no direct cash-flow effects are referred to as "cosmetic".[148]

---

144 Duvall et al. (1992, p. 6) report that, out of a sample of 485 firms having goodwill, only 115 (23.7%) disclosed the amount of goodwill amortization *anywhere* within their financial statements. Only 24 of these disclosures were made in the income statement.

145 See Osterland (2002).

146 According to Deng and Lev (1998, p. 17), it "is widely known that acquiring managers generally prefer the 'pooling' method of recording acquisitions over the 'purchase' method, since pooling avoids the recognition of goodwill and the subsequent drain on earnings from goodwill amortization". See also Nathan (1988, p. 187).

147 Duvall et al. (1992, p. 2) refer to the following arguments as the "user's perspective".

148 See, for example, Lev and Ohlson (1982, p. 250). A typical example of an accounting choice that *does* affect cash flow directly is the choice between the LIFO and FIFO methods of inventory valuation. This choice directly affects taxable income in the U. S. See, for example, Lindahl, Emby and Ashton (1988).

Stated differently, proponents of the efficient markets hypothesis (EMH) in its semi-strong form maintain that security prices fully reflect all publicly available information and are immediately updated to impound "news", regardless of the source of information.[149] If this hypothesis holds, investors should be indifferent whether a given business combination is accounted for using the pooling method or the purchase method, provided that the choice of accounting method has no cash flow effects.[150] They would be able to "see through" the financial statement presentation, using alternative sources of information to assess the underlying economics (cash flows) of the deal and value the combined firm accordingly.[151] Managers, then, should not incur costs either by lobbying with standard setters in favor of the pooling method or by structuring a business combination to satisfy the pooling requirements.[152]

Preparers' concerns appear to be in stark contrast with this view: Managers apparently assume that investors fixate on earnings, which leads them to argue that the lower earnings implied by purchase accounting depress stock prices.[153] Stated differently, "investors and financial analysts focus on earnings per share (EPS) and price-to-earnings (P/E) ratios in valuing companies."[154] This *functional fixation hypothesis* "maintains that individual investors interpret earnings numbers the same way regardless of the accounting procedures used to calculate them."[155] If all investors made decisions in this way, there would be a mechanical relation between earnings and stock prices (*mechanistic hypothesis*). Investors exhibiting this behavioral pattern are "fooled" or "misled" by firms' accounting methods and choices and therefore referred to as "unsophisticated" or "na-

---

149 See Fama (1970). The implications of this paradigm for accounting research are discussed by Beaver (1981), Brown (2001, pp. 13-4), Kothari (2001, pp. 110-1), and Mayer-Sommer (1979). Also, refer to section 3.3.2.4.1 below for a discussion of the relation between the EMH and "cosmetic" accounting differences.

150 See, for example, Jenkins (1999).

151 Brown, Tucker and Pfeiffer (1999, p. 13) argue as follows: "Given a properly specified conditional expectation of securities returns, as well as information efficiency in the securities market, we would not expect to observe any systematic relations between goodwill amortization and subsequent securities returns." See also Davis (1996, p. 53). Early research, including Beaver and Dukes (1973), suggests that investors can "see through" cash-neutral accounting differences. In the words of Kaplan and Roll (1972, p. 245): "Earnings manipulation may be fun, but its profitability is doubtful." See also Archibald (1972) and Lindahl, Emby and Ashton (1988).

152 See Wyatt (1983, p. 60).

153 See Martínez-Jerez (2001, p. 24).

154 Vincent (1997, p. 5).

155 See Watts and Zimmerman (1986, p. 160).

ïve".[156] The mechanistic hypothesis is consistent with the classical approach to accounting theory.[157] However, it directly contradicts the efficient market hypothesis.[158]

In summary, the extent to which preparers' concerns are justified depends on two empirical questions: First, stock price effects are expected to the extent that the accounting method used changes investors' expectations regarding the firm, either by providing incremental information on the firm's future cash flows or by changing these cash flows directly.[159] Second, in the absence of such cash flow effects, stock price effects are expected only when the EMH is not descriptive and, instead, the functional fixation hypothesis explains the behavior of at least some investors.[160]

The method used to account for a given business combination does not automatically affect the direct cash flows of the combined firm.[161] Because the pooling method is only available in stock-for-stock acquisitions,[162] tax differences do not arise since amortization of goodwill resulting from such acquisitions is not tax deductible.[163] As Nobes (1996) points out, goodwill charges arising from goodwill in a firm's consolidated financial

---

156 See Watts (1992, p. 3) and Watts and Zimmerman (1986, p. 160). Hand (1990) investigates an "extended functional fixation hypothesis", which he contrasts with the "traditional" one. The extended version assumes that not all investors are equally (un)sophisticated. Then, stock price implications of accounting data depend on the degree of sophistication of the marginal investor setting a firm's stock price.

157 See, for example, White, Sondhi and Fried (2003, p. 168).

158 Kothari (2001, pp. 186-207) reviews of a body of literature that tests market efficiency in an accounting context. With specific regard to the literature relevant here, on accounting method differences/changes and the functional fixation hypothesis, Kothari (2001, p. 199) concludes that the evidence "rules out noticeable magnitudes of market fixation on reported financial statement numbers." This literature is reviewed in more detail in section 2.4.4.

159 See, for example, Day and Hartnett (1999/2000, p. 199).

160 Martínez-Jerez (2001, p. 5) argues in essentially the same way when he specifies three conditions under which the choice of pooling or purchase should have no impact on the capital market assessment of a merger: Capital markets are efficient, the purchase/pooling choice does not proxy for the economic attributes of the deal, the purchase/pooling choice does not affect the contracting environment of the firm.

161 See Desai et al. (2001, p. 2) and Vincent (1997, p. 5).

162 See APB Opinion 16.45.

163 See Blackburn Norris and Ayres (2000, p. 79 fn. 1), Hong, Kaplan and Mandelker (1978, p. 31), Hopkins, Houston and Peters (2000, p. 258 fn. 2), Lindenberg and Ross (1999, p. 32), and Robinson and Shane (1990, p. 31). For the U. K., see Nobes (1992, p. 156 fn. 13). With respect to cash acquisitions, Davis (1996, p. 53) points out that those accounted for as purchases are taxable, meaning that goodwill amortization is tax deductible. This fact results, ceteris paribus, in a future tax benefit for the acquirer. However, due to the acquisition's taxability, the sellers will incur capital gains taxes that should, ceteris paribus, raise purchase price. Therefore, the net tax effect on future cash flows is difficult to assess. It seems justified to assume that no future cash flow effects are associated with the purchase/pooling choice.

statements are tax deductible in virtually *no* jurisdiction, since consolidated financial statements are in most cases irrelevant for tax purposes.[164] Authors suggesting tax deductibility of goodwill either refer to purchased goodwill in a company's individual financial statements or are mistaken.[165]

However, indirect cash flow differences between the two methods might arise from contracts between the company and internal or external participants which are stated in accounting terms. Such contracts include debt covenants and compensation agreements.[166] Due to such interdependencies, Lev and Ohlson (1982) conclude that "the conventional dichotomy between accounting changes having 'cosmetic' and those having real (cash-flow) effects is clearly simplistic."[167]

In addition, the choice of accounting method might lead investors to alter their expectations about the firm's future prospects. Management might be *signaling* information with their exercise of that choice, exercising their discretion about reported accounting numbers so as to reduce the information asymmetry that might exist in their favor about the distribution of future cash flows.[168]

Goodwill accounting might present a special challenge which will make it problematic even for sophisticated investors to "see through" the cosmetic earnings effect. It has been argued that, while financial statement users have no difficulties in disentangling goodwill amortization from other, "real" expenses for relatively recent acquisitions, they are much less able to unravel the financial statement effects of the purchase method when acquisitions occurred several periods ago.[169] This difficulty might lead them to penalize firms using the purchase method for their, ceteris paribus, lower earnings relative to firms us-

---

164 See also Nobes and Norton (1996) for a summary of the tax treatments of goodwill in different jurisdictions.

165 Nobes (1996) explicitly directs this criticism at Dunne and Ndubizu (1995) but notes that a large number of other papers suffer from the same problem. See Nobes (1996, p. 591). Beatty and Weber (2004, fn. 1) note that SFAS 142 did not affect the accounting treatment of goodwill amortization.

166 For example, Aboody, Kasznik and Williams (2000) claim that the form of top management compensation may affect the choice of accounting in mergers. This "contracting" theory is explored in more detail in section 3.3.2.3 below.

167 Lev and Ohlson (1982, p. 250).

168 For an application of the information asymmetry and signaling arguments to accounting research, refer to Gonedes (1978) and Watts and Zimmerman (1986, pp. 165-6). A literature review is provided by Gonedes and Dopuch (1974).

169 Duvall et al. (1992) document that accounting information related to goodwill (e.g. book value, amortization expense and amortization policy) is frequently difficult to infer from published financial statements.

ing the pooling method.[170] Interestingly, in Hopkins, Houston and Peters' (2000) experimental setting, analysts could accurately recall the total amount of goodwill and of amortization included in the most recent income statement. Consequently, the authors argue that the failure to adjust income for the effect of amortization was not necessarily, as has been suggested in the literature,[171] because investors could not find information about goodwill or goodwill amortization in later years.[172] Rather, they maintain that people use simplifying strategies in complex task environments and that people tend to use data the way they are provided.[173]

2.4 Empirical evidence relevant to the goodwill debate

2.4.1 Overview

The discussion presented in sections 2.3.2.3 and 2.3.3 above has not only influenced standard setting, but has also motivated a vast area of research. It suggests two empirical issues relevant to this dissertation: First, the arguments produced by financial statement preparers imply this group's *belief* that the financial statement effects of alternative goodwill accounting treatments influence the behavior of financial statement users, even in the absence of cash flow effects.[174] Preparers' financial reporting decisions will be influenced by the expected impact of such user behavior on preparers' utility. Empirical research into the actual determinants of preparers' goodwill-related accounting decisions provides evidence on whether these decisions are actually influenced by how preparers *believe* that users will respond to them. Second, another empirical question is how financial statement users' actually view goodwill-related accounting issues that do not impact cash flows. Empirical research into actual user behavior allows researchers to infer whether preparers' beliefs and concerns are justified.

---

170 This assertion presents a challenge to the semi-strong form information efficiency hypothesis. See Desai et al. (2001, p. 2 fn. 3).

171 See Palepu (1987, p. 88) and Lys and Vincent (1997, p. 374).

172 See Hopkins, Houston and Peters (2000, p. 259).

173 See Hopkins, Houston and Peters (2000, p. 263).

174 This belief is contrary to what the EMH suggests. Refer to section 3.3.2.4.1 for the importance of managers' beliefs. White, Sondhi and Fried (1997, p. 224 fn. 14) note, albeit in a different context, "that market efficiency does not mean that everyone (in this case, management) believes it is efficient."

The evidence reviewed in this section addresses both of these issues.[175] Obviously, the extent to which inferences from prior research findings generalize to the transitional SFAS 142 setting is limited. However, the findings are nonetheless expected to improve formulation of hypotheses about managers' transitional SFAS 142 goodwill write-off behavior for two reasons: First, this research provides insights into different aspects of managers' financial reporting behavior regarding goodwill in general. Actual management behavior is more informative in this respect than managers' publicly stated assertions. Second, from the empirical findings inferences can be drawn about financial statement users' actual position regarding goodwill accounting, regardless of what preparers believe this position to be. Observing users' actual responses to goodwill accounting might even challenge managers' formerly held beliefs and thereby influence their goodwill-related financial reporting behavior in the context of SFAS 142. In summary, these findings are expected to contribute to an understanding of how managers are likely to exercise their discretion regarding the accounting for goodwill in the year in which SFAS 142 is initially applied.[176]

As with other areas of financial reporting, empirical research on goodwill accounting cannot lead to prescriptions how goodwill *should* be accounted for.[177] Also, as White, Sondhi and Fried (2003) point out, "any transactions ... or change in market prices [induced by accounting data make] some people better off than others. Thus, deciding the best alternative necessarily [involves] judgment affecting social consequence and the general welfare, which [are] deemed to be 'political' in nature and beyond the realm of academic research".[178] Therefore, the purpose of the following literature review is ex-

---

175 Reviews of the relevant literature include Clinch (1997) and Davis (1997). While every effort is made to give a comprehensive overview of this field of research, it cannot be ruled out that individual studies have escaped consideration, given the enormous wealth of literature published on these issues.

176 The research presented in this section draws on theories about the determinants and consequences of financial reporting decisions in general. These theories are not reviewed before chapter 1, where they are placed in the context of discretionary asset write-off studies. The focus of this section is predominantly on research results and implications for the question at hand as opposed to theoretical and methodological considerations. Transitional SFAS 142 goodwill write-offs are argued to have more in common conceptually with other discretionary asset write-offs, which are the subject of chapter 1, than with the wide array of goodwill-related financial reporting decisions reviewed here.

177 See Clinch (1997, p. 342), Holthausen and Watts (2001).

178 White, Sondhi and Fried (2003, p. 170). See also Huijgen (1996, p. 30): "Although [market-based accounting research] is capable of showing the welfare implications of accounting disclosures, it is the task of policymakers to ultimately judge whether these welfare implications are desirable."

pressly *not* to generate normative prescriptions about how business combinations and goodwill *should* be accounted for.[179]

2.4.2 Research questions

The degree of persuasiveness of this body of literature depends on how *directly* the respective studies analyze preparers' and users' attitudes towards goodwill write-offs recorded in the year of transition to an impairment only-based goodwill accounting standard. The evidence reviewed here relates to preparers' and users' past behavior with regard to a wide array of goodwill-related accounting decisions. The research questions pursued can be summarized as shown in Figure 4.

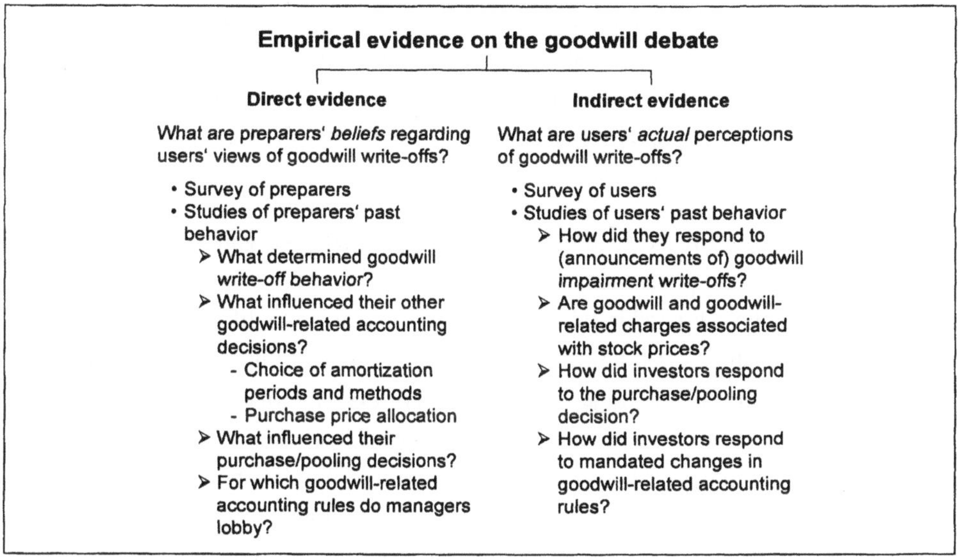

Figure 4: Empirical evidence on the goodwill debate

Perhaps most directly related to the problem at hand are studies of the factors influencing goodwill write-off behavior, preferably under SFAS 142.[180] In addition, research on managers' goodwill-related accounting decisions involving issues such as the choice of

---

179 White, Sondhi and Fried (2003, pp. 165-6) summarize this "classical approach" to accounting research from an American point of view. Much of the academic literature on goodwill accounting in Germany has adopted this methodology. Refer to section 2.2. Furthermore, the focus is not on criticizing the research questions and methods used to arrive at the findings presented. Instead, most of the results are taken at face value, and their respective contributions to the question at hand are analyzed.

180 The only such studies to date, to my knowledge, are Henning, Shaw and Stock's (2002) and Segal's (2003). The determinants of goodwill write-offs under an earlier accounting regime are the subject of Francis, Hanna and Vincent's (1996) analysis.

acquisition accounting method, amortization periods and procedures, or the approach used to allocate the purchase price after an acquisition, is also potentially informative. Finally, inferences can be drawn from management's lobbying behavior in the standard-setting process preceding goodwill-related accounting rules.

Since, as discussed above, managers' incentives are primarily shaped by their *beliefs* concerning investors' reactions to their goodwill-related accounting decisions, studies of investors' *actual* past reactions to such decisions are, strictly speaking, not direct evidence in this context. However, to the extent that managers are aware of research on investors' actual past reactions to goodwill-related accounting decisions, deem this research credible, and believe the findings to be indicative of investors' future behavior, their beliefs are likely to be influenced by that research. Therefore, analyses of investors' actual past reactions to different goodwill-related accounting decisions are also reviewed here. However, it is noted here that individual investors' perceptions are not observed directly. Instead, stock price behavior is used as an aggregate proxy for the unobservable perceptions and reactions of investors in most cases.

The predictive ability of these findings for managers' SFAS 142 goodwill write-off behavior is open to debate. In essence, it depends on the extent to which the empirical and institutional setting investigated in this dissertation is perceived to differ from the settings analyzed in prior studies. First, an impairment-only approach to goodwill accounting as prescribed under SFAS 142 is largely unprecedented, even internationally. Managers as well as capital market participants, e.g. financial analysts, had no experience, prior to the date of adoption, in applying these rules and interpreting the data reported under them, respectively. Therefore, results from previous research might not generalize because most of them originate from different time periods, accounting regimes, and economic settings. Second, the fact that the period of initial application of a new accounting standard is analyzed, with the transition effects being reported as changes in accounting principle, might have certain implications in itself.[181]

2.4.3 Direct evidence

In this section, a body of literature on managers' past goodwill-related accounting decisions and their determinants is summarized. This literature provides relatively *direct* evidence of how managers think goodwill-related accounting issues are perceived by financial statement users.

---

181 Refer to section 3.3.2.4.8 below.

2.4.3.1 Survey evidence

Conceptually, the most direct way of learning about managers' *beliefs* regarding users' perception of transitional SFAS 142 goodwill write-offs would be to elicit their views in a survey. To my knowledge, such survey evidence does not exist at present. It is doubtful, even if a sufficient number of managers could be motivated to participate in that type of survey, whether their responses would be entirely and verifiably truthful. When the FASB issued SFAS 141 and 142, the financial press conducted polls to elicit constituents' views on the subject. However, while these results are interesting to note in passing, they are by no means representative and are therefore not further relied on here.[182]

However, scientific survey evidence of managers' attitudes toward goodwill accounting in a more general setting does exist. Gore, Taib and Taylor (2000) use a postal questionnaire to explicitly analyze management's beliefs regarding a proposed change in mandatory goodwill accounting standards in the U. K.[183] Usable responses from 212 firms show, among other things, "that corporate managements' goodwill accounting preferences are .. influenced to a great extent by their beliefs about how the stock market (represented by financial analysts) would respond to the financial statement impact of changes in standards."[184] Specifically, responding managers believe "that analysts would downgrade their rating if their company's profits were lower due to enforced goodwill amortisation".[185] The authors form hypotheses regarding cross-sectional differences in manager preferences for either capitalization-based or immediate write-off approaches to goodwill accounting. Cross-sectional regression analysis shows that these preferences are significantly related to contracting-based incentives as well as capital markets-based in-

182 For example, CFO magazine established on its website (www.cfo.com) a whole section on the new rules and conducted an online survey of managers' expectations regarding the new rules. (The results are reported in the "Discussion" section of the website.) Two polls are worth mentioning here: (1) Asked whether they expected to take a goodwill write-off during the adoption period, responding managers answered "yes" (127 votes/42%), "no" (114/38%) and "not sure" (57/19%). Interestingly, these results reflect managers' expectations as of October 2001, suggesting that most managers (81%) were already sure what write-off behavior would be long *before* they had actually had the opportunity to conduct an impairment test. (2) In another poll, CFO magazine asked about managers' main concerns with regard to the new rules. The responses, as of June 2001, suggest that managers find most troublesome the costly appraisal of reporting units (172 votes/51%). Other concerns include the stricter amortization requirements for intangible assets (46/14%), possible SEC scrutiny of the purchase price allocation (41/12%), the elimination of the pooling method (25/7%), and investors' alleged ignorance of related disclosures (55/16%).

183 See Gore, Taib and Taylor (2000, pp. 216-7).

184 Gore, Taib and Taylor (2000, p. 224).

185 Gore, Taib and Taylor (2000, p. 224).

centives.[186] More specifically, the authors find that managers' preferences are related to the way in which the proposed accounting rules would affect that restrictiveness of their firms' accounting-based debt covenants and their own accounting-based compensation.[187] Furthermore, the results indicate managers' belief that analysts are misled by goodwill accounting: Among other things, analysts are believed to penalize firms for the earnings drag caused by goodwill amortization and to favor, in an international setting, firms that write off goodwill to reserves.

2.4.3.2 Determinants of goodwill write-offs

Given the scarce survey evidence, other areas of research are reviewed for evidence of preparers' beliefs regarding users' perception of goodwill write-offs. These beliefs can, to some extent, be deduced from preparers' past reporting behavior in conjunction with this decision. If managers believe that, ceteris paribus, transitional goodwill write-offs (especially when they occur unexpectedly early and are unexpectedly large) will cause negative reactions by investors, they will use their financial reporting discretion to avoid, delay and/or understate these charges. Conversely, if management supposes that, ceteris paribus, transitional goodwill write-offs will produce positive stock price effects, they will record these charges, using their discretion to accelerate and/or overstate them.[188]

Therefore, the analysis in section 3.3 of what previous research implies about managers' goodwill write-off behavior is referred to here. The primary finding reported by Francis, Hanna and Vincent (1996) is that "incentives ... play a substantial role in explaining goodwill write-offs".[189] They provide evidence that, consistent with a "big bath" conjecture, a previous change in top management is positively related to the amount of goodwill write-off, while unexpectedly good earnings performance is negatively associated with it.[190] The authors note that the latter finding contradicts the income smoothing hy-

---

186 See Gore, Taib and Taylor (2000, p. 221). The latter incentives are referred to by the authors as "information effect" incentives (p. 217).

187 Theoretical background on these incentives is given in section 3.3.2.3 below.

188 Similarly, if managers think goodwill write-offs are viewed as noise in the transition period whereas goodwill write-offs occurring in later periods are not, goodwill write-off behavior will be determined, as outlined above, by how managers believe users will view these charges in later periods.

189 Francis, Hanna and Vincent (1996, p. 134).

190 See Francis, Hanna and Vincent (1996, p. 125).

pothesis, under which unexpectedly good performance would be predicted to trigger a write-off that brings earnings in line with expectations.[191]

In one of the first, preliminary studies of SFAS 142 goodwill write-offs, Henning, Shaw and Stock (2002) report that, of a "transition sample" consisting of 1,482 firms, 681 firms announced the results of their transitional impairment tests as early as the first quarter of 2002.[192] 205 (30.1%) of these firms indicated that they were going to record an impairment loss. The authors further indicate an association of write-off behavior with prior stock performance: Over 90% of transition firms with significantly negative abnormal stock returns decided to recognize goodwill impairments.[193] These firms also wrote off larger portions of their goodwills and had higher debt-to-capital ratios. The authors note that managers apparently maximized transitional goodwill impairment, consistent with "big bath" behavior, because the impairment is displayed "below the line" in the adoption year.[194]

Using an approach similar to that of Francis, Hanna and Vincent (1996), Segal (2003) analyzes, among other things, the determinants of goodwill write-offs in the adoption year of SFAS 142. This component of Segal's approach is similar to the one proposed in this dissertation. Segal largely extends the Francis, Hanna and Vincent (1996) study by adding more recent SFAS 121 data and including SFAS 142 data. However, he focuses on firms that publicly announced SFAS 142 write-offs, which results in a biased sample. Also, the sample only includes write-offs announced during the first half of 2002, which neglects firms that made use of the whole year available to them to complete the impairment test under SFAS 142.

Segal (2003) investigates whether certain economic factors (impairment) as well as financial reporting incentives are associated with the amount written off.[195] In terms of

---

191 See Francis, Hanna and Vincent (1996, p. 133). The amount of goodwill write-off is further found to be higher when the firm has a history of previous write-offs. See Francis, Hanna and Vincent (1996, p. 125). However, Francis, Hanna and Vincent's (1996) might have to interpreted with caution because they do not examine a really comprehensive set of potential incentives. For example, they focus on capital market-related incentives, failing to address incentives suggested by contracting theory.

192 It must be noted that the authors address a wide array of research questions in this paper, of which the determinants of transitional SFAS 142 goodwill write-off behavior are only a minor component. Also, they do not include the entire transition period, but focus on a "transition sample" of first-quarter disclosures. Their findings do not generalize because firms did not have to complete their transitional goodwill impairment test before the end of the adoption year.

193 See Henning, Shaw and Stock (2002, p. 20). This percentage was significantly lower for firms with insignificantly negative or even positive abnormal returns.

194 See Henning, Shaw and Stock (2002, p. 21).

195 See Segal (2003, pp. 15-7).

economic variables, he hypothesizes that poor historical firm and industry performance makes a write-off more likely. With regard to financial reporting incentives, he conjectures that a change in top management as well as unexpectedly high (income smoothing) and low (big bath) earnings will tend to induce a write-off, while the amount written off will tend to be limited by debt covenant restrictions. In contrast to Francis, Hanna and Vincent (1996), he finds that the income smoothing variable is a significant explanatory factor of goodwill write-offs, suggesting that managers record write-offs in an attempt to smooth their companies' earnings over time. Since financial reporting incentives play a more significant role in explaining SFAS 121 write-offs in his study, Segal concludes that "SFAS No. 142 write downs are more associated with economic variables [than SFAS No. 121 write-offs] and less associated with reporting incentives."[196]

In a recent working paper that adopts an approach widely similar to the one pusued here, Beatty and Weber (2004) interpret firms' adoption of SFAS 142 not so much as a goodwill-related accounting decision but rather as a tradeoff between the timing of expense recognition and the question where to report an expense item. Consequently, they abstract from goodwill-specific issues relating to SFAS 142 adoption. They find that firms have incentive to accelerate expense recognition (and secure the benefit of below-the-line treatment) where debt covenants, bonus plans, or delisting status are affected by goodwill impairment. Conversely, firms are found to defer expense recognition (and report goodwill impairment within income from continuing operations) where the CEO has been recently appointed and where a firm's earnings from continuing operations are highly priced.

2.4.3.3 Determinants of other goodwill-related financial reporting decisions

As discussed in section 2.3.2.3 above, managers are widely assumed to believe that investors respond negatively to the future earnings drag from goodwill charges subsequent to acquisitions.[197] The above-mentioned survey conducted by Gore, Taib and Taylor (2000) sheds some light on "the effects on management preferences of their beliefs about revisions in market perceptions of their companies resulting from changes in goodwill accounting" in a general sense.[198] It documents that the responding U. K. firm managers' inclination towards different goodwill-related accounting approaches is in part influenced

196 Segal (2003, p. 26).

197 See, for example, Davis (1996, p. 50): "[T]he question is whether the acquirer's share price will be affected ... by the big negative impact of goodwill amortization on the bottom line? Many merger participants and observers appear to think so." For further references, see Davis (1996, p. 51).

198 Gore, Taib and Taylor (2000, p. 13).

by how they expect financial statement users to behave when these different approaches becoming mandated accounting rules. Again, it must be noted that, since their focus is not on goodwill write-offs, their findings do not necessarily generalize to the issue focused on here.[199] However, their results do suggest that managers are generally concerned with a potential adverse effect of goodwill-related charges on earnings.[200] Cross-sectional differences in managers' choices among accepted goodwill-related accounting rules allow inferences regarding managers' beliefs pertaining to users' perception of goodwill-related accounting decisions. Similarly, management's beliefs can be inferred from the way they exercise their goodwill-related financial reporting discretion.

2.4.3.3.1 Influence of goodwill accounting rules on acquisition premiums

The underlying theme of the goodwill debate is that the availability of favorable goodwill-related accounting treatments puts firms at a competitive advantage over firms that are subject to less beneficial rules. That advantage is argued to translate into a willingness to bid higher in acquisitions. For example, an argument frequently put forward is that those firms are put at a competitive advantage which either have the option of applying the pooling method instead of the purchase method or which, when required to use purchase accounting, can charge any resulting goodwill directly against equity. Firms domiciled in jurisdictions where purchase accounting is mandatory and goodwill must be charged against income, then, are viewed to be at a competitive disadvantage. This alleged disadvantage refers primarily to the international takeover market. While the acquirer's determination of purchase price is not strictly an accounting issue, the related evidence is relevant here and is therefore reviewed in some detail next.[201]

---

199 For example, the survey is primarily concerned with what managers believe a *mandated* accounting change, not some *voluntary* goodwill-related accounting decision given a fixed set of rules, will do to users' perception of their firm. Also, the authors did not specifically elicit management's belief regarding users' perception of goodwill write-offs.

200 To reiterate this point, this does not say anything about the empirical validity of the EMH. However, it does suggest that managers' belief in the EMH might not be very strong, and that the occurrence of earnings management behavior inconsistent with the EMH cannot be ruled out *a priori*.

201 The question whether managers are willing to pay for the avoidance of down-the-road goodwill charges is relevant in its own right, and must be viewed independently of users' actual reaction to those, allegedly overpaid, transactions. It calls for a direct analysis of managers' goodwill-related accounting decisions, which in turn will yield insights into managers' beliefs and incentives. If empirical evidence can document that the availability of favorable accounting treatment influences managers' willingness to pay, this suggests that the "cosmetic" costs associated with future goodwill charges are perceived to outweigh the "real" benefits of a lower acquisition price. A related issue is the choice of payment method. See, for example, Gregory (2000).

Harris and Ravenscraft (1991), in an analysis of 1,273 acquisitions of U. S. firms by domestic (1,114) and foreign (159) acquirers during the period 1970-87, show that foreign buyers pay substantially higher purchase prices than U. S. acquirers.[202] They investigate several explanatory factors, not including, however, the accounting treatment of the acquisition in the acquirer's financial statements. Since most of these potential determinants (industry characteristics, tax effects, exchange rate levels, and bidder experience) fail to explain the purchase price difference, there is potential that the accounting treatment is, at least partially, responsible for this effect. Other researchers have tried to explicitly consider the accounting treatment as an explanatory variable.

Choi and Lee (1991) examine whether national differences in accounting standards on the treatment of purchased goodwill help explain any differences in merger premiums.[203] In an analysis of 1,160 acquisitions of U. S. firms by domestic (1,056) and U. K. (104) acquirers announced during the period 1985-89, they find that U. K. firms pay higher premiums in acquisitions than do U. S. firms, concluding that these "higher premium differences on the part of U.K. acquirers do appear to be associated with not having to amortize goodwill to reported earnings."[204] In addition, premiums paid by U. K. firms tend to be more highly associated with goodwill than those paid by U. S. firms. Clinch (1997) criticizes that Choi and Lee (1991) do "not explicitly specify and test the link between goodwill accounting and subsequent economic consequences."[205] While the authors do speculate that goodwill-related accounting rules encourage U. S. acquirers to bid less than U. K acquirers because of possible compensation repercussions of goodwill amortization,[206] they do not explicitly test this conjecture,[207] e.g. by analyzing the relation between compensation schemes and merger premiums. Clinch (1997) concludes that the results of Choi and Lee (1991) are difficult to interpret because the amount of premium paid might be influenced by several factors, to which the accounting treatment of goodwill might or might not belong.[208] This point is acknowledged by the authors who

---

202 See Harris and Ravenscraft (1991, p. 842).

203 Choi and Lee (1991, p. 223) estimate the merger premium as "the difference between the total offering price quoted on the deal announcement date and the market value of the acquired firm ... prior to the announcement date". This measure is different from what is commonly referred to as "acquisition premium" in accounting, the difference between purchase price and book value of net assets.

204 Choi and Lee (1991, pp. 235-6).

205 Clinch (1997, p. 346).

206 See Choi and Lee (1991, p. 226).

207 See Clinch (1997, p. 347).

208 See Clinch (1997, p. 346). For example, he cites differences in "the tax treatment of acquired subsidiaries" as a possibility.

note that "[o]ther variables such as strategic considerations may very well account for the merger premium differences observed."[209]

A follow-up study by Lee and Choi (1992) yields similarly ambiguous results. Lee and Choi (1992) replicate Choi and Lee's (1991) analysis for a small sample of German, Japanese and U. S. acquirers. Again, the firms domiciled in the more "favorable" accounting environment (Germany) pay, on average, higher premiums than those operating under an accounting system where application of the pooling method is either prohibited or subject to restrictive criteria, and where goodwill amortization is mandatory. The authors interpret this finding as showing "that goodwill accounting does explain merger premia."[210] Again, the authors are careful to point out that, while the accounting treatment of goodwill might be an important determinant of the amount of merger premium paid, other factors, not controlled for in their regression models[211] might be driving this behavior much more strongly.[212]

Dunne and Ndubizu (1995) further corroborate the notion that "unfavorable" accounting rules put firms at a competitive disadvantage in the international market for corporate acquisitions. They study the effect of international differences in accounting treatments of goodwill on prices paid in acquisitions. Their sample consists of 95 acquisitions of U. S. firms by foreign bidders from seven different countries during the period 1983-88. Firms that have the option to write off goodwill directly to reserves apparently transfer greater wealth to target shareholders than do firms required to amortize goodwill against earnings.[213]

2.4.3.3.2 Determinants of purchase price allocation decisions

While most of the studies summarized below report evidence from the Asia-Pacific area,[214] the fact that the purchase price allocation process involves considerable discretion is by no means limited to this region.

---

209 Choi and Lee (1991, p. 236).

210 Lee and Choi (1992, p. 220).

211 Control variables, e.g. industrial affiliations and mode of payment, are presented in Lee and Choi (1992, pp. 228-9).

212 See Lee and Choi (1992, p. 233), referring to "strategic considerations and cost of capital differences."

213 The authors also investigate the effects of differing tax treatments. As noted in section 2.3.3 above, Nobes (1996) criticizes Dunne and Ndubizu's (1995) failure to distinguish between goodwill from consolidations and other purchased goodwill, because only the latter is deductible for tax purposes.

214 Goodwill-related rules for Australia and New Zealand are nearly identical. See Dunstan (1999, p. 5).

Wong and Wong (2001) investigate the determinants of New Zealandian firms' accounting choices relating to allocating the acquisition price in a business combination to identifiable assets and goodwill.[215] They point out that the presence of accounting-based debt covenants that restrict the ratio of consolidated debt to consolidated tangible assets is widely assumed to induce managers to allocate only the smallest possible portion of the purchase price to goodwill, suggesting a negative relation between leverage (a proxy for the restrictiveness of the covenant) and acquired goodwill.[216] However, the authors point out that such relation might also be due to "joint effects between each of these variables and the firm's investment opportunity set" represented by assets-in-place and the market-to-book (MTB) ratio.[217] Their empirical results indicate an "endogenous relation among the firm's asset structure, financing policy, and acquired goodwill",[218] casting doubt on whether certain findings in prior research were interpreted correctly as supporting the debt covenant hypothesis.

Dunstan's (1999) paper directly addresses the inference problems identified by Wong and Wong (2001).[219] Her analysis "provides insight into the factors that motivate management's discretionary accounting policy choices for goodwill."[220] She investigates "both *ex ante* and *ex post* explanations for the accounting treatment .. of goodwill"[221] in 163 Australian acquisitions occurring during the period 1988-94. Specifically, she is interested in "the determinants of the decision to proportionately allocate the purchase price between goodwill and identifiable assets."[222] Her *ex ante* explanations deal with the question if, in the absence of any earnings management and due to the acquired investment opportunity set (i.e., the economic nature of the given acquisition), the portion of purchase price recorded as goodwill is likely to be higher in some acquisitions than in others. In contrast, her *ex post* explanations are intended to clarify how managers are likely to exercise their discretion within the accepted set of accounting procedures, given the *ex ante* restrictions imposed on this discretion. The latter hypotheses include variants

---

215 See Wong and Wong (2001, pp. 191-2).

216 See Wong and Wong (2001, p. 180).

217 Wong and Wong (2001, p. 191).

218 Wong and Wong (2001, p. 191).

219 Dunstan's (1999, pp. 5-6) paper contains an at-length review of the pre-publication version of Wong and Wong's (2001) article.

220 Dunstan (1999, p. 33).

221 Dunstan (1999, p. 2).

222 Dunstan (1999, p. 3).

of the bonus plan and debt covenant hypotheses.[223] In summary, Dunstan (1999) reports that her overall model explains 8.5% (R^2) of the cross-sectional variation in the proportion of purchase price recorded as goodwill. Not all of the individual hypotheses are supported.[224] Of the *ex post* predictions, the debt covenant hypothesis is sustained.[225] According to the data, managers allocate more of the purchase price to tangible assets (and less to goodwill) when they operate under debt covenants that restrict the ratio of total liabilities to total tangible assets.[226] Further, Dunstan (1999) finds a positive indirect relation between the investment opportunity set of the acquirer, represented by the proportion of growth options, and goodwill. The rationale is that high growth option firms, due to their assumed lower leverage (higher relevance of equity financing) and non-existence of accounting-based compensation plans (higher relevance of market-based performance measures in compensation schemes), have less incentive to minimize reported goodwill.[227]

Wines and Ferguson (1993) document firms' reluctance to incur goodwill amortization expenses by examining the accounting procedures adopted for goodwill and identifiable intangible assets by a sample of 150 Australian listed companies over the period 1985-89. They find that, while goodwill accounting policies tended to converge over that period, the opposite seemed to be true of accounting policies for identifiable intangible assets. Increasingly, firms chose, in conflict with then effective GAAP, to recognize and not amortize identifiable intangible assets, often reclassified from goodwill, allegedly "in an effort to reduce the impact on reported operating profits of the requirement for the amortization of goodwill balances."[228]

Grinyer, Russell and Walker (1991) analyze the determinants of the purchase price allocation decision for a sample of 392 U. K. firm years during the period 1982-86. During that time, U. K. GAAP allowed firms to choose between immediately writing off good-

---

223 See Dunstan (1999, pp. 14-7). For a detailed explanation of these hypotheses, refer to sections 3.3.2.3.3 and 3.3.2.3.4 below, respectively.

224 See Dunstan (1999, pp. 30-2). The intuitive *ex ante* prediction that the goodwill proportion would be positively associated with the level of growth options (versus assets in place) acquired, is supported. However, this finding does not allow any conclusions as to management's financial reporting incentives.

225 See Dunstan (1999, pp. 31-2).

226 See Dunstan (1999, p. 14). Apparently, this type of restriction is common in Australian debt covenants. See also Wong and Wong (2001).

227 See Dunstan (1999, pp. 17-8).

228 Wines and Ferguson (1993, p. 104).

will against reserves versus capitalizing and amortizing it.[229] Due to considerable discretion with regard to purchase price allocation, managers could effectively control the portion of purchase price to be allocated to separable assets and, consequently, to goodwill. The authors find that firms with high leverage tended to allocate a greater portion of purchase price to separable assets, strengthening their leverage-related balance sheet ratios.[230] Grinyer, Russell and Walker (1991) conclude that the presence of accounting-based debt covenants influences managers' purchase price allocation decisions.[231]

2.4.3.3.3 Determinants of amortization parameters

Exploiting a unique institutional setting,[232] Day and Hartnett (1999/2000) investigate "what might motivate the use of *differential* amortisation methods amongst firms and whether some sort of cash effect (direct or indirect) might feasibly flow from the [abandonment of the inverted-sum-of-years-digits method]."[233] The hypotheses draw on the positive accounting theory introduced in section 3.3.2.3 below. Specifically, the bonus plan, debt covenant, and political costs hypotheses as well as a contracting efficiency perspective are proposed.[234] The authors find significant differences in the goodwill-related properties of the nine firms using the inverted-sum-of-years-digits method compared to 38 other firms that do not use deferred amortization methods.[235] While the political costs and debt covenant hypotheses are rejected, goodwill expense and the goodwill asset are significantly larger in firms that use the inverted-sum-of-years-digits method.[236] This finding is consistent with predictions from both the bonus plan and contracting efficiency hypotheses, which creates interpretation problems. At best, the data

---

229 Due to a unique provision in the U. K. Companies Act, firms were able to mitigate the equity-decreasing effect of the immediate write-off under certain circumstances. Therefore, the immediate write-off gave firms the opportunity to obtain the favorable income statement effect of no amortization without having to incur fully the adverse balance sheet effect of reduced equity reserves.

230 Conversely, firms that did not face the equity-decreasing consequences of the immediate write-off alternative tended to allocate a greater portion of purchase price to goodwill.

231 See also the at-length review in Dunstan (1999, pp. 3-5).

232 The setting is unique insofar as the authors exploit the window of opportunity that opened in Australia during the first half of the 1990s and closed when Australian accounting regulators banned the controversial inverted-sum-of-years-digits method of goodwill amortization in 1996. This procedure essentially defers most of the goodwill amortization towards the end of the goodwill's useful life, thereby minimizing the present value of total goodwill-related charges. The debate is outlined in considerable detail in Day and Hartnett (1999/2000, pp. 195-8). See also Brown (1995).

233 Day and Hartnett (1999/2000, p. 200 [emphasis in original]).

234 See Day and Hartnett (1999/2000, pp. 200-2).

235 It must be noted that the small sample size might call into question the *economic*, if not the statistical, significance of the results.

236 See Day and Hartnett (1999/2000, pp. 204-8).

documents that managers, for whatever reason, will defer goodwill-related charges when it is nearly costless to do so due to a downright choice in applicable accounting guidance.

Hall (1993a) explores the determinants of goodwill amortization period under APB 17 in a cross-sectional study of 149 firms that reported goodwill amortization in 1985. His hypotheses also draw on the positive accounting theory introduced in section 3.3.2.3 below. Hall's (1993a) results indicate that the choice is affected by firm size and by the proximity of a firm's accounting data to violating covenant restrictions. Henning and Shaw (2003) analyze the determinants of goodwill amortization behavior from a different angle. On a sample of 1,741 acquisitions from 1990-94, they test whether the choice of amortization period predicts the acquirer's post-acquisition earnings and, therefore, might be interpreted as strategic. Their findings suggest that firms with expectations of high post-acquisition earnings are likely to amortize goodwill more aggressively, presumably because they can "afford" the earnings dilution caused by shorter amortization periods.

2.4.3.4 Determinants of the purchase/pooling choice

As discussed in section 2.3.2.3 above, it is a common conjecture that managers prefer the pooling method of accounting for business combinations because under this procedure, no goodwill is recognized and no future goodwill charges occur. Since the effects of the purchase/pooling decision mirror the effects of other goodwill-related accounting decisions, it is plausible to assume that determinants of the purchase/pooling choice are also likely to influence other goodwill-related accounting decisions such as the goodwill write-offs under SFAS 142. Therefore, empirical findings surrounding the purchase/pooling choice are presented next. Special emphasis is placed on research findings that document managers' willingness to bear substantial costs to obtain the pooling treatment, which indicates that managers perceive this treatment to involve substantial benefits.[237]

2.4.3.4.1 Factors influencing the purchase/pooling choice

According to Weber (2000), research on the factors associated with the decision to use the pooling method provides evidence that "man[a]gers use pooling-of-interests to increase future accounting income."[238] This is also the bottom-line of Robinson and Shane's (1990) summary of five early studies, reviewed in this section, of "an income

---

237 See Lys and Vincent (1995, p. 368).

238 Weber (2000, p. 6).

maximization hypothesis as a decision rule for predicting the acquisition accounting method".[239]

In an early "progress report", Gagnon (1967) tries to find a predictor for whether a merger will be accounted for as a purchase or as a pooling, in order to be able to infer the decision rule that underlies the choice of treatment. Especially, he is interested in distinguishing between the income maximization and income smoothing hypotheses.[240] Using data on "approximately 500 mergers"[241] occurring in the period 1955-58, he applies discriminant analysis to infer the separating characteristics of pooling and purchase acquisitions. His results suggest that firms whose future expected earnings are likely to be decreased by the future amortization of a high acquisition premium tend towards using the pooling method.[242] These findings are corroborated in Gagnon's (1971) later study. Copeland and Wojdak (1969) discuss Gagnon's (1967) article and replicate Gagnon's study with more current data (1966-1967). They find as well that "firms record mergers by the method that maximizes reported income".[243] Anderson and Louderback (1975) test whether the Copeland and Wojdak (1969) results still hold after APB Opinion 16 restricted the purchase/pooling choice. They compare 114 mergers in the pre-APB Opinion 16 period with 64 transactions taking place after that rule was issued. They conclude that, although "the two treatments are no longer alternatives" post-APB Opinion 16, "the lack of significant decline in [pooling transactions] is evidence that managements have continued to select and 'follow GAAP' in a manner consistent with the income maximizing hypothesis."[244]

Crawford (1987) invokes contracting theory to explain the purchase/pooling choice. He reports results "consistent with the hypothesis that managers consider the effect on their compensation packages when they choose a merger's structure ... [but] ... weakly consistent with the hypothesis that merger structure is influenced by the presence of debt cove-

239 Robinson and Shane (1990, pp. 26-8).

240 See Gagnon (1967, pp. 191-6).

241 Gagnon (1967, p. 196).

242 Sapienza (1967) and Wyatt (1967) provide discussions of the Gagnon (1967) paper. Sapienza (1967, p. 205) argues that the purchase/pooling choice was not actually a choice during the period analyzed, because "widespread knowledge of the pooling concept was not the case". Also, he notes that the pooling method might in some cases have been adopted for tax reasons. Wyatt's (1967, pp. 211-2) most notable criticism relates to the notion that the accounting treatment of a given acquisition is determined jointly with other variables of the transaction. Therefore, simulating, as Gagnon (1967) does, the accounting acquisition premium that would have arisen had a given acquisition been accounted for as a purchase versus as a pooling, generates potentially irrelevant values.

243 Copeland and Wojdak (1969, p. 195).

244 Anderson and Louderback (1978, p. 343).

nants".[245] This latter finding is somewhat contrary to the results reported in most of the other studies described below.

Davis (1990) analyzes 108 pooling and 69 purchase method mergers completed during the period 1971-82. He finds that "leverage for the purchase method sample ... is significantly higher than for the pooling method sample".[246] Similar to Aboody, Kasznik and Williams (2000), Desai et al. (2001) and Ayers, Lefanowicz and Robinson (2000a),[247] this could be interpreted as supportive of the debt covenant hypothesis, since highly leveraged firms have incentive to recognize the asset step-up often occurring under the purchase method, thereby reducing leverage. However, Davis (1990) concludes that "highly leveraged firms may prefer purchase method accounting to reduce profits."[248] The author goes on to argue, consistent with the political costs hypothesis, that reduced reported earnings will also reduce "regulators' attention".[249] However, it is not made clear why especially highly leveraged firms should have an interest in escaping regulators' scrutiny.[250]

Dunne (1990) investigates the factors influencing the purchase/pooling choice of 158 acquirers during the period 1983-85. She expects that manager-ownership, accounting-based compensation, debt covenant, and political cost considerations affect that decision. Her findings indicate that manager-controlled firms[251] tend to opt for the income-increasing pooling method.[252] Also, Dunne finds that, "when management chooses between the two accounting treatments for a business combination, they consider the accounting method's effect on their compensation."[253] High-debt firms tend to use the purchase method, possibly in an attempt to strengthen their asset bases.[254] Finally, the evi-

---

245 Crawford (1987, p. 109), as quoted by Robinson and Shane (1990, p. 28).

246 Davis (1990, p. 705).

247 These studies are reviewed shortly.

248 Davis (1990, p. 708).

249 Davis (1990, p. 696).

250 Usually, firm *size* is assumed to be positively related to a firm's exposure to adverse regulation. Refer to section 3.3.2.3.5 below. This is also acknowledged by the author. See Davis (1990, p. 704). Another reported finding is that the relative bargaining strength of the firms engaged in a merger appears to influence the choice of accounting method to report that merger. According to his results, acquirers having high bargaining power tend towards using the purchase method. See Davis (1990, p. 696).

251 In a manager-controlled firm, management has only a limited stake in the firm's equity.

252 See Dunne (1990, p. 125).

253 Dunne (1990, p. 126).

254 See Dunne (1990, p. 126).

dence suggests that "firms with higher earnings may prefer purchase accounting because of political cost considerations."[255]

Using a case study approach, Lys and Vincent (1995) discuss at length possible motives of AT&T to obtain pooling treatment for its acquisition of NCR, among others shareholder communications, debt covenants and bonus plans.[256] They conclude that "AT&T's willingness to pay a premium for the pooling-of-interests method of accounting was to avoid a sustained decrease in *EPS* because of the importance of investors' perceptions."[257] The authors find no evidence to suggest that the income-increasing choice was due to debt covenants, but "cannot dismiss the possibility that the preference was due to executive compensation".[258]

Aboody, Kasznik and Williams (2000) provide evidence that the purchase/pooling choice does not appear to be driven by managers' beliefs regarding investors' perceptions but rather by contracting incentives.[259] Specifically, managers subject to accounting earnings-based compensation schemes are more likely than others to incur costs to obtain pooling treatment for acquisitions, especially where there is a large gap between purchase price and the target's net assets that will lead to a future "earnings penalty". However, managers rewarded on the basis of their firms' stock performance do not appear to be concerned with the allegedly negative accounting effects of the purchase method, suggesting that they do not believe investors to respond negatively to this method. The findings also suggest that firms with high DTE ratios tend towards using the purchase method, according to the authors because of its favorable balance sheet effects. The authors also find that the likelihood to use pooling decreases in the potential costs of complying with the pooling criteria. With regard to the question of main interest here, Aboody, Kasznik and Williams's (2000) findings suggest that, while managers are willing to incur costs to obtain pooling treatment, this is mainly due to contracting considerations and not necessarily to investors being assumed to respond negatively to goodwill and the accompanying earnings drag.

---

255 Dunne (1990, p. 127).

256 Refer to Lys and Vincent (1995, pp. 369-74).

257 Lys and Vincent (1995, p. 377 [emphasis in original], pp. 373-4).

258 Lys and Vincent (1995, p. 377).

259 Refer to Aboody, Kasznik and Williams (2000, pp. 283-4).

Ayers, Lefanowicz and Robinson (2000a) also investigate the factors that influence the purchase/pooling choice. Results for a sample of 198 stock-for-stock acquisitions[260] made during the period 1990-96 suggest that "acquiring firms select their accounting method to enhance the financial statement presentation of the combined firm".[261] Specifically, in transactions where large premiums over acquired net assets are paid, firms tend towards the pooling method, supposedly in order to avoid the severe "earnings penalty" from future depreciation and amortization. Conversely, where the target firm's leverage is high, the purchase method tends to be used more frequently, purportedly since it improves the DTE ratio.[262]

Desai et al. (2001) also report that "acquirers in purchase mergers have higher leverage relative to pooling acquirers."[263] In addition, their analysis of 129 purchase and 366 pooling mergers completed between 1978 and 1999 documents that the targets in pooling mergers have superior prior stock and accounting performance. This might suggest that acquirers that "acquire performance" have incentive to use an income-increasing accounting method to report the acquisition.[264] Desai et al. (2001) declare that these "characteristics significantly influence the choice of accounting method in a merger."[265]

Overall, the evidence summarized here is again consistent with the notion that managers are concerned about the financial statement effects of goodwill-related accounting decisions. Especially, they fear an erosion of earnings due to future amortization and, albeit documented less frequently, an increase in financial leverage, possibly due to the existence of accounting-based debt covenants.

2.4.3.4.2 Managers' willingness to "purchase" the pooling method

Some of the earlier studies discussed in the previous section have interpreted the purchase/pooling decision as a downright choice. However, when APB Opinion 16 was issued in 1970, the pooling method was made mandatory for transaction that satisfied certain restrictive – and potentially costly-to-satisfy – criteria.[266] At that time, a costless

---

260 While 49 of these acquisitions were accounted for under the purchase method, 149 were subjected to the pooling treatment.

261 Ayers, Lefanowicz and Robinson (2000a, p. 27).

262 These findings correspond to those reported by Aboody, Kasznik and Williams (2000).

263 Desai et al. (2001, p. 5).

264 Desai et al. (2001, p. 17) use the term "income maximization hypothesis".

265 Desai et al. (2001, p. 5).

266 Refer to section 2.3.2.2.1 above.

"choice" between the two treatments ceased to exist. The fact that the pooling method did not lose much of its appeal in the aftermath suggests that managers were willing to incur the pooling costs, possibly because the benefits associated with this favorable accounting treatment outweighed the costs to meet the pooling criteria. In this section, evidence is presented, first, on the costs of obtaining pooling treatment and, second, on managers' willingness to incur these costs.

Davis (1996) notes that application of the pooling method is subject to "12 restrictive provisions, some of which can be quite difficult and costly to satisfy."[267] In addition to direct transaction costs, structuring an acquisition to fulfill these conditions is "likely to be costly for shareholders because it requires the firm to forego valuable real options", such as "the ability to do share repurchases and asset divestures".[268] Moreover, as Desai et al. (2001) point out, an acquirer's ability to satisfy the pooling criteria in effect hinged on the cooperation of the target's management, which often entailed higher premiums in pooling mergers.[269] Another interesting cost item is pointed out by Gagnon (1967): He argues that, before APB Opinion 16 specified criteria to govern the purchase/pooling decision, a company had to "convince both the SEC and its independent [auditors] that [the pooling] treatment [was] appropriate under the circumstances."[270] Finally, Martínez-Jerez (2001) argues that the pooling method increases shareholders' monitoring costs due to reduced financial statement transparency.[271] Using a case study approach, Lys and Vincent (1995) give an extensive overview of the incremental costs of pooling in AT&T's acquisition of NCR.[272]

In view of the substantial costs of meeting the pooling criteria, researchers have argued that managers' willingness to incur these costs could be viewed as evidence of their strong belief in the desirable accounting effects of this method. This belief is highlighted by the frequently made assertion that several acquisitions were made contingent on the

---

267 Davis (1996, p. 51).

268 Martínez-Jerez (2001, p. 6). In a similar vein, Robinson and Shane (1990, p. 29) refer more generally to "an opportunity cost associated with satisfying one or more APBO No. 16 criteria".

269 See Desai et al. (2001, pp. 2-3) and Nathan (1988, p. 187). Unless stated otherwise, "premium" in this context does not refer to the difference between purchase price and fair value of acquired net assets (i.e., goodwill plus any fair value increments) but to some market-based measure of the acquirer's willingness to pay more than the target's market value before the market learned of the acquisition plan.

270 Gagnon (1967, p. 189).

271 See Martínez-Jerez (2001, p. 8). Transparency is reduced because the acquired assets and liabilities are not adjusted to their fair values but carried over at their book values.

272 See Lys and Vincent (1995, pp. 367-8).

availability of the pooling treatment.[273] However, the exact nature of these perceived benefits is open to debate. Nathan (1988) suggests managers' belief in the mechanistic hypothesis when he notes: "Managers of acquiring firms will pay to pool if they *believe* the market is fooled by the higher net income number. Whether the market actually is fooled (implying market inefficiency) is an empirical question".[274] However, if managers are found to "pay to pool" although shareholders consistently penalize this behavior, this is evidence that managers, acting in a self-interested way, derive private benefits from the pooling treatment.[275] Next, studies on managers' willingness to incur the pooling costs are analyzed. Shareholders' reactions to the purchase/pooling decision are reviewed in section 2.4.4.4 below.

Evidently, the substantial extra costs of obtaining the pooling treatment are willingly incurred by many firms. In their detailed account of AT&T's acquisition of NCR, Lys and Vincent (1995) document that AT&T's management was willing to expend "between $50 and $500 million of corporate assets" for the perceived benefits of pooling.[276]

Desai et al. (2001) analyze whether firms are "willing to 'pay' to report higher earnings even in the absence of any incremental effect on cash flow" for a large sample of stock-for-stock mergers spanning the period 1978-97.[277] They find no significant association between the acquisition premium[278] and the choice between the purchase and pooling methods, after other significant influencing factors of that choice are controlled for.[279] All this indicates is that managers are not necessarily, *on average*, willing to incur significant costs in the form of a higher merger premium for the ability to use pooling. Similarly, Aboody, Kasznik and Williams' (2000) conclude that "firms for which the pooling requirement of no post-acquisition share repurchases appears to be binding ... are less likely than others to use pooling."[280] Of course, the notion that the perceived pooling benefits are likely to be foregone when opportunity costs are higher stands to economic reason. However, pending further analysis, these results should not be taken as evidence

---

273 See, for example, Gagnon (1967, p. 189). Empirical evidence on this fact is presented by Nathan (1988, p. 198).

274 Nathan (1988, p. 187 fn. 2 [emphasis in original]). See also Robinson and Shane (1990, p. 29).

275 See Robinson and Shane (1990, p. 29).

276 Lys and Vincent (1995, p. 373).

277 Desai et al. (2001, p. 2).

278 Desai et al. (2001 p. 11): "Merger (Acquisition) Premium is measured as the target's matching-firm-adjusted return ... over two holding periods."

279 See Desai et al. (2001, p. 5).

280 Aboody, Kasznik and Williams (2000, p. 284).

that managers believe the accounting choice does not matter to investors. Only, in certain circumstances they deem the pooling costs to exceed the benefits.

Robinson and Shane (1990) investigate whether benefits derived from the accounting treatment are reflected in bid premiums for target firms. Their sample consists of 59 pooling and 36 purchase acquisitions occurring during the period 1972-82. They conclude that "the acquisitions accounted for as poolings involved higher average bid premia than the acquisitions accounted for as purchases." The authors attribute this difference to the fact that "bidders are willing to pay for benefits derived from accounting method." However, pointing to an identification problem, they caution that the difference may be due to omitted intervening variables that jointly determine bid premia and accounting method, e.g. the percentage of shares acquired,[281] or to the possibility that "higher bid premia lead to a higher probability of pooling."[282] The latter suggestions would contradict the notion that the accounting treatment of a given acquisition is determined before the transaction actually takes place, and is established jointly with other variables of the transaction.[283]

In a more recent paper, Ayers, Lefanowicz and Robinson (2000b) document firms' willingness to pay higher acquisition premiums in mergers accounted for using the pooling method. They address the identification problem documented above by "controlling for known economic determinants of acquisition price and differences across purchase and pooling acquisitions" and report that "on average, firms incur in excess of $60 million in additional acquisition premiums to structure the average sample acquisition as a pooling-of-interests."[284]

Nathan (1988) is interested in the impact of APB Opinions 16 and 17 on the purchase prices paid in stock-for-stock pooling acquisitions in the period 1963-78. While his study is not exactly an investigation of the purchase/pooling choice (only pooling transactions are examined), he does contribute insights of relevance here. He predicts that the increased restrictiveness of the pooling criteria brought about by APB Opinion 16 increases offer prices because the acquirer must secure, certainly at a price, the target's cooperation in fulfilling these criteria. In addition, he hypothesizes that the pooling method's income-increasing properties induce managers, who are subject to loan covenants and account-

[281] See also Clinch (1997, p. 347).

[282] Robinson and Shane (1990, p. 47 [all quotes]).

[283] See Wyatt (1967, pp. 211-2).

[284] Ayers, Lefanowicz and Robinson (2000b, p. 30 [both quotes]).

ing-based compensation contracts, to offer higher premiums[285] for larger amounts of potential goodwill that pooling would avoid, a proxy for the accounting benefits of this method.[286] Linear regression results suggest that the offer premium, contrary to the prediction, is *negatively* related to the amount of potential goodwill, especially in post-APB Opinion 16 acquisitions.[287] Nathan (1988) draws on arguments advanced by Walkling and Edmister (1985) to explain his findings:[288] First, low-goodwill firms might appear to be bargain purchases that can be had at not much more than their replacement value, making them more attractive for bidders. Second, low potential goodwill might be an indicator of poor management, suggesting to acquirers a high potential for value-increasing restructuring efforts. Additional tests of the income maximization hypothesis show that, after APB Opinion 16 prohibited pooling transactions paid for with preferred stock, the frequency of common-stock pooling acquisitions and not that of preferred-stock purchase acquisitions increased.[289] Nathan (1988) concludes that management, on average, preferred incurring the costs of common-stock versus preferred-stock payment [290] over foregoing the perceived benefits of the income-increasing pooling method.[291] Overall, the findings seem to indicate that the perceived accounting benefits derived from the pooling treatment exceed the costs from the dilution of control. However, the author fails to find substantiation for the hypothesis that higher potential goodwill increases the acquirers' offer premiums.

Overall, the evidence presented is largely consistent with the assumption that "managers prefer [the pooling] method and are willing to incur significant costs to avoid the recognition of additional assets and expenses associated with the purchase method".[292]

---

285 Nathan (1988, p. 187) defines the premium as the "offer price per share minus the target's preannouncement share price ... divided by the target's preannouncement share price".

286 See Nathan (1988, p. 188). This relation is expected to be more pronounced after APB Opinion 16 became effective than before.

287 Several control variables that have been shown in prior research to be related to the size of offer premium are included in the models. See Nathan (1988, pp. 188-9).

288 See Nathan (1988, pp. 193-5).

289 See Nathan (1988, pp. 195-7).

290 These costs are, in effect, "opportunity cost associated with the dilution of control due to the use of common stock". Robinson and Shane (1990, p. 47).

291 See Nathan (1988, p. 198).

292 Ayers, Lefanowicz and Robinson (2000b, p. 2).

2.4.3.5 Managers' lobbying for goodwill-related accounting rules

A final source of information about managers' beliefs regarding the stock market effects of their goodwill-related accounting decisions is their lobbying behavior with financial accounting standard-setters and other regulatory agencies. It is straightforward to assume that managers lobby for the accounting rules they consider most beneficial for them.[293] Any cross-sectional variation in firms' lobbying behavior is likely to help reveal the determinants of managers' goodwill-related accounting preferences.

The influence of "political lobbying" on the standard-setting process has interested researchers for a long time. It is frequently argued that several U. S. accounting rules can only be interpreted as the results of such lobbying taking place.[294] As discussed in section 2.3.2.2.1 above, there is a wealth of, mostly anecdotal, evidence that the impairment-only approach adopted in SFAS 142 is the outcome of political lobbying. It is maintained that the *de facto* opportunity to avoid or at least defer goodwill charges resulting from the abolishment of the goodwill amortization requirement was the political price the FASB had to pay to compensate firms for the elimination of the pooling method. Dennis R. Beresford, former chairman of the FASB, documents the extent of political involvement in standard setting.[295] For example, he notes that Senator Phil Gramm, then chairman of the responsible Senate committee, personally recommended that an impairment-only approach to goodwill accounting be required.[296] Furthermore, the SEC Chief Accountant is cited demanding that the FASB abandon the pooling method because SEC staff "spends nearly 40 percent of its time dealing with interpreting the complicated pooling criteria under APB Opinion No. 16."[297] A representative of the so-called "new economy" argued strongly in favor of retaining the pooling method, because "[t]he elimination of pooling will constrain companies from engaging in business combinations that make sense".[298] Another claimed that the U. S. "are the premier capital market of the world, and pooling has no doubt contributed to our fast growth and expansion."[299]

---

293 For example, refer to Watts and Zimmerman (1978).

294 First and foremost, SFAS 123, *Accounting for Stock-Based Compensation*, comes to mind in this respect. Zeff (2002, p. 50) argues that, "under the gun from key members of Congress, the FASB could do no more than issue SFAS No. 123, ... requiring footnote disclosure of the estimated dilutive effect of stock options on reported earnings". See also Zeff (1997) and the literature cite there.

295 Refer to Beresford (2001).

296 See Beresford (2001, p. 74).

297 Beresford (2001, p. 75).

298 Beresford (2001, p. 76).

299 Beresford (2001, p. 77).

These and other *ad hoc* suggestions that politicians and, possibly through them, other lobbyists significantly shaped SFAS 141 and 142, the outcomes of the FASB's business combinations project. More systematic evidence can be obtained from the comment letters that the FASB received from its constituents in various stages of the project. Wyrwich (2002) suggests that, while the impairment-only approach was predetermined by Congressional pressure, the details were open to debate.[300] His analysis of comment letters indicates that financial statement preparers as well as Big Five auditors principally influenced the final wording of SFAS 141 and 142.[301]

The study by Gore, Taib and Taylor (2000) documents "the positions taken by managements of UK-listed companies during the heated debate surrounding proposals for a new standard on goodwill accounting".[302] As discussed above, the authors find that managers prefer goodwill-related accounting rules that avoid future charges and are especially in favor of an immediate charge of goodwill against equity.[303] In his analysis of goodwill accounting standard setting in the U. K., Nobes (1992) discusses the influences exercised by several interested parties.[304] He concludes standard setting follows a cyclical pattern, where perceived variety in accounting practices, economic developments, and international regulatory initiatives induce standard setters to act. The ensuing process is shaped by competing "downward" and "upward forces", which are in favor of less or more standardization, respectively. The downward force is usually represented by self-interested managers, possibly supported by audit firms, whereas the upward force is frequently constituted by "individual senior members of the profession", backed by government, the press and international organizations.[305]

2.4.4 Indirect evidence

It is interesting to examine whether the beliefs apparently held by some preparers of financial statements are corroborated by market data. If market reactions consistently turn out contrary to management's beliefs, revisions in these beliefs to reflect actual market

---

300 See Wyrwich (2002, p. 48).

301 Wyrwich's (2002) analysis includes 208 comment letters on the FASB's February 2001 Exposure Draft, *Business Combinations and Intangible Assets – Accounting for Goodwill*, with a combined length of 1,002 pages. Methodologically, his approach draws on McLeay, Ordelheide and Young's (2000) study.

302 Gore, Taib and Taylor (2000, p. 213).

303 See Gore, Taib and Taylor (2000, p. 221).

304 Refer to Nobes (1992, pp. 157-9).

305 Nobes (1992, p. 158).

behavior are likely to occur. Accordingly, in this section a body of research that sheds light on investors' perceptions of goodwill accounting and the purchase/pooling choice is reviewed.

2.4.4.1 Experimental evidence

According to some authors, management's doubts in the EMH, implying that investors are unable to fully see through the financial statement effects of goodwill-related accounting decisions, are not entirely far-fetched. For example, Duvall et al. (1992) suggest that then current U. S. reporting requirements made it difficult for investors to disentangle the financial statement effects of goodwill accounting. Especially, they report that a substantial number of firms, amounting to 76.3% of the sample,[306] do not disclose goodwill amortization, even when it is material.[307] Furthermore, estimation of this charge when it is not disclosed can result in material errors.[308]

Hopkins, Houston and Peters' (2000) experimental study of financial analysts' information processing behavior suggests a similar conclusion: The authors ask 113 buy-side equity analysts[309] to estimate the price of a company's stock, depending on the method chosen to account for a recent stock-for-stock business combination and on the amount of time elapsed since the transaction occurred. They hypothesize that application of the purchase method and subsequent amortization of any resulting accounting acquisition premium[310] results in lower estimated stock prices than does either immediately expensing the premium or use of the pooling method. The authors also predict that the negative effects of amortization are stronger in association with business combinations that occurred a longer time previously because investors fail to remember that the amortization originated from a cash-neutral accounting decision. It is further assumed that separate income statement presentation of goodwill amortization, combined with a display of pre-goodwill-amortization income, diminishes the negative effects of this accounting treatment. They report that, with respect to the same business combination, test persons' stock-price judgments depend on the method chosen to account for the business combi-

---

306 See Duvall et al. (1992, p. 6).

307 See Duvall et al. (1992, p. 11).

308 See Duvall et al. (1992, pp. 8-10). The estimation procedure is reported in Duvall et al. (1992, pp. 12-4).

309 An analyst employed by an entity, such as a mutual fund, that invests on its own accounts. Unlike that of the sell-side analysts employed by brokerage firms or other firms that manage client accounts, research produced by buy-side analysts is usually unavailable outside of the firm that hired the analyst.

310 The difference between the fair value paid for the target and the book value of the target's net assets. See Hopkins, Houston and Peters (2000, p. 258).

nation and on the time passed since the transaction. Analysts' judgments are lowest when a business combination is accounted for using the purchase method and any resulting premium is amortized. With respect to the timing issue, they find support for the assumption (e.g. made by AT&T in its acquisition of NCR[311]) that analysts tend to forget over time that income-decreasing financial statement repercussions from past transactions are purely cosmetic in nature and not indicative of economic decline. It is important to keep in mind not only that Hopkins, Houston and Peters' (2000) experimental setting does not realistically simulate actual market behavior,[312] but also that "market prices are determined by an aggregation of the beliefs of a myriad of participants, not a set of isolated financial analysts".[313] However, the experimental setting has at least one advantage: It inherently controls for factors other than the choice of accounting method that are likely to influence market perception of a merger.[314] In market-based studies, these factors must be controlled for in the research design, which poses problems of model misspecification and other errors. In conclusion, Hopkins, Houston and Peters' (2000) results do challenge the EMH in that they document that analysts tend to forget after several reporting periods that lower earnings due to goodwill amortization are merely cosmetic and not resultant from lower cash flows.[315]

2.4.4.2 Information content of goodwill write-offs

Ceteris paribus, statistically significant associations between goodwill write-offs and stock prices is likely to induce management to influence, within their discretion, the existence, amount, and timing of these charges in order to either achieve or, if desirable, avoid the expected stock price effect associated with them. If the sign and/or extent of any association between goodwill write-offs and stock price were documented to vary cross-sectionally, different incentives would exist depending on firm characteristics and other factors found to be statistical determinants of this association.

While there is a substantial body of literature on investors' reactions to other discretionary asset write-offs,[316] there is little direct evidence on the association of goodwill write-offs with share prices. At this point, empirical tests of stock market reactions to transi-

---

311 See Lys and Vincent (1995, p. 370)

312 See Hopkins, Houston and Peters' (2000, pp. 277-8).

313 Hong, Kaplan and Mandelker (1978, p. 34).

314 See Hopkins, Houston and Peters (2000, p. 258).

315 See also Hong, Kaplan amd Mandelker (1978, pp. 33-4).

316 Refer to section 3.4 below.

tional SFAS 142 goodwill write-offs have relied on preliminary data. Segal (2003) analyzes such market reactions. However, his study includes write-off announcements published between October 2001 and June 2002 only. He controls for the expected portion of the write-off by estimating these amounts using, first, a "market price drop" estimation method and, second, a residual income estimation method.[317] Also, any earnings surprise as well as other information inherent in the write-off announcement is controlled for. The unexpected portion of the write-off is found to be significantly associated with a negative stock price response, whereas the expected portion is insignificant.[318] The earnings surprise and "other information" variables are insignificant. A comparison of the market reactions under the SFAS 121 regime and under the SFAS 142 regime generates only a weak indication that "the market reaction to goodwill write-downs is more negative under the new rule".[319] Regarding the timeliness of the write-offs, Segal claims that SFAS 142 may have caused some "catching up" of write-offs not recognized under the previous regime.[320] However, under both accounting standards, goodwill write-offs, on average, lag the corresponding stock price declines.[321]

Henning and Stock (1998) conduct a value-relevance study of pre-SFAS 142 goodwill write-offs.[322] They find that the association of stock prices with write-offs depends on the type of goodwill. Write-offs of goodwill related to valuable intangible assets are associated with both advance and contemporaneous stock price decreases. The anticipation of the write-offs by market participants is greater for firms with poor results than for firms with strong results.

In contrast, Francis, Hanna and Vincent (1996) use an event study design to document an insignificantly *positive* association between two-day abnormal returns and goodwill write-off amounts for a sample of 44 goodwill write-off announcements made during the

---

317 See Segal (2003, p. 26). The methods are explained in more detail in the appendix to the paper.

318 See Segal (2003, pp. 27-8). This result relates to the unexpected portion estimated using the residual income estimation method. In contrast, the alternative method generates a significantly negative coefficient for the *expected* portion of the write-off, which is not easily interpreted.

319 Segal (2003, p. 28).

320 An alternative explanation would be big bath behavior because transitional goodwill write-offs are displayed "below-the-line".

321 See Segal (2003, p. 28).

322 Since the Henning and Stock (1998) paper is no longer available for full download on SSRN, the published abstract is used. According to an email from contact author Steven L. Henning, the Henning and Stock (1998) study was continued by Henning, Shaw and Stock (2002). However, unlike the former paper, the Henning, Shaw and Stock (2002) analysis does not consider market reactions to goodwill write-offs.

period 1989-92.[323] They interpret this finding as suggesting that, since "incentives ... play a substantial role in explaining goodwill write-offs",[324] these write-offs reveal less information about any economic value declines than other write-off types (e.g. inventory write-offs) where reporting managers have less discretion over existence, amount, and timing. Overall, "investors' response is driven more by write-offs revealing information about asset impairments than by write-offs conveying positive signals about future performance".[325]

Finally, in an event study of 80 pre-SFAS 142 goodwill write-off announcements made during the period 1992-96, Hirschey and Richardson (2002) document statistically significant negative event-day market reactions. They interpret their findings as suggesting that goodwill write-offs are perceived as bad news, signaling a deterioration of the firm's future proft-making potential. In a cross-sectional regression analysis, they find no evidence that the size of the write-off influences the strength of the market response. In a long-window extension of this study, Hirschey and Richardson (2003) find that investors initially underreact to goodwill write-off announcements. They document significant negative returns in the one-year pre-announcement period as well as the one-year post-announcement period, the latter of which are more pronounced for larger write-offs.

2.4.4.3 Value relevance of goodwill book value and amortization

Investors' overall assessment of goodwill accounting in general has also been tested in several studies of the association of goodwill accounting numbers and either stock prices or long-window stock returns.[326] Especially, researchers perform regression analyses to examine (1) whether the "goodwill asset" has incremental explanatory power for stock prices, and/or (2) whether goodwill amortization has incremental explanatory power for stock returns.[327] Evidence on these questions is reviewed next.[328] While the relevance of these studies for the question at issue here is less direct than the literature presented ear-

---

323 See Francis, Hanna and Vincent (1996, pp. 130, 133).

324 Francis, Hanna and Vincent (1996, p. 134).

325 Francis, Hanna and Vincent (1996, p. 134).

326 The methodology used in such studies is briefly introduced in section 3.4.2 below.

327 These questions are frequently addressed jointly within a single paper. "Incremental" in this context means that, while other explanatory variables are frequently included in the regression models, the researchers' main interest is in the sign and significance of the coefficient on the goodwill-related variable.

328 For a review of part of the literature, refer to Clinch (1997, pp. 342-4). Most of the evidence presented concerns U. S. firms.

lier, investors' perception of goodwill-related accounting numbers is a potential source of management's beliefs in this matter.[329]

2.4.4.3.1 Balance sheet approach

Chauvin and Hirschey (1994), interpreting accounting goodwill "as a potentially useful, albeit imperfect, indicator of intangible assets which give rise to higher rates of profitability", investigate whether accounting goodwill numbers are "a useful proxy or instrument for the size and duration of economic goodwill".[330] In a three-equation system of simultaneous equations, they test whether goodwill, profitability and the market value of the firm are related. They show for a pooled sample of 1,353 firm years (1989-1991) from non-manufacturing sectors that the reported goodwill asset is related positively to market value, suggesting that this balance sheet item is regarded by investors "as a proxy useful for the favorable influence of brand-name recognition, good customer relations, and good management, among other factors." They "infer that accounting goodwill data offer a useful perspective on the hard-to-measure ongoing concern (reputational) value component of the economic value of the firm."[331]

McCarthy and Schneider (1995) analyze whether goodwill book values have incremental explanatory power, beyond other assets, liabilities and income, for the market value of equity.[332] They find, for a sample of 6,216 U. S. firm years in the period 1988-92, that goodwill is significant in explaining firm value and that the value attached to it by investors is at least as high as that of other assets.[333] However, the authors indicate several econometric issues that potentially limit the validity of their findings.[334]

Similar to McCarthy and Schneider (1995), Wang (1993) conducts a study of the explanatory power of goodwill book value for the market value of equity, incremental to that of other assets' and total liabilities' book values. Making no specific prediction, he tests whether goodwill book value overstates (understates) its market value and whether, therefore, goodwill amortization is understated (overstated) due to too long (short) amor-

---

329 However, it must be noted that a statistical relation between market variables and goodwill-related variables does not necessarily imply causality. All it indicates is that some of the information that investors use to determine share prices is also reflected in the goodwill-related variables. See Clinch (1997, p. 343 fn. 3).

330 Chauvin and Hirschey (1994, p. 161 [both quotes]).

331 Chauvin and Hirschey (1994, p. 178 [both quotes]).

332 The model is explained in McCarthy and Schneider (1995, pp. 73-4).

333 See McCarthy and Schneider (1995, pp. 77-9).

334 See McCarthy and Schneider (1995, p. 80).

tization periods.[335] He tests his hypothesis on two samples of firms from the service industry (1988: 67 firms; 1989: 69 firms) because of the high significance of goodwill (amortization) for these firms. He finds positive coefficients on goodwill book value in excess of +1 for both the 1988 and the 1989 samples, suggesting that "the security market perceived the reported goodwill assets as being understated under the current amortization requirement".[336] A further study by Wang (1995), motivated by the IASB's then plans to reconsider goodwill accounting, draws heavily on Wang's (1993) analysis[337] and yields similar results,[338] albeit for a larger sample.[339]

2.4.4.3.2 Combined balance sheet and income statement approaches

Henning, Lewis and Shaw (2000) use a model developed by Bradley, Desai and Kim (1988) to partition goodwill into the components suggested by Johnson and Petrone (1998).[340] They first analyze each component's explanatory power for contemporaneous stock prices in the context of a balance sheet model. They find that a disaggregation of the goodwill number provides explanatory power incremental to that of goodwill book value itself. Especially, the results show that "investors attach positive *and* negative weights to components of goodwill."[341] An income statement model reveals "no significant relation between returns and the amortization of the going-concern or synergy components."[342] This suggests that the amortization procedure used does not capture the actual value decline, if any, in the underlying goodwill components or that these components are perceived by the market to be non-wasting assets altogether.

Jennings et al. (1996) examine a sample of 259 U. S. firms over the period 1982-88. They find a "strong positive cross-sectional association between equity values and re-

---

335 See Wang (1993, pp. 128-9).

336 See Wang (1993, p. 129). The results are robust to several alternative specifications. See Wang (1993, pp. 129-32).

337 The two papers are widely similar, including their recommendations for further research, namely to extend his balance sheet approach by an analysis based on an income statement approach. Interestingly, Wang's (1993) study is nowhere referred to in Wang (1995).

338 See Wang (1995, p. 46).

339 See Wang (1995, p. 42).

340 This component approach is introduced in section 2.2 above.

341 Henning, Lewis and Shaw (2000, p. 385 [emphasis in original]). Both "core" components of goodwill exhibit a positive relation to market value. The synergy component is apparently viewed to be even more relevant than other assets. Conversely, the residual component, intended to capture any overpayment, is related negatively to market value. For a detailed description of the components and the empirical variables designed to proxy for them, refer to Henning, Lewis and Shaw (2000, pp. 375-8).

342 Henning, Lewis and Shaw (2000, p. 385).

corded goodwill asset amounts, after controlling for other components of net assets" as well as "evidence of a negative association between equity values and goodwill amortization, after controlling for other components of expected earnings."[343] Upon these findings, the authors base the recommendation of "recording purchased goodwill as an asset that is reduced in value only when its value is clearly impaired."[344] In effect, they advocate a "capitalization and annual review" approach to goodwill accounting that had been under consideration by the Accounting Standards Board (ASB) in the U. K. at the time. However, they caution that, for this approach to realize its perceived potential of representational faithfulness, "the financial reporting incentives of managers must be aligned with those of financial statement users."[345] However, no suggestions are made as to how this alignment of interests could be achieved.

Lindenberg and Ross (1999) find that goodwill book values are unrelated to firm value-to-EBITDA multiples of 3,633 large public U. S. companies, suggesting that there is no "market bias against balance sheet goodwill or against known future amortization charges".[346] The authors further examine the association of goodwill amortization and P/E ratios when industry effects and other variables are controlled for.[347] They find that P/E ratios are positively related to goodwill amortization, i.e. P/E ratios adjust upward where goodwill amortization is present in earnings, effectively offsetting the income-decreasing effect goodwill amortization and, on average, leaving stock prices unaffected. They interpret this result as supportive of the EMH, stating that "equity analysts who fail to see through goodwill amortization may find themselves undervaluing firms with relatively large amounts of goodwill."[348]

Vincent (1997) includes both purchase and pooling firms in her study of the value relevance for stock prices of goodwill and goodwill amortization, incremental to that of reported book value of equity and reported net income. She examines data from the five years of and following 57 purchase and 35 pooling transactions that occurred during the period 1979-86 in the U. S. Since goodwill and goodwill amortization are reported only

---

343 Jennings et al. (1996, p. 530). Regarding the latter finding, they stress that this association is weak and exhibits substantial cross-sectional variation, suggesting that "investors may view purchased goodwill as an economic resource that does not decline in value for some firms."

344 Jennings et al. (1996, p. 513).

345 Jennings et al. (1996, p. 530).

346 Lindenberg and Ross (1999, p. 40).

347 See Lindenberg and Ross (1999, pp. 36-9).

348 Lindenberg and Ross (1999, p. 38 fn. 16).

in purchase transactions, she uses the estimated accounting acquisition premium[349] and its accompanying amortization to approximate the goodwill and goodwill amortization that would have been reported had the pooling transactions been accounted for under the purchase method. She argues that, if the EMH holds, "investors would similarly value implicit acquisition goodwill for pooling firms."[350] Under the precondition that both reported equity and net income are value relevant, she expects coefficients to be zero for the goodwill and goodwill amortization proxies in the purchase transactions, since both should be captured by the other variables, reported equity and net income. If, contrary to popular conjectures, "pooling and purchase firms are valued equivalently",[351] the author expects the goodwill proxy (the goodwill amortization proxy) of pooling firms to be positively (negatively) associated with pooling firms' stock prices, because for those firms it is not included in reported book value of equity (reported net income). Results are not entirely in line with predictions. The coefficient on the goodwill proxy is insignificant for pooling firms, suggesting that investors do not perceive the goodwill proxy as an asset for those firms. For purchase firms, it has a positive association with stock price, indicating that goodwill is perceived to be undervalued on the books. Also unpredicted, the goodwill amortization proxy is positively associated with the stock prices of pooling firms in most years, suggesting that it is viewed as positively value relevant, not as an expense. In contrast, the goodwill amortization proxy is negatively associated with the stock prices of purchase firms in the years most recent to the acquisition. The author partly attributes her inconsistent (for example, for purchase firms, goodwill seems to be undervalued and at the same time underamortized) results to the research design and follows up with a ratio analysis in which she compares the purchase and pooling firms' MTB and P/E ratios.[352] She finds that unadjusted median MTB ratios for pooling and purchase firms are equal in the pre-acquisition year but that pooling firms' median MTB ratios significantly exceed those of purchase firms in later years.[353] However, when the firms' equity values are adjusted to an "as if pooling" or an "as if purchase" basis, the difference in MTB ratios disappears. These results are corroborated in an industry comparison.[354] According to the author, this "analysis confirms that, on average, the market adjusts pooling firms to an 'as if purchase' basis, and values purchase and pooling firms

---

349 This premium represents goodwill and the asset write-up recognized in the business combination. See Vincent (1997, p. 7).

350 Vincent (1997, p. 8).

351 Vincent (1997, p. 11).

352 See Vincent (1997, pp. 12-5).

353 See Vincent (1997, p. 13).

354 See Vincent (1997, p. 13).

similarly, at least during the first five years following the acquisition."[355] However, in an analysis of P/E ratios, the author finds that "pooling P/E ratios tend to be higher regardless of whether earnings are adjusted for accounting differences, especially in the year of and the first year after the acquisition."[356] Overall, the author draws the following conclusions: "The results overall suggest that concerns about the negative valuation implications of purchase accounting are not unjustified. Firms that choose (or that structure transactions to achieve) the pooling-of-interests method of accounting for a business combination appear to enjoy a valuation premium relative to purchase firms and relative to their industry, especially as measured using P/E ratios."[357] However, she cautions that, since the "evidence also suggests investors adjust accounting numbers for pooling and purchase firms to an approximately equivalent basis, .. the accounting method, in and of itself, does not explain the valuation differences."[358] She points out that the differences in market perception of purchase and pooling firms might be due to differences along other dimensions between pooling and purchase firms.[359]

The EMH is backed by Deng and Lev (1998), who conduct a comparative value relevance study for a sample of 375 purchase and 186 pooling acquisitions that occurred during the period 1985-96.[360] They analyze whether "investors [treat] differently acquisitions recorded by the purchase method than those recorded as pooling".[361] Based on a regression of stock price on assets, liabilities, earnings and the acquisition price, they find evidence suggesting that "the reliability of asset and liabilities' values under purchase accounting ... is higher than the reliability of assets/liabilities under pooling".[362] They summarize that "in acquisitions accounted for as pooling investors largely ignore the accounting practice used and focus on the economics of the transaction".[363]

Motivated by proposed changes in IAS, Wilkins, Swanson and Loudder (1998) analyze the value relevance of book value of goodwill and other intangible assets. For a sample

355 Vincent (1997, p. 13).
356 Vincent (1997, p. 14).
357 Vincent (1997, p. 17).
358 Vincent (1997, pp. 17-8).
359 See Vincent (1997, p. 16). This problem of self-selection bias is also stressed in other studies.
360 See Deng and Lev (1998, pp. 17-20).
361 Deng and Lev (1998, p. 18).
362 Deng and Lev (1998, p. 18).
363 Deng and Lev (1998, p. 20).

of 8,230 firm-years from the period 1988-96, they find that "investors do view the balance sheet disclosure of goodwill as value-relevant."[364]

Petersen (2002) presents evidence from the Danish stock exchange. Using methodology following Jennings et al. (1996) and Vincent (1997), he finds a significant positive association between stock prices and goodwill book values,[365] suggesting that investors view goodwill as an asset.[366] The coefficient on the goodwill variable is considerably higher than that on the other assets variable. In addition, an income statement approach yields mixed results regarding the explanatory power of levels and change components of goodwill amortization for stock returns, depending on alternative specifications of the dependent variable. According to the author, this evidence does not substantiate the hypothesis that investors view goodwill as an asset with a limited economic life.[367] He notes that his findings might suggest that goodwill amortization *per se* is viewed as an expense, but reported goodwill amortization is based on inappropriately short amortization periods. However, the results might also reflect the fact that what little incremental explanatory power goodwill amortization might have is difficult to detect due to "noise" introduced by the research design.

Huijgen (1996) adopts a research program similar to those of Jennings et al. (1996), Vincent (1997), and Petersen (2002).[368] He considers 90 large Dutch non-financial firms listed on the Amsterdam Stock Exchange in the period 1990-94. The value relevance of goodwill book value is assessed using the Ohlson (1995) model that interprets market value as a function of reported book value and earnings. Since goodwill is charged directly to equity by most sample firms, the author had to add back those amounts, gathered from footnote disclosures, to arrive at a book value of equity that would have been reported had the goodwill not been charged to equity. He finds that these "as if capitalized" goodwill amounts have significant incremental explanatory power for market values in the sample period. A risk analysis based on firm betas supports the same conclusion: Purchased goodwill, even if not reported on the face of the financial statements but only disclosed in footnotes, appears to be viewed as an asset by investors. Also, consistent with results reported by Vincent (1997), Petersen (2002), and Wang (1993), Huijgen

---

364 Wilkins, Swanson and Loudder (1998, p. 129).

365 The sample consists of 307 firm-year observations. The period over which these observations are drawn is not reported in the paper.

366 See Petersen (2002, p. 7).

367 See Petersen (2002, p. 5).

368 Refer to Huijgen (1996, ch. 4). Main results are reported in Huijgen (1996, pp. 111-3).

finds higher positive coefficients on goodwill than on other components of reported equity, suggesting that investors value goodwill higher than other components of reported equity. Finally, an analysis of returns does not indicate that goodwill amortization adds explanatory power over and above that of other components of net income.

Empirical evidence on the information content of goodwill accounting in Germany is presented by Krämling (1998). Adopting an approach similar to that of Huijgen (1996), he tests the value relevance of the goodwill asset, incremental to that of reported equity and earnings, conditional on the methods used to account for this balance sheet item. He expects that, if the goodwill asset reflects economic benefits, the value relevance of the summary measures equity and earnings will be higher when goodwill is capitalized and amortized over a long period, as opposed to charged directly against equity.[369] He finds that goodwill's incremental explanatory power for market value exceeds that of other components of net assets.[370] Further, he documents that equity and earnings are more value relevant when goodwill is capitalized and charged against income over time than when it is charged against equity directly after the acquisition, bypassing the income statement.[371] Finally, Krämling (1998) fails to find evidence suggesting that the length of amortization period significantly affects value relevance.[372] These findings basically corroborate what has been found in other jurisdictions.

2.4.4.3.3 Income statement approach

A number of studies challenge especially the notion that goodwill amortization is value relevant.[373] Moehrle, Reynolds-Moehrle and Wallace (2001) investigate the explanatory power for market-adjusted returns of different earnings and cash flow measures of the S&P 1500 firms in the period 1988-98. They conclude from their results that goodwill amortization disclosures were not decision-useful during that period. Jennings, LeClere and Thompson (2001) report for a large sample of publicly traded U. S. firms in the period 1993-98 that "earnings before goodwill amortization explain significantly more of the observed distribution of share prices than earnings after goodwill amortization and that when share valuations are based on earnings alone, goodwill amortization simply adds noise to the measure."[374] The authors interpret this finding as supportive of the

---

369 Results are presented in Krämling (1998, pp. 184-246).

370 See Krämling (1998, pp. 185-9).

371 See Krämling (1998, pp. 190-226).

372 See Krämling (1998, pp. 226-37).

373 See the conclusions in Clinch (1997, p. 345) and Davis (1996, p. 57).

374 Jennings, LeClere and Thompson (2001, p. 20).

FASB's decision to eliminate goodwill amortization.[375] Brown, Tucker and Pfeiffer's (1999) study is motivated by the FASB's initial 1999 exposure draft on accounting for business combinations, in which the FASB suggested separate income statement reporting of goodwill charges. The authors investigate, among other aspects of this topic, whether firms that use the purchase method to account for acquisitions are indeed at a competitive disadvantage due to the income-decreasing effects of goodwill amortization. In a regression of security returns on goodwill amortization and a number of control variables, they find no evidence that stocks of firms with high goodwill amortization are systematically undervalued.[376]

2.4.4.3.4 International comparison studies

In recent years, researchers have turned to comparing the value relevance of outputs of different accounting regimes.[377] Using form 20-F reconciliations of national GAAP financial statements to reflect U. S. GAAP, Amir, Harris and Venuti (1993) and Barth and Clinch (1996) compare, among other things, the association of goodwill book values and market values of equity for firms from different countries. For their sample of 467 firms from various countries,[378] Amir, Harris and Venuti (1993) find that "capitalizing goodwill is consistent with the way investors price this asset."[379] Since most of their firms are from the U. K., their analysis bears on the value relevance of the immediate write-off approach then available under U. K. GAAP. The authors conclude that some national GAAP regimes require goodwill to be accounted for in a manner inconsistent with how investors view it.

In a similar study, Barth and Clinch (1996) investigate whether differences between, on the one hand, U. K., Australian, and Canadian GAAP and, on the other hand, U. S. GAAP are associated with share prices and returns. With regard to goodwill, the authors conclude that "[g]oodwill amortization under U.S., U.K., and Australian GAAP is 'too

375 See Jennings, LeClere and Thompson (2001, p. 26). However, this conclusion appears to be premature because the explanatory power of goodwill impairment losses likely to occur under SFAS 142 has yet to be examined systematically.

376 See Brown, Tucker and Pfeiffer (1999, pp. 13-5).

377 This body of literature has grown considerably over the past decade. Refer to Bonse (2004, ch. III) for an overview and to Holthausen and Watts (2001) and Barth, Beaver and Landsman (2001) for critical perspectives. However, this section focuses on studies that explicitly analyze issues relevant to goodwill accounting.

378 Of these, roughly 42 % are from the U. K., whereas the next largest numbers of firms are registered in Australia, the Netherlands and Sweden. The rest is distributed across 16 other countries, not including Germany. See Amir, Harris and Venuti (1993, pp. 233-6).

379 Amir, Harris and Venuti (1993, p. 259).

small' relative to the expense reflected in returns, and a portion of U.S. GAAP goodwill is priced as an asset, suggesting that, by electing to write off goodwill, U.K. managers reduce the relevance of reported balance sheet amounts."[380]

2.4.4.4 Market reactions to the purchase/pooling decision

Figure 5 gives an example how different market reactions to the purchase/pooling decision might be interpreted.[381] Some managers apparently consider well spent the costs of obtaining what they believe to be a favorable accounting treatment. If investors respond positively or neutrally, interpretation of this finding will depend on the researcher's view of the EMH: Skeptics would point to the mechanistic hypothesis, claiming that management's attempt at "fooling" investors was successful. In contrast, proponents of the EMH would assert that the positive (or non-existent) response is due to the fact that investors do see through the cosmetic accounting effects but derive other (unobserved) benefits from the pooling treatment that (over-) compensate for the costs of obtaining this treatment. Conversely, if the market reacts negatively, this suggests that investors are not entirely fooled: They see through the accounting effects and understand that management has incurred costs that are quite real for alleged benefits that, to shareholders, are non-existent.

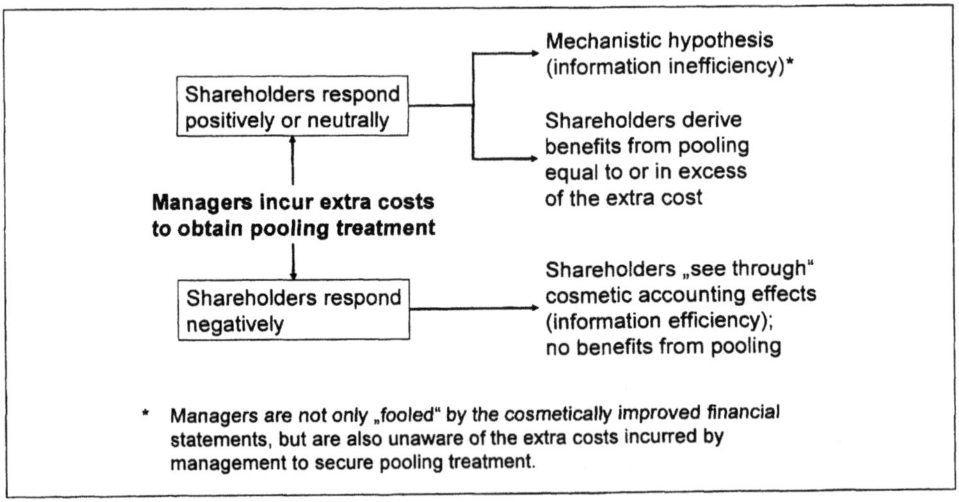

Figure 5: Market reactions to overpayment in pooling acquisitions

---

380 Barth and Clinch (1996, p. 164).

381 The following discussion is purely conceptual and ignores empirical problems of measuring market response.

In this section, studies on the market reactions to firms' choices of accounting methods in business combinations are reviewed. According to persistent popular conjectures, pooling firms enjoy a valuation premium due to the allegedly favorable, but ultimately cosmetic, earnings effects of this method.[382] In effect, this is a challenge to the EMH.[383]

Research findings are largely contrary to this hypothesis in that purchase method acquisitions are generally found to outperform pooling mergers. Two relatively early studies, Hong, Kaplan and Mandelker (1978)[384] and its replication by Davis (1990),[385] report evidence suggesting that firms using the purchase method to account for acquisitions on average outperform those using the pooling method.[386] The latter firms essentially stay even with the broad market. These findings are documented over various test periods surrounding the transactions.[387]

Desai et al. (2001) find no substantiation for the widely held belief that the purchase/pooling choice is a significant determinant of the acquirer's post-acquisition stock performance.[388] They interpret this finding as corroboration of the EMH, since "the market is able to see through this choice in accounting method that has no cash flow implications."[389]

Lindenberg and Ross's (1999) results of a study of stock market reactions to 1,442 business combination announcements also indicate that the market does not seem to penalize acquirers that use the purchase method. On the contrary, they find a significant, positive announcement effect for purchase business combinations, whereas the average stock

---

382 Refer to section 2.3.2.3 above.

383 See Hong, Kaplan and Mandelker (1978, p. 33): "If stock prices were to be affected by the choice of an accounting method for a merger, then we might have evidence in conflict with the Efficient Markets Hypothesis since information on the effects of using either method is generally available."

384 Hong, Kaplan and Mandelker (1978, p. 33) hypothesize that "the market is efficient and thus able to distinguish between higher earnings caused by pooling-of-interests from higher earnings caused by real economic events of the firm".

385 See Davis (1990, p. 707).

386 See reviews by Davis (1996, pp. 54-5) and Clinch (1997, p. 347). While Hong, Kaplan and Mandelker (1978) use a sample of 205 tax-free pooling and purchase transaction occurring in the pre-APB Opinion 16 period 1954-1964, Davis (1990) analyzes 177 tax-free mergers that were completed during the period 1971-1982.

387 Davis (1990, p. 700) uses a period from 26 weeks before the merger announcement date to 26 weeks after the merger effective date. The interim period between those dates varies across mergers. Hong, Kaplan and Mandelker (1978, pp. 37-42) use different time periods, the first centered on the first (annual and/or interim) earnings announcement after the merger, and the second centered on the merger date.

388 See Desai et al. (2001, p. 5).

389 Desai et al. (2001, p. 5).

price response to the announcement of pooling acquisitions is significantly negative. The authors offer possible interpretations of this result, including pooling acquirers' (1) alleged propensity to overpay for an acquisition, (2) inability, due to the restrictive pooling criteria, to implement certain value-enhancing activities in the combined entity, and (3) apparent preoccupation with accounting cosmetics rather than with value creation.[390] However, as the authors concede, their results might be influenced by their failure to control for the effects of different forms of purchase price consideration. The fact that some of the purchase business combinations studied were effected by a cash payment might drive the market's preference of this type of transaction over pooling business combinations.[391] Replication of their study with stock-for-stock purchase transactions confirms this assumption: While the stock price effect of cash-only purchase business combinations is significantly positive, the market appears to be indifferent to stock-only purchase transactions.[392]

Similar to Lindenberg and Ross (1999), Martínez-Jerez (2001), examining a sample of 355[393] stock-for-stock acquisitions completed in the U. S. during the period 1990-98,[394] finds significant, negative acquirer stock price effects of an average 4% surrounding announcements of transactions accounted for using the pooling method,[395] while "returns for purchase transactions are not significantly different from zero"[396] He states that this statistically significant difference is not attributable to systematic differences, other than the choice of accounting method, between the 246 pooling and 89 purchase firms. This finding is interpreted as being "inconsistent with [both] the accounting irrelevance and earnings fixation hypotheses".[397] The negative reaction to pooling acquisitions is found to be especially pronounced "in companies with poor corporate governance", presumably due to shareholders' increased concerns about the costs associated with pooling accounting when corporate control mechanisms are poor.[398]

Based on the notion that management incurs additional costs to obtain the perceived favorable pooling treatment for acquisitions, Weber (2000) examines whether shareholders

---

390 See Lindenberg and Ross (1999, p. 35).

391 See Lindenberg and Ross (1999, p. 35).

392 See Lindenberg and Ross (1999, p. 36).

393 Martínez-Jerez (2001, p. 24): 345.

394 See Martínez-Jerez (2001, p. 24).

395 See Martínez-Jerez (2001, pp. 24-5).

396 Martínez-Jerez (2001, p. 14).

397 Martínez-Jerez (2001, p. 24).

398 See Martínez-Jerez (2001, p. 24).

consider these costs well spent and benefit from managers' use of pooling. Since the SEC restricts firms' ability to repurchase shares subsequent to pooling transactions, using the pooling method restricts firms' scope of actions, forcing them to forego what some perceive to be valuable options.[399] Weber finds that "shareholders do not consider the favorable financial reporting effects of pooling to be beneficial, when they are obtained at the cost of firms' share repurchase programs",[400] since "the market considers the benefits of a firm's share repurchase program to exceed the financial reporting advantages of pooling-of-interests."[401] This result is arrived at, among other analyses, by an event-study analysis of abnormal security returns earned by firms with pending pooling transactions following the SEC's adoption of Staff Accounting Bulletin (SAB) 96.[402] Weber (2000) argues that SAB 96 reduces the likelihood that (1) pending pooling transactions will be completed, (2) the pooling method will be applied, and (3) future share repurchase programs will occur.[403] Based on this assumption, he finds statistically significant negative abnormal stock returns associated with firms' decision to go through with pooling transactions at the expense of future options to initiate share repurchase programs.[404] This finding sheds light on the issue of whether managers act in the shareholders' best interest or, rather, opportunistically when making financial reporting choices: "Managers appear to be willing to incur the increased costs associated with the use of pooling-of-interests and continue to use pooling even though the results from this study suggest that the current shareholders do not derive a benefit from the financial reporting effects of pooling."[405]

The findings of Blackburn Norris and Ayres (2000) are somewhat in contrast with those presented previously. The authors examine stock price responses to the first earnings announcements subsequent to the completion of acquisitions accounted for by either the purchase or the pooling method.[406] According to their results, "it appears that a negative reaction occurs on the first earnings announcement date in response to the book reduction in reported earnings from the goodwill amortization."[407] The alternative explanation that

---

399 For a discussion of the benefits of share repurchases, refer to Schremper (2002, especially ch. III).

400 Weber (2000, p. 1).

401 Weber (2000, pp. 28-9).

402 SAB 96 restricts firms' ability to engage in share repurchase programs for up to two years subsequent to pooling transactions.

403 See Weber (2000, pp. 19-20).

404 See Weber (2000, pp. 26-8).

405 Weber (2000, p. 29).

406 Their sample includes 116 acquisitions that occurred in the U. S. during the period 1984-1990.

407 Blackburn Norris and Ayres (2000, p. 87).

the extent of any overpayment drives the negative response is rejected on the grounds that it is not necessarily on the date of the first earnings announcement that investors would learn of the existence and extent of any overpayment.[408]

While these findings appear to refute the conjecture that, contrary to the EMH, the market is "fooled" into responding positively to the favorable financial statement effects of the pooling method, it is far from established that this phenomenon is causally related to the accounting choice. In most of the studies reviewed in this section, the authors concede that cross-sectional differences, if any, are not necessarily due to the purchase/pooling choice, but might be caused by omitted variables.[409] Alternative interpretations include the following: Clinch (1997) argues that Davis' (1990) results are subject to cautious interpretation because much of the stock price response occurs before the acquisitions are consummated and before the respective accounting treatments are made public, suggesting explanatory variables other than the accounting treatment.[410] Davis (1990) examines this possibility and finds that abnormal returns decrease as the acquirer's bargaining strength decreases, consistent with the notion that weak acquirers tend to overpay.[411] Since he documents that the purchase method is associated with positive abnormal returns and that acquirers in a strong bargaining position tend towards using the purchase method, the low abnormal returns to pooling mergers might be associated with the acquirer's low bargaining power and resulting overpayment, and not with the fact that the merger is accounted for as a pooling of interests. This evidence would support the EMH in so far as, apparently investors are not mislead by the financial statement effects of the pooling method. However, the bargaining strength explanation is not the only convincing one: It is possible that investors not only are not fooled by the improved earnings under pooling but do in fact detect that managers incur substantial costs to secure these "phantom" benefits.[412] A similar explanation is offered by Lindenberg and Ross (1999): If managers believe that the market punishes purchase business combinations, only the economically soundest transactions should accounted for using that method, and an effi-

---

408 See Blackburn Norris and Ayres (2000, p. 87 fn. 15).

409 Refer also to the individual reviews above.

410 See Clinch (1997, p. 347).

411 See Davis (1990, pp. 706-7).

412 Davis (1996, p. 50) states that "companies that overpay for acquisitions are penalized by financial markets". See also Davis (1996, p. 55). Lys and Vincent's (1995) case study evidence shows that AT&T's willingness to incur additional costs of up to $500 million in order to be able to use the pooling method for the acquisition of NCR was apparently not rewarded by the market: An enormous stock price decline (between $3.9 and 6.5 billion) occurred during the time the acquisition was being carried into execution.

cient market's reaction to them should tend to be positive.[413] Martínez-Jerez (2001) summarizes that "the choice of pooling of interests is likely to be a sign that managers' interests have dominated those of shareholders, leading stock prices to decline."[414]

2.4.4.5 Market reactions to mandated changes in accounting rules for business combinations

A final body of literature relevant here is concerned with assessing market reactions to mandated changes in accounting rules, as opposed to voluntary accounting decisions, related to goodwill. These analyses predominantly take the shape of event studies, where abnormal returns to key events preceding the issuance of new accounting standards are measured.[415] The existence and sign of any market reactions to mandated changes in goodwill-related accounting rules allow conclusions about the market perception of goodwill accounting, especially if these reactions vary across firms. For example, the existence (or absence) of any response to a cash-neutral accounting change will potentially shape managers' belief in the EMH.

Day and Hartnett (1999/2000) investigate stock market reactions to distinct milestones within the standard-setting process preceding the abolishment of the favorable inverted-sum-of-years-digits method of goodwill amortization in Australia.[416] However, they fail to find significant excess returns associated with any of the events or announcements investigated, which refutes the assumption that "the market actually perceived a material economic consequence in banning the [inverted-sum-of-years-digits] method."[417]

Leftwich (1981), also in an event-study approach, tests abnormal stock performance related to the deliberations preceding the APB's change in accounting rules for business combinations. Hypotheses are derived from contracting theory, predicting that this apparently "cosmetic" rule change will affect firms according to their exposure to restrictive covenants in lending agreements.[418] While significant abnormal returns are found for nine of 21 events considered, these abnormal returns can only partially be attributed to effects as predicted by contracting theory.[419] Leftwich (1981) reports a strong and unpre-

---

413 See Lindenberg and Ross (1999, p. 36).

414 Martínez-Jerez (2001, pp. 6-7).

415 Refer to section 3.4.3.1 below.

416 See Day and Hartnett (1999/2000, pp. 208-12).

417 Day and Hartnett (1999/2000, p. 211).

418 See Leftwich (1981, pp. 7-9).

419 See Leftwich (1981, p. 31).

dicted indication that larger firms were less negatively affected by the mandated accounting rule change, which he interprets as suggestive of omitted variables. Overall, Leftwich (1981) concludes that, while contracting theory cannot fully account for the results, there are "few competing theories to explain why apparently cosmetic accounting changes affect the equity value of firms."[420]

2.5 Summary and implications

The literature analyzed in section 2.4 provides empirical evidence on the goodwill debate presented earlier in this chapter. The first part of the review deals with the question whether managers' actual goodwill reporting behavior is consistent with their beliefs stated in the discussion. In the second part, financial statement users' goodwill-related behavior is analyzed in order to infer whether managers' capital market-related beliefs are justified. This dichotomy is appropriately summarized by Day and Hartnett (1999/2000) who highlight management's *beliefs* as important determinants of management's financial reporting behavior:

> "In light of widely accepted efficient market concepts, mandated changes in goodwill amortisation policy may appear to be of little relevance to share price. However, in view of such strong and sustained public debate concerning goodwill and its perceived value, it is clear that business communities are divided on this issue. The divergence of opinion is in itself important because it may also suggest the possibility of dysfunctional decision-making and a continued need to better understand the various perceptions, thought processes and decision criteria of key market participants."[421]

According to Dunstan (1999), "evidence regarding the determinants of the accounting treatment of goodwill is limited" within existing literature.[422] The literature presented in section 2.4.3 above contributes direct evidence to suggest that, in most settings and under most circumstances, managers prefer income-increasing goodwill-related accounting treatments. They are also concerned about the effect of goodwill accounting on their financial leverage ratios. These preferences are found to be consistent with contracting-based incentives as well as the notion that investors are believed to react negatively to goodwill-related charges. Firms generally prefer the pooling method over the purchase method to account for business combinations, and are frequently willing to incur substantial costs to obtain the perceived accounting benefits associated with this procedure. Fur-

---

420 Leftwich (1981, p. 33).

421 Day and Hartnett (1999/2000, p. 212).

422 Dunstan (1999, p. 2).

ther, in the political process managers and their allies lobby for firms' preferred goodwill-related accounting treatments.

Again, this result suggests in no way that the EMH does not hold. However, it does indicate that managers do not necessarily *believe* that it does. Apparently, managers do not in general trust investors to "see through" goodwill charges to the underlying substance of the firm. To them, the downside risk remains that investors might just be "fooled" by appearances after all, penalizing the firm for its superficially poor financial status.[423] For example, the costs of pooling are quite real and a large portion of the expected accounting benefits will, in the absence of any direct cash flow effects of the purchase/pooling choice, only accrue to management to the extent that investors in fact fail to see through the allegedly desirable, albeit cosmetic financial statement effects of the pooling method. Since this risk does not seem to preclude managers from "paying to pool", their belief that different accounting methods for goodwill "matter" beyond any direct cash flow effects must indeed be strong.

In section 2.4.4, indirect evidence on management's preferences is derived from studies of investors' responses to goodwill-related accounting decisions. The experimental results imply that not all users of financial statement information are at all times able to see through goodwill-related accounting effects under an amortization approach with inadequate disclosure requirements. Maybe this circumstance can account for managers' apparent doubts in the EMH: Knowing that goodwill-related accounting information is sometimes hidden (or not contained at all) in financial reports, they worry about negative stock price effects of goodwill amortization because they do not think investors are able to see that sometimes it is cash-neutral goodwill charges that drive weak earnings performance. However, while these findings present a potential challenge to the EMH, similar deficiencies are much less likely to occur under SFAS 142, where any goodwill write-offs will be communicated much more clearly to the capital markets through separate-line disclosure in the income statement.

Given the scarce and inconclusive evidence on stock market reactions to goodwill write-offs, it is unclear whether managers have any reason to be concerned about (hopeful of) adverse (positive) stock price effects of SFAS 142 goodwill write-offs. Therefore, that

---

423 Desai et al. (2001) note that a "necessary condition for acquirers to pay more in pooling transactions is that some parties to the merger believe that market participants cannot see through the differences in earnings."

particular body of research has little potential, at this point, to inform hypotheses regarding write-off behavior.

The research findings on the value relevance of goodwill-related accounting amounts suggest that, on the whole, goodwill book values are positively and significantly associated with market values of equity.[424] Not in all of the studies reviewed here, however, this association is equally strong for goodwill and for other balance sheet items.[425] Value relevance is found although the goodwill asset is likely to be subject to substantial earnings management.[426] Consequently, one would expect investors to adjust stock prices downward, ceteris paribus, when goodwill book values fall. Goodwill write-offs cause goodwill book values to fall. If goodwill book values reflect information used by capital market participants in determining stock prices, one would likewise expect goodwill write-offs, on average, to provide value-relevant information to investors. Then, goodwill write-offs would, on average, be associated with downward stock price movements.[427] If managers believe that investors, for whatever reason,[428] respond negatively to changes in goodwill book value *and* if managers' utility is positively associated with their firms'

---

424 See Clinch (1997, pp. 342-4) and Davis (1996, p. 57).

425 Also, as Clinch (1997, p. 344) notes, there should be cross-sectional differences in the sign and strength of the association. For example, different degrees of negotiating power exercised in the takeover negotiations will influence the extent to which the purchase price reflects the present value of anticipated future economic benefits of the acquisition. Acquirers with high bargaining power will, on average, have to pay less than the present value of all expected future economic benefits, whereas acquirers with low bargaining power will, on average, have to remunerate the acquiree's owners for the full present value of expected future economic benefits associated with the acquisition. Goodwill book values resulting from the former group's acquisitions will tend to understate the true economic benefits, whereas goodwill book values from acquisitions made by firms with low bargaining power will more accurately reflect or even overstate present value of expected future economic benefits associated with these acquisitions. These and other factors will contribute to cross-sectional variation in the value relevance of goodwill-related accounting numbers. Therefore, goodwill write-offs made by some firms should be associated with stronger stock price declines than that would be expected for goodwill write-offs recorded by other firms. In turn, managers of firm belonging to the former group will be less inclined to record (accelerate/overstate) goodwill write-offs than will be the case with managers of firms belonging to the latter group, because the former will expect goodwill write-offs to be associated with a more pronounced stock price decline than will the latter.

426 See, for example, Francis, Hanna and Vincent (1996).

427 A separate issue is whether such write-offs occur in a timely manner. A write-off is timely when it reflects the economic value decline of the underlying asset in the period in which it occurs. If a write-off is not recorded in a timely manner, it might be preempted by other information. Refer to Segal (2003) for an empirical study of the timeliness of certain SFAS 121 and SFAS 142 goodwill write-offs.

428 Again, a critical point is management's perspective on the EMH. If managers accept the EMH, earnings management for capital market-related reasons (i.e., to "fool" investors) is pointless since investors will see through any "cosmetic" (i.e. cash-neutral) accounting decisions. However, incentives remain to manage goodwill write-offs for other, primarily contracting reasons. Refer to section 3.3.2.3 below.

stock prices,[429] they have incentive to avoid or, depending on the circumstances, to delay and/or understate any goodwill write-offs as long as the costs of any expected associated stock price decline outweigh any benefits of these write-offs.

While the goodwill asset does appear to capture information used by investors in setting share prices, the goodwill amortization rule prevalent in most accounting systems in the past apparently does a poor job at capturing the value decline, if any, of this asset. Apparently, while goodwill is perceived by investors as a valuable asset, its value does not appear to develop in the manner suggested by linear amortization over some arbitrarily chosen period. Rather. goodwill amortization is apparently viewed as "noise". The FASB, in line with the recommendation by Jennings et al. (1996),[430] claims that the impairment-only approach in SFAS 142 is more relevant to investors.[431] This might be taken as *prima facie* evidence that managers will believe that shareholders' will view (unexpected) goodwill write-offs under SFAS 142 as value relevant, which would result in negative stock price reactions. In view of extant criticism of the high degree of discretion inherent in the details of SFAS 142,[432] this new method represents a considerable leap of faith by standard setters. Managers' use of their discretion in this context will depend not only on their contracting-related incentives but also in their assumptions as to how investors will react to transitional goodwill write-offs under SFAS 142.

The persistent belief apparently held by managers, that investors respond less favorably to purchase acquisitions than they do to pooling acquisitions, amounts to an expression of doubt regarding the EMH, specifically in the market's ability to adjust for differences in

---

429 Refer to section 3.3.2.4.2 below.

430 See Jennings et al. (1996, p. 513). Interestingly, this recommendation is subject to the reservation that "the financial reporting incentives of managers must be aligned with those of financial statement users."

431 See, for example, SFAS 142.B74-8. However, the finding that goodwill amortization apparently does not reflect information used by investors does not automatically imply that an impairment-only approach, despite its conceptual appeal, is superior in that respect. All it suggests is that goodwill amortization does not accurately reflect any decline in the value of goodwill as perceived by investors. However, simply omitting goodwill amortization is not what occurs under an impairment-only approach, at least not when an impairment write-off actually takes place. It is not self-evident that a goodwill write-off measured according to SFAS 142 will accurately capture the "real" extent and timing of any goodwill value decline as perceived by market participants. Especially, the apparent "value irrelevance" of goodwill amortization does not necessarily mean that goodwill does not decline in value in the market's view at all. However, arguments put forward in favor of the impairment-only approach by both the FASB and members of the academic community might induce management to feel justified in avoiding goodwill write-offs because they might think that the market feels that goodwill is an asset that does not decline in value.

432 Refer to chapter 4 below.

financial reporting methods that have no accompanying direct cash flow differences.[433] However, the data reviewed here suggests that, on average, purchase business combinations appear to outperform pooling transactions. The apparent lack of positive market response to the pooling method suggests that investors do not appear to respond mechanistically to the financial statement effects of a given accounting treatment.

What little evidence there is on the stock price effects of mandated changes in goodwill-related accounting rules does not allow a consistent conclusion. While some abnormal returns are found, they apparently cannot be fully explained by theory consistent with the EMH. On the other hand, where abnormal returns are not observed, the EMH is only supported under the assumption that no unanticipated indirect cash flow effects, as assumed to exist under contracting theory, will result from the rule change.[434]

As stated earlier, while the research analyzed above contributes valuable information to the question at hand, the findings do not fully generalize for various reasons. While, under the pre-SFAS 142 reporting regime, avoiding charges to earnings had to be traded off against maintaining leverage, SFAS 142 offers "the best of both worlds". Therefore, the evidence presented here suggests that managers are likely to avoid goodwill charges altogether. However, since the transitional SFAS 142 goodwill write-off is disclosed as a change in accounting principle, managers might prefer the adoption year over later periods for recording large write-offs.

---

433 Even the FASB cited as a reason for taking on the business combinations project concerns that a competitive advantage were bestowed on firms that qualified for use of the pooling method to account for their acquisitions. See SFAS 141.B6.

434 This mixed evidence can be at least partly attributed to problems with the research design. It is particularly difficult to identify the key event(s) within a lengthy rule-making process that caused revisions in investors' expectations. Also, since virtually all firms are affected by the change, calculating abnormal returns is exceptionally problematic.

3 Empirical research on discretionary asset write-offs

3.1 Chapter overview

In chapter 2, goodwill write-offs according to SFAS 142 were presented as the latest episode in the long-standing goodwill debate. It was argued that the relevant theoretical arguments and empirical findings have implications for possible determinants of firms' behavior related to the adoption of SFAS 142. In this chapter, another facet of the transitional SFAS 142 goodwill write-off is analyzed: It has been claimed that the new rules make accounting for goodwill even more flexible than it was before – and therefore increasingly susceptible to management's financial reporting incentives.[435] In this sense, SFAS 142 goodwill write-offs belong to a category of accounting phenomena frequently referred to as *discretionary asset write-offs*, which are interesting objects of study due to their economic significance and other specific characteristics. The hypotheses, theoretical background, and main findings generated in this well-developed discretionary asset write-off literature appear to be largely applicable to the SFAS 142 setting and might help predict managers' financial reporting behavior upon adoption. Therefore, this chapter is devoted to an in-depth analysis and review of this research area, the insights of which are taken up in section 5.2 to form specific hypotheses.

This investigation proceeds as follows: In section 3.2, discretionary asset write-offs are introduced and established as an interesting and fruitful area of accounting research. The remainder of this chapter is dedicated to analyzing the two facets of the discretionary asset write-off literature in turn: In section 3.3, research on the determinants of discretionary asset write-offs is analyzed. Special emphasis is placed on the theoretical origins of the main hypotheses, in order to ascertain applicability of predictions and findings to the SFAS 142 setting. The literature on financial statement users' perception of these charges is the subject of section 3.4. Investors' responses to discretionary asset write-offs in general are instructive in predicting managers' transitional SFAS 142 goodwill write-off behavior. In both of these sections, the literature review occasionally goes beyond the limited number of discretionary write-off studies to include instructive research findings from neighboring areas, e.g. the earnings management and value relevance literatures.[436] Finally, section 3.5 contains a summary of the evidence and a discussion of possible implications for transitional SFAS 142 goodwill write-off behavior.

---

435 The discretionary nature of SFAS 142 goodwill write-offs is established in chapter 4 below.

436 However, since the empirical study presented in chapter 5 below contributes to the research reviewed in section 3.3, this section is more detailed and comprehensive than section 3.4.

3.2 *Discretionary asset write-offs as a subject of accounting research*

A *write-off* is an "accounting event where a firm recognizes a loss and reduces an asset's balance sheet value".[437] In theory, it is triggered by an *impairment* of the underlying asset, i.e. a situation in which the carrying amount of that asset on the company's books exceeds its fair value or similar benchmark amount.[438] Francis, Hanna and Vincent (1996) refer to write-offs as *discretionary* when there is "little authoritative guidance" on the accounting for them.[439] It is debatable to what extent an area of accounting can be termed "discretionary" when accounting standards do exist for it. In this study, however, it is argued that the existence of accounting standards as such does not necessarily eliminate all discretion. Consequently, a write-off is referred to as discretionary if its existence, amount, and/or timing either are not regulated explicitly under existing GAAP or are governed by rules that allow an unusually high degree of flexibility and discretion.[440]

It has been briefly discussed in section 1.2 that discretionary asset write-offs have drawn the attention of accounting researchers, policy-makers and other interest groups for a number of reasons.[441] First, the write-offs studied are economically significant, having a large impact on firms' financial statements item such as accounting earnings and the book value of (net) assets.[442] Second, long-term assets, especially intangible assets, are inherently difficult to value. As has been discussed at length in section 2.3.2 above, this problem is particularly severe where the unidentifiable intangible asset "goodwill" is

---

437 Heflin and Warfield (1997, p. 1). Similar definitions are provided by Bartov, Lindahl and Ricks (1998, p. 327), Bunsis (1997, p. 1385), Hirschey and Richardson (2002, p.178), and Zucca and Campbell (1992, p. 30). The terms "write-off" and "write-down" are used as synonyms. See Alciatore et al. (1998, p. 1). Bartov, Lindahl and Ricks (1998, p. 343) note that "write-off" is "a very general term, one that encompasses a wide array of financial events". Elliott and Hanna (1996, p. 139) include in their analysis of write-offs all "large negative special items", noting that these potentially comprise accruals other than write-offs.

438 See SFAS 144.7: Impairment "is the condition that exists when the carrying amount of a long-lived asset (asset group) exceeds its fair value." See also IAS 36.5: "An impairment loss is the amount by which the carrying amount of an asset exceeds its recoverable amount". With respect to the goodwill impairment test, refer to SFAS 142.19. According to section 253 par. 2 HGB, "außerplanmäßige Abschreibungen" are recorded to account for the fact that an asset's book value no longer reflects its lower fair value as of the balance sheet date. Breidert (1994, pp. 20-7) discusses conceptual differences between impairment write-offs and changes to the amortization schedule as well as between temporary and permanent declines in asset value. See also Coenenberg (2003, pp. 112-6), Schildbach (2000, pp. 245-7), and Streim (1988, pp. 102-4).

439 See Francis, Hanna and Vincent (1996, p. 117).

440 Corresponding to the stance taken here, Segal (2003, p. 5) refers to "discretionary write-offs" as "situations in which little authoritative guidance on accounting exists *or* the discretion afforded to managers is large" (emphasis added).

441 For an overview, refer to Alciatore et al. (1998, pp. 1-2).

442 This point is made by Alciatore et al. (1998, p. 1) and Bartov, Lindahl and Ricks (1998, p. 327).

concerned. This circumstance makes detecting and quantifying any impairment a challenging task, even in the absence of incentives to manage financial statements.[443] Third, most GAAP allow firms a high degree of discretion and flexibility in determining the existence, magnitude and timing of any write-offs.[444] For example, before the issuance of SFAS 121, in December of 1994, write-offs of long-lived assets were argued to be discretionary in nature due to the lack of available authoritative guidance.[445] Therefore, such write-offs were argued to be well suited for earnings management, especially in the form of "big bath" behavior.[446] Fourth, new accounting pronouncements recently issued in several jurisdictions around the world, prompted mainly by the reasons stated above, have sparked renewed interest in the analysis of write-offs. Apart from SFAS 142, these include, for example, SFAS 144, *Accounting for the Impairment or Disposal of Long-Lived Assets*, issued in 2001, and the IASB's revised IAS 36, *Impairment of Assets*, dated March 2004. Many commentators hold that even these pronouncements have not been successful in severely restricting discretion.[447] Taken together, these characteristics make write-offs of long-lived assets ideal instruments of earnings management and, in turn, interesting objects of study.

Consequently, empirical accounting researchers have mainly focused on two aspects:[448] First, due to the high degree of discretion involved in the relevant accounting pronouncements, the *reliability* of discretionary asset write-offs is frequently questioned. Consequently, academics investigate the determinants of discretionary asset write-offs in order to ascertain the extent to which these write-offs are used by managers to achieve their own self-interested financial reporting objectives. If asset write-offs are primarily explained by earnings management incentives, it can be argued that they do not actually represent what they purport to represent, i.e. an economic decline in the value of the underlying assets (impairment). Second, the sheer magnitude and infrequent occurrence of these charges raises questions regarding their *relevance* to users of financial statements. Therefore, another area of research deals with the association of discretionary asset write-offs and the market value of write-off firms. Aspects of this literature are possible stock

---

443 See Segal (2003, p. 6).

444 See Elliott and Shaw (1988, p. 92). See also Schildbach (2001, p. 130).

445 See Francis, Hanna and Vincent (1996, pp. 117-8).

446 See, for example, Alciatore et al. (1998, p. 1).

447 Riedl (2002, pp. 1-2) argues that, even after the issuance of SFAS 121, write-offs of long-lived asset remain a discretionary item, possibly even more so than before.

448 These two aspects of the research are addressed jointly in many studies.

price responses to write-off announcements as well as the value relevance of accounting amounts that reflect the write-offs.

The core of this literature, and consequently the review in this section, focuses on write-offs of long-lived assets. A number of other accounting items are also touched upon due to their structural similarity with asset write-offs in terms of the criteria discussed above. First and foremost, restructuring charges are an exemplar of this equivalence, especially because they are also potential vehicles of "big bath"-type charges.[449] Equivalently, write-offs of acquired in-process R&D share some of the characteristics of other discretionary asset write-offs.[450] Other accounting events, including upward revaluations of long-lived assets, special items, write-offs of current assets, severance payments, liability accruals, and asset disposals are too structurally dissimilar to be included in the literature of interest here.[451] Also, several studies analyze industry-specific accruals (e.g. loss-reserve accruals in the insurance industry or bank loan loss reserves) that, while similar to discretionary asset write-offs in a number of respects, are not considered here due to their limited scope.[452] Finally, a number of industry-specific studies analyzing non-discretionary write-offs in the oil and gas industry are also omitted here.[453]

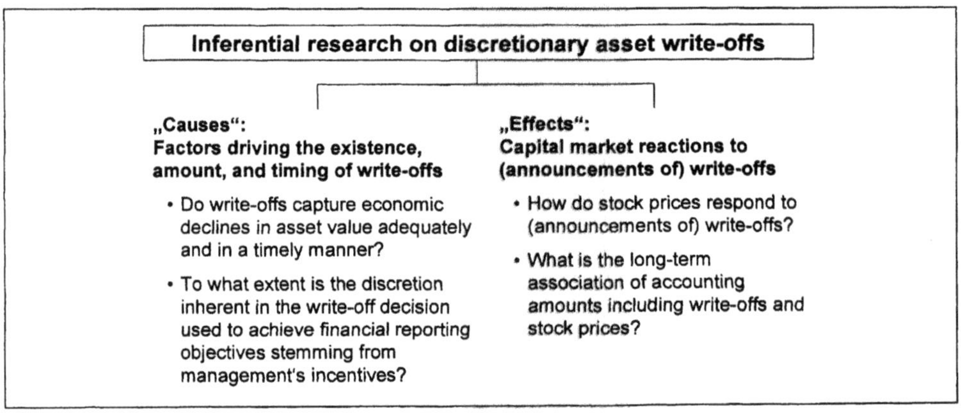

Figure 6: Research questions in discretionary write-off studies

---

449 See, for example, Chaney, Hogan and Jeter (2000), who consider write-offs as a possible component of a larger restructuring effort. See also the literature reviewed in Bartov, Lindahl and Ricks (1998, pp. 329-332).

450 See, for example, Deng and Lev (1998).

451 Empirical investigations of upward asset revaluations include those by Black, Sellers and Manly (1998) and Easton, Eddey and Harris (1993). Bartov (1993) analyzes asset sales as an instrument of earnings manipulation.

452 Refer to McNichols (2000, pp. 316-7, 333-5) for a detailed discussion of part of this literature.

453 Refer to Alciatore et al. (1998, pp. 22-6) and Alciatore, Easton and Spear (2000).

Figure 6 on the previous page summarizes the research agendas pursued in the discretionary write-off literature.[454]

First, researchers are commonly interested in the *causes* of discretionary asset write-offs. Therefore, they analyze the statistical association between write-offs and a range of variables that proxy for possible determinants of the write-off decision and the amount written off. Since available methodology cannot ascertain causality,[455] reference is made to "determinants" of or "factors" associated with, as opposed to "causes" of write-offs. However, researchers try to establish the root causes of write-offs and therefore try to present evidence that allows them to decide whether their hypotheses about potential causes must be rejected. On the one hand, it is possible that the existence, amount, and timing of these accounting events reflect the existence, amount, and timing of economic declines in the values of the underlying assets accurately and in a timely manner. On the other hand, the discretion inherent in the (or the complete lack of) rules governing the write-off may be used by management to engage in earnings management, motivated by any of the earnings management incentives discussed in section 3.3.2 below.[456] It is difficult to disentangle the two factors, a fact that is not always sufficiently accounted for.[457]

Second, researchers are also interested in the *effects* of discretionary write-offs on the market value of the write-off firms' equity. While information content studies mainly focus on the short-term stock price effects of write-off announcements, association studies investigate the association of write-off amounts and longer-term stock returns. The theory presented in section 3.4.1 below explains why such associations would be expected. Again, available methodology cannot determine causality. Rather, levels of statistical significance are established at which a given hypothesis is either refuted of refutation of a given hypotheses is rejected.[458]

---

454 Another area not separately discussed here concerns descriptive investigations of the characteristics of write-offs, especially their magnitude and significance relative to other balance sheet and income statement items. See Alciatore et al. (1998, pp. 2, 26, 29).

455 See, for example, Huijgen (1996, p. 9 fn. 5).

456 Consequently, Francis, Hanna and Vincent (1996, p. 118) "investigate the extent to which proxies for managerial incentives to manipulate earnings and proxies for asset impairment explain write-off decisions".

457 Riedl (2002, p. 7) argues that "the reporting of asset impairment is conceptually a function of economic factors and reporting incentives". Wilson (1996, p. 172) states that the "credibility of a manipulation study's research findings depends on the extent to which the experimental design controls for .. economic factors".

458 Bearing this in mind, Francis, Hanna and Vincent's (1996) choice of title ("Causes and Effects of Discretionary Asset Write-Offs") raises somewhat false expectations. See also Wilson (1996, p. 177).

It should be noted that these two apparently separate and distinct research agendas influence each other: As discussed above, when trying to grasp the factors driving write-offs, consideration must be given to economic developments likely to have caused the underlying asset's value decline. Some investigate whether poor performance, as a proxy for value declines, is related to subsequent write-offs.[459] If a statistically significant relation can be shown to exist, it might be interpreted as evidence of the causality outlined above. But the relation might as well work the other way round: The fact that an economic decline in (part of) the firm's asset base has occurred might lead investors to adjust downwards their expectations regarding the firm's future cash flows. Provided that market participants learn about these developments through sources other than the firm's financial reporting disclosures, a stock price drop is bound to occur even before the corresponding write-off is actually recorded, let alone announced.[460]

Research on causes and effects is linked in another way: Investors are unlikely to react to each write-off in the same, predictable way regardless of its underlying cause. Each investor's reaction will depend on the information that the write-off is perceived to convey, i.e. on the way in which a specific write-off changes her expectations about the firm's future cash flows. For example, a surprising write-off reflecting an asset's obsolescence will probably trigger a response different from the one observed if that same write-off were purely motivated by management's desire to signal a strategic change that is planned to improve future earnings power. Therefore, market reactions may be different for different types of write-offs and in different settings in which write-offs occur. This notion is explicitly analyzed in studies testing for cross-sectional differences in market reactions to (announcements of) asset write-offs.[461]

Occasionally, the question whether or not a write-off is recorded in a *timely* manner (timeliness) is presented as a separate issue.[462] A write-off can be characterized as timely when it is recorded contemporaneously with the underlying asset becoming economically

---

459 For example, as Strong and Meyer (1987, p. 646) point out: "If an asset writedown is at heart a recognition of valuation declines that occurred in the past, the prior effects are likely to be apparent in past financial and operating performance".

460 See also Comprix (2000, p. 4).

461 For example, Francis, Hanna and Vincent (1996, p. 128) maintain that a write-off announcement potentially conveys information on three types of underlying facts: Economic value decreases, changes in management strategies, and management's inclination and ability to exercise earnings management discretion. For each type, they hypothesize different effects. See also Elliott and Shaw (1988, pp. 105-107).

462 See, for example, Alciatore et al. (1998, p. 3), Heflin and Warfield (1997, pp. 3, 9-15), and Riedl (2002, pp. 14-9).

impaired.[463] In analyzing the factors underlying discretionary asset write-offs, researchers must address the question whether or not these accounting events are caused by economic factors, i.e. declines in the economic values of the assets in question. When analyzing these economic factors, one will necessarily have to consider timing issues, i.e. whether contemporary economic developments underlie the write-off or whether the write-off only reflects the related economic decline with a time lag. For example, explanatory variables for the write-off amount might include current as well as lagged stock returns.

In "effects" studies, the timeliness issue is more complicated, which makes drawing inferences is difficult: For example, a stock price decline following a write-off announcement can be interpreted as evidence that the announcement contained information that caused investors to revise their expectations regarding firm value. In this respect, the write-off would have been timely. However, the fact that no stock price effect is observed is ambiguous: Either the write-off is preempted by other information that influences stock price before the write-off announcement (then it is not timely), or it is *caused* by the stock performance prior to the write-off announcement (then it might or might not be timely).[464]

3.3 Determinants of write-off behavior

3.3.1 Earnings management as an explanatory factor

3.3.1.1 Earnings management defined

A common issue in this literature is the choice of terminology, and corresponding definition, regarding its subject. The term *earnings management* is by far the most common.[465] It is frequently acknowledged that finding an appropriate term and definition is not a trivial task.[466] The following quote is representative of the definitions mainly found in the literature:

---

463 This discussion should not be confused with the descriptive issue of the distribution of write-offs among fiscal quarters, which is more a matter of disclosure. See, for example, Alciatore et al. (1998, p. 29).

464 The latter explanation would suggest a relevance of stock prices for accounting earnings. See Brown (2001, ch. 9). See also White, Sondhi and Fried (2003, p. 687).

465 For example, refer to the titles of the articles by Beneish (1998, 2001), Dechow and Skinner (2000), Healy and Wahlen (1999), McNichols (2000), and Schipper (1989).

466 See Beneish (2001, p. 2), Dechow and Skinner (2000, pp. 238-40).

> Earnings management is "the process of taking deliberate steps within the constraints of generally accepted accounting principles to bring about a desired level of reported earnings."[467]

This definition suggests a very limited focus on earnings versus other financial statement items and components that can be used to achieve managerial financial reporting objectives. Interestingly, the most common German term, "Bilanzpolitik", suggests a similarly narrow focus, albeit on the balance sheet.[468] Schipper (1989) suggests the broader term "disclosure management" to clarify that the actual focus is not exclusively on earnings.[469] The same objective is achieved by Fields, Lys and Vincent's (2001) similarly broad term "accounting choice".[470] In Germany, the term "Jahresabschlusspolitik" has been suggested to indicate this boader focus.[471]

It should also be noted that the above definition implies some form of "prejudice", as it were, regarding a certain managerial intent to self-interestedly manipulate the financial statements.[472] As discussed above, it is impossible to ascertain empirically the causality of managerial intentions for a given financial reporting decisions. While researchers may have some idealized sort of intentional management behavior in mind when studying specific accounting phenomena, statistical methodology can only document, not posi-

---

467 Sidney Davidson, Clyde P. Stickney and Roman L. Weil, Accounting: The language of business, 7th ed. 1987, as cited in Schipper (1989, p. 92).

468 See, for example, Baetge and Ballwieser (1977, p. 200) and Schmidt (1977, pp. 2-5). Heintges (1997, pp. 5-7) provides an in-depth discussion of different aspects of this definition. The fact that the German term is centered on the balance sheet as opposed to the income statement documents different emphases that are deeply rooted in dissimilar concepts of accounting theory. Brecht (2002, pp. 152-3, esp. fn. 13) explores the relation between "Bilanzpolitik" and "earnings management", concluding that earnings management is the wider concept.

469 "By 'earnings management' I really mean 'disclosure management' in the sense of a purposeful intervention in the external financial reporting process, with the intent of obtaining some private gain (as opposed to, say, merely facilitating the neutral operation of the process)." See Schipper (1989, p. 92).

470 "An accounting choice is any decision whose primary purpose is to influence (either in form or substance) the output of the accounting system in a particular way, including not only financial statements published in accordance with GAAP, but also tax returns and regulatory filings". See Fields, Lys and Vincent (2001, p. 256). Arguably, this definition is *too* broad: It should be every manager's objective to influence reported earnings upwards, primarily by making sound operating, investment, and financing decisions. Such non-accounting decisions would be comprised by "accounting choice".

471 See, for example, the literature cited in Veit (2002, p. 3).

472 This is also true of Schipper's (1989) definition. Refer to fn. 469. In contrast to that, Küting and Dawo's (2002a, p. 1157) definition implies that "Bilanzpolitik" is motivated a desire to obtain the firm's, not management's own, objectives: "Die willentliche und hinsichtlich der *Unternehmensziele* zweckorientierte Einflussnahme auf Form, Inhalt und Berichterstattung des handelsrechtlichen Jahresabschlusses wird allgemein als Bilanzpolitik bezeichnet" (emphasis added). Possibly, the concept of methodological individualism has not profoundly taken root in German accounting scholarship. For an introduction to that concept, refer to Furubotn and Richter (2000, pp. 2-3).

tively prove, empirical regularities suggestive of certain causal relations.[473] Although some managerial purpose or intent is an integral element of a meaningful definition,[474] presuming self-interested, opportunistic intentions,[475] as is the standard assumption in new institutional economics,[476] might be beside the point in some cases. Advocates of a "signaling" view argue that earnings management can serve to align managers' and stakeholders' interests, when managers use their financial reporting discretion to reduce information asymmetries regarding the firm's future prospects.[477] Most definitions appear to exclude signaling as an explanation of financial reporting decisions, suggesting that earnings management is always opportunistic.

Another issue has to do with the concrete actions potentially taken by management when pursuing its financial reporting objectives. The following definition by Healy and Wahlen (1999) explicitly considers this point:

> "Earnings management occurs when managers use judgment in financial reporting and in structuring transactions to alter financial reports to either mislead some stakeholders about the underlying economic performance of the company or to influence contractual outcomes that depend on reported accounting numbers."[478]

Schipper (1989) also acknowledges that financial reports can be influenced by "real" investment, financing, and operating decisions, as well as pure financial reporting steps

---

473 To mitigate this potential problem, Dechow and Skinner (2000, p. 241) propose to focus on managerial incentives in order to infer indirectly whether earnings management has been engaged in.

474 For example, according to Merchant and Rockness (1994, p. 79), "[e]arnings management can be defined as any action on the part of management which affects reported income and which provides no true economic advantage to the organization and may, in fact, in the long-term, be detrimental". This definition is too broad in that includes just *any* income-affecting management action that, regardless of original intent, turns out to be detrimental in the long term. It centers on the *outcome*, not the a priori intent. Other broad definitions do include a wide range of actions as well, but they rely on managerial intent to qualify those decisions as earnings management.

475 According to Christie and Zimmerman (1994, p. 541), "[o]*pportunism* occurs when a manager's decision increases the manager's wealth, but does not create a net increase in aggregate wealth. Since claim holders are price protected, opportunism is the *excess* opportunism over that expected" (emphasis in original).

476 Refer to Furubotn and Richter (2000, pp. 2-8, esp. 4).

477 See, for example, Beneish (2001, p. 3) and Rees, Gill and Gore (1996, p. 157). This signaling or information perspective dates back to Holthausen and Leftwich (1983).

478 Healy and Wahlen (1999, p. 368). This definition is also wide in that it does not focus on earnings alone, but on "financial reports" in a more general sense.

to account for a given "real" decision.[479] Furthermore, it should be noted at this point that the purpose of earnings management can be either to shift income across periods (intertemporal earnings management) or to achieve a certain financial statement presentation (classificatory earnings management).[480]

Healy and Wahlen's (1999) use of the term "judgment" highlights another point common to much of the terminology: Earnings management, achieved by taking advantage of subjective and discretionary GAAP guidance, is strictly distinct from *fraudulent accounting*, which implies clear violations of GAAP.[481] Where a self-interested management is assumed, possible types of financial reporting behavior can be thought of as a continuum ranging from neutral, unbiased financial reporting, via earnings management within GAAP, to earnings manipulation violating GAAP. Motivations might or might not be similar.

Considering the aspects discussed above, the more neutral term "financial reporting decisions" is defined here to comprise any purposeful management behavior intended to achieve management's financial reporting objectives, whatever these objectives might be. This behavior, while keeping within the borders set by GAAP, involves all aspects of the financial reporting process, and could therefore also be referred to as "financial statements management".[482]

---

479 See Schipper (1989, p. 92). The German terms "Sachverhaltsgestaltungen" and "Sachverhaltsabbildungen", respectively, represent these actions. See, for example, Veit (2002, pp. 10-1). See also Degeorge, Patel and Zeckhauser (1999, pp. 2-3) who similarly distinguish "direct" earnings management from "misreporting", both constituting earnings management. Beneish (2001, p. 3) argues that excluding all "real" decisions is problematic because it neglects at least two types of such decisions that earnings management researchers are interested in. These involve the structuring of transactions (solely) to obtain a desired accounting treatment (e.g. the pooling method) and the timing of transactions during the short time span around the closing date of the accounting period in order to achieve certain financial relations or ratios (*window-dressing*).

480 This distinction is discussed in more detail in section 3.3.2.4.4 below.

481 See Dechow and Skinner (2000, pp. 238-40). This notion is consistent with the definition used by Davidson, Stickney and Weil (see fn. 467), who specifically stress the "within the constraints of GAAP" aspect. On the other hand, Brecht (2002, p. 153) argues that earnings management does include fraudulent conduct.

482 However, since the term "earnings management" is by far more common and essentially comprises the same aspects, it will be used synonymously throughout the text.

3.3.1.2 Overview of the earnings management literature

Several authors have compiled overviews of the wide array of research questions and, mainly empirical, methodological approaches spanned by this extensive topic area.[483] Typically, these summary articles are structured around different types of earnings management incentives. Perhaps the most comprehensive synopsis of the more recent research in this area is provided by Fields, Lys and Vincent (2001),[484] who organize their review around three market imperfections that managers seek to exploit with their financial reporting decisions.[485] These imperfections, including agency costs, information asymmetries, and externalities,[486] give rise to financial reporting behavior motivated by contracting considerations (management compensation, debt covenants), stock price considerations, and a potential impact on third parties.[487] Concluding that the research in the 1990s has generated relatively little progress, they recommend that researchers widen the scope of accounting issues addressed, improve their empirical research designs, increasingly incorporate theoretical guidance from analytical models, and examine more closely the consequences of different aspects of financial reporting behavior, including its costs and benefits.[488] Beneish (2001) also discusses earnings management incentives. However, in contrast to Fields, Lys and Vincent (2001), he chooses to distinguish between income-increasing and income-decreasing earnings management as resulting from different incentives.[489] He acknowledges that this distinction is somewhat simplistic because, depending on the situation, one type of incentives may lead to both income-increasing and income-decreasing earnings management.[490] Dechow and Skinner's (2000) review

---

483 A list of 55 articles on earnings management, published during the 1993-99 period in The Accounting Review, Contemporary Accounting Research, Journal of Accounting and Economics, Journal of Accounting, Auditing and Finance, Journal of Accounting and Public Policy, Journal of Accounting Research, Journal of Business Finance and Accounting, and Review of Accounting Studies, has been compiled by McNichols (2000, p. 316).

484 The authors focus on studies published in the "three top accounting journals" in the 1990s. These journals are the Journal of Accounting and Economics, the Journal of Accounting Research, and The Accounting Review. They suggest that "roughly 10 percent of papers" in these periodicals deal with accounting choice. See Fields, Lys and Vincent (2001, p. 256 [both quotes]).

485 That article is reviewed by Francis (2001).

486 Refer to Fields, Lys and Vincent (2001, pp. 261-3).

487 Refer to Fields, Lys and Vincent (2001, pp. 265-88). These categories are presented in more detail in section 3.3.2 below.

488 Refer to Fields, Lys and Vincent (2001, pp. 288-99).

489 Refer to Beneish (2001, pp. 7-11).

490 See Beneish (2001, p. 11).

focuses on capital market-related incentives for earnings management and market participants' responses to such behavior.[491]

Beneish (2001) further examines different methodological approaches used in the literature to detect whether earnings management is present.[492] This approach is also adopted by McNichols (2000), who explicitly focuses on research design issues in earnings management studies. She distinguishes between three main methodological approaches, including studies based on aggregate (total or discretionary) accruals, on specific accruals (such as discretionary asset write-offs), and on the distributional patterns of "managed" earnings.[493] McNichols (2000) concludes that future progress in earnings management research is unlikely to be made in aggregate accruals studies because the empirical methodology employed in this research is not powerful and reliable enough to assess earnings management behavior in many interesting contexts. She encourages tests of specific accruals, which make use of detailed institutional knowledge, as well as of earnings distributions. Specifically, she highlights studies that focus on particular industries or economic setting in which a certain earnings management incentive is especially strong.[494] For example, banks and insurance companies have specific discretionary accruals available in which earnings management should manifest itself. Also, income-decreasing earnings management might be observed most frequently where firms are in wage negotiations with labor unions or are preparing a management buy-out, whereas income-increasing behavior is mostly likely in firms preparing for an initial public offering (IPO). Schipper's (1989) seminal commentary on earnings management is also preoccupied with research design issues. However, the author also reviews analytical work on conditions giving rise to earnings management.[495]

Healy and Wahlen's (1999) overview represents an attempt to extract implications for financial accounting standard setting from the research findings concerning earnings management. Focusing on the research questions most likely of interest to regulators, they document the specific accruals used to manage earnings and the pervasiveness in times of frequency and magnitude of earnings management behavior. Furthermore, they assess whether earnings management is "successful" in that it actually influences investor

---

491 Refer to Dechow and Skinner (2000, pp. 242-7).

492 Refer to Beneish (2001, pp. 4-7). See also Beneish (1999b, 1998, 1997).

493 Refer to McNichols (2000, pp. 316-9). Bernard and Skinner's (1996) review of papers by Subramanyam (1996) and Kasanen, Kinnunen and Niskanen (1996) is focused on discretionary accruals studies.

494 See McNichols (2000, p. 334).

495 Refer to Schipper (1989, pp. 93-8).

behavior. However, Healy and Wahlen's (1999) paper also considers different types of incentives and methodological approaches. They conclude that the earnings management literature to date has had only limited success in clarifying the questions of main interest to standard setters.[496]

Finally, the earnings management literature is reviewed in some of the more comprehensive review articles, where it is considered as a specific facet of accounting research in general.[497] Earnings management research is generally regarded under the aspect of the informativeness or "quality" of "managed" earnings, from which inferences are drawn regarding, among other things, capital market efficiency. Also, where "managed" earnings turn out to be informative, it might not be desirable that standard setters eliminate *all* discretion from financial reporting standards.[498]

In this dissertation, much of the earnings management research beyond the discretionary asset write-off literature is reviewed in the appropriate sections below.

3.3.1.3 Discretionary asset write-offs and earnings management

While accounting rules pertaining to asset write-offs are intended to capture asset impairment, the discretionary nature of most of this guidance makes such write-offs a potential instrument used by managers to achieve their financial reporting objectives. In this context, researchers interested in managers' financial reporting behavior and its underlying motives have turned to examining the determinants of discretionary asset write-offs in order to ascertain the extent to which these write-offs actually reflected impairment versus financial reporting incentives. In this sense, research on the determinants of discretionary asset write-offs is a distinct subset of the earnings management literature, a larger body of research into managers' incentives and behavior pertaining to accounting method choice and other, more subtle financial reporting decisions.

This "earnings management literature attempts to understand why managers manipulate earnings, how they do so and the consequences of this behavior".[499] Within the categories suggested by McNichols (2000), discretionary asset write-off studies represent tests of

---

496 See Healy and Wahlen (1999, p. 380).

497 These articles include, among others, Beaver (2002, pp. 466-8), Beaver (1998, pp. 98-9), Beaver (1996, pp. 116, 119), Lev and Ohlson (1982, pp. 266-275), Kothari (2001, pp. 161-7, 196-204), Bernard (1989, pp. 85-6).

498 See, for example, Schipper (1989, p. 91).

499 McNichols (2000, p. 313). In this section, the focus is on the former part, while the consequences of managers' financial reporting decisions are the subject of section 3.4 below.

financial reporting incentives using specific accruals. The specific characteristics of discretionary asset write-offs, including transitional SFAS 142 goodwill write-offs, have important implications for their suitability as earnings management instruments. This fact must be taken into consideration when forming hypotheses about management's behavior regarding these charges. For example, the effects of write-offs on the financial statements are usually considerable and must in most cases be disclosed separately. For this reason, it is not plausible to assume that managers use discretionary asset write-offs to achieve some subtle financial statement effect, which they hope will go undetected by capital market participants.[500] Rather, it is likely that managers use discretionary asset write-offs strategically as a one-off effect. "Advertised" to investors as a change in accounting method or a "cash-neutral" restructuring charge, managers hope that write-offs are viewed neutrally, or even favorably, at the time they occur. For this reason, write-off effects are frequently and backed out of "pro forma" earnings numbers that allegedly represent firm performance much more accurately than GAAP figures can. The true benefits of this effect, then, accrue to management in later periods, when financial statement ratios appear more favorable as a result of the prior write-off. This notion that investors view such transitory items differently from other earnings components is an important aspect of the discretionary write-off literature. It is a reason why not all of the hypotheses used in the broader earnings management literature can be applied in an unmodified way to discretionary write-off settings. In section 3.3.2.4.8, this issue is elaborated upon.

3.3.2 Theory, hypotheses, and main findings

3.3.2.1 Overview

As has been noted in section 3.2 above, applicable accounting guidance requires a write-off to be recorded upon impairment of the underlying asset. However, the assets of interest to the discretionary asset write-off literature share the common characteristic that their fair values (or similar benchmark amounts compared to book values in an impairment test) cannot be measured without recourse to management's subjective judgment. Consequently, researchers interested in ascertaining the determinants of discretionary asset write-offs face the challenge of discriminating between, on the one hand, economic factors and, on the other hand, management's financial reporting incentives as potential causes of discretionary asset write-offs.

---

500 See also Moses (1987, p. 366 fn. 11).

In section 3.3.2.2 below, the concept of economic impairment and researchers' approaches to ascertaining the extent to which actual impairment is behind discretionary asset write-offs are discussed. In a manner of speaking, where a discretionary asset write-off reflects management's incentives rather than the asset's actual economic obsolescence, the applicable accounting guidance introduces measurement error into the write-off amount, which might harm financial statement relevance and reliability.

Management's financial reporting objectives stem from the multiple functions of financial accounting information.[501] As will be discussed in more detail below, financial accounting information provided by firms, voluntarily or due to legal or contractual obligations, potentially serves numerous purposes.[502] In several countries, financial statements established according to local GAAP are used to bring about legal consequences. For example, taxable income of German firms is to a large extent determined by the same rules that also govern the establishment of accounts for financial reporting purposes. In addition, according to corporation law, the amount of accounting earnings calculated under German GAAP influences the level of dividends that can or must be distributed to stockholders of German stock corporations. However, since most of the research discussed here, as well as the empirical study presented in chapter 5, focuses on jurisdictions where such close links between discretionary asset write-offs, taxation, and dividend policy do not exist,[503] financial reporting incentives stemming from possible consequences for taxes and dividend payouts are not at the center of attention in this section.

Rather, two types of financial reporting incentives that are most frequently discussed in the discretionary write-off research and in the broader earnings management literature are focused on here. As depicted in Figure 7, financial reporting incentives potentially result when the outcome of firms' explicit and implicit contracts with outside parties depends on reported accounting numbers. Such contracts include management compensation plans as well as restrictive clauses in debt covenants and, where the concept of "contract" is interpreted broadly, political and regulatory costs that depend on a firm's financial statements. Furthermore, financial reporting incentives also ensue because financial

---

501 Refer to Heintges (1997) for a detailed discussion of financial reporting incentives depending on differing capital market and legal conditions in Germany and the U. S. See also Sieben and Coenenberg (1997, pp. 1045-7).

502 The purposes of financial accounting information are discussed in most accounting textbooks and countless academic articles. Examples include Kieso, Weygandt and Warfield (2001, pp. 2-6), Pellens (2001, pp. 9-21), Schildbach (2001, pp. 39-47), Schildbach (2000, pp. 23-73), Streim (1988, pp. 8-26), Schneider (1997, pp. 27-66), and White, Sondhi and Fried (2003, pp. 2-5).

503 For example, the tax linkage is regulated in the U. S. only with respect to the LIFO method. See Watts and Zimmerman (1986, p. 233).

statement information is believed by managers to be an important factor in the decision-making processes of capital market participants, including investors and rating agencies. Sections 3.3.2.3 and 3.3.2.4 below provide background on each of these categories and contain discussions of the relevant literature.[504]

Management's financial reporting incentives

Economic-consequences incentives	**Capital market-related incentives**
Influence contractual outcomes and (potential) regulation to *directly* affect management's utility	Influence market perceptions to *directly or indirectly* affect management's utility
• Accounting-based compensation plans • Accounting-based covenants in debt contracts • Accounting-based regulation	• Benevolent view (signaling): Convey privately held information about timing, magnitude and risk of future cash-flows through exercise of accounting discretion • Malevolent view (manipulation): Influence earnings for self-interested reasons, chiefly in order to increase stock price

Figure 7: Management's financial reporting incentives

3.3.2.2 Economic factors

As indicated in section 3.2 above, an asset write-off is supposed to reflect an economic value decline (impairment) that causes the carrying amount of the asset in question to fall below its fair value (or other relevant benchmark amount).[505] Therefore, researchers interested in identifying the factors underlying asset write-offs are required to expose the extent to which write-offs can be explained by indicators of economic developments that affect negatively the values of the assets under scrutiny. In the attempt to distinguish empirically between economic and incentive causes behind discretionary asset write-offs, researchers model write-off behavior under the assumption that it is made "true to the spirit" of the applicable guidance. Under that assumption, a write-off would be unaffected by management's incentives, but would purely reflect the underlying asset's economic value decline. Cotter, Stokes and Wyatt (1998) argue that incentives might also be

---

504 A similar classification is used by Fields, Lys and Vincent (2001). Beneish (2001, pp. 7-11) chooses a different categorization when he discusses earnings management incentives based on whether earnings are likely to be increased or decreased because of them.

505 See, for example, SFAS 121.7, SFAS 144.7. The term "fair value" is most common under U. S. GAAP, whereas the relevant IAS 36.5 refers to "recoverable amount", "the higher of an asset's net selling price and its value in use." For ease of exposition, the term "fair value" will be used throughout. Francis, Hanna and Vincent (1996, p. 122) refer to "economic value" instead.

behind the extent to which managers actually report any economic value declines in assets. They point out that managers have "economic and legal liability incentives and responsibilities to recognise writedowns."[506] Similarly, Healy and Palepu (1993) argue that reflecting asset value declines in the financial statements enhances managers' reputation for credible reporting. If economic factors behind discretionary asset write-offs are not controlled for, researchers are vulnerable to jumping to the conclusion that managers manipulate earnings when in fact they only account for asset obsolescence as required by financial reporting standards.[507]

Most accounting standards on asset write-offs specify impairment indicators as well as more or less detailed impairment testing procedures.[508] Where the underlying asset's fair value can be objectively measured, most frequently due to the existence of an active market, the researcher can readily model the amount of impairment, if any. Such marketable assets do not offer much room for discretionary financial reporting behavior, since objective benchmarks for impairment testing are usually available. Wilson (1996) suggests that accounting numbers be decomposed into three components, distinguishing between a fictitious "true" measurement construct, a measurement error (due to difficulties in observing the "true" value) absent earnings management, and an intentionally "managed" component.[509] He notes that, for marketable assets, the measurement error component will, on average, be much smaller than for firm-specific assets such as goodwill that are difficult to value.

The discretionary write-off literature is primarily interested in the latter type of assets, for which active markets do *not* exist. The fact that management has significant discretion in making the write-off decision and in determining the amount, if any, to write off (i.e., Wilson's (1996) second and third components are potentially large) directly implies that researchers have little hope in developing reasonably correct predictive models of that decision. Stated differently, if researchers were able to ascertain the extent of economic impairment (i.e., Wilson's (1996) first component) in a given asset with sufficient certainty, auditors as well as capital market participants could use these models to verify managers' write-off behavior, limiting management's financial reporting discretion. Consistent with this notion, Francis, Hanna and Vincent (1996) report that incentives play a

---

506 Cotter, Stokes and Wyatt (1998, p. 160).

507 See, for example, Wilson (1996, p. 172).

508 Impairment indicators relevant to SFAS 142 goodwill write-off behavior are analyzed in section 4.3.2 below. For an investigation of the testing procedure itself, refer to sections 4.5 and 4.6 below. See also SFAS 144.7-22 for assets other than goodwill and indefinite-lived intangibles.

509 Refer to Wilson (1996, p. 173).

substantial role in explaining discretionary financial reporting decisions such as goodwill write-offs or restructuring charges, whereas write-offs of inventory and PP&E appear to be significantly less "managed".[510] Due to this difficulty in modeling the "unmanaged" portion of a discretionary asset write-off, conclusions from extant modeling on the extent to which a given set of write-offs correctly reflects economic obsolescence should be drawn with caution. Similarly, researchers focusing on write-off firms alone are likely to waste information, since the decision *not* to record but to avoid a write-off potentially has an economic and an incentive portion as well.

Most researchers include in their models proxy variables designed to capture the firm's economic development surrounding the write-off. For example, Francis, Hanna and Vincent (1996) use indicators of the firm's as well as the industry's financial and accounting performance as "variables indicating the likelihood that the firm has impaired assets and the extent of any impairment", assuming that "impairment is associated with both poor historical firm performance and declining industry trends."[511] They find that most types of write-offs examined are significantly associated with past stock price declines. Goodwill write-offs in particular are additionally found to be related changes in both to firm and industry MTB ratio and ROA. However, not all of these associations have the predicted sign.[512]

While adopting a similar approach, Riedl (2002) focuses on change in firm sales and change in industry ROA as economic factors behind asset write-offs under SFAS 121 compared with the pre-SFAS 121 regime.[513] These variables are found to be highly significant, in both Tobit and ordinary least squares (OLS) specifications,[514] in the pre-SFAS 121 regime, but not under SFAS 121. In a related study of goodwill write-offs under SFAS 121 versus SFAS 142, Segal (2003) uses the same proxies for economic factors that are employed by Riedl (2002).[515] In addition, he includes the change in firm market value (ΔMV). In both regimes, only ΔMV is found to be significant.[516] Cotter,

---

510 See Francis, Hanna and Vincent (1996, p. 125).

511 Francis, Hanna and Vincent (1996, p. 122 [both quotes]). Proxy variables used include several lagged stock returns, the book-to-market ratio and its change over time, the change in return on assets (ROA) and sales, as well as the corresponding 4-digit SIC industry values.

512 See Francis, Hanna and Vincent (1996, p. 125).

513 See Riedl (2002, pp. 9-10).

514 For a discussion of methodological details peculiar to discretionary asset write-off studies, refer to section 5.4.1 below.

515 See Segal (2003, p. 17).

516 In contrast to Riedl (2002) and Francis, Hanna and Vincent (1996), Segal (2003, pp. 40-1) exclusively relies on an OLS specification.

Stokes and Wyatt (1998) also document that write-offs are associated with economic value declines.[517] Heflin and Warfield (1997), Rees, Gill and Gore (1996), Elliott and Shaw (1988), as well as Strong and Meyer (1987) report largely similar results for univariate comparisons between write-off firms and their industries, concluding that write-off firms significantly underperform their industry peers on a variety of performance measures.[518] Loh and Tan (2002) find that macroeconomic factors such as GDP growth, change in interest rate, property vacancy rate, and change in unemployment rate are associated with the frequency and magnitude of fixed-asset and investment write-offs recorded by firms in Singapore.[519] Overall, "the evidence seems to indicate that firms write down assets during periods of poor performance."[520]

Commentators on the discretionary asset write-off literature (and the more general earnings management research) suggest that researchers should make more explicit use of their institutional knowledge of accounting standards and financial reporting practice.[521] For example, the studies discussed above rely on proxy variables that capture some general notion of economic firm and industry decline. In most cases, these variables are not specifically modeled to emulate the method according to which the relevant accounting guidance requires asset impairment to be measured.[522] For example, SFAS 142 goodwill write-offs should be observed whenever the MTB ratio of a firm's reporting unit falls below one.[523] In a recent working paper, Beatty and Weber (2004) adopt a different approach to controlling for economic developments in the context of an SFAS 142 write-off causes study. They model the expected portion of the transitional goodwill write-off as "the amount by which the tangible book value of equity exceeds the market value of equity".[524]

---

517 See Cotter, Stokes and Wyatt (1998, pp. 170-4).

518 See Heflin and Warfield (1997, p. 25), Rees, Gill and Gore (1996, pp. 160-2), Elliott and Shaw (1988, pp. 98-103), and Strong and Meyer (1987, pp. 646-8).

519 See Loh and Tan (2002, pp. 138-40, 150). The importance of controlling for the state of the economy at the time of the write-off is also stressed by Alciatore et al. (1998, p. 32).

520 White, Sondhi and Fried (2003, p. 279).

521 See, for example, Wilson (1996, pp. 171-3), McNichols (2000, pp. 337-8), Fields, Lys and Vincent (2001, p. 301).

522 See Wilson (1996, p. 173).

523 Refer to section 5.2.2 below for a more detailed discussion of the use of the MTB ratio as a proxy for economic impairment in the SFAS 142 setting. The SFAS 142 impairment testing procedure is described in SFAS 142.19-22. For a detailed discussion, refer to sections 4.5 and 4.6 below.

524 Beatty and Weber (2004, p. 14). According to the authors, this method is outlined in Tergesen (2002).

Determining the "unmanaged" portion of a financial reporting decision is highly relevant to another aspect of the discretionary write-off literature. When modeling the expected portion of a discretionary asset write-off in the context of a write-off effects study,[525] researchers must make assumptions regarding the amount of write-off, if any, expected by capital market participants, based on the information available at the time of the write-off. Usually, the extent to which a write-off is assumed to be expected depends on economic developments preceding the write-off. In other words, capital market participants are not, on average, assumed by researchers to be able to anticipate earnings management.

As noted above, discretionary asset write-off studies can be characterized as tests of specific accruals.[526] However, a substantial segment of the broader earnings management literature is interested in ascertaining the extent to which financial reporting incentives are reflected in earnings, the aggregate of the entirety of a firm's financial reporting decisions. Such studies rely, perhaps to a larger extent than studies of individual financial reporting decisions, on the researcher's ability to correctly specify the amount of earnings that would be observed in the absence of earnings management.[527] However, early research such as Healy (1985) relied on unadjusted total accruals, represented by the difference between reported earnings and operating cash flow,[528] as a proxy for the "managed" portion of a firm's earnings.[529] This approach has been widely criticized because total accruals can be disaggregated into a discretionary and a non-discretionary component and total accruals are thought to be a noisy measure of the discretionary component.[530]

In order to better predict the expected amount of "unmanaged" accruals, researchers have developed models to isolate from total accruals the discretionary portion, i.e. the amount

---

525 Such studies are discussed in section 3.4 below.

526 See, for example, McNichols (2000, p. 316).

527 In the former context, the "earnings management potential" available to management is restricted to a single balance sheet or income statement item, perhaps made fairly predictable by accounting guidance and/or industry practice, whereas aggregate accruals studies deal with a much wider array of financial reporting decisions.

528 See, for example, Healy (1985, p. 94) and DeAngelo (1986, p. 408).

529 See Healy (1985, p. 94). Another proxy used by Healy (1985) is "the effect of voluntary changes in accounting procedures on earnings".

530 For example, refer to Dechow, Sloan and Sweeney (1995). Healy (1985, p. 94) and DeAngelo (1986, p. 408) acknowledge this potential weakness of total accruals. DeAngelo (1986, p. 409) uses prior-period total accruals as "a benchmark for what the current accrual would be, absent income manipulation", assuming that nondiscretionary accruals follow a random walk pattern. However, this method assumes that prior-period total accruals were "unmanaged".

of potentially "managed" accruals. One of the earliest studies to propose such a discretionary accruals model is Jones (1991), who developed what became known as the "Jones model". Discretionary accruals models attempt to estimate the discretionary portion of total accruals under the assumption that nondiscretionary accruals are a function of the firm's operating characteristics. More technically, total accruals are regressed on firm size, the change in revenues, and the level of property, plant and equipment (PP&E) over some estimation period. The resulting regression coefficients are then used to estimate, for the period under consideration, the expected level of non-discretionary accruals. The difference between this estimate and total accruals is then interpreted as the amount of discretionary accruals. Dechow, Sloan and Sweeney (1995) provide an overview of these models.[531] Recently, discretionary accruals model have been widely criticized on the grounds that they produce potentially noisy estimates of the "managed" portion of earnings, and that they therefore lack power to actually detect earnings management.[532]

3.3.2.3 Economic-consequences incentives

Since financial reporting rules provide discretion to management, financial reporting decisions such as asset write-offs are likely to be influenced by factors other than economic value declines. The determinants of these financial reporting decisions can be further explained by investigating management's incentives. An approach introduced in this section analyzes any *direct* cash flow consequences of these decisions. These *economic consequences* are theorized to result from specific contracts (explicit or implicit) that the firm is a party to.[533] For this reason, this category of incentives has also come to be termed *contracting* incentives,[534] as opposed to incentives derived from an *information perspective*:

> "[T]he contracting and information perspectives agree that there is an association between accounting methods and cash flows, but they disagree on the causality. The contracting perspectives (either efficient contracting or opportunistic behavior) suggest that the accounting methods chosen affect the firm's cash flows (choose the most efficient methods to maximize firm value or behave opportunistically to trans-

---

531 See Dechow, Sloan and Sweeney (1995, pp. 197-200). Identifying certain weaknesses, they suggest a "modified Jones model". See also Beaver (2002, pp. 466-8), Bernard and Skinner (1996), and Kothari (2001, pp. 161-7).

532 Wilson (1996, p. 173) suggests that researchers "stop decomposing accounting numbers into discretionary and nondiscretionary components". See also McNichols (2000, pp. 337-8).

533 In the spirit of Lev and Ohlson (1982, p. 250), a "broader view" is adopted here that includes all direct cash flow consequences of financial reporting decisions.

534 See White, Sondhi and Fried (2003, p. 173). See also Fields, Lys and Vincent (2001, pp. 265-75).

fer wealth), while the information perspective suggests the methods chosen provide information about the future cash flows of the firm, but do not affect them directly."[535]

Economic-consequences incentives have been derived from a literature most frequently referred to as *positive accounting theory*, which is introduced next. This research developed into three main branches, each of which is discussed in turn subsequently. As the previous quote indicates, financial reporting decisions made to influence cash flows from contracts may be made by management for either *efficiency* or *opportunistic* reasons. This distinction, including the problems it creates for empirical analyses of the motivations of financial reporting decisions, is discussed further in section 3.3.2.3.6.

3.3.2.3.1 Intellectual roots: Positive accounting theory

Prior to the 1960s, accounting research was largely concerned with prescribing how firms *should* report. It was attempted to *normatively* recommend accounting procedures that fulfill some theoretical ideal or principle. Under this normative approach, alternative accounting procedures were evaluated based on the extent to which they align net income with this perceived ideal.[536] *Positive accounting theory* evolved in the 1970s and was originally intended by its initiators, Watts and Zimmerman, to form a counter-proposal to that normative approach.[537] Inspired by contemporary developments in economics and finance, a *positive* approach was adopted, shifting the focus to explaining and predicting current observable accounting practice.[538] Watts and Zimmerman looked to the contracting and political processes, in which the firm and its constituents are embedded, for explanatory factors of observable accounting practice.[539] Under the assumption of nonzero contracting and information costs, accounting methods have the potential to affect the cash flows accruing to the firm and its managers.

---

[535] Holthausen (1990, pp. 208-9). In the words of White, Sondhi and Fried (2003, p. 173), "accounting data do not merely *describe* reality – they in effect *define* reality, as real economic consequences flow from the reported numbers" (emphasis in original).

[536] See Beaver (1998, pp. 2-3).

[537] The evolution of positive accounting theory is outlined in Watts and Zimmerman (1990, pp. 132-140). Haller (1994) provides an introduction to this theory (pp. 597-601) and a review of related research findings (pp. 601-3) from a German perspective. See also Kelly (1983). Critical appraisals are provided, among others, by Ballwieser (1993, pp. 125-8), Tinker and Puxty (1994), and Wagenhofer (1988).

[538] The seminal paper is Watts and Zimmerman (1979). See also Watts and Zimmerman (1978).

[539] The original idea of positive accounting theory has been widely criticized. The proponents reply to this criticism in Watts and Zimmerman (1990, pp. 140-9). See also their views on the terminology (p. 148).

This *contracting role of accounting* is based on an economic theory of the firm that draws on the property rights literature.[540] This literature views a firm as a nexus of (formal and informal, explicit and implicit) contracts that govern the *agency relationships* between, essentially, owners, debtholders (the *principals*), and managers (the *agents*).[541] The assumption that the costs to establish and maintain these contracts are non-zero provides a link between accounting procedures and the cash flows accruing to the firms and/or their managers: Accounting is an integral part of the firm's contracts in that accounting numbers are used to determine the outcomes of these contracts. Relevant contracts include management's compensation schemes and private lending agreements with creditors.

Since the agent's utility is assumed to increase in the amount of money and non-pecuniary benefits she receives or consumes on the job, the agent has incentive to engage in *opportunistic behavior*, i.e. behavior that increases the agent's wealth but reduces firm value.[542] However, under the assumption of rational expectations,[543] the principal will anticipate these actions and adjust the prices she is willing to pay for stock or debt accordingly (*price protection*), causing the agent to bear *agency costs*.[544] Therefore, as an owner-manager with a relatively large stake in the firm's equity, she has incentive to incur costs for bonding and monitoring actions to reduce agency costs. However, as is common in today's large, public corporations, when the agent is a professional manager with a relatively small stake in the firm's equity, she bears only a small fraction of the agency costs, which reduces her incentive to act in the principal's best interest. In this scenario it is the principal who has incentive to align the agent's interests with her own (maximization of firm value) in order to reduce agency costs.[545]

Two concrete instruments to minimize agency costs have been the focal points of the contracting literature: Incentive compensation plans that align managers' and sharehold-

---

540 See Watts and Zimmerman (1990, p. 133). For much the following, refer to Watts and Zimmerman (1986, ch. 8). For references see Fülbier (1998, pp. 121-34).

541 The role of managers differs depending on whether they are owner-managers or professional managers who own no more than a small percentage of the firm's equity.

542 See Watts and Zimmerman (1986, p. 192). The concept of opportunism is discussed in Williamson (1975, pp. 26-30). See also Fülbier (1998, pp. 128-9).

543 See, for example, Furubotn and Richter (2000, pp. 3-4).

544 The costs of conflicts of interest between agent and principal, which result in value-reducing actions taken by the agent. See Watts and Zimmerman (1986, pp. 196, 198).

545 The manager is additionally disciplined by the labor market. Refer to Watts and Zimmerman (1986, pp. 191-3).

ers' interests and debt covenants that align managers' and debtholders' interests.[546] These contracts are often defined in terms of accounting numbers.[547] For example, lending agreements between firms' managers and their creditors often specify certain covenants, defined in terms of accounting ratios such as interest coverage[548] or DTE[549], the violation of which triggers default on the loan.[550] Therefore, incentives exist for managers to influence the accounting numbers that are used in these contracts and also in corporate charters and bylaws.[551]

3.3.2.3.2 Application to financial reporting decisions

Early capital markets-based accounting research assumed that, at any point in time, the publicly available information set was instantaneously impounded in security prices.[552] Stated differently, researchers relied on the EMH in its semi-strong form.[553] Under this assumption, "cosmetic" (i.e., cash-neutral) accounting decisions were not expected to have any influence on the market value of the firm. More specifically, announcements of mandated or voluntary changes in accounting methods were not expected to affect stock prices in the absence of tax consequences or any other "direct" cash-flow effects.[554] Nor were firms that followed different accounting methods expected to be priced differently by the market *because* of their different accounting procedures. However, when early research found some evidence that cosmetic accounting decisions did actually appear to have stock price effects,[555] a debate ensued concerning possible explanations of these findings which apparently contradicted the semi-strong-form EMH.[556] Suggested interpretations range from functional fixation, investors punishing income-increasing manipu-

---

546 Watts and Zimmerman (1986, p. 200) point out that these types of contracts are most frequently studied because "data are available on those contracts", whereas data "are not readily available for many other formal and informal firm contracts". Other such contracts include sales and other contracts. Refer to Watts and Zimmerman (1990, pp. 134 [especially fn. 5], 145, 151).

547 Refer to sections 3.3.2.3.3 and 3.3.2.3.4 below for empirical evidence on the actual extent to which accounting numbers are used in contractual relations.

548 EBIT divided by interest expense.

549 Debt divided by shareholders' equity.

550 See Watts and Zimmerman (1986, p. 210).

551 See Watts and Zimmerman (1986, p. 196).

552 See, for example, Fields, Lys and Vincent (2001, p. 264), Holthausen and Leftwich (1983, pp. 80-2).

553 According to Beneish (2001, p. 9), informational efficiency is "a central hypothesis in capital market research". Refer also to the discussion section 2.3.3 above.

554 See, for example, the review of early research in this area by Lev and Ohlson (1982, pp. 266-75).

555 For concrete examples, refer to Lev and Ohlson (1982, pp. 267-9).

556 See, for example, Lev and Ohlson (1982, pp. 273-5) and Bernard (1989).

lation, signaling, and cosmetic accounting choices as proxies for firms' economic characteristics.

As explicitly encouraged by Lev and Ohlson (1982),[557] the types of contracts discussed above have been considered by the "Rochester school" as an explanation for (1) such seemingly "cosmetic", i.e. cash-neutral, financial reporting decisions (mainly mandatory and voluntary accounting choices) and for (2) market movements observed in association with these decisions, which could not be readily explained when the EMH was assumed to hold (so-called "anomalies"[558]). The existence of contracts that relied on accounting numbers to generate "real" economic, cash-relevant consequences has been viewed as presenting a theoretically sound explanation consistent with the EMH not only for, at first sight, "cosmetic" financial reporting decisions, but also for firms' lobbying behavior in the standard-setting process and, ultimately, standard setters' regulatory decisions. According to positive accounting theory, these financial reporting decisions have cash-flow and resulting stock price effects through the use of accounting numbers in contracts. However, early empirical tests of these hypotheses generated inconclusive results, possibly because research methods at that time were insufficient to detect the minuscule stock price movements associated with the contracting-induced cash-flow consequences of financial reporting decisions.[559] White, Sondhi and Fried (1997), summarizing the evidence on the economic-consequences incentives hypotheses, state that "research results are consistent, albeit weakly, with the predicted relationships for mandated accounting changes but not for voluntary ones."[560]

Besides the use of accounting information in the firm's contracts, positive accounting theory also considered the role of accounting in the *political and regulatory environment*.[561] The political process was viewed as a medium through which constituents competed for wealth transfers, with accounting information serving as an indicator of wealth. For example, it was assumed that large reported earnings were used as evidence of a monopoly from which wealth had to be transferred away by regulation. This provided man-

---

557 See Lev and Ohlson (1982, pp. 274-5).

558 Brown (2001, p. 85) paraphrases Kuhn's (1970) definition of an anomaly as "systematic evidence that appears scientifically precise but is inconsistent with the tenets of basic theory". Lev and Ohlson (1982, p. 274) prefer the term "surprises", wondering why "some still insist on referring to them as anomalies."

559 See, for example, Zmijewski and Hagerman (1981). Literature reviews by, for example, Bernard (1989, p. 80), Christie (1990), Haller (1994), Holthausen and Leftwich (1983), and Leftwich (1990) report a growing disenchantment with this line of research.

560 White, Sondhi and Fried (2003, p. 242).

561 Refer to Watts and Zimmerman (1986, ch. 10).

agers with an incentive to influence accounting numbers in order to minimize the likelihood of exposure to adverse regulation.

Since Watts and Zimmerman, focusing on explaining and predicting accounting decisions, primarily identified explanatory factors that stemmed from the role of accounting numbers in contracts and regulation,[562] this line of reasoning has also become known as *contracting theory*. However, Watts and Zimmerman (1990) defend the term positive accounting theory, which they prefer over contracting theory and other terms that have been suggested, e.g. *economic-consequences* literature.[563] According to them, it was originally chosen to "distinguish research aimed at explanation and prediction from research whose objective was prescription",[564] of which contracting theory is only a small fraction.[565]

In this dissertation, financial reporting incentives derived from assumed "real" cash-flow consequences of accounting numbers are referred to as *economic-consequences incentives*, because (1) the term *contracting theory* falls intuitively short of including political and regulatory considerations, and (2) the term *positive accounting theory* is too broad: The incentives discussed in this section are distinct from the capital markets-related motivations discussed in section 3.3.2.4.[566] However, all financial reporting incentives are part of positive accounting theory, while not all are considered to stem from assumed "real" cash-flow consequences of accounting numbers.[567] Three branches of the economic-consequences literature are discussed in some detail below: Accounting-based compensation schemes, accounting-based debt covenants, and accounting-based political and other regulatory costs.[568] Problems stemming from the fact that accounting-based contracts are possibly endogenous are the subject of section 3.3.2.3.6.

---

562 Watts and Zimmerman (1990, p. 150): "The [positive accounting] literature ... emphasizes the central role of contracting costs in accounting theory".

563 See Watts and Zimmerman (1990, p. 148).

564 Watts and Zimmerman (1990, p. 148).

565 In that sense, all research interested in the determinants of actual financial reporting decisions is "positive". Tinker and Puxty (1994, p. 8) argue that positive accounting theory denotes the whole paradigm that replaced normative accounting research: "This contracting research is still 'positive' in that it explores the factors influencing management's choice of one accounting policy over others."

566 These latter incentives are studied, according to Watts and Zimmerman (1990, p. 132 fn. 1), from an "information perspective".

567 The term *positive accounting theory* does not only include that contracting role of accounting but also, as Watts and Zimmerman (1990, p. 148 fn. 14) explicitly state, "noncontractual variables ... [such as] taxes or information for the capital markets". Most generally, according to Watts and Zimmerman (1990, p. 150), "[accounting choices] are made in terms of individual objectives and the effects of accounting methods on the achievement of those objectives."

568 These categories are described fundamentally in Watts and Zimmerman (1986, chapters 9 and 10).

3.3.2.3.3 *Accounting earnings-based compensation schemes*

The fact that the principal is interested in motivating the agent to increase firm value explains the existence of management incentive compensation schemes as such.[569] However, it is less straightforward why the principal, especially in a publicly traded firm, should reward the agent not on the basis of her impact on firm value but on the basis of accounting earnings.[570] Watts and Zimmerman (1986) argue that the proliferation and long history of accounting earnings-based compensation plans indicate that these are efficient contracts. They point to several factors that possibly motivate the use of these schemes:[571] First, much of a firm's (debt) capital might not be publicly traded. Earnings before interest, then, could be a useful indicator of the firm's performance, i.e. of changes in the total value of the firm, since it may be reasonable to assume that overall firm value varies with earnings before interest like stock price varies with earnings.[572] Second, even where (a large portion of) total firm value is observable, it need not be the adequate basis for compensating managers that are not responsible for the whole firm. Subunit managers should be rewarded based on divisional performance. For most divisions, market values are not observable, but divisional accounting earnings that are indicators of those subunits' market value can be calculated.[573] Third, since performance and bonus plans defer compensation for one or more years, a tax benefit is realized by the manager if the firm's corporate tax rate exceeds the manager's personal tax rate. However, an offsetting effect is the plan's influence on the manager's risk. Compared to the present value of a fixed salary, the present value of accounting earnings-based bonus compensation adds more risk to the manager's overall portfolio. Risk-averse managers will require greater compensation when they are subject to a bonus plan. The fact that such plans nonetheless do exist suggests that other (incentive) benefits are derived from their use.[574] Finally, com-

---

569 Hypotheses that explain the existence and composition of management compensation schemes are presented by Watts and Zimmerman (1986, p. 201). See also Smith and Watts (1992).

570 Shareholders may be interested in high accounting earnings as such, because accounting earnings are a determining factor of the amount of dividends that can be paid. A bonus plan that ties (part of) management's compensation to the accounting earnings reported in a given period, then, should help align management's interests with those of shareholders. In a related paper, Lewellen. Loderer and Martin (1987) investigate the composition of executive compensation packages in terms of current versus deferred and stock-related versus cash-based elements.

571 Refer to Watts and Zimmerman (1986, pp. 202-3).

572 According to Healy (1985, p. 93), 33.5% of bonus contracts examined included an earnings definition that involved adding back interest.

573 Guidry, Leone and Rock (1999, p. 121) explicitly investigate business-unit managers' earnings-based bonus plans that are based on business-unit earnings, arguing that the signal-to-noise ratio of aggregate firm-level earnings is likely to be low in a decentralized firm.

574 Hypotheses why compensation contracts include accounting performance (in addition to stock price performance) are also discussed by Boschen et al. (2003, pp. 146-7).

pensating a manager based on stock performance alone would involve rewarding and, as the case might be, penalizing her for market fluctuations that might not be under her influence.

Compensation schemes that rely on accounting earnings are widespread. Management compensation usually consists of base salary and incentive compensation. Two types of the latter are distinguished:[575] (1) *Performance plans* tie management's reward to three- or five-year targets, frequently defined in terms of stock performance, while (2) *bonus plans* specify annual goals based on accounting measures such as net income, ROA, and ROE.[576] Healy (1985) cites evidence documenting that, in 1980, 90% of the 1,000 largest U. S. manufacturing firms used an accounting earnings-based bonus plan to remunerate managers, and that bonus plans accounted for a larger proportion of managers' overall compensation than did performance plans.[577]

If compensation is based on accounting measures generated by management, it is not intuitively clear, why discretion should be allowed in determining these measures.[578] However, *some* discretion appears to be economically efficient since it can be used by managers to signal the firm's future performance. Also, it is simply too costly to eliminate all discretion. Possibly, management's manipulation accounting earnings upward to increase their bonus payments might even be in the shareholders' best interest, since higher earnings are also likely to result in higher stock price and/or a lower likelihood of debt covenant violation. Furthermore, discretion in accounting-based contracts allows managers to use their superior knowledge about the accounting methods that best motivate subordinates. Ultimately, investors' assumed rational expectations provide that management's overall compensation package anticipates opportunistic financial reporting decisions. One cost of more rather than less discretion is the increased likelihood of *ex post* opportunism due to unanticipated redistribution.[579]

---

575 See Healy (1985, p. 87).

576 See Fields, Lys and Vincent (2001, p. 266).

577 See Healy (1985, pp. 85, 87). For more recent evidence, especially on the determinants of CEO compensation, refer to Boschen et al. (2003, pp. 147-9).

578 In the words of Watts and Zimmerman (1986, p. 204 [both quotes]), "[i]f managers controlled the calculation of earnings to the extent that they could report any number they wished, earnings-based bonus plans would not exist for incentive purposes". "If earnings-based plans are used to reward managers for incentive reasons, there must be some restriction of the methods managers use to calculate earnings".

579 See Watts and Zimmerman (1990, pp. 135-6) and Fields, Lys and Vincent (2001, p. 266). For more detail on this issue, refer to section 3.3.2.3.6 below.

In practice, compensation committees are frequently responsible for administering accounting-based compensation schemes. It has been investigated whether compensation committees undo certain transactions/accounting entries to adjust accounting earnings, or other accounting data relevant for compensation purposes, in order to generate enhanced incentive effects.[580] Generally speaking, opportunistic earnings management to maximize bonus payments could be precluded by adjusting for bonus-increasing earnings management. Conversely, managers could be shielded from bonus-decreasing events that either are outside their responsibility or benefit shareholders by enhancing firm value. Healy, Kang and Palepu (1987) examine the effect of two distinct accounting procedure changes on CEOs' cash compensation. They find no evidence that changes between inventory valuation methods and depreciation procedures are adjusted in order to compute CEO compensation. The authors are surprised by this finding since correcting earnings numbers to pre-change levels would have been low-cost for compensation committees, since the accounting changes studied are well visible and apparent from publicly available financial data.[581] In a related study, Abdel-khalik (1985) finds opposite results. Dechow, Huson and Sloan (1994) report evidence on a specific aspect of this issue. They argue that restructuring charges are of specific interest in this context because they usually produce reverse short-term earnings versus long-term shareholder value effects. Their empirical evidence suggests that restructuring charges are backed out of CEO cash compensation. Interestingly, the fact that restructuring charges are backed out is not necessarily stated explicitly in the plans. Therefore, managers might still engage in bonus-related earnings management and only learn later on that avoiding, understating, or delaying restructuring charges was unnecessary.[582] Gaver and Gaver (1998) examine the extent to which different components of earnings influence CEO cash compensation. They distinguish above-the-line earnings from below-the-line earnings, i.e. the results of discontinued operations and extraordinary items. Their regression results suggest that positive components flow through to affect compensation while negative components do not. This result holds even for other unusual, non-recurring gains and losses that do not qualify for below-the-line treatment. The authors suggest several explanations for this interesting finding:[583] First, they argue that executives have high bargaining power in negotiations

[580] See, for example, Dechow, Huson and Sloan (1994, p. 138). Healy (1985, p. 85) declares that earnings "are often defined so that certain accounting decisions do not affect bonuses". Pertaining to the financial reporting decisions of interest here, Francis, Hanna and Vincent (1996, p. 123 fn. 7) note that "manipulations will affect management compensation if bonus calculations are not adjusted for write-offs and restructuring charges."

[581] See Healy, Kang and Palepu (1987, p. 32).

[582] See Dechow, Huson and Sloan (1994, p. 155).

[583] See Gaver and Gaver (1998, p. 252).

with compensation committees since replacement is not easily found for their specialized knowledge and shareholders have incentive to avoid potential decreases in firm value caused by the departure of the CEO. Second, managers are rewarded for the value-increasing decisions that are behind the non-recurring items. This explanation corresponds to the frequent assertion that goodwill write-offs and other charges, e.g. restructuring charges,[584] are part of a strategic review that leads to enhanced future prospects. Finally, executives are shielded from exogenous losses for which they are not responsible.[585] Finally, Boschen et al. (2003) document that CEO compensation initially responds positively to unexpected accounting performance, but falls below prior levels in later periods. However, they point that economic interpretation of this finding is open to debate: Performance standards might be raised for periods following unexpected earnings, making them more difficult to attain. Alternatively, unexpected earnings due to earnings management might reverse in later periods because future earnings had been accelerated to achieve them.[586] Taken together, the evidence presented in these studies suggests that the extent to which earnings management decisions affect compensation is not a priori known to management. Therefore, bonus-related earnings management cannot be ruled out in most situations, especially where unprecedented financial reporting decisions are made due to mandatory changes in GAAP such as the initial application of SFAS 142.

The bonus plan hypothesis has originally been formulated by Watts and Zimmerman (1986) as follows:

> "Ceteris paribus, managers of firms with bonus plans are more likely to choose accounting procedures that shift reported earnings from future periods to the current period."[587]

Healy (1985) expands this simple relation by explicitly taking into account that bonus plans frequently have upper and lower bounds and that bonus payments are an increasing function of reported accounting earnings only when earnings are within the corridor defined by these thresholds. When managers make financial reporting decisions so as to maximize multi-period compensation, they have incentive to manage earnings upward only when unmanaged earnings are expected to fall within the corridor or when they are

---

584 For example, Dechow, Huson and Sloan (1994) report that CEO cash compensation does not decrease as a result of restructuring charges taken.

585 Lambert (2001) documents that incentive constructs have a discouraging effect when they are based on measures that are highly volatile and not under the manager's influence. See also Hitz and Kuhner (2002, p. 284) and Kahle (2002b, pp. 903-4).

586 See Boschen et al. (2003, p. 164).

587 Watts and Zimmerman (1986, p. 208).

sufficiently close to the lower end that income-increasing earnings management can level out the remaining difference. When unmanaged earnings are either above the upper bound or (far) below the lower bound, managers will have incentive to manage earnings downward instead, a fact not recognized by the simple bonus plan hypothesis as stated originally by Watts and Zimmerman. While Healy (1985) finds evidence supporting his hypotheses, his study has been criticized, not least on methodological grounds and with respect to competing hypotheses.[588] Several papers, including Gaver, Gaver and Austin (1995), Holthausen, Larcker and Sloan (1995), and Guidry, Leone and Rock (1999) expand upon Healy (1985) and partly challenge his conclusions.

Another reason why the Watts and Zimmerman (1986) hypothesis may be overly simplistic is the fact that bonus plans frequently exhibit a "ratchet effect". This means that the target earnings numbers are not fixed from one period to the next, but next period's target earnings are a function of the current period's actual earnings. In this setting, the incentive to manage earnings upward is dampened because future targets are escalated, and therefore more difficult to meet, when the current target is overachieved.[589] Finally, bonus considerations must be viewed in the context of other, potentially conflicting earnings management incentives, some of which may suggest different predictions regarding management's financial reporting behavior.[590]

Several asset write-off studies invoke the bonus plan hypothesis to explain the determinants of write-off behavior. These studies assume, implicitly or explicitly, that management's accounting-based compensation reflects the effect of the write-off.[591] Heflin and Warfield (1997) posit that managers delay write-offs to maximize bonus payments.[592] Francis, Hanna and Vincent (1996) argue that earnings-based compensation plans present an incentive to accelerate write-offs in bad years, in order to shelter future bonus payments, suggesting a negative association between pre-write-off earnings and write-off

---

588 For example, refer to Fields, Lys and Vincent (2001, pp. 267-9), Guidry, Leone and Rock (1999, pp. 116-21).

589 See Guidry, Leone and Rock (1999, p. 116). The opposite effect, i.e. a downward adjustment of the target after a shortfall in the current year, is much less pronounced.

590 For example, income smoothing has been suggested as an alternative explanation of Healy's (1985) findings. See Guidry, Leone and Rock (1999, p. 117).

591 For example, Francis, Hanna and Vincent (1996, p. 123) explicitly state that acceleration of a write-off where pre-write-off earnings are already short of a target "will affect management compensation if bonus calculations are not adjusted for write-offs". For financial reporting incentives relative to earnings targets, refer to section 3.3.2.4.5 below.

592 See Heflin and Warfield (1997, p. 9). However, more interested in the stock price effect of write-off announcements, they do not explicitly test this notion.

amounts. However, they note that the opposite association might also be observed, consistent with income smoothing behavior. In order to empirically discriminate between these two settings, they develop proxy variables of unexpectedly high versus low operating ROA.[593] However, throughout their regression analysis, these variables were either insignificant or significant with the wrong sign.[594] Riedl (2002) follows Francis, Hanna and Vincent's (1996) choice of variables, finding that unexpectedly low earnings have a significantly negative relation to write-off amounts in both the pre-SFAS 121 and post-SFAS 121 regimes.[595] Using the same variables as the two previous studies, Segal (2003) reports a significantly positive relation of unexpectedly high earnings and write-off amounts in both the SFAS 121 and SFAS 142 regimes,[596] suggesting the use of write-offs as an income-smoothing device.[597] Beatty and Weber (2004) find that firms with earnings-based bonus plans, on average, are less likely to record SFAS 142 write-offs and record lower write-offs. Loh and Tan (2002) also allude to the management compensation hypothesis; however, they end up using generic variables of firm profitability and a change in top management that bear no explicit relation to the existence and/or specification of accounting-based bonus plans.[598] Overall, the evidence from the discretionary asset write-off literature seems to suggest that these charges are not particularly suited to influence management's accounting based compensation, but might be used to either smooth earnings or accelerate expenses in an attempt to shelter future earnings levels.

3.3.2.3.4 Accounting-based debt covenants in lending agreements

Creditors are interested in ensuring that management has enough funds available to pay interest and repay existing debt. Debt covenants are designed to restrict the amount of additional debt capital that management can raise to finance operations and/or additional investments. They are also intended to limit management's ability to increase the firm's (financial and operating) risk and take value-reducing investment and financing actions, such as liquidating dividends.[599] For this purpose, debt covenants frequently define accounting-based heuristics, the violation of which often constitutes an "event of default".

---

593 See Francis, Hanna and Vincent (1996, pp. 123-4).

594 See Francis, Hanna and Vincent (1996, p. 125). They note that this result sharply contrasts with Zucca and Campbell's (1992) findings.

595 See Riedl (2002, p. 39). This finding is robust to both OLS and Tobit specifications.

596 See Segal (2003, p. 40). In contrast to that, the proxy variable for unexpectedly low earnings is insignificant.

597 See Segal (2003, p. 25).

598 See Loh and Tan (2002, pp. 136-8).

599 See Smith and Warner (1979, p. 117) and Watts and Zimmerman (1986, pp. 186-91, 210-7).

If a firm is in technical default, its debt is due to be repaid immediately. Recent debt contracts increasingly include performance pricing features, which tie the interest rate on the debt to some set of measures of the borrower's creditworthiness.[600] In some cases, however, the violations are simply waived, especially where the borrower is not in immediate danger of bankruptcy.[601] Beneish and Press (1993) document empirically the different cost components associated with technical covenant violations for 91 firms in the period 1983-87. They estimate that refinancing costs, resulting from interest rate increases, range from 0.84 to 1.63% of the market value of the borrower's equity. Restructuring costs, stemming from the lender's demand for accelerated repayment, are approximately 0.37% of the market value of equity. In addition, other consequences, such as forced changes in operations and increased lender control, are found to be associated with technical default.[602] As Beneish and Press (1995) document, these costs also translate into decreases in shareholder wealth when technical default is publicly announced.[603] However, Frost and Bernard (1989) find that no observable adverse consequences related to loan covenant violations for a sample of oil and gas firms that recorded write-downs mandated by the SEC.[604]

Standard covenants frequently require that management uphold sufficient levels of working capital and similar financial variables and ratios.[605]A variety of accounting-based ratios used in debt covenants exists.[606] These are often based on debt ratios (also referred to as leverage ratios), which measure the portion of debt within a firm's overall capital structure. A common example is the DTE ratio.[607] Furthermore, direct measures of a firm's ability to make current debt-related payments are used, for example interest coverage ratios such as times-interest-earned or capital expenditure ratios,[608] which take into

---

600 See Beatty and Weber (2003, p. 120) and Dichev (2002).

601 See Dichev and Skinner (2002, p. 1122).

602 See Beneish and Press (1993, pp. 233-4). However, the extent to which these consequences actually impose costs on the borrower is not sure. See Beneish and Press (1995, p. 338).

603 El-Gazzar (1993) documents that the anticipation of a mandated accounting change that is likely to increase the tightness of covenant restrictions results in negative stock returns for the affected firms. The debt covenant effects of mandated accounting changes are also analyzed by Collins, Rozeff and Dhaliwal (1981), Espahbodi, Espahbodi and Tehranian (1995), Leftwich (1981), and Lys (1984).

604 See Frost and Bernard (1989, p. 807).

605 See White, Sondhi and Fried (2003, p. 174). Also, refer to Smith and Warner (1979).

606 Refer to Watts and Zimmerman (1986, pp. 211-3) and White, Sondhi and Fried (2003, pp. 130-2). For recent evidence, refer to Dichev and Skinner (2002, pp. 1101-1104).

607 Total debt divided by total equity.

608 Cash flow from operations divided by capital expenditures.

consideration capital expenditures in excess of interest charges.[609] Smith (1993) structures the wide array of observable covenants by distinguishing affirmative and negative covenants.[610]

Accounting-based restrictions in debt covenants are calculated on the basis of original GAAP or rely on accounting methods that either represent modified GAAP or are entirely outside GAAP.[611] Where GAAP is the relevant basis, the applicable accounting rules can either be "frozen" at the time of the debt issuance or be allowed to "roll". In the latter case, the calculation is based on GAAP effective at the date of the calculation. Departures from GAAP are common; however, they occur most frequently in private rather than public lending agreements.[612] Watts and Zimmerman (1986) assume that most debt covenants observed in large, publicly traded firms rely on reported and audited accounting numbers that are based on promulgated GAAP.[613] Beatty, Ramesh and Weber (2002) find that the interest rate charged on the debt is lower where the covenant is based on "frozen" GAAP, which prohibits voluntary as well as mandatory accounting changes. Their interpretation is that managers incur costs to retain accounting flexibility that enables them to avoid covenant violations.[614]

In its most general and theoretically correct form, the debt covenant hypothesis has been formulated as follows:

> "The debt covenant hypothesis states that managers are motivated to choose accounting methods that minimize the likelihood that covenants would be violated."[615]

Since the actual restrictions imposed by lending agreements are not necessarily known to the researcher, empirical tests of the debt covenant hypothesis frequently rely on variables that capture the proximity to the restrictions imposed by actual debt covenants. The most frequently used indicator is the DTE ratio.[616] Early research adopting this approach

---

609 EBIT (or operating cash flow) divided by interest expense.

610 See Smith (1993, p. 290).

611 El-Gazzar and Pastena (1990) investigate to what extent such "tailoring" of GAAP depends on the contracting parties' characteristics.

612 See Leftwich (1983, p. 36). Refer to section 5.2.3.1.2 below for discussion of the assumption that firms' transitional SFAS 142 goodwill write-off behavior will have effects on accounting-based debt covenants.

613 See Watts and Zimmerman (1986, p. 213).

614 See Beatty, Ramesh and Weber (2002, p. 222).

615 White, Sondhi and Fried (2003, p. 174).

616 See Duke and Hunt (1990, p. 48). Other ratios, used less frequently, are listed in fn. 4 of that article. See also Press and Weintrop (1990, pp. 65-6) and Smith (1993, p. 290).

includes Collins, Rozeff and Dhaliwal (1981), Daley and Vigeland (1983), Leftwich (1981), and Lys (1984). However, researchers seem to increasingly rely on actual covenant data to test the debt covenant hypothesis. Among these studies are Beneish and Press (1993), El-Gazzar (1993), Healy and Palepu (1990), Mohrman (1993), Press and Weintrop (1990), Smith (1993), and Sweeney (1994).

The DTE hypothesis has been operationalized as follows:

> "Ceteris paribus, the larger a firm's debt/equity ratio, the more likely the firm's manager is to select accounting procedures that shift reported earnings from future periods to the current period."[617]

Watts and Zimmerman (1986) argue that the DTE ratio is a reasonable approximation of most actual debt covenant restrictions because the likelihood of these other restrictions being violated can be shown to increase when the DTE ratio increases. Nonetheless, they encourage researchers to increasingly rely on actual debt covenant details.[618] Duke and Hunt (1990) examine empirically the accounting-based debt covenant proxies used in prior research and their association with actual debt covenant restrictions.[619] Based on their finding that different variations of the DTE ratio capture the most common accounting-based restrictions used in actual debt covenants, they conclude that researchers are comparatively safe in using this proxy.[620] Beneish and Press (1993) also show that leverage is a suitable proxy for the magnitude of debt covenant violation costs, with similar findings being reported by Press and Weintrop (1990).[621] However, recent large-sample evidence reported by Dichev and Skinner (2002) suggests that leverage is only to a small extent correlated with firms' actual closeness to covenant restrictions.[622]

---

617 Watts and Zimmerman (1986, p. 216).

618 See Watts and Zimmerman (1986, p. 216).

619 Data was obtained from the American Bar Foundation's 1971 publication "Commentaries on Indentures" and from a random 20-firm sample retrieved from "Moody's Industrial Manual" of 1985. See Duke and Hunt (1990, p. 52). White, Sondhi and Fried (2003, pp. 350-4) caution that these data are general in nature and may provide only an incomplete understanding of what actual covenant constraints look like. Like Press and Weintrop (1990), they recommend the use of original bond indentures filed with the SEC upon issuance of the bond.

620 See Duke and Hunt (1990, p. 61). Earlier analyses of actual covenants used in debt contracts were carried out by Smith and Warner (1979, especially pp. 125-146) and Leftwich (1983, especially pp. 31-41), who, like Duke and Hunt (1990), rely on data published in 1971 in the American Bar Foundation's "Commentaries on Indentures". See Smith and Warner (1979, p. 118).

621 However, Beneish and Press (1995, p. 338) caution that leverage is not associated with abnormal returns around announcements of technical default. They conclude that the debt covenant hypothesis is better specified when actual covenant data is used instead of a proxy variable. See Beneish and Press (1995, p. 352).

622 See Dichev and Skinner (2002, p. 1122).

The debt covenant hypothesis is frequently included in empirical tests of the determinants of discretionary asset write-offs and of the market reactions to those write-offs. Despite the mixed evidence on the DTE ratio's suitability as a proxy for imminence of covenant violation, this variable is widely relied upon in the discretionary asset write-off literature. Heflin and Warfield (1997) speculate that managers may defer write-offs in order to minimize debt covenant violation costs.[623] However, the scope of their paper does not include an empirical test of this assertion. Riedl (2002) invokes contracting theory to hypothesize that firms "take income-increasing accounting decisions to avoid costly violations of debt covenants."[624] Referring to Bartov's (1993) study of discretionary timing of asset sales, he uses the DTE ratio as a proxy variable of nearness to covenant restrictions. Since write-offs are never an income-increasing accounting decision, Riedl's prediction of "a negative association between write-offs and this variable" apparently implies that he expects to observe no write-offs where debt covenant violation is at hand.[625] However, this hypothesis is not corroborated in Riedl's empirical analyses of pre-SFAS 121 and SFAS 121 write-offs.[626] Similarly, Segal (2003) finds only marginal significance for the DTE ratio as an explanatory variable of SFAS 121 write-offs, and no association of this variable with SFAS 142 write-offs.[627] Beatty and Weber (2004) find that firms delay SFAS 142 write-offs where their covenants, e.g. net worth covenants, are affected by the write-off. Finally, Loh and Tan (2002) also adopt the DTE hypothesis.[628] Their analysis of asset write-offs in Singapore suggests that the debt-to-asset ratio is not a significant explanatory factor of write-off behavior.

3.3.2.3.5 Political costs

Another earnings management incentive stems from the fact that accounting numbers may influence the degree to which firms are subjected to (potentially adverse) regulation that imposes "political costs" on them.[629] In economic theory of regulation, the political

---

623 See Heflin and Warfield (1997, p. 9).

624 Riedl (2002, p. 11).

625 Riedl (2002, p. 12).

626 See Riedl (2002, pp. 22, 39-40).

627 See Segal (2003, p. 40).

628 See Loh and Tan (2002, p. 138).

629 The seminal paper, Watts and Zimmerman (1978, p. 115) distinguishes regulatory from other political costs. However, both terms are used synonymously here. Likewise, the term "regulation" is commonly meant to include legislation and other political or regulatory actions. For example, according to Gowland (1990), "[r]egulation means the laying down of rules".

process is viewed as a competition for wealth transfers between different constituents.[630] In this process, accounting numbers are frequently used to determine the direction and amount of wealth transfers. First, the amount of allowable profit in certain industries is restricted *ex ante* by regulation based on reported accounting numbers. Second, adverse economic consequences for "politically visible" firms are assumed to arise *ex post* from their reported income numbers.[631] These different aspects are summarized in Figure 8.

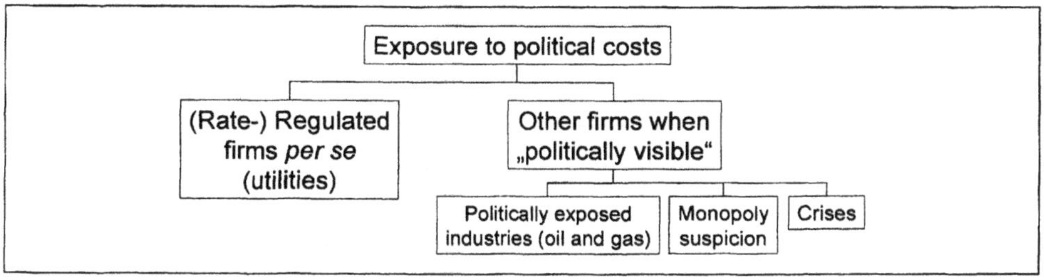

Figure 8: Firms' exposure to potential costs from adverse regulation

Several regulated industries, predominantly the utilities industry,[632] have been the subject of political cost-based studies.[633] In these industries, firms' profits are restricted to some "fair rate of return" on assets, estimated as a weighted-average cost of debt and equity capital.[634] Allowable earnings are calculated on the basis of GAAP,[635] with occasional adjustments where certain costs are considered abnormal.[636] Based on this relation, several researchers have studied (1) the effects of (the standard-setting process preceding) new accounting standards on the market value of regulated and non-regulated firms as well as (2) the question whether firms engage in earnings management to increase regulated allowable profit. Khurana and Loudder (1994) and Espahbodi, Strock and Tehra-

---

630 For an overview of the role of accounting in the political process and related literature, refer to Watts and Zimmerman (1986, pp. 222-43) and Watts and Zimmerman (1990, pp. 115-6).

631 See Watts and Zimmerman (1978, p. 115).

632 Watts and Zimmerman (1978, pp. 115-6) focus on rate-regulation in the public utilities industry. However, other industries (including banking, insurance, and oil) are also mentioned.

633 For the very reason that researchers interested in the political cost hypothesis find regulated firms a promising object of study, these firms are often excluded from general earnings management studies. For example, Burgstahler and Dichev (1997, p. 101 fn. 3) exclude from their analysis firms from the utilities industry, because "conflicting incentives to report lower earnings or decreases in earnings arise whenever there are economic benefits from reporting lower earnings to regulators."

634 The mechanics of a typical rate-regulation formula are explained in Watts and Zimmerman (1986, pp. 231-233).

635 See Watts and Zimmerman (1986, p. 232).

636 For example, SFAS 71, *Accounting for the Effects of Certain Types of Regulation*, explicitly considers the accounting by regulated firms. Certain expenses ordinarily charged to income in non-regulated firms are capitalized as "regulatory assets", which increases allowable profit in the future. See Khurana and Loudder (1994, p. 366).

nian (1991) examine the effect of pronouncements related to SFAS 106, *Employers' Accounting for Postretirement Benefits Other Than Pensions*, on regulated and non-regulated firms' stock price. While the former study finds a positive reaction stemming from regulated firms' increased cash flows due to the standard's effect on rate-setting, the latter study documents that this positive effect is compensated by negative debt covenant repercussions. Cahan (1993) refutes the political cost hypothesis in his analysis of nuclear power plant operators' accounting responses to a nuclear breakdown and the subsequent threat of adverse regulation.

Besides rate-regulated industries, where allowable firm profits are directly calculated in terms of accounting numbers, accounting data is also hypothesized to determine a firm's "political visibility", i.e. the likelihood of adverse regulation and, consequently, the expected value of political costs.[637] Certain industries, e.g. the oil industry, have been a particular object of political exposure. Hall (1993b) states that the oil industry has "historically been tied to the political process."[638] Han and Wang (1998) show that oil firms expected to benefit from the rapid oil price upsurge following the 1990 Persian Gulf crisis have responded with income-decreasing earnings management to that event. The alleged reason for this behavior was that higher profits resulting from these "unjustified" product price increases were likely to trigger adverse regulation, such as antitrust investigations or a special "profits tax" for oil firms.[639] In a more general setting, Hall (1993b) finds similar behavioral patterns, suggesting that oil firms manage earnings in response to the development of gasoline prices and, consequently, oil firm earnings. Although not exactly related to political costs, Hall and Stammerjohan (1997) document that oil firms threatened with potentially large damage awards, e.g. from environmental litigation, respond by income-decreasing earnings management.

Irrespective of industry, however, "obscenely" high accounting earnings are more generally assumed to indicate monopoly or "windfall" profits.[640] Such earnings, as well as large fluctuations in earnings,[641] increase the likelihood of adverse legislation or other

---

637 For the following, refer to the right branch of Figure 8.

638 Hall (1993b, p. 325).

639 See Han and Wang (1998, p. 104). As a side result, firms were found to have reversed their previous tendency to disclose "good" earnings news early.

640 Watts and Zimmerman (1986, p. 223) argue that it is irrational for voters to become informed about the real reasons behind high profits. Knowing this, politicians try to gain media exposure and improve their (re-) election chances by responding with regulation to the perceived "crisis".

641 See Moses (1987, p. 363).

regulation.[642] Because it is costly for firms to lobby for favorable (or the absence of adverse) regulation, managers have incentive to exercise discretion to reduce reported earnings.[643] Cahan (1992) reports that firms under monopoly-related antitrust investigation adopted more income-decreasing accounting methods while being investigated than in periods of non-investigation.[644] Watts and Zimmerman (1986) argue that high profits due to price increases in consumer products are more likely to trigger adverse regulation since they are more visible and of concern to voters.[645]

Researchers have attempted to increase the power of empirical tests by focusing on specific settings in which firms' political cost-related incentives were assumed to be particularly strong. Such situations, regularly signaled by high earnings reported by certain firms, are perceived in the political process as (potential) "crises" that must be overcome by additional regulation.[646] An example is oil companies' high profits following oil embargoes or other rapid oil price increases,[647] which spurred political scrutiny directed at imposing price controls or even breaking up individual firms. Affected firms are expected to manage earnings downward in order to escape such political repercussions.[648] Several papers focusing on such narrow settings have been cited elsewhere in this section, e.g. Cahan (1992), Cahan (1993), and Han and Wang (1998). Jones (1991) focuses on firms hoping to benefit from potential import relief, and finds that these firms practice income-decreasing earnings management during import relief investigations. Key (1997) analyzes cable television firms' earnings management behavior during periods of Congressional scrutiny, arguing that this setting "provides an opportunity to investigate political costs theory directly."[649] Consistent with expectations, she finds that firms expected to be especially exposed to political costs manage earnings downwards during those periods.

---

642 Watts and Zimmerman (1990, p. 133) state that "[p]olitical costs are a function of reported profits." See also Watts and Zimmerman (1978, p. 115), Watts and Zimmerman (1986, p. 223), Beatty and Verrecchia (1989, pp. 473-4). For example, the pharmaceutical industry is constantly under the suspicion of extracting monopoly rents from proprietary, patented drugs.

643 See Watts and Zimmerman (1986, p. 231), Watts and Zimmerman (1978, p. 115).

644 See Cahan (1992, pp. 84-90).

645 See Watts and Zimmerman (1986, pp. 361-2).

646 Refer to Watts and Zimmerman (1986, pp. 230-1). An overview of "crisis theory", a branch of the positive theory of regulation, and the related literature, is provided by Fülbier (1999, p. 472).

647 Refer to the discussion above.

648 This assumes that it is costly for outsiders to undo such earnings management. See Watts and Zimmerman (1986, p. 231).

649 Key (1997, p. 311).

The likelihood of adverse regulation has frequently, especially in earlier research, been assumed to increase in the absolute size of the firm since "[s]ize is a proxy variable for political attention."[650] Therefore, larger firms are predicted to tend towards using income-decreasing accounting methods. This "size hypothesis" has been formulated by Watts and Zimmerman (1986) as follows:[651]

> "Ceteris paribus, the larger the firm, the more likely the manager is to choose accounting procedures that defer reported earnings from current to future periods."[652]

However, the size proxy has been criticized as crude, since it is not explicitly linked to political costs.[653] According to Ball and Foster (1982), size might proxy for a variety of other aspects of firm, including industry membership.[654] Also, the original suggestion by Watts and Zimmerman (1978) that political costs are positively associated with firm size might be based on superficial and partially misunderstood evidence.[655] On the contrary, where compliance with regulation causes fixed costs, relative regulatory costs actually *decrease* in firm size.[656] However, despite these criticisms, Watts and Zimmerman conclude that, at the time, there were no alternative theories available to explain the empirical regularity that large firms tend to use income-decreasing accounting methods.[657]

Since the suspicion that a firm earns monopoly rents has been argued to be associated with political costs,[658] the extent of a firm's market power, approximated by market

---

650 Watts and Zimmerman (1990, p. 139). See also Gagnon (1967), White, Sondhi and Fried (2003, p. 175), and Watts and Zimmerman (1986, pp. 287, 295).

651 For an early empirical test of the size hypothesis, refer to Zmijewski and Hagerman (1981).

652 Watts and Zimmerman (1986, p. 235).

653 Refer to Holthausen and Leftwich (1983), Ball and Foster (1982, pp. 182-4). Watts and Zimmerman (1990, pp. 139-40) and Watts and Zimmerman (1986, pp. 234-40) provide overviews of this debate and respond to some of the criticisms.

654 See Ball and Foster (1982, pp. 190-1) and also Christie (1990, p. 15). It has been shown that political exposure is driven by industry membership, and especially by oil and gas firms. This point is conceded by Watts and Zimmerman (1986, p. 239). See Gupta (1995, p. 493). Also, the size hypothesis appears to be confined to only the very largest firms. See Zmijewski and Hagerman (1981).

655 See Ball and Foster (1982, p. 183) allege that Watts and Zimmerman (1978) misunderstood the conclusions reached in Siegfried's (1975) study on the determinants of antitrust activity.

656 See Ball and Foster (1982, pp. 182-4). However, it must be noted that the expected value of political costs depends on both the absolute amount of these costs and the likelihood of their being imposed through regulatory action. If this likelihood is extremely high (only) for very large firms, the expected value of political costs might increase in firm size nonetheless.

657 See Watts and Zimmerman (1990, p. 140) and Watts and Zimmerman (1986, pp. 239-40).

658 See Hagerman and Zmijewski (1979), Watts and Zimmerman (1978, p. 115), and Zmijewski and Hagerman (1981).

share, has been used along with, or instead of, the size variable.[659] Gupta (1995) uses a measure of industry concentration to identify industries in which monopolistic conditions are most likely to be present.[660]

Political costs hypotheses are not popular in the discretionary asset write-off literature. Among the studies in that category, Francis, Hanna and Vincent (1996) include firm size, measured as the log of sales, as an explanatory variable.[661] However, that variable is intended to "control for any disclosure and publication biases",[662] not to pick up any political cost incentives. This variable turns out to be significantly positively related with goodwill write-offs and write-offs in general.[663] This finding might be interpreted in the sense of positive accounting theory, suggesting that "politically visible" firms minimize earnings by taking write-offs.[664]

3.3.2.3.6 Discriminating between competing hypotheses

The theory introduced in section 3.3.2.3 so far predicts that managers use financial reporting decisions to influence the outcomes of contracts based on accounting numbers. Empirical support for these predictions has commonly been interpreted as evidence that managers act *opportunistically*, i.e. transfer wealth from other stakeholders to themselves by exploiting the discretion inherent in applicable financial reporting rules in a self-interested way.[665] However, an analysis of the whole contracting process shows that this interpretation is not necessarily correct and might be premature in some cases.[666]

---

659 See, for example, Moses (1987, p. 363), who defines market share as firm sales by total industry sales, where the industry is comprised of all firms with identical four-digit SIC codes.

660 See Gupta (1995, p. 499). Further, Gupta (1995) and El-Gazzar, Lilien and Pastena (1986) use the effective tax rate to surrogate for political costs. However, Zimmerman (1983) cautions that the quality of the effective tax rate as a proxy for political costs potentially varies intertemporally as well as cross-sectionally. See also Watts and Zimmerman (1986, pp. 235-8).

661 See Francis, Hanna and Vincent (1996, p. 126).

662 Francis, Hanna and Vincent (1996, p. 124).

663 See Francis, Hanna and Vincent (1996, p. 125).

664 This explanation is only briefly alluded to by the authors. See Francis, Hanna and Vincent (1996, p. 124 fn. 10).

665 According to Holthausen (1990, p. 208), the opportunistic behavior perspective implies that "a manager's utility is affected by the firm's stock price and the manager's compensation." When the firm's contracts are taken as given, the opportunistic behavior perspective predicts that "the accounting method a manager would choose is driven by how the choice affects the existing contracts without considering how future contracts might be written." To Holthausen, this interpretation clearly underestimates the level of sophistication of the contracting parties.

666 See, for example, Fields, Lys and Vincent (2001, p. 271), Skinner (1993, p. 411), and Watts and Zimmerman (1990, pp. 134-7).

It has been argued that two major factors influence financial reporting decisions in a contracting setting. First, the existence of accounting-based contracts and the accepted set of accounting rules employed to administer these contracts are not necessarily exogenous, but more likely to stem from economic efficiency reasons: For some firms, accounting-based contracts apparently present an effective way to resolve agency problems.[667] The accepted set of accounting rules, or GAAP, referred to in these contracts evolves over time and represents some form of best practice to minimize agency costs.[668] Therefore, observable financial reporting decisions are (pre-) determined *ex ante* (i.e. before the contracts are in place) by the fact that some firms use accounting-based contracts at all and by the accepted set of GAAP that is deemed to be efficient for these firms.[669] This notion that accounting-based contractual provisions and the resulting financial reporting behavior might be in the best interest of all contracting parties has been referred to as the *efficient contracting perspective*.[670]

Second, if the accepted set of GAAP were to restrict managers' discretion completely, (opportunistic) *ex post* (i.e. after the contracts are concluded) earnings management would not arise. Therefore, researchers have addressed the question why the accepted set leaves room for discretion at all.[671] The decision (to be made by those administering the

---

667 For example, Bushman and Smith (2001, pp. 248-9) criticize that earnings management studies using the bonus plan hypothesis treat managerial incentive plans as *exogenous* and earnings management behavior motivated by these plans as dysfunctional. They argue that rational investors should be able to predict the incentives provided by these plans and thus the earnings management behavior likely to result from them. Consequently, the empirical earnings management research following the "exogenous contract approach" is likely to lead to misguided conclusions because earnings management behavior interpreted as opportunistic might well be in the investors' best interest.

668 According to Watts and Zimmerman (1990, p. 136), the set of accounting procedures within which managers have discretion is called the "accepted set". Since managers have incentive to act opportunistically, the accepted set includes "conservative" and "objective" procedures. The accepted set of GAAP is a component of the "firm's implicit and explicit contracts including the firm's capital structure, compensation plans, and ownership structure" (p. 137). However, it is difficult to predict exactly which accepted set of GAAP is efficient in a given contracting situation. Watts and Zimmerman (1986, pp. 246-7) note that "[e]xplaining the choice of accounting procedures to use in contracts (the choice *of* accepted procedures) requires a theory explaining the detailed structure of contracts. Contracting theory is not yet developed to that point" (emphasis in original).

669 Leftwich (1983, p. 31) argues that the accounting choices that have evolved as "best practice" in debt contracts (and that are specified in "boiler-plate" type models) represent procedures that have turned out over time to minimize the agency costs between the firm and its creditors.

670 As stated by Holthausen (1990, p. 207), "[t]he efficient contracting perspective ... implies that accounting methods, like the form of organization chosen or the form of contracts written, will be selected to minimize agency costs amongst the various parties to the firm." See also Watts (1977), Skinner (1993, pp. 410-2).

671 In the words of Dunstan (1999, p. 6), this question can be interpreted as the search for *ex ante* explanations for financial reporting decisions. In contrast to that, *ex post* explanations deal with the question how managers use their discretion *within* a given accepted set of GAAP.

contract) to what degree discretion should be allowed involves a tradeoff.[672] On the one hand, if managers are completely free to choose among financial reporting alternatives, accounting-based contracts are unsuited to control their actions, i.e. restrict their behavior.[673] On the other hand, stakeholders incur different costs when restricting managers' discretion completely: (1) It might be cost-effective to allow managers discretion when managers have specific knowledge about which financial reporting procedures maximize firm value. For example, managers might know best which methods minimize political costs or which procedures are most suitable to motivate subordinates. Therefore, there is a potential that managers use their discretion in a way that is optimal from the perspective of all stakeholders. (2) Non-trivial costs are involved in monitoring and enforcing restrictions on management's financial reporting discretion. (3) Finally, there is potential that managers exercise their discretion within the accepted set to signal private information about the firm's future prospects to stakeholders.[674] Foregoing this potentially valuable information also represents costs. Despite these potential benefits of leaving some room for discretion, the risk remains that managers exploit this leeway to make themselves better off at the expense of the other contracting parties, i.e. act opportunistically. However, where researchers jump to the conclusion that observed financial reporting behavior is motivated by opportunism alone, other, potentially more appropriate explanations are often overlooked.[675]

In order to discriminate empirically between efficient contracting and opportunism reasons behind observed financial reporting behavior, theories have been developed to predict the accepted set of GAAP by examining firms' economic characteristics.[676] Specifi-

---

672 Refer to Skinner (1993, p. 411).

673 For example, if a manager's annual bonus was 10% of accounting earnings, little motivational effect would result from this scheme if the manager were completely free to choose from alternative procedures to calculate accounting earnings. See Skinner (1993, p. 411).

674 Holthausen (1990, p. 208) states that "the information perspective suggests that accounting methods are chosen to reveal managers' expectations about the future cash flows of the firm." Managers are assumed to have private information about the firm and their hypothesized incentive to reveal this information through choice of accounting techniques stems from the assumption that they are "compensated in part on the basis of their ability to provide information about the future cash flows of the firm."

675 As discussed in section 3.3.2.3.1, stakeholders are price-protected from any *anticipated* opportunistic behavior. Opportunism can only arise where (1) stakeholders had no way of anticipating certain actions on the part of management and where (2) there is no *ex post* adjustment of contractual outcomes to adjust for these actions due to prohibitive search and monitoring costs. According to Watts and Zimmmerman's (1990, p. 135) wording: "If managers elect to exercise discretion to their advantage *ex post, and* the discretion has wealth redistributive effects among the contracting parties, then we say managers acted 'opportunistically.'"

676 Watts and Zimmerman (1990, p. 136) stress that it is difficult to distinguish empirically between opportunistic, efficient contracting, and signaling explanations.

cally, it has been argued that the relative costs and benefits of restricting managers' *ex post* discretion vary across firms, depending on firms' investment opportunities.[677] Therefore, the cost-effective accepted sets of GAAP, specified *ex ante*, are likely to vary with firms' *investment opportunity sets* (IOS).[678] Consequently, since observed financial reporting behavior is likely to vary with firms' accepted sets of GAAP, there should be an association between firms' financial reporting behavior and their IOSs. However, it is difficult to predict exactly *how* the IOS is likely to affect the accepted set of GAAP and, thus, management's financial reporting behavior. For example, Watts and Zimmerman (1986) posit that managers of growth firms have more accounting flexibility because the assets of these firms are more difficult to value than those of established firms with a large portion of assets-in-place.[679] Managers from firms with different IOSs are likely to have made their financial reporting decisions with respect to different accepted sets of GAAP.

This discussion has certain implications for researchers interested in the determinants of financial reporting decisions. The existence of accounting-based contracts is frequently taken as given. If researchers rely on proxy variables to surrogate for contract-based incentives (e.g. the DTE ratio as a proxy for the incentive to manage earnings upward in order to avoid debt covenant violation) without knowing whether these contracts are actually present in the firm analyzed, conclusions may be inappropriate. The same problem occurs when accounting-based contracts are in place, but the financial reporting decision of interest does not influence their outcomes because it is adjusted by one of the contracting parties.[680]

Also, even if the hypothesized contracts exist in a given firm, the risk of a type II error is present, i.e. the contract-based hypothesis might be upheld although the assumed causality is not present. Where the predicted relation is found in the data, a type II error occurs when management's behavior, while consistent with the prediction (e.g. firms with high DTE ratios tend to make income-increasing financial reporting decisions), is not caused by contracting motivations but by correlated variables omitted from the predictive

---

677 See Skinner (1993, p. 411) and Watts and Zimmerman (1986, pp. 360-1).

678 According to Smith and Watts (1992, p. 264), a firm's IOS is defined by its "prospective investment opportunities and associated payoff distributions".

679 See Watts and Zimmerman (1986, pp. 360-1).

680 For a discussion of possible adjustments to reported GAAP figures by compensation committees or in debt contracts, refer to sections 3.3.2.3.3 and 3.3.2.3.4 above.

model.[681] However, Skinner (1993) concludes that, "while I find that firms' investment opportunities do affect the nature of their contracts, I also find that the 'traditional' explanations for accounting choice are important after controlling for the effects of the investment opportunity set."[682]

For the reasons discussed here, it is important to consider the factors that determine, first, which firms are likely to have accounting-based contracts at all and, second, which accepted set of accounting rules these contracts are likely to specify. Especially the latter question is difficult to solve in the context of newly promulgated accounting standards such as SFAS 142. In section 5.2 below, it is discussed at length how transitional SFAS 142 goodwill write-off behavior is expected to affect the outcomes of accounting-based contracts of adopting firms, and the implications for management's expected financial reporting behavior.

3.3.2.4 Capital market-related incentives

3.3.2.4.1 Theoretical fundamentals

In contrast to the economic-consequences incentives discussed above, the capital market-related incentives presented in this section rest on the notion that, under certain circumstances, management will engage in earnings management for reasons other than generating (contract-related) *direct* cash flow effects. Stated generally, management's financial reporting decisions may be intended to influence favorably capital market participants' perceptions of the firm's future prospects. In the words of Heflin and Warfield (1997), one earnings management objective may be "influencing perceptions of managerial performance",[683] partly because of "the need to raise external financing".[684] Here, management's utility is not affected directly, but only via the market reaction expected to be triggered by the financial reporting decision at issue. Capital market-related earnings management can only be expected when information asymmetries exist between management and capital market participants.[685] Fields, Lys and Vincent (2001) stress this

---

681 See Skinner (1993, p. 409. In this example, an alternative explanation might be that firms with relatively low growth options, which rely on debt financing and thus have high DTE ratios, also have high levels of accounting earnings. See Gaver and Gaver (1993).

682 Skinner (1993, p. 408). In the context of goodwill amortization periods, Bradbury, Godfrey and Koh (2003) report that IOS-related variables have greater explanatory power than traditional contracting variables.

683 Heflin and Warfield (1997, p. 9).

684 Beneish (2001, p. 2).

685 See Fields, Lys and Vincent (2001, pp. 257, 262, 275-81).

point, referring to the incentives described here as *asset pricing motivations*, i.e. attempts to influence asset prices that are driven by information asymmetries. It is only when such information asymmetries exist that management can send informative or manipulative "signals" that constitute information to the market and cause revisions in expectations.

Although alleged capital market-related financial reporting strategies take different forms,[686] they are assumed to share a common ultimate objective: Management's financial reporting decisions are motivated by the desire to, in the current and/or future periods, fulfill or exceed investors' expectations and thus bring about an increase in share price.[687] This motivation need not be opportunistic; management might as well strive to foster shareholders' interests along with their own. Stated differently, "firms with a greater capacity to absorb the financial statement effects of the writedowns (those with greater financial slack) are more likely to disclose greater writedowns."[688]

While conceptually different, capital market-related incentives may lead to the same predicted behavior as economic-consequences incentives. Income-increasing earnings management might be motivated by contracting considerations and/or the desire to increase stock price. For example, while Healy's (1985) evidence suggests that managers manipulate accruals to maximize bonus payments, Gaver, Gaver and Austin (1995) find that the income smoothing hypothesis better explains management behavior.[689] This makes empirical findings difficult to attribute to a specific set of motivations.[690] Conversely, since contradictory capital market-related and economic-consequences incentives might be present in a given situation, empirical investigations might return inconclusive evidence because conflicting effects compensate each other.

Although discussed in sections 2.3.3 and 3.3.2.3.2 above, the importance of management's beliefs regarding the way the capital markets process information is reiterated here: Since management's intention is to influence market perceptions, predictions about management behavior must take into consideration how management *expects* the market to respond to management's actions. In other words, it is not primarily important whether

---

686 See Fields, Lys and Vincent (2001, p. 275).

687 This is also true for signaling, at least in the long run, even when management signals that difficult times lie ahead: When managers signal private information to shareholders, their objective is to correct shareholders' (upward or downward) biased expectations. Once the bias is removed, management will continue trying to fulfill expectations.

688 See Cotter, Stokes and Wyatt (1998, p. 163).

689 The financial reporting strategy of income smoothing is explained in more detail in section 3.3.2.4.4 below.

690 See Fields, Lys and Vincent (2001, p. 277).

the EMH actually holds.[691] Rather, predicting management's capital market-related financial reporting behavior requires assumptions about management's *beliefs* regarding the EMH. For example, Mayer-Sommer (1979) reports survey evidence indicating low levels of understanding and even lower levels of acceptance of the EMH and its accounting implications.[692] Cosmetic financial reporting decisions are meaningful when the EMH is not assumed to hold.[693] If managers do not believe in the EMH, one might observe financial reporting decisions that could not otherwise be explained.[694] For example, Moses (1987) refers to income smoothing as a financial reporting strategy that "may be practiced to directly reduce market risk", although "in an efficient market the relationship between accounting numbers and market parameters should not be mechanistic and use of visible accounting techniques to affect risk should be ineffective."[695]

Although "[e]arnings management to influence stock values ... is taken as a given in capital markets",[696] its existence is difficult to justify theoretically, especially when it is assumed that management successfully tries to "fool" or "mislead" investors.[697] This notion does not sit well with proponents of the semi-strong form EMH, who claim that investors are not misled by cosmetic earnings management but "see through" management's misrepresentations, using public information – available to them at low cost – to

---

691 The EMH has frequently been cast in doubt with respect to the effects of financial reporting decisions. For example, Lev and Ohlson (1982, p. 250) conclude from their comprehensive evaluation of the relevant literature that "the existence of some investor irrationality (often termed 'functional fixation' cannot be precluded." This phenomenon is often explained with reference to the behavioral finance literature; see for example Lakonishok, Shleifer and Vishny (1994).

692 See Mayer-Sommer (1979, pp. 97-103) and, with a similar conclusion, Wyatt (1983, p. 56).

693 Cosmetic financial reporting decisions are also likely to be successful when capital markets are efficient but participants' information processing costs to adjust for these decisions exceed the perceived benefits. See Moses (1987, p. 366 fn. 11).

694 See Wyatt (1983, pp. 57-62), who cites financial reporting decisions that dispute the validity of the EMH. It is not essential that *all* managers share the same beliefs. If only a subgroup of managers believed that capital markets are informationally inefficient, certain financial reporting decisions would be made in order to favorably influence ("fool") investors. Managers belonging to a second subgroup of EMH proponents would be forced to behave similarly, if only in order to be comparable. If, however, the former subgroup's behavior were found to be successful, the EMH proponents would have to start "playing the same game" or suffer a competitive disadvantage. The financial press frequently alludes to financial reporting strategies that are not meaningful from an EMH standpoint, but are nonetheless observed in practice because "everybody's doing it".

695 See Moses (1987, p. 366 fn. 11).

696 Abarbanell and Lehavy (2000, p. 5).

697 A frequently cited example is a speech entitled "The Numbers Game", given in 1998 by Arthur Levitt who was chairman of the SEC at the time: "In the zeal to satisfy consensus earnings estimates and project a smooth earnings path, wishful thinking may be winning the day over faithful representation." See Levitt (1998).

estimate the firm's "true" future prospects.[698] Consequently, they dismiss an *information hypothesis*, according to which managers' financial reporting decisions are driven by the assumption that financial statements are investors' main, if not only, source of information for valuing firms and making investment decisions.[699] As Watts and Zimmerman (1986), the main advocates of the contracting hypothesis, point out:

> "Researchers have been able to generate links between accounting procedures and the firm's or manager's cash flows under the contracting hypothesis, links that are consistent with the EMH. Based on these links, they can generate predictions about the accounting procedures used by firms. Under the information hypothesis researchers have not been able to generate links consistent with the EMH."[700]

As a consequence, the fact that they should not exist "if investors are rational may explain why academics have been slow to examine capital market incentives for earnings management."[701] Increasingly, anecdotal as well as systematic evidence calls into question the empirical descriptiveness of the semi-strong form EMH.[702] However, even the empirical validity of this theory would not necessarily rule out that those managers who happen not to believe in the EMH may still attempt to influence market participants' perceptions, albeit probably with little success. Because of this, a considerable body of literature now examines "whether managers act as if they *believe* users of financial reporting data can be misled into interpreting reported accounting earnings as equivalent to economic profitability."[703]

A more benign interpretation of capital market-related financial reporting behavior is compatible with the theory: Management may use financial reporting, from an *information perspective*, as a means of signaling private information to investors.[704] Since the semi-strong form EMH assumes that private information is not reflected in stock prices at any given point in time, timely financial reporting disclosures containing such information have the potential to affect stock prices:

> "[R]esearchers have generally not considered the premise that the market could react, either positively or negatively, to a write-down if it provides any new informa-

---

698 See Abarbanell and Lehavy (2000, p. 6).

699 Fields, Lys and Vincent (2001, p. 275) refer to this phenomenon as *investor irrationality*.

700 Watts and Zimmerman (1986, p. 198).

701 Dechow and Skinner (2000, p. 245).

702 Refer to Brown's (2001, p. 14, ch. 8) review of the literature on stock market anomalies that contradict the EMH. Further discussion and references are provided, for example, by Coenenberg et al. (1978), Fülbier (1998, pp. 157-9) and Möller and Hüfner (2002).

703 Fields, Lys and Vincent (2001, p. 279 [emphasis added]).

704 See, for example, Zarowin (2002).

tion that would cause investors to *revise their estimates* of expected future cash flows from that asset".[705]

This *information perspective* is compatible with the EMH, because it assumes that managers signal new, private information that, according to the semi-strong form EMH, has not previously been included into investors' beliefs and therefore has the potential to alter stock price.[706] With respect to discretionary asset write-offs, positive market reactions have frequently been observed upon write-off announcements.[707] Such positive stock price effects can be expected where management successfully passes off write-offs as "good news", e.g. as part of a larger restructuring effort,[708] or where investors expected a larger "bad news" write-off. As will be discussed in greater detail below, it is difficult in practice to distinguish between the manipulation and signaling explanations for an observed financial reporting decision.[709] For example, a write-off might reflect both of management's intent to signal that prospects are improving ("clear the decks") or worsening ("show how bad the situation really is").

3.3.2.4.2 Management's interest in the firm's stock price

The above-mentioned incentives rest on the assumption that management has a stake in the firm's stock price, i.e. when a manager's utility is a function of her firm's stock price.[710] In today's publicly owned corporations, managers do not necessarily have substantial ownership. Therefore, they will only to a small extent derive capital gains from stock price increases that result from their financial reporting decisions.

Regardless, it is a common conjecture that management utility increases with the level and growth rate of stock price and decreases with its variability.[711] In recent years, it has been widely argued that the main reason for management's preoccupation with stock price is the growing importance of employee stock options as a component of corporate decision makers' incentive plans.[712] In fact, much of the earnings management activities

---

705 Alciatore et al. (1998, p. 31 [emphasis in original]).

706 See also Fields, Lys and Vincent (2001, p. 275).

707 White, Sondhi and Fried (2003, pp. 278-9) discuss this signaling view of write-offs. This branch of the literature is presented in section 3.4 below.

708 See, for example, White, Sondhi and Fried (2003, p. 59).

709 See Fields, Lys and Vincent (2001, p. 259).

710 See propositions 1 and 2 in Gordon (1964, p. 261).

711 See, for example, proposition 2 in Gordon (1964, p. 261).

712 According to Levitt (1998), "companies try to meet or beat Wall Street earnings projections in order to ... increase the value of stock options." See also Fields, Lys and Vincent (2001, p. 259).

alleged by the financial press have been attributed to management's attempts to increase stock prices and, consequently, their income from this specific component of their remuneration.[713]

Additional links between management utility and stock price include the following: From the perspective of the market for managers, executives of growing firms are likely to enjoy better reputations, enhancing their current income as well as their prospects for future employment.[714] These firms are also less likely to be targets of hostile takeovers that jeopardize management's job security. Managers are also likely to derive a sense of status and prestige from their firm's size and growth.[715] Further, to the extent that management participates in earnings, increasing stock prices and thereby reducing cost of capital is in its best interest.

These considerations suggest that management is interested in a (steady) growth in stock price,[716] which they attempt to achieve through a number of capital market-related financial reporting strategies discussed in the subsequent sections.

3.3.2.4.3 Maximizing earnings

The most intuitive strategy is for management to maximize earnings in a given period.[717] Early research on this hypothesis is reviewed by Robinson and Shane (1990).[718] As will be discussed at length below, this strategy has several drawbacks because it neglects intertemporal effects. Maximum earnings are not an end in itself because capital market participants and managers alike are usually concerned with the time series of earnings.

---

713 Bernstein (1993, p. 757) stresses the importance of management's greed as the primary driver of earnings management behavior.

714 See, for example, Fudenberg and Tirole (1995), Murphy and Zimmerman (1993), and Weisbach (1988).

715 See, for example, DeFond and Park (1997, p. 117).

716 Unique situations might occur when it is in management's interest to *decrease* stock price. For example, managers planning to initiate a management buyout can be expected to understate earnings in an attempt to reduce share price. However, this specific setting is fundamentally similar to other capital market-related situations in that management is assumed to (1) have a stake in the firm's stock price, (2) attempt to self-interestedly influence stock price, and (3) bring about future increases in stock price. The interest in decreasing stock price is temporary at best. Perry and Williams (1994) find evidence consistent with this prediction, whereas DeAngelo (1986) does not. This is possibly due to management's conflicting incentive to impress potential creditors through high earnings, since these transactions are often highly leveraged. See Fields, Lys and Vincent (2001, p. 276).

717 See Fields, Lys and Vincent (2001, p. 275). Early evidence on this hypothesis is reported by Gagnon (1971, 1967).

718 Robinson and Shane (1990, pp. 26-8). For a discussion of income-maximization incentives in the context of the purchase/pooling decision, refer to 2.4.3.4.1 above.

However, in situations where the long-term development of earnings is of little concern to management, maximizing earnings might be an effective strategy. Erickson and Wang (1999) argue that managers planning a stock-for-stock acquisition have incentive to manage earnings upwards in order to increase share price and thus decrease acquisition costs. They find evidence consistent with this prediction, especially where transactions are large. For managers planning to initiate a management buyout (MBO), diametrically opposed incentives are reported.[719]

3.3.2.4.4 *Income smoothing*

"The variance of a firm's earnings is a direct measure of the uncertainty (risk) of its earnings stream. A smooth earnings stream is assumed to be desirable by firms, their creditors, and the financial markets. To the extent that accounting earnings mirror a firm's economic well-being, the variance in that measure would be expected to measure a firm's risk."[720] Stated differently, investors may equate steady earnings with low risk, which will, *ceteris paribus*, increase stock price[721] and, as a side effect, managers' job security[722] and income.[723] In addition, political cost considerations may support income smoothing:[724] While regulatory sanctions might be imposed on firms with rapid profit increases,[725] large downward fluctuations may signal crisis, prompting regulators to act.[726]

For these reasons, income maximization might in some circumstances be an inferior strategy. Rather, these considerations imply an incentive to engage in what has been called earnings smoothing or *income smoothing*:[727]

> "Income smoothing describes an earnings pattern in which management aspires to maintain a steady and predictable rate of earnings growth".[728]

---

719 See, for example, DeAngelo (1986), Perry and Williams (1994), and Wu (1997). Also, see fn. 716.

720 White, Sondhi and Fried (2003, p. 647).

721 See Barth, Elliott and Finn (1999), Copeland (1968, pp. 101-2), Fischer and Haller (1993, p. 37), Gordon (1964), Ronen and Sadan (1981), Shank and Burnell (1974), and Trueman and Titman (1988).

722 Fudenberg and Tirole (1995) develop the theory that managers smooth income to enhance their reputation and, consequently, job security. Empirical support for this hypothesis has been reported by DeFond and Park (1997). See also Lambert (1984, p. 604) and Weisbach (1988).

723 Moses (1987) explores the linkage between income smoothing behavior and economic-consequences incentives. See also Gaver, Gaver and Austin (1995, p. 6).

724 Refer to section 3.3.2.3.5 for a discussion of political cost incentives for earnings management.

725 See Watts and Zimmerman (1986, p. 234).

726 See Ronen and Sadan (1981).

727 A review of the income smoothing literature is provided by Fischer and Haller (1993).

Managers might attempt to attain a smooth earnings stream by using the discretion inherent in existing GAAP to dampen earnings fluctuations as well as by lobbying with standard setters for regulations that increase the extent of this discretion.[729]

Two types of smoothing behavior are usually distinguished:[730] *Intertemporal smoothing* involves shifting gains and losses between reporting periods so as to reduce earnings in good periods and inflate earnings in bad periods. This objective can be achieved either by timing real business decisions, such as expenditures or disposals, or by choosing accounting methods that allocate earnings over time in the desired manner.[731] German corporation law links earnings to dividends.[732] Therefore much emphasis is placed there on the concept of an intertemporally smooth dividend stream.[733] In contrast, *classificatory smoothing* deals with the presentation of reported income.[734] Under the assumption that investors concentrate on income from continuing operations, income components that are incompatible with the smoothing strategy currently pursued (e.g., losses) are classified as non-recurring or otherwise extraordinary, "below-the-line" income. These "undesired" components, it is hoped, are then ignored by investors. Arguably, this distinction is blurred since classificatory smoothing deals with the *object* of intertemporal smoothing by making assumptions about *which* earnings figure is smoothed over time.

The literature on income smoothing dates back to the 1950s.[735] Hepworth (1953) states that "the owners and creditors of an enterprise will feel more confident toward a corporate management which is able to report stable earnings than if considerable fluctuations of reported earnings exist."[736] Originally, researchers were primarily interested in

---

728 Zucca and Campbell (1992, p. 35). To Beidleman (1973, p. 653), income smoothing is the "intentional dampening of fluctuations about some level of earnings that is currently considered to be normal for a firm". See also Beidleman (1975), Gaver, Gaver and Austin (1995, p. 6), and Imhoff (1975).

729 For example, the income smoothing devices of SFAS 87, *Employers' Accounting for Pensions*, have often been cited as evidence that a smoothed time series of earnings is desired by management. See Kieso, Weygandt and Warfield (2001, p. 1125) and Schildbach (1999, pp. 968, 973). Evidence on earnings management under pension accounting standards is reported by Ali and Kumar (1993).

730 Refer to Ronen and Sadan (1981) and Lambert (1984, p. 605).

731 See, for example, Fudenberg and Tirole (1995, p. 76). A narrower definition is employed by Bernstein (1993, p. 755), according to whom income smoothing excludes the influencing of "real" transactions.

732 Refer to sections 58 and 150 of the German Stock Corporation Act (Aktiengesetz, AktG).

733 For example, refer to Süchting (1995, pp. 548-51).

734 See, for example, Barnea, Ronen and Sadan (1976, 1975) and Ronen and Sadan (1975a, 1975b).

735 Summaries of the literature are provided by White, Sondhi and Fried (2003, pp. 59-61) and, more extensively, by Schmidt (1977). See also the references in Ronen and Sadan (1975a, p. 133). A review of more recent theory and evidence is given by DeFond and Park (1997, pp. 117-9).

736 Hepworth (1953, p. 33).

whether smoothing actually occurred at all,[737] which involved the problem of devising a financial model that could detect the existence of smoothing by distinguishing a "smoothed" from an expected, "natural" time series of earnings. A simple approach suggested by Gordon (1964) considers the accounting choices made and their relation to the trend in (pre-managed) earnings.[738] Later, the attention shifted to the question whether the commonness of smoothing behavior was influenced by the degree to which a firm's ownership and (management) control are separated.[739] Results indicated that manager-controlled firms engaged in income smoothing more frequently than did owner-controlled firms.[740]

It was not until approximately the 1980s that researchers accounted more explicitly in their empirical research designs for the determinants of smoothing behavior.[741] In the early literature, a negative connotation was most frequently associated with income smoothing.[742] Later, it became more accepted that income smoothing could be used as both a manipulative and a signaling device.[743] In the latter event, management uses its discretion to indicate the future prospects of the firm, thereby increasing the predictive ability of earnings. Lambert (1984) shows analytically that smoothing can possibly arise as rational equilibrium behavior. The potentially value-enhancing effects of income smoothing are also shown by Trueman and Titman (1988). Barnea, Ronen and Sadan (1976) specifically highlight the conceivable signaling use of classificatory smoothing.[744]

The literature providing theoretical and empirical evidence on income smoothing further fanned out in the 1990s. For example, DeFond and Park (1997) find support for Fudenberg and Tirole's (1995) theory that managers smooth income and dividends for job security reasons under the assumption that their current performance is considered more important than their past performance (*information decay*).[745] Kirschenheiter and Melumad (2002) provide theory to suggest that income smoothing and "big bath" can co-exist

---

737 Gagnon (1967) examined whether firms used the purchase/pooling choice to smooth their income. See also the reviews by Sapienza (1967) and Wyatt (1967).

738 See Gordon (1964, p. 262). See also Copeland and Licastro (1968).

739 While not tested empirically until a substantially later time, this notion was already brought up in the 1960s. Refer to Gordon (1964) and Monsen and Downs (1965).

740 See Kamin and Ronen (1978) and Smith (1976).

741 See the criticism in Ball and Foster (1982, pp. 214-5).

742 Refer to the discussion in Lambert (1984, p. 604). See also Ball and Foster (1982, p. 214).

743 See, for example, Moses (1987).

744 See Barnea, Ronen and Sadan (1976, p. 110).

745 A critical reassessment of this paper is provided by Elgers, Pfeiffer and Porter (2003).

as equilibrium financial reporting strategies, depending on the extent and direction of any earnings surprise.[746] According to Zarowin (2002), managers reveal private information about the firm's future profitability by smoothing income.

Discretionary asset write-off studies testing the income smoothing hypothesis include those conducted by Riedl (2002), Zucca and Campbell (1992), Francis, Hanna and Vincent (1996), and Segal (2003).[747] The results found in these papers are mixed. While Zucca and Campbell (1992) conclude that some write-off firms appear to be smoothing earnings, Francis, Hanna and Vincent (1996) find a significantly negative association of write-off amounts and unexpectedly high earnings, suggesting that managers do not, on average, use write-offs to bring down excess earnings to a "smoothed" level. Riedl (2002) reports no significant association of the smoothing proxy with the write-off amount. However, in Segal's (2003) data, the smoothing variable is highly significant in the SFAS 121 regime, while it is the only significant explanatory variable of SFAS 142 goodwill write-offs.

3.3.2.4.5 Target accounting

A financial reporting strategy that makes immediate intuitive sense when the EMH is not believed to hold is the attempt to meet or exceed certain one-period thresholds regarding reported income numbers (target accounting).[748] To the extent that actual earnings represent a positive (negative) surprise, investors are assumed to revise their expectations regarding the firm's prospects upward (downward), which results in an immediate stock price increase (decrease).

This "numbers game", heavily criticized by regulators,[749] has only recently received extensive attention from the academic community.[750] Researchers analyze, first, whether earnings are indeed managed with respect to certain thresholds, second, why these thresholds appear to be important, third, whether threshold-based earnings management

746 The financial reporting strategy referred to as "big bath" is explained in section 3.3.2.4.6 below.

747 For the following, refer to Francis, Hanna and Vincent (1996, pp. 123-8), Heflin and Warfield (1997, p. 16), Riedl (2002, pp. 10-2, 39-40), Segal (2003, p. 16 fn. 17, p. 40), and Zucca and Campbell (1992, pp. 35, 40-1).

748 In contrast, income smoothing deals with earnings management to achieve a multi-period benchmark. A brief literature review is provided by Dechow and Skinner (2000, pp. 242-5). See also Moehrle (2002, pp. 400-1). The terms "threshold", "target" and "benchmark" are used synonymously here, as is the custom in the literature.

749 See Levitt (1998).

750 See Bartov, Givoly and Hayn (2002, pp. 176-7) for a brief literature review. See also White, Sondhi and Fried (2003, p. 60).

incentives vary between firms, and, fourth, whether "making the numbers" (failing to "make the numbers") is rewarded (punished) by investors. So far, target accounting has not been explicitly tested as a determinant of discretionary write-off behavior.[751]

3.3.2.4.5.1 Prevalence of target accounting

Anecdotal as well as systematic evidence suggests that firms do manage earnings to meet or beat different types of targets (see Figure 9).[752]

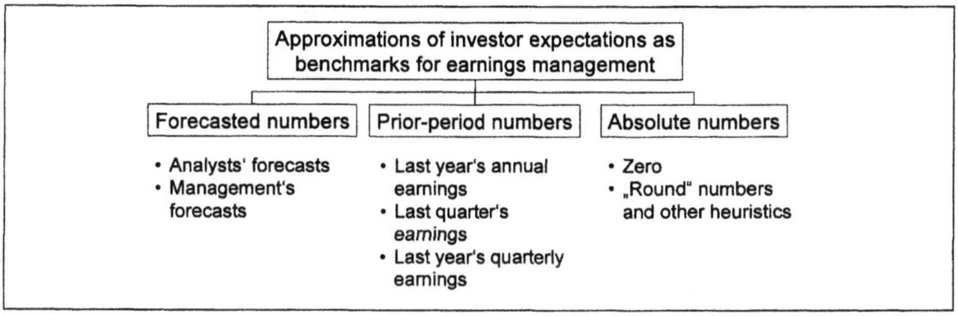

Figure 9: Targets for earnings management

While some of these thresholds, such as published forecasts by analysts or management itself, are direct proxies for the expectations of (sophisticated) investors,[753] others include prior-period earnings figures[754] and certain absolute numbers, e.g. zero. Degeorge, Patel and Zeckhauser (1999) argue in favor of a hierarchy of behavioral thresholds for earnings management: It "is most important first to make positive profits, second to report quarterly profits at least equal to profits of 4 quarters ago, and third to meet analysts' expectations".[755] According to Brown and Caylor (2003), these priorities have apparently shifted over time, with avoiding negative earnings surprises becoming the most important moti-

---

751 Moehrle (2002) considers restructuring charge reversals as a means to meet or beat earnings targets.

752 For example, Burgstahler and Dichev (1997, pp. 99-100) cite several firms' explicitly stated intentions to present a consistently increasing earnings stream.

753 See Schipper (1991, p. 105).

754 The former can be subdivided to include previous year's annual earnings in the case of an annual earnings announcement as well as, in the event of a quarterly earnings announcement, the preceding quarter's earnings and previous year's quarterly earnings, i.e. the earnings reported in the same quarter of the previous year.

755 Degeorge, Patel and Zeckhauser (1999, p. 1).

vation in recent years.[756] It should be noted that intertemporal income smoothing, discussed above, is actually a special case of meet-or-beat behavior, where the relevant benchmark is prior period's earnings.

In this literature, the presence of earnings management is usually not detected by analyzing a subset of accruals or by using a discretionary accruals model. Instead, time series and/or cross sections of reported earnings numbers are analyzed and "unusual" distributional patterns are interpreted as evidence of earnings management.[757] In a pioneering study, Hayn's (1995) findings of an unexpected concentration of small above-zero earnings suggest that earnings are managed to avoid losses.[758] Burgstahler and Dichev (1997), for annual earnings, and Burgstahler (1997) and Skinner and Myers (1999), for quarterly earnings, report similar evidence and conclude that earnings management is used to avoid earnings decreases and losses.[759] Earlier research undertaken by Carslaw (1988) and Thomas (1989) indicates that round numbers, not necessarily zero, are important benchmarks that managers attempt to meet by exercising financial reporting discretion.[760] Degeorge, Patel and Zeckhauser (1999) document that managers engage in earnings management to avoid losses, sustain earnings from four quarters ago, and meet analysts' expectations. Moehrle (2002) finds that restructuring charge reversals are used to meet or beat these three thresholds. Libby and Kinney's (2000) experiments imply that managers – with auditor approval – are likely to not correct immaterial earnings overstatements if consensus earnings forecasts would be missed as a result. Brown (2001) documents that median earnings surprise has shifted from small negative to zero to small positive over the period 1984-99.

---

756 Degeorge, Patel and Zeckhauser's (1999) results cover the 1974-96 time period, while Brown and Caylor's (2003) data is taken from the 1986-2001 period. During 1994-2001, meeting analysts' forecasts seems to be management's overriding goal.

757 See the discussion in McNichols (2000, pp. 316-7, 335-7).

758 Burgstahler, Elliott and Hanlon (2003) provide further evidence that this is in part achieved by use of deferred taxes.

759 Burgstahler and Dichev (1997) estimate that about 10% of firms with small decreases in unmanaged earnings use their discretion to achieve an earnings increase, and that 30-44% of firms with small premanaged losses manipulate earnings to report earnings above zero. Marquardt and Wiedman (2002) argue that earnings are managed using different items, depending on the context. In order to avoid reporting an earnings decrease, they find that transitory items are used, e.g. special items.

760 Carslaw (1988) finds that earnings numbers ending with zero, such as $2.00, appear with unexpectedly high frequency in the earnings reports of New Zealand firms, while those ending with nine, such as $1.99, occur unexpectedly seldom. Thomas (1989) reports similar findings for U. S. firms.

Research considering analyst forecasts[761] as the best proxy for investors' expectations and, therefore, as the relevant earnings target must deal with the fact that there are two components to an earnings surprise: the benchmark number and the actual number. Consequently, earnings management intended to meet or exceed analysts' forecasts need not be limited to manipulating the actual earnings number, but might include attempts to influence analysts' expectations as well. While this latter phenomenon, frequently referred to as *expectations management*,[762] does not strictly fall under the term "earnings management" as defined in section 3.3.1.1, it is nevertheless considered here.[763]

It has been shown by Brown (1998), Burgstahler and Eames (2001), Degeorge, Patel and Zeckhauser (1999), Payne and Robb (2000), and Richardson, Teoh and Wysocki (1999) that analysts' forecast errors (i.e., the differences between consensus forecasts and actual earnings numbers) also exhibit unusual properties: They are unusually often zero or just positive and unusually seldom just negative.[764] While unusual earnings patterns relative to fixed, "natural" benchmarks (zero, prior-period numbers) suggest earnings management, the evidence on forecast errors calls into question the process by which these forecasts are generated.[765] For example, a small positive earnings surprise might be caused by management manipulating earnings upward, analysts "walking down" their estimates, or, most likely, a combination of both. Burgstahler and Eames (2001) find in this context that managers not only manage reported earnings upwards but also give guidance to analysts that influences their forecasts downward.[766] In a similar vein, Schrand and Walther (2000) demonstrate that prior-period benchmarks reported in earnings announcements are selected strategically to compare favorably with current figures. This is achieved by highlighting non-recurring prior-period gains.

One possible alternative set of simple targets that management tries to attain by earnings management is its own voluntarily disclosed forecasts.[767] Kasznik (1999) finds that man-

---

761 Frequently, individual forecasts are aggregated to a summary measure referred to as "consensus" forecasts. See Schipper (1991, pp. 106-7).

762 See, for example, Bartov, Givoly and Hayn (2002) and Kasznik and Lev (1995).

763 In contrast to the contracting-based earnings targets discussed in section 3.3.2.3, capital market-based targets derived from investors' expectations change over time because they are revised to include new information as it becomes available during the reporting period. See Abarbanell and Lehavy (2000, p. 5). Apparently, management actively influences these revisions.

764 Abarbanell and Lehavy (2000) use analyst forecasts to predict the direction of earnings management.

765 Since the focus here is on earnings management, research on the characteristics of analysts' forecasts and forecast errors is not reviewed in detail.

766 Matsumoto (2002, p. 484) refers to this behavior as "forecast guidance".

767 For an overview of the literature on certain aspects of voluntary disclosure, refer to Healy and Palepu (2001, p. 425).

agers whose forecasts would otherwise turn out to be overly optimistic use discretionary accruals to manage earnings upward. He argues that managers avoid the costs of falling short of their own forecasts, which include potential shareholder litigation and reputation loss.[768] In a related paper, Dutta and Gigler (2002) theorize that asking managers to issue earnings forecasts will limit their future earnings management potential. For several reasons, earnings management studies based on management's own forecasts are relatively rare and are not further considered here.[769]

3.3.2.4.5.2 Importance of earnings targets

Where thresholds proxy for market participants' expectations, earnings management to meet or exceed them makes intuitive sense. When, due to assumed high information costs, investors are expected to rely on simple earnings-based heuristics, such as analysts' consensus estimates, to evaluate firm performance, managers will fear that a failure to live up to these expectations is likely to be penalized. Therefore, it is not surprising that "making the numbers" is important to managers.

However, it is much less clear why the net benefits of earnings management should be especially high around simple thresholds such as zero, prior-period earnings, or round numbers. Essentially, managers "focus on thresholds for earnings because the parties concerned with the firm's performance do."[770] Burgstahler and Dichev (1997) invoke transaction cost theory to argue that managers assume stakeholders' decisions to be "based on heuristic cutoffs at zero levels or zero changes in earnings",[771] making transactions with them disproportionately more costly when these targets are not met.[772] Alternatively, prospect theory suggests that "decision-makers derive value from gains and losses with respect to a reference point, rather than from absolute levels of wealth", implying that changes in investors' utility are greatest around these cutoff points.[773] Using

---

768 If managers fail to meet their own forecasts, this could signal to investors that the firm operates in a volatile, high-risk environment, causing share price to fall. See Kasznik (1999, p. 61).

769 First, only few firms issue quantitative forecasts, possibly due to substantial costs associated with forecasts that turn out to be inaccurate. Second, firms that do issue voluntary management forecasts self-select into the group studied. The causal relation between the fact that forecasts are issued and the fact that earnings management is practiced is not clear, causing complex methodological problems. Third, a long research tradition in this area has been further precluded by the fact that the SEC did not always allow managers to disclose forecast information. For a review of the management forecast literature, refer to Cameron (1986).

770 Degeorge, Patel and Zeckhauser (1999, p. 5).

771 Burgstahler and Dichev (1997, p. 122).

772 This reliance on simplifying heuristics amounts to a challenge of the EMH.

773 Burgstahler and Dichev (1997, p. 123).

similar theoretical reasoning, Degeorge, Patel and Zeckhauser (1999) conclude that stakeholders exhibit a "threshold mentality".[774] With respect to round numbers, e.g. the avoidance of the figure nine in favor of the figure zero in earnings numbers, Carslaw (1988) cites psychological evidence on the role of key numbers, especially factors of ten, as cognitive reference points. Das and Zhang (2003) document that firms engage in earnings management in order to be able to round up reported EPS figures. Finally, Matsunaga and Park (2001) document that missing quarterly earnings benchmarks has negative repercussions on CEOs' annual bonus payments.

3.3.2.4.5.3 Cross-sectional differences in target-accounting behavior

After early studies established that target accounting indeed occurred, researchers' attention shifted to cross-sectional differences in this behavior. Several firm characteristics were assumed to explain why some firms were more likely to engage in threshold-based earnings management than others. For example, Beatty, Ke and Petroni (2002) single out differences in ownership structure as one of these factors. They argue that publicly held firms have different incentives to engage in earnings management than those held privately, because the former's shareholders are more likely to focus on simple earnings thresholds. Consistent with this prediction, they find that public bank holding companies appear to manage earnings more frequently than do their privately held counterparts.[775] Matsumoto (2002) explores a number of other firm characteristics associated with particularly strong incentives to meet or beat earnings benchmarks. She hypothesizes and finds that high institutional ownership, high dependence on a positive image with stakeholders other than investors, and low value relevance of earnings are positively associated with the frequency to which firms achieve simple earnings benchmarks.

3.3.2.4.5.4 Market reactions to target accounting

Given the mounting evidence that meeting or exceeding benchmarks induces earnings management, researchers ask whether this purely "cosmetic" financial reporting behavior is actually rewarded by capital market participants.

Barth, Elliott and Finn (1999) demonstrate that firms with a history of earnings increases have higher price-earnings multiples than other firms, and that these premiums are higher

---

[774] Degeorge, Patel and Zeckhauser (1999, p. 6).

[775] Most frequently, the loan loss provision is used to achieve the desired earnings effect.

for longer sequences.[776] This incentive to maintain a time series of increasing earnings for as long as possible is further strengthened by the finding that price-earnings multiples decrease substantially once that pattern is broken. Similarly, DeAngelo, DeAngelo and Skinner (1996) find that breaking a string of increasing annual earnings triggers a significantly negative abnormal stock return. With respect to the benchmark "zero", Burgstahler (1997) predicts and finds that the marginal benefits of earnings management are especially high around zero.

Focusing on analyst forecasts as the benchmark, several authors find favorable market reactions to positive earnings surprises, as well as stock price declines associated (especially in the case of "growth" stocks) with negative earnings surprises. Bartov, Givoly and Hayn (2002) document that positive quarterly forecast errors are associated with higher returns, even when the earnings surprise has apparently been achieved by either earnings or expectations management.[777] Significant negative responses to even small earnings disappointments are found by Kinney, Burgstahler and Martin (2002) and Skinner and Sloan (2001). Lopez and Rees (2002) document an interesting dichotomy: The market reward for beating forecasts is significantly smaller than the penalty associated with missing them.

3.3.2.4.6 Big bath

The so-called "big bath" strategy, frequently alluded to in the financial press and criticized by regulators,[778] has been widely investigated by researchers. A phenomenon especially associated with discretionary asset write-offs and therefore of particular relevance here,[779] "the big bath hypothesis suggests that management will report additional losses in bad years in the hope that, by taking all available losses at one time, they will 'clear the decks' once and for all. The implicit assumption is that future profits will increase."[780]

This hypothesis assumes that investors do not mechanistically fix on a reported earnings number but carefully evaluate the implications of current financial reporting announce-

---

776 These differences are not due to differences in growth or risk. See Barth, Elliott and Finn (1999, p. 410).

777 Similar results are reported by Kasznik and McNichols (2002) and Lopez and Rees (2002).

778 Levitt (1998) disapproves, among other things, of "'big bath' restructuring charges".

779 See White, Sondhi and Fried (2003, p. 279).

780 White, Sondhi and Fried (2003, p. 60). See also Moehrle (2002, p. 399) in the context of restructuring charges.

ments for the firm's future cash flows, even if that implies ignoring large one-time charges.[781] Under this assumption, management can "sell" a large and possibly overstated write-off as "good news". This phenomenon is frequently said to follow changes in top management.[782] Incoming executives allegedly have inventive to engage in *house cleaning* to signal that "the worst is over", a strategic reorientation has occurred and, generally, problems left behind by the predecessor management are being dealt with.[783]

"Big bath" is not strictly a financial reporting incentive in itself, but a financial reporting behavior that might be observed as a result of several motivations, not all of which necessarily stem from capital market-related considerations: Healy (1985) argues, and provides evidence that, managers "take a bath" when earnings fall below a threshold in their bonus plan. In general, "big bath" behavior is assumed to occur when earnings are expected to fall short of any threshold that management considers important to achieve. In that sense, it can be considered the fallback option to be exercised when the attempt to meet or exceed earnings thresholds, discussed at length above, fails. In the context of SFAS 142, the "big bath" strategy would allow management to store up reserves for future periods through accelerated and/or overstated goodwill impairment losses in the transition year.[784]

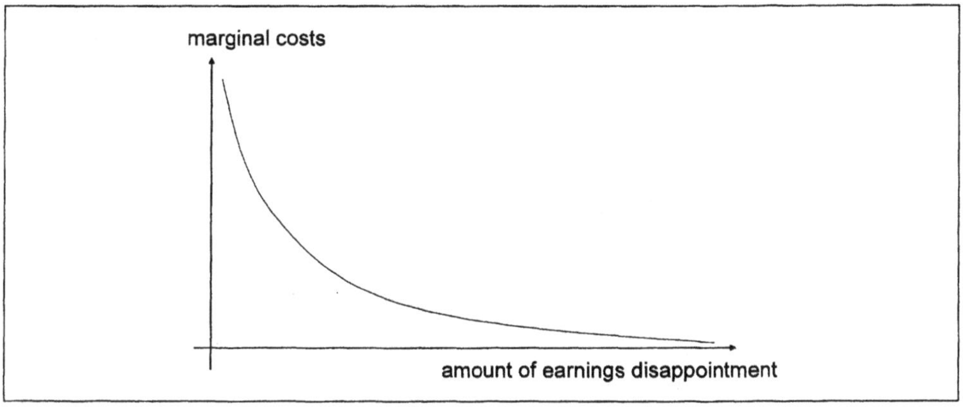

Figure 10: The marginal costs associated with missing a threshold

---

781 See, for example, Levitt (1998).

782 This assertion has been documented and investigated as early as the 1970s. See Moore (1973, p. 100). See also Cotter, Stokes and Wyatt (1998, pp. 163-4), Strong and Meyer (1987), Pourciau (1993), and Segal (2003, p. 7).

783 See White, Sondhi and Fried (2003, p. 278).

784 See Abarbanell and Lehavy (2000, p. 7).

Given that the marginal costs associated with falling short of earnings expectations or other thresholds have been found to decline in the amount of the deficit (see Figure 10), the costs of taking a "big bath" (i.e., reporting an "overstated" loss) are only slightly higher than the costs of disappointing investors by a narrow margin. Therefore, to ensure that future thresholds are attained, it might be rational for managers in some circumstances to "save" earnings for future periods by accelerating losses.[785]

Despite this convincing rationale as well as frequent reports in the financial press, empirical evidence concerning big bath hypothesis is mixed.[786] Several researchers, including Elliott and Shaw (1988),[787] have found that most asset write-offs do not appear to be considered good news by investors, as would be expected under the big bath hypothesis.[788] Based upon the claim that write-off announcements might convey different types of information, Bartov, Lindahl and Ricks (1998) report that "restructurings" meet with positive market reactions, while purely accounting write-offs generate negative responses. Riedl (2002) finds a significantly negative relation between unexpectedly negative earnings and the amount of SFAS 121 and pre-SFAS 121 write-offs, suggesting a "big bath" explanation.[789] However, in Segal's (2003) analysis of SFAS 121 and SFAS 142 goodwill write-offs, no such relation is found. Fried, Schiff and Sondhi (1989), Elliott and Hanna (1996), and Francis, Hanna and Vincent (1996) document that a write-off is rarely a one-time event, but is often followed by another one soon after, suggesting that write-offs are underestimated rather than overstated as implied by the big bath hypothesis.[790] However, while write-offs frequently coincide with poor performance and negative

---

785 Abarbanell and Lehavy's finding (2003) that firms rated by analysts as "sell" tend to engage in big bath behavior. See also Degeorge, Patel and Zeckhauser (1999, p. 30). Kirschenheiter and Melumad (2002) develop a model suggesting that the big bath strategy is appropriate when investors do not know the precision of reported earnings and pre-managed earnings are already below expectations. By additionally understating earnings, i.e. engaging in big bath behavior, management introduces "noise" into the earnings figure, which reduces the inferred precision of the earnings report. Investors are led to believe that the "true" earnings figure is in fact higher than the reported one.

786 White, Sondhi and Fried (2003, pp. 60, 278-9) review the discretionary asset write-off literature for evidence on the big bath hypothesis.

787 Elliott and Shaw (1988, p. 110) report that analyst forecasts of year-ahead earnings are adjusted downward upon write-offs. Also, write-off announcements trigger negative market reactions.

788 Similar findings are documented by Bunsis (1997). Analyzing restructurings, Brickley and Van Drunen (1990) and Kross, Park and Ro (1996) report that the announcements of such activities and the related charges generate positive abnormal returns.

789 See Riedl (2002, pp. 22-3, 39-40).

790 Anecdotal evidence exemplified by AOL Time Warner's repeated revisions of its estimated goodwill write-off amount corroborate this notion. See Taub (2003).

discretionary accruals,[791] write-off firms are not necessarily the worst performing firms within their industries.[792] Evidence reported by Cotter, Stokes and Wyatt (1998), DeAngelo (1988), Elliott and Shaw (1988), Godfrey, Mather and Ramsay (2003), Moore (1973), Murphy and Zimmerman (1993), Pourciau (1993), and Strong and Meyer (1987) suggests that big bath behavior follows management changes.[793] Beatty and Weber (2004) argue similarly when they predict that a recently appointed CEO has incentive to accelerate goodwill write-offs, whereas the CEO who made the original acquisition decision does not.[794] Finally, big bath behavior has also been suggested to explain certain restructuring charges.[795]

In summary, the big bath hypothesis does not explain the majority of observed write-offs,[796] and even where it does appear to do so, it is not clear whether earnings management is really at the heart of the empirical findings.

A financial reporting strategy closely related to target accounting and "big bath" behavior is suggested where a firm exceeds an earnings target by a substantial amount. In order to establish earnings reserves for future earnings management use, firms engage in "cookie jar reserving", i.e. decreasing earnings just enough to bring them just above the target.[797]

3.3.2.4.7 Rating

In recent years, the dominance of credit of rating agencies has increased in the global capital markets. Basically, four firms (Standard & Poor's,[798] Moody's Investors Service, Inc., Fitch, Inc., and Dominion Bond Rating Service Limited) share the market for bond

---

791 See, for example, Elliott and Shaw (1988), Fried, Schiff and Sondhi (1989), Rees, Gill and Gore (1996), and Heflin and Warfield (1997).

792 Refer to Strong and Meyer (1987).

793 DeAngelo's (1988, pp. 30-4) findings pertain to newly elected dissident managers following proxy contests, while Pourciau (1993) focuses on "non-routine" executive changes. Both authors caution that their findings are compatible not only with an earnings management hypothesis but might also be caused by economically sound decisions. Furthermore, both the management change and the apparent "big bath" could be caused by a third variable such as poor performance. See DeAngelo (1988, p. 32) and Pourciau (1993, p. 334). In Smith's (1993) review of the two papers, these issues are expanded upon.

794 See Beatty and Weber (2004, p. 11).

795 See for example Brickley and Van Drunen (1990) and John, Lang and Netter (1992).

796 According to Fried, Schiff and Sondhi (1989, p. 109), write-offs are determined by economy- and industry-wide developments rather than by firm-specific factors such as financial reporting decisions.

797 See, for example, Abarbanell and Lehavy (2000, p. 7).

798 Standard and Poor's is a division of the publishing company McGraw-Hill.

ratings.[799] These organizations operate independently, disseminating their ratings to the public, and relying on investors' willingness to accept their judgments. Like financial analysts, they are not strictly capital market participants themselves; rather, they function as information intermediaries between firms and investors.[800]

Firms are concerned about possible downgrades in their rating status, because of the increased cost of capital such downgrades often bring about. In the event of a downgrading, a firm's costs of debt capital usually rise due to worsening terms with its creditors. Indirectly, the costs of equity capital frequently rise also, because such events are often accompanied by severe declines in stock price.[801] Anecdotal evidence suggests that these concerns have the potential to influence managers' financial reporting decisions. For example, Gore, Taib and Taylor's (2000) survey evidence indicates UK managers' concerns that the income-decreasing effect of goodwill amortization might impair their firms' rating status.[802] Similarly, Nelson, Elliott and Tarpley (2002) report that concern over bond ratings is among the reasons behind earnings management attempts observed by auditors.[803]

In fact, the procedures employed by the agencies to arrive at their appraisals rely at least in part on financial ratios derived from GAAP financial statements. For example, Standard & Poor's "Corporate Ratings Criteria" publication contains the methodologies employed to arrive at the agency's rating decisions.[804] While S&P emphasizes that "[t]he rating process is not limited to an examination of various financial measures",[805] it does

---

799 These four agencies are recognized by the staff of the SEC as "nationally recognized statistical rating organizations". Their bond ratings today are "widely used as benchmarks in federal and state legislation, rules issued by financial and other regulators, foreign regulatory schemes, and private financial contracts." See SEC Concept Release "Rating Agencies and the Use of Credit Ratings under the Federal Securities Laws".

800 By way of example, S&P's role in the financial markets is outlined in S&P (2003, pp. 3-6). For a more general description of the bond rating process, refer to Crouhy, Galai and Mark (2001, pp. 50-55) and Ederington and Yawitz (1987).

801 On February 21, 2003, the German heavy industry group ThyssenKrupp was downgraded by Standard & Poor's, whereupon market capitalization dropped by roughly 20% or about three quarters of a billion Euro. See Hennes (2003). Interestingly, while Standard & Poor's downgraded ThyssenKrupp by two notches to junk bond status (BB+), the Moody's rating remained unchanged at Baa1.

802 See Gore, Taib and Taylor (2000, p. 221).

803 See Nelson, Elliott and Tarpley (2002, p. 190).

804 While Moody's and Fitch's approaches vary from that of S&P's in some minor details, S&P's methodology is considered here to be representative of the way that rating organizations process accounting information. This simplifying assumption seems reasonable given S&P's superior market position. For a summary of Moody's approach, refer to Crouhy, Galai and Mark (2001, pp. 50-55).

805 S&P (2003, p. 5).

state that "[f]inancial risk is portrayed largely through quantitative means, particularly by using financial ratios."[806] In computing these ratios, S&P relies on audited data, although specific accounting issues are reviewed and certain adjustments to reported GAAP figures are made in order to improve comparability and "to better portray reality."[807] When assessing the degree of leverage, different ratios are employed.[808] A firm's asset mix and business risk are considered when assessing appropriate levels for these leverage measures.[809] Key ratios to measure leverage are, among others, long-term debt to capital and total debt to capital.[810]

Managers might be inclined to believe that financial ratios play a dominant role in the rating process. For example, Standard & Poor's downgrading of Thyssen-Krupp was justified by the firm's high provisions for future pension obligations.[811] These provisions, until then regarded as similar to equity-type financing, were for the first time considered to be debt in nature, which caused a marked increase in ThyssenKrupp's financial leverage.[812] In contrast, U. S. firms frequently use external funding agencies, therefore reporting on the balance sheet not the entire future pension obligation, but, under SFAS 87, *Employers' Accounting for Pensions*, only a portion of any deficit not covered by the plan assets held by the funding agency. ThyssenKrupp officials disputed Standard & Poor's decision on the grounds that it did not reflect any worsening of ThyssenKrupp's financial condition but exclusively resulted from a change in Standard & Poor's methodology. Other European firms chimed in, hinting at managers' belief that rating agencies might take financial statement information at face value instead of autonomously considering the economic substance of the pension obligations. This belief might have further implications for management behavior: To the extent that rating agencies are believed to rely mechanistically on certain financial ratios, managers' concerns about possible downgrades might be justified, even where the deterioration of financial ratios is brought about by a mandatory accounting change. Therefore, managers

806 S&P (2003, p. 22).

807 S&P (2003, p. 22).

808 While the traditional measure of debt to capital has recently lost some its former significance, it does remain in the focus of rating organizations. See S&P (2003, pp. 30-1).

809 Refer to S&P (2003, pp. 24, 56). Specific adjustments with regard to the accounting for business combinations and goodwill are discussed in section 5.2.3.2.

810 See S&P (2003, p. 55). Long-term debt to capital is long term debt divided by long-term debt plus shareholders' equity (including preferred stock) plus minority interest. In the total debt to capital ratio, long-term debt is supplemented by current maturities, commercial paper, and other short-term borrowings. These ratios are adjusted for the amount to which operating leases are in fact debt equivalents.

811 See, for example, o. V. (2003).

812 S&P's treatment of pension and similar obligations is explained in S&P (2003, pp. 107-24).

about by a mandatory accounting change. Therefore, managers have incentive to influence the relevant financial ratios.[813]

3.3.2.4.8 Specific considerations regarding accounting changes and other transitory earnings components

Transitional SFAS 142 goodwill write-offs, possibly even more than other discretionary asset write-offs, are distinct from other components of earnings, which might influence the extent to which they are suitable as instruments to achieve capital market-related financial reporting incentives. It is commonly assumed that (the time series of) a firm's earnings are relevant to investors' assessment of the firm's future prospects.[814] Therefore, investors are interested in certain properties of this earnings stream, frequently referred to as the *quality of earnings*.[815] High-quality earnings contain a high proportion of permanent, sustainable components, which have predictive ability for future earnings. In contrast to that, earnings have low quality when they are affected by one-off effects and other transitory or non-recurring components, which complicate the forecasting of future earnings.[816] Therefore, one of financial statement users' primary tasks is to remove transitory components from reported earnings in an attempt to "normalize" reported income and assess a firm's underlying earnings power.[817]

Such transitory components, or non-recurring items, are comprised of unusual or infrequent items, extraordinary items, discontinued operations, and accounting changes.[818] While the first category, also referred to as "special" items,[819] are reported "above the line" as income from continuing operations, the other three components are presented net of tax as "below-the-line" items. Extraordinary items are unusual in nature, infrequent in

---

813 Although firms pay fees to be rated, potential costs arising from adverse rating changes are not considered here to be "contracting costs" (refer to section 3.3.2.3.1), since they are imposed on firms not by the rating agencies directly but by investors relying on the agencies' judgments. Therefore, earnings management incentives stemming from a desire to influence rating status are capital market-related as opposed to economic consequences-type incentives.

814 Hirst and Hopkins (1998) state that "equity analysts typically use earnings-based valuation models". See also Barker (1999), Block (1999), and Brown, Finn and Hope (2000, p. 1235) for evidence on valuation models used by analysts.

815 See, for example, White, Sondhi and Fried (2003, p. 637), to whom earnings quality is represented by "the degree of conservatism in a firm's reported earnings."

816 See, for example, Beaver (1998, pp. 92-6). Early research on the value relevance of permanent versus transitory earnings components includes Beaver and Morse (1978) and Lipe (1986).

817 See Hopkins, Houston and Peters (2000, p. 263) and White, Sondhi and Fried (2003, pp. 631-6).

818 For much of the following, refer to White, Sondhi and Fried (2003, pp. 52-56).

819 These entries are either unusual in nature or infrequent in occurrence but not both.

occurrence and material in amount.[820] APB Opinion 30 states explicitly that write-offs of intangible assets do not belong in this category.[821] Income from discontinued operations, governed by SFAS 144, is segregated in the income statement because these activities will not contribute to future earnings or cash flows. The treatment of accounting changes is regulated in APB Opinion 20, *Accounting Changes*. Usually, the cumulative effect on prior period earnings is reported net of tax below the line. This treatment is required by SFAS 142.56 for transitional SFAS 142 goodwill write-offs.[822] White, Sondhi and Fried (2003) note that "accounting changes also affect future operating results. That impact is rarely disclosed but can sometimes be estimated."[823]

The fact that a transitional SFAS 142 goodwill write-off is presented separately as a cumulative effect-type accounting change makes it an extremely visible item, which might not lend itself to subtle earnings manipulation.[824] Therefore, it is unreasonable to assume that managers use transitional SFAS 142 goodwill write-offs in the context of a financial reporting strategy that hinges on the notion that the earnings manipulation goes unnoticed by financial statement users. Furthermore, transitional SFAS 142 goodwill write-offs reduce net income while having no influence on operating income or other earnings measures such as EBITDA. Subsequent to the transitional impairment test, however, SFAS 142 goodwill write-offs will represent a separate line item in the income statement before the subtotal "income from continuing operations".[825]

These considerations suggest a strategic use of transitional SFAS 142 goodwill write-offs. Financial reporting incentives related to the adoption of SFAS 142 are likely to differ from those regarding "regular" goodwill write-offs. Consistent with the classificatory smoothing literature, Henning, Shaw and Stock (2002) expect "transition period firms [to] announce large goodwill impairments based on a belief that, as 'below-the-line' items, the market would view such impairments as relating to a past problem and having

---

820 Refer to APB Opinion 30, *Reporting the Results of Operations--Reporting the Effects of Disposal of a Segment of a Business, and Extraordinary, Unusual and Infrequently Occurring Events and Transactions*, par. 19-24.

821 See APB Opinion 30.23 lit. a. Kieso, Weygandt and Warfield (2001, p. 563) also argue that impairment losses do not have the characteristics of extraordinary items and should therefore be reported as part of income from continuing operations.

822 Refer to section 4.7.3 below.

823 White, Sondhi and Fried (2003, p. 55).

824 Beneish (2001, p. 6) states that managers intent on managing earnings "are likely to do so in a way that is difficult to detect".

825 See SFAS 142, par. 43. Such "regular" SFAS 142 write-offs represent "special" items like most other impairment write-offs. See White, Sondhi and Fried (2003, p. 53).

no impact on current firm value."[826] If that assumption holds, firms with present write-off potential and firms anticipating such potential in the near future will have incentive to engage in "big bath" behavior, accelerating future write-offs into the adoption period.[827]

In that sense, Beneish's (1998) assertion that "accounting changes [are] a rather blunt instrument for earnings management because it is not plausible to assume that the effects of the accounting change on earnings are difficult to unravel" is not entirely correct.[828] It assumes that earnings management works best where it cannot be detected by financial statement users in the period in which it is occurs. Quite on the contrary, precisely *because* accounting changes are visible and therefore likely to be ignored due to its transitory nature in the period of the change, users frequently overlook the strategic implications of these changes for earnings and other financial statement items in future periods.[829] Therefore, transitional SFAS 142 goodwill write-offs are suitable for strategic earnings management.[830] With respect to capital market-related financial reporting incentives,[831] it appears reasonable to assume that managers will expect investors to largely ignore transitional, but not regular SFAS 142 goodwill write-offs.[832] Transitional SFAS 142 goodwill write-offs, then, will be used strategically. As will be discussed in more

---

826 Henning, Shaw and Stock (2002, p. 8).

827 See also Osterland (2002), who quotes a Lehman Brothers associate with the statement that an initial goodwill write-off, reported as an accounting change is likely to be ignored or discounted by investors. That associate advises firms to record a transitional SFAS 142 goodwill write-off as early and as high as possible, in order to avoid regular write-offs in the near future.

828 Beneish (1998, p. 85).

829 Elliott and Philbrick's (1990) evidence suggests that analysts are unable to predict the earnings effect of a mandatory accounting change. It is reasonable to assume that analysts will assign less importance to earnings components that, to them, represent pure accounting events, the effect of which on future prospects cannot be estimated. Burgstahler, Jiambalvo and Shevlin (2002), Elliott and Hanna (1996) and Moffitt and Rai (2002) report that the presence of special items impairs investors' ability to form accurate earnings expectations. Similar evidence is reported by Chen, Danielson and Schoderbek (2003).

830 In the context of SFAS 87, Langer and Lev (1993) demonstrate that the adoption of a new standard is used by firms to engage in earnings management. Elliott and Philbrick (1990) find that managers make income-increasing (income-decreasing) voluntary accounting changes in response to analysts' downward (upward) earnings forecast revisions, suggesting an income-smoothing explanation of voluntary accounting changes. Evidence consistent with this finding is reported by Kinney and Trezevant (1997) in the context of special items.

831 The role of transitional SFAS 142 goodwill write-offs and other transitory items in accounting-based contracts is another issue. Refer to section 3.3.2.3 above and section 5.2.3.1 below.

832 This – alleged – opinion of the capital markets is portrayed in Osterland's (2002) article, suggesting that investors will ignore any transitional goodwill write-offs, while goodwill write-offs that occur after the transition period "will likely have a lot more negative impact in the market". Similarly, Riedl (2002, p. 2) argues that "asset impairments directly affect net income, suggesting incentives may exist for managers to manipulate write-off amounts".

detail in section 5.2.3.2 below, firms that anticipate future earnings to be above earnings targets will have incentive to avoid transitional write-offs, storing up write-off potential for future periods. Conversely, firms that anticipate future earnings to be below earnings targets will accelerate transitional write-offs in order to shelter future earnings.

A number of studies on target accounting[833] present evidence on whether the assumption that investors will ignore transitional SFAS 142 goodwill write-offs is representative of extant research approaches. Burgstahler and Dichev (1997) use both net income and earnings before extraordinary items as the earnings numbers relevant to analysts. They find that "the results are generally consistent for the two alternative measures of earnings."[834] Moehrle (2002) uses EPS based on net income, except where I/B/E/S backs out unusual items from reported earnings.[835] Burgstahler and Eames (2001) use the proprietary definition of *Zacks Investment Research* database for an "operating EPS before extraordinary and non-recurring items".[836] Degeorge, Patel and Zeckhauser (1999) use quarterly EPS before extraordinary items for the pre-1985 period. Post-1984, they use I/B/E/S forecasted and actual EPS, which, according to I/B/E/S, exclude unusual or non-recurring charges.[837] Bartov, Givoly and Hayn (2002) use "actual earnings" (not defined any further) and forecasts from I/B/E/S.[838] Abarbanell and Lehavy (2000) report difficulties in comparing EPS figures across databases. Marquardt and Wiedman (2002) use net income before extraordinary items.[839] Kasznik (1999), consistent with Jaggi and Sannella (1995), excludes changes in accounting principle and extraordinary items, because the management forecasts studied relate to earnings from continuing operations.[840] Hayn (1995) uses "income (loss) from continuing operations, before extraordinary items, discontinued operations, and the cumulative effect of accounting changes."[841] Finally, Phil-

---

833 Refer to section 3.3.2.4.5.

834 Burgstahler and Dichev (1997, pp. 101-2).

835 I/B/E/S is the Institutional Brokers Estimate System.

836 Burgstahler and Eames (2001, p. 5 fn. 10). The authors note that *Zacks*' actual (and forecast) EPS are not directly comparable to I/B/E/S actual EPS and that differences are sometimes substantial.

837 Degeorge, Patel and Zeckhauser (1999, pp. 15-6).

838 They delete observations where I/B/E/S earnings and COMPUSTAT earnings (not defined any further) differ substantially (> 50%) and the difference cannot be explained by a special item. They stress that I/B/E/S reports an "adjusted" earnings figure.

839 See Marquardt and Wiedman (2002, pp. 19, 38).

840 See Kasznik (1999, p. 63 fn. 10).

841 Hayn (1995, p. 129).

brick and Ricks (1991) report that extraordinary items are excluded from I/B/E/S forecasts.[842]

3.3.2.5 Factors restricting management discretion

The above discussion of different earnings management incentives does not imply that there are no limitations to management's discretion in managing earnings. Stated generally, the benefits managers associate with achieving their financial reporting objectives must be traded off with the costs of earnings manipulation.[843] Pertaining to the focus of this dissertation, managers will also trade off the particular costs and benefits of earnings manipulation associated with discretionary asset write-offs with those related to other discretionary financial reporting decisions.[844] For example, since write-offs are high-profile accounting events, using them for subtle earnings management is not feasible.[845]

Several factors determine the costs of earnings manipulation and thereby the extent to which management can achieve their financial reporting objectives by engaging in earnings management. First, the degree of rigidity, i.e. the absence of flexibility and discretion, in applicable financial reporting rules (GAAP) predefines the extent to which management can influence the reported numbers and accompanying disclosures. While a rules-based accounting system tends to be relatively rigid, a principles-based approach to standard setting necessarily introduces considerable discretion of application into the rules.[846] As has been discussed above, discretionary asset write-offs are characterized by the comparatively high degree of judgment and subjectivity involved in applying the relevant guidance, where any exists. This is argued to be especially true for transitional SFAS 142 goodwill write-offs.[847]

Second, the guiding principles of most accounting rules contain principles intended to limit randomness and enhance the decision usefulness of financial statements. Under

---

842 See Philbrick and Ricks (1991, p. 401).

843 For example, refer to Waymire (1988, pp. 123-5).

844 See Waymire (1998, pp. 125-6). A discussion of the relative costs and benefits of using different accounting items as earnings management instruments is provided by Marquardt and Wiedman (2002, pp. 8-18). They partition the relevant costs into costs of detected versus costs of undetected earnings management.

845 Refer to section 3.3.2.4.8.

846 In the theoretical extreme, a rules-based accounting system leaves no discretion. Earnings management, then, cannot occur in a strictly rules-based accounting system. However, such a system would be associated with prohibitive costs.

847 Refer to chapter 4 below.

U. S. GAAP, "[c]onsistency in applying accounting methods over a span of time has always been regarded as an important quality that makes accounting numbers more useful."[848] According to SFAC 2, consistency is defined as "[c]onformity from period to period with unchanging policies and procedures."[849] Due to this principle, the exercise in one period of what discretion exists usually limits the degree of discretion available in later periods.[850] This implies that discretion will be exercised strategically, taking into consideration the implications of current financial reporting decisions for the degree of discretion available in future periods. Applied to the SFAS 142 setting, the methods and basic assumptions used by management in the transitional goodwill impairment test will, at least to some extent, have to be carried over into future periods. At least, significant deviations will have to be justified by management to auditors and, possibly, SEC officials.

Third, management's financial reporting decision making is monitored by auditors in order to ensure compliance with GAAP and to prevent manipulation. Since earnings management is here defined to be strictly within the limits of GAAP, the role of the auditor with respect to earnings management is to prevent management from crossing the fine line to GAAP violation.[851] Stakeholders rely on auditors to limit earnings management.[852] For example, managers potentially face adverse consequences from auditors' decisions to raise audit fees, render qualified audit opinions or, in severe cases, terminate the audit engagement.[853] Since GAAP on discretionary asset write-offs rely heavily on management's judgment, the extent to which auditors limit management's discretion in this context is an open issue.[854] Some argue that it is precisely this discretionary nature

---

848 SFAC 2.120. With regard to financial statement measurement, presentation, and consolidation issues, this concept is also important in Germany ("Stetigkeit"). See Pellens (2001, p. 141) and Sieben and Coenenberg (1997, p. 1146-7).

849 SFAC 2 (Glossary of terms).

850 This relation is referred to by Marquardt and Wiedman (2002, p. 13) as the "reversal" of earnings management.

851 In addition, managers' incentives to abstain from manipulative or even fraudulent GAAP violations stems from the potential threat of litigation under applicable securities laws. See, for example, Waymire (1988, pp. 124-5). However, since the definition of earnings management given in section 3.3.1.1 above does not include GAAP violations, this aspect is not further pursued here.

852 See, for example, Heninger (2001, p. 112).

853 See, for example, Waymire (1988, p. 124).

854 DeFond and Subramanyam (1998, p. 40) stress that, "because the interpretation of GAAP requires professional judgment, management and auditors ... can hold legitimate divergent beliefs regarding its application".

that ensures close monitoring of asset write-offs and prevents potential abuse.[855] The role of auditors with respect to earnings management has been the subject of extensive research. For example, Krishnan's (2003b) analysis suggests that auditors with industry expertise limit the amount of discretionary accruals reported by client firms. Nelson, Elliott and Tarpley (2002) document survey evidence on clients' earnings management attempts and auditors' responses. Heninger (2001) finds that auditors' litigation risk increases in the extent of their clients' income-increasing earnings management. DeFond and Subramanyam's (1998) evidence suggests that auditor changes can frequently be explained by auditors' preference of conservative accounting due to litigation concerns, which conflict with managers' financial reporting incentives. Francis, Maydew and Sparks (1999) conclude from their evidence that Big Six auditors constrain aggressive and potentially opportunistic earnings management.[856]

Fourth, extensive disclosure requirements also help to ensure that managers make public their assumptions underlying write-offs and other discretionary financial reporting decisions. Where assumptions must be explicitly stated and are therefore made open to scrutiny, management's incentive to manipulate financial statements will tend to be further restricted. Such disclosures assist financial statement users in "seeing through" the possibly manipulative motivations behind managers' financial reporting decisions.[857]

Finally, assuming that managers maximize their own utility does not necessarily imply that financial reporting decisions are exclusively motivated by considerations such as income or job security, which ultimately have financial repercussions. To the extent that character traits such as honesty, decency, or, less solemn, a simple distaste for lying, are part of a manager's personality, making financial reporting decisions that faithfully represent economic reality will increase her utility.[858]

---

855 See Elliott and Hanna (1996, p. 137): "Management must use judgment to determine the size of a write-off. Because these large accounting write-offs are discrete and relatively infrequent, this managerial judgment may be more subject to investor and regulator scrutiny than similar recurring judgments by management regarding receivables collectability and other accruals."

856 Also, refer to Elder and Zhou's (2003, 2002) evidence on the association between audit quality and earnings management in the context of seasoned and initial equity offerings, respectively.

857 See also Baetge and Ballwieser (1977, p. 2003).

858 Evans et al. (2001, pp. 552-5) use an experimental design to analyze managers' preferences for wealth and honesty and their effect on managerial reporting. They show that subjects gave up a substantial portion of the available payoff by reporting (partially) honestly. These results challenge existing agency models that predict at most a weak role of honesty. Subjects were (partially) honest although they faced none of the negative consequences normally associated with lying due to the absence of monitoring, auditing, and reputation effects.

To summarize, factors restricting management's discretion can be interpreted as costs of manipulation. Due to the specific characteristics of discretionary asset write-offs, the costs resulting from their use of as earnings management instruments differ from those associated with other financial reporting decisions.

3.4 Financial statement users' view of discretionary asset write-offs

In this section, research on the relation between discretionary asset write-offs and market-based metrics such as stock prices or stock returns is reviewed. In contrast to the approach introduced in section 3.3.2.2 above, the focus of this research is not on whether the firm's market performance causes the write-off. Rather, investors' responses to discretionary asset write-offs are studied, where the write-off itself is interpreted as the cause.[859] The findings of this research area are of interest to both managers and researchers: Managers might want to pre-estimate the stock price effects of avoiding or recording discretionary asset-write-offs. Researchers are interested in learning about investors' perception of these charges.

3.4.1 Information perspective of financial reporting

The literature discussed here is primarily interested in the implications of discretionary asset write-offs for investors' assessment of the amounts, timing, and uncertainty of the write-off firms' future cash flows. These implications, if any, are expected to influence security prices in the instance they are disclosed to the market as well as over longer time periods. Therefore, researchers interested in financial statement users' perception of discretionary asset write-offs investigate empirically the relation between a write-off firm's accounting numbers and the market value of its stock.

Such relation is expected to exist because financial statements and other elements of financial reporting are commonly viewed from an *information perspective*, i.e. they are primarily intended to provide decision-useful information to present and potential users, primarily shareholders.[860] This information perspective has also been adopted by financial reporting standard setters. It is stipulated in the FASB's conceptual framework as follows:

---

[859] Since this aspect of the discretionary asset write-off literature is not taken up in the empirical analysis in chapter 5, the discussion in this section is less detailed and comprehensive than that in section 3.3 above.

[860] For example, refer to Beaver (1998, pp. 4-5) and Christensen and Demski (2003, ch. 1). See also Francis and Schipper (1999, p. 319).

> "Financial reporting should provide information that is useful to present and potential investors and creditors and other users in making rational investment, credit, and similar decisions ... Financial reporting should provide information to help present and potential investors and creditors and other users in assessing the amount, timing, and uncertainty of prospective cash receipts ... financial reporting should provide information to help investors, creditors, and others assess the amounts, timing, and uncertainty of prospective net cash inflows to the .. enterprise."[861]

In the IASB's framework for the preparation and presentation of financial statements,[862] the objective of financial statements is stated in this fashion:

> "The objective of financial statements is to provide information about the financial position, performance and changes in financial position of an enterprise that is useful to wide range of users in making economic decisions."[863]

Investors, especially shareholders, are identified in the Framework as the primary user group.[864] Their information needs are thought to be representative of those of most other users.[865] Shareholders are assumed to be "interested in information which enables them to assess the ability of the enterprise to pay dividends."[866]

Since a firm's dividend-paying ability is determined by its cash flows, financial reporting data is intended to help the firm's stakeholders in assessing the amount, timing, and risk of the firm's prospective cash flows. Information based on accrual accounting, which is primarily earnings-oriented, is useful for the assessment of future cash flows because accruals have normalizing properties that reduce the raw cash flows' inherent volatility. Therefore, they have predictive value over and above that of raw cash flows.[867] Since an accrual-based accounting system produces information incremental to that included in cash flows (e.g. management's expectations about an asset's future earnings power that

---

861 SFAC 1, *Objectives of Financial Reporting by Business Enterprises*, par. 34, 37. Also, refer to Pellens (2001, pp. 132-7).

862 Hereafter referred to as "Framework".

863 Framework, par. 12. Also, refer to Pellens (2001, pp. 437-8), and Pellens, Bonse and Fülbier (1996, pp. 271-6).

864 See Framework, par. 9.

865 See Framework, par. 10.

866 Framework, par. 9 (a).

867 For an in-depth discussion of this issue, refer to Dechow (1994, pp. 4-7, 35-6). She documents that, over short periods, earnings are more closely associated with stock returns than are realized cash flows, especially where forms operate in a "steady state". Where firms experience changes in their operating environment, cash flows suffer from timing and matching problems.

might get reflected in that asset being written off), earnings are viewed to be more informative and indicative of future cash flows than are past cash flows alone.[868]

3.4.2 Research approaches

To ascertain the informational properties of discretionary asset write-offs, two distinct approaches are adopted in the research, depending on whether short-term or long-term effects of (the announcements of) write-offs are studied.[869] In *information content studies*, a causal, short-term relation is assumed to exist between (announcements of) discretionary asset write-offs and security prices.[870] If such relation is found to exist, the discretionary asset write-off is said to have information content,[871] implying that it "conveys new information to market participants as reflected in changes in the level ... of security prices ... over a short time period around the event".[872] The maintained hypothesis in these studies is that the EMH holds, i.e. security prices reflect the new information in the instant it is made public.[873] Generally speaking, the information content of an earnings figure is "measured by market reaction to the announced earnings and its deviation from expected earnings."[874] Likewise, the information content of a discretionary asset write-off would be measured by the market reaction to the write-off announcement. To the extent that the write-off was unexpected, any market reaction can be interpreted as reflecting investors' assessment of the information conveyed by the write-off. Since the market reaction is most frequently measured in terms of the write-off firm's stock return over a short interval centered on the write-off announcement, this approach has also been labeled return analysis.[875]Because this type of analysis methodologically represents an

---

868 See, for example, Beaver (1998, p. 6).

869 See, for example, Alciatore et al. (1998, pp. 3-4).

870 In the words of Vincent (1997, p. 7), researchers are interested in "the information content (or 'news') of an event", i.e. of the write-off announcement.

871 Holthausen and Watts (2001, p. 6) label such research "marginal information content studies".

872 Kothari (2001, p. 116). See also Watts and Zimmerman (1986, ch. 3) and Brown (2001, pp. 14-6). According to Alciatore et al. (1998, p. 3), the "question implicit in these studies is: Do asset write-downs convey information to investors at the time they are *announced*?" (Emphasis in original.)

873 This, of course, assumes that the information is actually new and has not been previously conveyed to investors through mechanisms other than the write-off announcement. With respect to asset write-offs, Heflin and Warfield (1997, p. 9) argue that investors may obtain information about asset value declines through financial intermediaries and reported accounting data in the period before the write-off.

874 White, Sondhi and Fried (2003, p. 169).

875 Atiase and Tse (1986, p. 2) refer to the "returns approach". See also Alciatore et al. (1998, p. 3).

event study,[876] this branch of capital market-based accounting research has also become known under that label.[877] The archetypal event study, conducted by Fama, Fisher, Jensen and Roll (1969), was initiated even before, although published later than, the influential article by Ball and Brown (1968) that made the event study approach popular in accounting research.[878]

Association studies represent another approach found in the discretionary asset write-off literature. Here, researchers are interested in the correlation between write-off amounts and stock prices or returns measured over longer time periods, e.g. the fiscal period.[879] The hypothesized relation can be framed as the following research question: "Does the inclusion of the amount of the write-down in earnings result in an income number which provides a better *summary* of the information that investors have used in setting security prices over the fiscal period?"[880] Since write-offs affect earnings numbers, not cash flows, association studies primarily analyze the relation between stock returns and earnings. If such a relation is found to be significant and positive, this result can be interpreted as evidence that the write-off reflects some of the same information that has caused investors to lower their expectations regarding the write-off firms' future cash flows. However, no direct causal connection is hypothesized.[881] Because association studies examine whether accounting numbers capture information relevant to investors in their estimation of firm value, they are also referred to as value relevance studies.[882]

---

876 Synonyms include "residual analysis" and "abnormal performance index test". See Bowman (1983, p. 561).

877 See, for example, Kothari (2001, p. 116). For an introduction into the methodology employed in an event study, refer to Binder (1998), Bowman (1983), MacKinlay (1997), Peterson (1998), Peterson (1989), Schremper (2002, pp. 121-30), and Thompson (1995).

878 See Brown (2001, p. 14, 23). Another seminal, albeit methodologically somewhat different study is Beaver (1968). Reviews of this literature include those by Beaver (2002), Brown (2001), Coenenberg (1974), Coenenberg et al. (1978), Kothari (2001), Lev (1989), Lev and Ohlson (1982), and Watts and Zimmerman (1986, ch. 3).

879 See Kothari (2001, p. 116). Following Vincent (1997, p. 7), "the degree of association between reported accounting numbers and either stock prices or long window (twelve to fifteen months) security returns" is investigated.

880 Alciatore et al. (1998, p. 3 [emphasis in original]).

881 See Kothari (2001, p. 116).

882 Excellent reviews of this literature include Barth, Beaver and Landsman (2001), Bonse (2004), Coenenberg (1974), Coenenberg et al. (1978), Holthausen and Watts (2001), Lev (1989), and Lev and Ohlson (1982). Francis and Schipper (1999, p. 320) refer to this line of research as the "explanatory power approach" because the value relevance of financial statement information can be measured by the "explanatory power of accounting information for measures of market value".

3.4.3 Main findings

3.4.3.1 Information content studies

Strong and Meyer (1987) study 120 write-offs announced during the period 1981-85. Their results indicate that information about an impending write-off was available to the market before the write-off was actually made. Positive pre-write-off stock performance suggests that investors responded positively to the anticipated write-off, possibly because it was perceived as part of a larger restructuring plan. However, stock performance during the write-off announcement period was mostly negative, which might indicate that investors perceived the actual restructuring plan disclosed in the write-off announcement to be disappointing.[883] However, during the period subsequent to the write-off announcement, the negative announcement reaction was largely reversed.

Focusing on the same time period as Strong and Meyer's (1987) analysis, Elliott and Shaw (1988) examine 240 firms reporting discretionary asset write-offs during the period 1982-85. The write-off announcements are found to be associated with significantly negative industry-adjusted returns.[884] Cross-sectional variation in the returns is found to be associated with write-off size, the information signal conveyed ("good" or "bad" news), and concurrent stock repurchase announcements.[885] During the subsequent six months, write-off firms continued to experience negative industry-adjusted stock performance. The write-offs also appeared to trigger downward revisions in analysts' expectations regarding the write-off firms. Overall, Elliott and Shaw (1988) find no evidence to suggest that write-offs are either expected or perceived as "good news" by investors; rather, they "occur during a period of sustained economic difficulty".[886]

In their analysis of 77 write-offs taken during the period 1981-83, Zucca and Campbell (1992) find no significant stock price response to the write-off announcements.[887] An examination of several performance measures during the six years centered on the write-off leads the authors to conclude that write-offs are not "a precursor of improved financial health" due to "big bath"-type improvement projects with which write-off firms in-

---

883 See Strong and Meyer (1987, p. 660).

884 See Elliott and Shaw (1988, pp. 104-5).

885 See Elliott and Shaw (1988, pp. 105-7).

886 Elliott and Shaw (1988, p. 114).

887 See Zucca and Campbell (1992, p. 36). This finding might be associated with the fact that the announcement period was very long (120 days).

tend to strengthen their future prospects; instead, they appear to indicate economic problems.[888]

Francis, Hanna and Vincent (1996) analyze 507 write-off announcements disclosed during the period 1989-92.[889] On average, they find negative market reactions to these events.[890] However, reactions vary with the type of write-off under scrutiny. Non-discretionary write-offs of inventory are viewed negatively, while restructuring-type charges trigger a positive response. Write-offs of goodwill and PP&E, in contrast, are perceived neutrally.[891] The authors conclude that, "on average, investors' response is driven more by write-offs revealing information about asset impairments than by write-offs conveying positive signals about future performance."[892]

Bunsis' (1997) study is designed as an explicit test of the above notion that investors' reactions to write-off announcements depend on the signal conveyed. Examining 207 write-offs made during the period 1983-89, he finds that write-offs suggesting increases (decreases) in future cash flows are associated with positive (negative) market-adjusted stock returns. The extent of these responses also increases in the amount written off. The author concludes that "the stock price reaction to write-off announcements is associated with the expected cash flow implications of the events surrounding the write-off."[893]

In their study of 373 write-off announcements disclosed during the period 1984-85, Bartov, Lindahl and Ricks (1998) make a similar distinction between pure accounting events and write-offs suggestive of changes in firm operations.[894] They report that the first category of write-offs trigger a marginally significant negative response in terms of risk-adjusted returns, while the second group is associated with significantly positive reactions.[895] Furthermore, they provide evidence that market participants either expect part of the write-offs or postpone their reaction until more detailed information about the reasons behind the write-offs is available.

---

888 Zucca and Campbell (1992, p. 41).

889 See Francis, Hanna and Vincent (1996, p. 128).

890 See Francis, Hanna and Vincent (1996, pp. 129-31).

891 See Francis, Hanna and Vincent (1996, pp. 131-3).

892 Francis, Hanna and Vincent (1996, p. 134).

893 Bunsis (1997, p. 1398).

894 See Bartov, Lindahl and Ricks (1998, pp. 335-7).

895 See Bartov, Lindahl and Ricks (1998, p. 328).

In a similar vein, Chaney, Hogan and Jeter (2000) analyze market responses to 128 restructuring charges taken in the period 1990-92. These charges represent either asset write-offs or severance payments and other cash outflows.[896] The authors find that asset write-offs do not, on average, result in significant stock price reactions. The market reaction to severance and other cash charges depends on whether the firm had experienced prior losses or changes in management. A combination of the two components does not result in significant stock price responses. The authors conclude that, "on average, the nature and context of restructuring charges are important to ... users in formulating their responses to the charges."[897]

In a recent comparative study of SFAS 142 versus SFAS 121 goodwill write-offs, Segal (2003) examines stock price reactions to the unexpected portion of 177 write-offs announced during the period October 2001 through June 2002.[898] He expects markets reactions to be more negative for SFAS 142 write-offs, since these are expected to be more strongly associated with economic factors as opposed to earnings management incentives.[899] Regarding both types of write-offs, Segal (2003) finds negative reactions that are only marginally significant, with no significant differences discernable between the regimes.[900]

Overall, the evidence presented here appears to be consistent with the notion that investors' reactions to write-off announcements depend on the information conveyed and on the extent to which these events were anticipated at the time they are announced. This finding implies an interesting new aspect of management's financial reporting discretion: Regardless of the "true" reasons behind a write-off, management might be able to control the market response to this event by voluntarily disclosing the write-off and carefully phrasing the accompanying announcement. In that way, asset impairments might be passed off as good news to an investing public suffering from information asymmetries.

3.4.3.2 Association studies

Elliott and Hanna (1996) investigate the valuation implications of repeated asset write-offs. They analyze 6,073 write-offs recorded by 2,761 firms in the period 1975-94, where

---

896 See Chaney, Hogan and Jeter (2000, pp. 7-8).

897 Chaney, Hogan and Jeter (2000, p. 22).

898 Segal (2003, p. 23) estimates the expected write-off amount by applying market-based and residual-income valuation models, which might introduce measurement error into that variable.

899 See Segal (2003, p. 19).

900 See Segal (2003, pp. 27-8).

write-offs are defined as negative special items in excess of 1% of total assets. The authors document that the association of earnings (before special items) and special items with stock returns becomes less significant when several write-offs occur in sequence. Apparently, a series of write-offs impairs investors' ability to discern permanent and transitory components of firms' earnings.[901] Similarly, Burgstahler, Jiambalvo and Shevlin (2002) report that stock prices do not fully reflect the implications of special items for future earnings.[902]

Heflin and Warfield (1997) investigate 845 write-offs taken in the period 1985-91 in order to assess whether asset write-offs occur in a timely manner and whether they are intentionally overstated to improve earnings subsequent to the write-off.[903] Their examination of stock price and accounting performance during seven years centered on the write-off suggests that firms delay write-offs until a year where earnings are poor irrespective of the write-off. They report that write-offs, on average, lag downward developments in stock performance as well as accounting performance by several periods. Also, write-offs appear to be overstated.

In the context of their information content study summarized above, Bartov, Lindahl and Ricks (1998) also analyze the longer-term association of write-offs and stock prices. Since short-term reactions to large write-offs are found to be unexpectedly small, the authors are interested whether the write-offs are preempted by other information or whether investors initially under-react to them, adjusting their expectations in the post-announcement period as more background information becomes available.[904] They find that write-offs are generally preceded by significant stock price declines as long as two years before the announcement. This development continues during the post-write-off year. Bartov, Lindahl and Ricks (1998) conclude that, "while the market might partially anticipate the write-off announcements, it fails to fully incorporate all the value-relevant information into stock prices on a timely basis."[905]

Based on the notion that asset write-offs should realign the book value of assets with the future economic benefits associated with those assets, Comprix (2000) analyzes the valuation of assets surrounding write-offs. He argues that, if asset write-offs are eco-

---

901 See Elliott and Hanna (1996, p. 154).

902 Also, refer to section 3.3.2.4.8 above.

903 See Heflin and Warfield (1997, p. 1).

904 See Bartov, Lindahl and Ricks (1998, p. 328).

905 Bartov, Lindahl and Ricks (1998, p. 329).

nomically meaningful, they are equal to the difference between the book value of an impaired asset and its fair value. Consequently, if an asset write-off aligns the asset's book value closer with its fair value, the resulting new book value should be more useful to investors than before. Accordingly, Comprix (2000) predicts that the value relevance to investors of non-impaired assets is different from that of the pre-write-off amounts of impaired assets.[906] From this assumption, he derives his main hypothesis that the book value and value relevance of impaired and non-impaired asset should converge subsequent to a write-off announcement.[907] In this association study, the author finds that the pre-write-off book values of impaired assets had a significantly weaker association with stock prices than did the book values of non-impaired assets. This difference in coefficients is largely removed subsequent to the write-off, which the author interprets as evidence that write-offs align book values and fair values, making financial statement data more relevant to investors.[908]

Deng and Lev (1998) investigate acquiring firms' practice to immediately write off to earnings the fair values of in-process R&D costs acquired in a business combination.[909] Finding that investors reverse the immediate write-off of in-process R&D when pricing both earnings and asset values, they conclude that such R&D activities are value relevant to investors.[910]

Riedl (2002) compares the timeliness of asset write-offs under the pre-SFAS 121 versus SFAS 121 financial reporting regimes. However, write-offs do not appear to be related to contemporaneous or lagged stock returns.[911] In that sense, Riedl's (2002) results do not unambiguously show whether write-offs are taken in a timely manner or whether the timeliness of write-offs differs between the two regimes.[912]

---

906 See Comprix (2000, pp. 2-3).

907 See Comprix (2000, pp. 2-3). Comprix further investigates whether and to what extent investors anticipate write-offs. Consistent with economic factors causing the write-off (refer to section 3.3.2.2 above), he argues that it will to some extent lag the economic event(s) that caused the impairment. See Comprix (2000, p. 3).

908 See Comprix (2000, pp. 23, 26).

909 This procedure is required by FASB Interpretation (FIN) 4, *Applicability of FASB Statement No. 2 to Business Combinations Accounted for by the Purchase Method – An interpretation of FASB Statement No. 2.*

910 See Deng and Lev (1998, p. 5).

911 See Riedl (2002, p. 28).

912 See Riedl (2002, p. 3).

The study of asset revaluations conducted by Easton, Eddey and Harris (1993) is not explicitly considered here because, while the authors do include downward revaluations, i.e. write-offs, in their analysis, the incidence of such write-offs is very infrequent.[913]

3.5 *Summary and implications*

The research reviewed in this chapter has documented that asset write-offs represent accounting events that have substantial effects on companies' financial statements. Frequently, they relate to assets for which market values are not readily observed and applicable accounting guidance, if available, involves considerable judgment and subjectivity. These characteristics make discretionary asset write-offs interesting earnings management instruments as well as promising objects of empirical research.[914]

Empirical research regarding the determinants of discretionary asset write-offs suggests that such charges frequently coincide with declining stock performance of the write-off firm and, occasionally, its industry. To a lesser extent, accounting performance and macroeconomic factors appear to be related to write-offs. These relations are comparatively stable across different accounting regimes and time periods. Despite assertions that discretionary asset write-offs are primarily used to manipulate the financial statements, the evidence strongly suggests that firms record such charges during periods of poor performance. However, extant research has been criticized with respect to the validity of the variables used to capture economic developments behind write-offs. Where such variables are not modeled after the actual impairment test prescribed in the relevant accounting guidance, the interpretation of reported findings is open to debate. Consequently, emphasis will be placed in chapter 5 on selecting economic-factors variables that adequately depict, to the extent possible, the impairment testing procedure set down in SFAS 142.[915]

Financial reporting incentives also seem to play an important role in the write-off decision and the amount written off. Among the economic-consequences incentives, compensation considerations appear to be consistent with both accelerated write-offs in order to shelter future bonuses as well as delayed write-offs, aimed at smoothing the income

913 For a review of this paper, refer to Alciatore et al. (1998, p. 16).

914 For example, Francis, Hanna and Vincent (1996, p. 127) predict and find that "the importance of incentives in explaining write-offs depends on the existence of both independent sources of information for measuring impairment and authoritative guidance on when such impairment must be recognized."

915 Refer to section 5.2.2 below.

stream. In most cases, the variables used are not derived from actual compensation agreements; a fact that makes their interpretation difficult. The same is true for evidence on the debt covenant hypothesis, where the DTE ratio is largely relied upon as a proxy for the restrictiveness of actual covenants. Overall, evidence on the association of discretionary asset write-offs and economic-consequences incentives is inconsistent at best.[916] This result is not surprising: Applying economic-consequences hypotheses to discretionary asset write-off behavior is especially difficult because the extent to which such nonrecurring charges are allowed to affect the outcomes of accounting-based contracts is largely unclear, *a priori*, not only to the researcher, but possibly also to investors and even management. This caveat applies particularly to the SFAS 142 setting investigated here. Therefore, formulating hypotheses regarding managements' contracting-induced behavior must rely on prior research findings as well as economic reasoning regarding the strategic implications of transitional SFAS 142 goodwill write-off behavior.[917]

Capital market-related financial reporting incentives have long been ignored since they are not easily derived when the EMH is assumed to hold. However, such incentives have recently been found to account for financial reporting behavior that economic-consequences incentives have failed to explain. Thereby, recent research has increasingly acknowledged that theoretically and empirically irrelevant financial reporting decisions might nonetheless be made as long as decisions-making managers *believe* that they will have an effect.[918] Anecdotal evidence suggests that managers pursue a number of financial reporting strategies aimed at influencing capital market participants' perceptions. Some of these strategies have been found to be behind discretionary asset write-offs. For example, such charges have sporadically been related to income-smoothing behavior.

Although the broader earnings management literature documented overwhelming evidence that firms manage earnings to achieve certain targets, this notion has not played much of a role in the discretionary asset write-off research to date. However, the strategic implications (for future earnings) of such charges as well as the fact that investors might view them differently from other, more permanent earnings components suggests a vi-

---

916 In addition, even where such associations are found, inferences that manipulative earnings management is behind the findings might be misguided. Refer to section 3.3.2.3.6 above. A notable exception, the political costs hypothesis is not usually tested in the discretionary asset write-off research.

917 Refer to section 5.2.3.1 below.

918 See Fields, Lys and Vincent (2001, p. 260). In turn, these beliefs held by management might be influenced by theories about how capital markets work as well as by, for example, the financial press. Ultimately, the existence of financial reporting decisions aimed at "manipulating" capital market perceptions rests on the joint hypothesis that (1) management has a stake in firm value, and (2) believes that financial reporting decisions will affect firm value.

able avenue to be explored in this dissertation. In section 5.2.3.2.1 below, it is argued that the transitional SFAS 142 goodwill write-off behavior is influenced by management's interest in achieving *future* earnings targets. Due to their income-decreasing nature and their possible association with profit-enhancing corporate restructurings, discretionary asset write-offs uniquely lend themselves to being taken in the context of a "big bath"-type financial reporting strategy. Perhaps the most persistent finding in extant research is that write-offs are taken subsequent to changes in top management positions. While this result might be explained by new executives doing their job of terminating unprofitable lines of business, it is equally consistent with "big bath" behavior to signal an impending turnaround to investors.

Interested in the way investors actually perceive discretionary asset write-offs, extant research has documented convincingly that investors' reactions to write-off announcements depend on the information conveyed in the write-off announcement. Write-offs were frequently anticipated by investors and contributed to the alignment of book values and fair values. If they occurred unexpectedly, the market regularly punished write-off firms, except where the charges appeared to be part of an overall restructuring.

Although the research findings discussed in this chapter allow inferences to be drawn regarding managers' transitional SFAS 142 goodwill write-off behavior, the particular circumstances of this setting imply that these prior hypotheses cannot be adopted without modification. As noted by Francis, Hanna and Vincent (1996) and discussed in chapter 2 above, the goodwill asset has specific characteristics that distinguish it from other assets. Furthermore, the fact that transitional SFAS 142 goodwill write-offs are presented "below the line" as an accounting change might alter the way managers expect those charges to influence contractual outcomes and investors' perceptions. Furthermore, the specific discretionary parameters inherent in SFAS 142 must be taken into consideration in order to model adequately this financial reporting decision.[919] In section 5.2 below, testable predictions incorporating these aspects are derived.

---

919 A detailed analysis of these parameters is provided in chapter 4 below.

4 Discretionary properties of the impairment-only approach

4.1 Chapter overview

Detecting earnings management behavior is most likely to be successful when focusing on accounting items involving a high degree of discretion. In this sort of setting, earnings management behavior is relatively low-cost and therefore more likely to be observed. Such behavior is unlikely to be penalized, since management can argue that a given financial reporting decision is within the bounds of the authoritative literature.[920] For that reason, it can be expected that accounts with a high discretionary component will be most frequently used to achieve managers' financial reporting objectives. In a review of research design issues related to earnings management studies, McNichols (2000) suggests that future progress in this area is likely to come from studies of specific accruals, rather than from studies using aggregate accruals models.[921] Elliott and Shaw (1988) perceive that material, separately disclosed asset write-offs involve "greater discretion as to their magnitude and timing" than other types of accruals.[922] Consequently, they examine the relations between material write-offs, underlying economic events, and the goals of management regarding financial disclosures. For the same reason, Riedl (2002) argues that SFAS 142 write-offs are an adequate setting for an earnings management study.[923]

Contrary to the FASB's reasoning, critics of SFAS 142 argue that – especially due to the replacement of goodwill amortization by an impairment-only approach – this standard affords management unprecedented discretionary freedom regarding the accounting for goodwill.[924] Empirical research has addressed the question whether discretion increased or decreased as a result of the new standard. Henning, Shaw and Stock (2002) argue in

---

920 Refer to section 3.3.2.5 above.

921 See McNichols (2000, pp. 337-9).

922 Elliott and Shaw (1988, p. 92). See also Marquardt and Wiedman (2002).

923 See Riedl (2002, p. 4). See also Moehrle (2002, p. 399), who cites similar reasons for his conjecture that restructuring charges and subsequent reversals of such charges are a likely object of earnings management.

924 See Brecht (2002, pp. 212-8), Busse von Colbe (2001a), Busse von Colbe et al. (2003, p. 248), Gentz and Kauffmann (2003, pp. 81-93), Hitz and Kuhner (2002, p. 286), Hommel (2001a, p. 809), Hommel (2001b, p. 1948), Hütten and Lorson (2002, pp. 31-2), IDW (2001), Janschek (2002, pp. 15-6), Kahle (2002b, p. 902), Küting, Weber and Wirth (2002, pp. 65-6), Küting, Weber and Wirth (2001, pp. 196-8), Küting and Koch (2003, p. 54), Lückmann (2001), Pejic and Buschhüter (2001, pp. 111-2), Pellens and Sellhorn (2002a, p. 114), Pellens and Sellhorn (2002b), Pellens and Sellhorn (2001a, pp. 1685-6), Pellens and Sellhorn (2001b, p. 720), Pfeil and Vater (2002a, pp. 78-9), Pfeil and Vater (2002b, p. 588), Richter (2004), and Stauber and Ketterle (2001, p. 961). For the notion that this substantial discretion makes these rules difficult to audit, refer to Ruhnke (2003) and Schurbohm and Ganssauge (2003). Articles focusing explicitly on the discretionary elements inherent in SFAS 142 include Haring (2002) and Pfeil and Vater (2002c).

favor of a decrease in discretion compared to the pre-SFAS 142 regime.[925] Similar findings are reported by Segal (2003).[926] In the empirical study presented in chapter 5, the focus is placed on one specific accrual: Transitional goodwill write-offs under SFAS 142. This choice of research object is based on the notion that this is an exemplar of a discretionary accrual, particularly in the period of transition. Much of this chapter is dedicated to substantiating the notion that the subjective elements inherent in the new standards afford management a high degree of discretion with regard to goodwill write-off behavior.

While measuring the degree of discretion associated with a given account is a difficult task, a detailed understanding of the applicable accounting guidance and the financial reporting process allows an assessment of the managerial flexibility involved.[927] Therefore, this chapter provides a detailed analysis of the provisions in SFAS 142 and other relevant standards as they relate to the transitional goodwill impairment test.[928] Subsequent to a brief introduction of the new standards' main provisions (section 4.2), it seems appropriate to organize the following detailed analysis of discretionary elements around these issues:[929]

1. *Frequency* – How frequently is goodwill tested for impairment and what are the occasions that trigger a goodwill impairment test (section 4.3)?

2. *Level of aggregation* – What is the level of aggregation at which goodwill is allocated to sub units of the reporting entity for impairment testing (section 4.4)?

3. *Existence* – How is the existence of impairment determined (section 4.5)?

---

925 See Henning, Shaw and Stock (2002, p. 1).

926 See Segal (2003, pp. 8-9).

927 See Schipper (1989, p. 100).

928 For a brief overview of SFAS 142, see also Jennings, LeClere and Thompson (2001, pp. 21-2), Segal (2003, pp. 9-11), and most of the articles cited in fn. 924 above.

929 Riedl (2002, p. 5) uses a similar approach in his analysis of SFAS 121. This chapter is not intended to provide a detailed discussion of *all* the provisions in SFAS 142, let alone SFAS 141. A thorough analysis of a given rule is conditional on the extent to which that rule is relevant to goodwill write-off behavior, i.e. the existence, amount, and timing of any goodwill impairment loss. See SFAS 141.61. Equity method goodwill is also not considered here since it is not subject to the SFAS 142 goodwill impairment test. Instead, starting with the firm's adoption of SFAS 142 it is no longer amortized (SFAS 142.59), and reviewed for impairment in accordance with APB Opinion 18, *The Equity Method of Accounting for Investments in Common Stock.* See SFAS 142.40, which refers to APB Opinion 18.19 lit. h. Further, issues of initial recognition and measurement of goodwill under SFAS 141, including those related to determining the cost of the acquired entity (SFAS 141.20-34) and to allocating the cost of the acquired entity to assets acquired and liabilities assumed (SFAS 141.35-46) are beyond the scope of this chapter.

4. *Measurement* – How is the amount of an impairment loss measured, if any (section 4.6)?

5. *Transition* – How is the transition from an amortization approach to an impairment-only approach organized (section 4.7)?[930]

A summary of implications of this analysis and a discussion of factors that potentially limit management's financial reporting discretion in the adoption year conclude this chapter in section 4.8.

4.2 Main provisions of SFAS 141 and 142

SFAS 142 took effect for fiscal years beginning on or after December 15, 2001.[931] The beginning of the fiscal year was designated to be the date of initial application. Given that most public U. S. firms are calendar-year firms,[932] most entities initially applied SFAS 142 as of January 1, 2002. In other words, these firms had to use the information available to them as of January 1, 2002, to make the transitional SFAS 142 goodwill write-off decision and determine the amount, if any, to write off. The provisions that deal with the accounting for goodwill are codified in SFAS 142.18-40.

Goodwill amortization is eliminated in favor of what has come to be called an impairment-only or non-amortization[933] approach.[934] That is, goodwill is to be tested for impairment at least annually at a level of reporting referred to as a reporting unit.[935] The FASB was reluctant to abandon goodwill amortization although it agreed that "straight-line amortization of goodwill over an arbitrary period does not reflect economic reality and thus does not provide useful information".[936] However, board members' willingness to consider a non-amortization approach was contingent on the possibility of developing

---

930 The discussion of transition provisions includes issues of financial statement presentation that are argued here to be specifically influential on goodwill write-off behavior in the year of transition.

931 SFAS 142.48a. Early adoption was permitted for firms with fiscal years beginning after March 15, 2001, except when the first interim financial statements for the fiscal years had already been issued. With that provision, the FASB intended to ensure that early adopters would not switch to SFAS 142 half-way through an annual financial reporting period. Retroactive application was not permitted.

932 Out of 11,764 public firms included in the COMPUSTAT industrial annual database, 7,776 (66%) were calendar-year firms as of June 2002.

933 See Busse von Colbe (2001c).

934 Regardless of whether acquired before or after adoption of SFAS 142, amortization is prohibited for all of goodwill, starting with the date of adoption (SFAS 142.50).

935 See SFAS 142.18.

936 SFAS 142.B79.

a conceptually sound impairment test that would be rigorous enough to detect a decline in value. The two-step impairment testing procedure laid down in SFAS 142.19-25 is considered by the FASB to possess these qualities.[937] Its mechanics are summarized in Figure 11:[938]

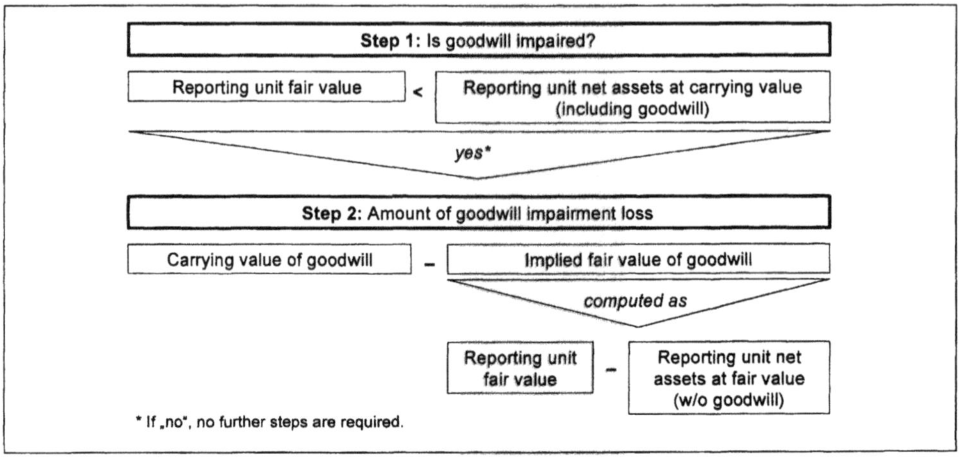

Figure 11: Goodwill impairment test procedure

The first step deals with the issue of recognition. It is used to identify a potential impairment by comparing the fair value of a reporting unit with its carrying amount, including goodwill.[939] The second step measures the amount of any goodwill impairment loss. It is "triggered" only when the first step indicates that reporting unit fair value is lower than its carrying amount, indicating that the goodwill assigned to the reporting unit under scrutiny might be impaired. The amount of any impairment loss is measured by weighing the implied fair value of goodwill against its carrying amount.[940]

The implied fair value of goodwill is a construct that accounts for the fact that goodwill cannot be measured separately since it does not exist apart from other assets. It is measured under the fiction that the reporting unit to which goodwill has been allocated is purchased at the date of the impairment test, with the purchase price being the reporting unit's fair value.[941] Allocating that notional purchase price to the fair value of the reporting unit's net assets (excluding goodwill) yields the implied fair value of goodwill, the

937 See SFAS 142.B95-100.

938 For details, refer to sections 4.5 and 4.6 below.

939 See SFAS 142.19.

940 See SFAS 142.20.

941 See SFAS 142.21.

residual. The goodwill impairment loss, if any, is the amount by which the carrying amount of goodwill exceeds its implied fair value. Consistent with other U. S. GAAP pronouncements, any impairment loss, once its measurement is completed, cannot be reversed.[942]

Any impairment loss resulting from initial application of SFAS 142 as of the transition date is to be presented in the financial statements as the effect of a change in accounting principle.[943] In contrast, regular impairment losses incurred after the initial impairment test has been completed are to be presented as a separate line item in the income statement as a component of income from continuing operations.[944]

4.3 Frequency

"Goodwill of reporting unit shall be tested for impairment on an annual basis and between annual tests in certain circumstances".[945] In this section, the discretionary parameters associated with the choice of annual test date and with the interpretation of impairment indicators are discussed.

4.3.1 Annual testing

4.3.1.1 Rule

The requirement of an annual test is rather straightforward and does not at first sight seem to give management any discretionary freedom. However, the annual impairment test may be conducted *at any time* during the fiscal year, and a different test date may be chosen for each reporting unit.[946] The transition provisions, discussed at length in section 4.7.2 below, require the *transitional* impairment test to be conducted as of the first of the year of initial application. Consequently, the first *regular* annual test must also be carried out within this first year, implying that two goodwill impairment tests must be conducted for each reporting unit within the transition year. This obligation to perform two parallel

---

942 See SFAS 142.20. This principle applies to most assets accounted for under U. S. GAAP. See Kieso, Weygandt and Warfield (2001, p. 564).

943 See SFAS 142.56.

944 See SFAS 142.43. Exempt from this rule are impairment losses associated with discontinued operations.

945 SFAS 142.26. The FASB had originally proposed a so-called "events-and-circumstances approach" that did not require annual testing but relied on triggering events alone. See SFAS 142.B137.

946 See SFAS 142.26. However, once chosen, the test dates for the different reporting units must remain fixed for each reporting unit in subsequent periods.

tests is only waived if the designated annual testing date for a reporting unit is the first of the year.[947]

Since firms are free to define arbitrary test dates for each reporting unit, management has the opportunity to strategically choose impairment test dates consistent with their financial reporting objectives. Assume that management's financial reporting strategy is to shift income from future periods to the present by avoiding/delaying/understating goodwill impairment losses. In this case, goodwill associated with reporting units that operate in seasonal industries are likely to be tested during a time of year when reporting unit fair value is highest, e.g. at the beginning of a cyclical high.[948] Conversely, if management intends to shift income from the present into future periods by recording/accelerating/overstating goodwill impairment losses, impairment test dates will be chosen to minimize reporting unit fair values. However, to the extent that financial reporting strategies change over time, the requirement to hold test dates constant in subsequent periods in effect limits management's discretion.[949]

4.3.1.2 Exception

SFAS 142 provides one exception to the annual testing rule: According to SFAS 142.27, the determination of reporting unit fair value can be carried forward from the previous goodwill impairment test under certain circumstances: First, the assets and liabilities that comprise the reporting unit "have not changed significantly" since reporting unit fair value was last determined.[950] Recent significant acquisitions or reorganizations of the segment reporting structure are given as examples of events that might lead to such a significant change. However, since only these two examples are given, management will possibly be justified in arguing that this first criterion is met whenever major acquisitions or reorganizations have not recently occurred. Further, the Board let it suffice to state that these events "might" significantly change a reporting unit's composition. This implies that there is elbowroom for management to argue that, under specific circumstances, a reporting unit has remained unchanged although a major acquisition and/or reorganiza-

---

947 See SFAS 142.58.

948 It could be argued that, given an infinite forecasting period, the date at which reporting unit fair vale is measured does not make a difference. However, in practice forecasting periods are usually shorter and terminal value is not necessarily defined as a perpetuity. Also, where reporting unit fair value is not measured as the present value of future cash flows, the timing of the measurement is likely to be relevant.

949 Refer to section 3.3.2.5 above.

950 See SFAS 142.27 lit a.

tion has recently taken place. Aided by such reasoning, management might be able to sidestep the testing requirement altogether in some years.

Second, when reporting unit fair value was determined in detail last time, it exceeded the reporting unit's carrying amount (including the carrying amount of the reporting unit's goodwill) "by a substantial margin".[951] It is not at all clear what constitutes a *substantial* margin. Given the potential sensitivity of reporting unit fair value, determined based on either quoted market price or some valuation method,[952] to changes in circumstances or valuation assumptions, it is likely that even a relatively large difference between reporting unit fair value and reporting unit carrying value may erode within a year's time.

Therefore, the third criterion requires that an analysis of events and changes in circumstances since the last determination of reporting unit fair value be conducted. Based on this analysis, the likelihood that the current reporting unit fair value is less than the carrying amount must be *remote*. According to SFAS 5, *Accounting for Contingencies*, the term "remote" implies that the "chance of the future event or events occurring is slight."[953] Application of this criterion inherently calls for management's subjective judgment regarding the occurrence probability of some event.[954]

In summary, SFAS 142.27 gives management the option to avoid the annual goodwill impairment test. The condition is that management successfully argues that there is no evidence to suggest that reporting unit fair value has declined below carrying amount since the last time both were determined and compared with each other. If so inclined, management can assert a certain minimum reporting unit fair value without actually measuring it, provided that three criteria are met. These criteria rely heavily on ill-specified terms such as "significant", "substantial", and "remote". While *remote* is arguably the most clear-cut of these terms, a great deal of discretion remains when management is required to apply it to real-life circumstances in order to make a likelihood assessment. This is even truer for the other two expressions, as is discussed in more detail below.

---

951 SFAS 142.27 lit b.

952 Refer to section 4.5.1.

953 SFAS 5.3 lit. c. See also SFAS 90, *Regulated Enterprises-Accounting for Abandonments and Disallowances of Plant Costs—an amendment of FASB Statement No. 71*, par. 9 lit. a, SFAS 114, *Accounting by Creditors for Impairment of a Loan*, par. 10, and SFAS 133.464.

954 For a fundamental discussion of the use of probability assessments in financial reporting, albeit in an IAS context, refer to Lüdenbach and Hoffmann (2003).

4.3.2 Unscheduled testing when circumstances warrant

Since a fixed test date each reporting period might preclude timely reporting when economic circumstances change, SFAS 142.28 provides a non-exhaustive list of impairment indicators:[955] These events and changes in circumstances that would *more likely than not* reduce reporting unit fair value below its carrying amount trigger additional impairment tests.[956] As shown below, most of these indicators are inherently subjective, in effect providing management with the opportunity to either actively seek or avoid additional, unscheduled impairment tests, depending on the financial reporting strategy pursued.

The first indicator is a "significant adverse change in legal factors or in the business climate".[957] The term "significant" is not defined in the context of SFAS 142. Thus, various perceptions are likely to exist regarding exactly what constitutes that type of event.[958] The term "significant", in contrast to the admittedly vague but well-understood financial accounting concept of materiality,[959] is used throughout the FASB's statements in a rather casual and not strictly defined manner. Two examples will demonstrate this: A reference to the term "significant" under U. S. GAAP is found in APB Opinion 18.17. The equity method of accounting is to be applied to an investment that gives the investor "the ability to exercise significant influence over operating and financial policies of an investee". The Board recognized that "determining the ability of an investor to exercise such influence is not always clear and applying judgment is necessary". Therefore, it established the rebuttable presumption that significant influence can be exercised when the investor controls between 20 and 50% of the investee's voting stock. Another reference to the term "significant" is found in SFAS 95, *Statement of Cash Flows*, where certain "significant noncash transactions" are to be omitted from the body of the statement and instead disclosed in the notes.[960] Existing does not provide sufficient guidance to strip the term "significant" of excessive subjectivity.[961]

---

955 See SFAS 142.B138.

956 Unscheduled impairment tests are also required in the period of initial application (SFAS 142.57).

957 SFAS 142.28 lit a.

958 Likewise, it is not clear how large a "portion of a reporting unit" or an "asset group within a reporting unit" must be in order to be deemed significant in the context of SFAS 142.28 lit. e and f, and by what criteria the size of a reporting unit is to be measured.

959 Refer to SFAC 2.123-132. See also Pellens (2001, p. 142).

960 See SFAS 95.32 and Kieso, Weygandt and Warfield (2001, pp. 1336-7).

961 It is not discussed whether the terms "significant" and "material" are equivalent, which would imply that, in SFAS 142.28 lit. a, an adverse change in legal factors or in the business climate is significant when "the judgment of a reasonable person" regarding the fair value of the reporting unit in question "would have been changed or influenced" by the knowledge of it (SFAC 2, Glossary).

According to SFAS 142.28 lit. e, a "more-likely-than-not expectation" that a (significant portion of a) reporting unit will be disposed of triggers an unscheduled impairment test. According to SFAS 109, *Accounting for Income Taxes*, the term *more likely than not* implies "a likelihood of more than 50 percent".[962] Although this definition seems, at first sight, to imply a relatively fixed cut-off point, the criterion is very open to management preferences since the likelihood of disposal is primarily determined by management's intent. Furthermore, deciding whether some future event is more likely than not to occur is much vaguer than applying criteria such as "remote"[963] that lean towards one end of the likelihood range. A clear judgment is only possible where the likelihood is either very small or very large, and a gray area exists in the center of the range.

Equally subjective are the following questions, to name but a few: When is competition "unexpected"?[964] What constitutes "key" personnel?[965] These questions cannot be answered without intimate knowledge of a company's business, and decisions based on them are therefore inherently difficult to verify. They demonstrate that management has the opportunity to exploit the information asymmetry that exists in its favor in judging whether or not an unscheduled impairment test is called for.

The two secondary criteria in SFAS 142.28 lit. f and g require an unscheduled impairment test under the condition that other financial reporting events have occurred elsewhere within the reporting entity. These criteria shift the discretion to the decision makers responsible for determining whether or not a significant asset group within a reporting unit is tested for impairment under SFAS 144[966] or a goodwill impairment loss is recognized in the separate financial statements of a subsidiary that is a component of a reporting unit. SFAS 144 contains a high degree of management flexibility in its own right, which, by this mechanism, is perpetuated for the purpose of applying SFAS 142.28 lit. f.

An unscheduled impairment test is only required when it is *more likely than not* that reporting unit fair value is reduced below its carrying amount because of the presence of one or more impairment indicators. The wording in SFAS 142.28 is somewhat ambigu-

---

[962] SFAS 109.17 lit. e, 97.

[963] SFAS 5.3 lit. c: "*Remote*. The chance of the future event or events occurring is slight." (Emphasis in original.)

[964] SFAS 142.28 lit. c.

[965] SFAS 142.28 lit. d.

[966] SFAS 144 superseded SFAS 121 for fiscal years beginning after December 15, 2001.

ous,[967] and allows different interpretations: First, one alternative is that the presence of any one of these indicators *in itself* is sufficient to assume that reporting unit fair value is more likely than not reduced below its carrying amount. Stated differently, under the first interpretation, the term "impairment indicator" means an event or change in circumstances that more likely than not reduces reporting unit fair value below its carrying amount. In that case, discretion does not go beyond that already described above. Impairment indicators would trigger an unscheduled impairment test regardless of how high reporting unit fair value was *before* the impairment indicator occurred.

Second, another reading would imply that management is not only required to determine whether these indicators are present, but also to judge the extent to which their presence is likely to influence reporting unit fair value. This interpretation suggests that an "impairment indicator" is an event or change in circumstances that might or might not be more likely than not to reduce reporting unit fair value below its carrying amount. The discretion inherent in the "more-likely-than-not" condition, which is invoked again here, has been discussed above. Determining the likelihood of a reduction of reporting unit fair value below its carrying amount also requires some preconception regarding how high reporting unit fair value was before the event or change in circumstances occurred. The obligation to conduct unscheduled impairment tests would mainly hinge on management's estimate of reporting unit fair value *before* that value had actually been measured.[968] This "second-guessing" about the likelihood of impairment has been a powerful argument against an "events-and-circumstances approach" to goodwill impairment testing, under which impairment tests would not have been required annually but only in the presence of impairment indicators.[969]

Since the list contained in SFAS 142.28 is non-exhaustive, management is free to find additional impairment indicators that it thinks are more likely than not to have reduced reporting unit fair value below its carrying amount. To the extent that timely/accelerated recognition of goodwill impairment losses is consistent with management's financial reporting strategy, management has incentive to adduce events and circumstances other than those listed as impairment indicators. Overall, while some discretion exists in the context of impairment indicators, the effect of this discretion on goodwill write-off be-

---

967 SFAS 142.28: "Goodwill of a reporting unit shall be tested for impairment between annual tests if an event occurs or circumstances change that would more likely than not reduce the fair value of a reporting unit below its carrying amount. Examples of *such* events or circumstances include ..." (emphasis added).

968 The problem is similar to that discussed in section 4.3.1.2.

969 See SFAS 142.B140.

havior is not very severe since SFAS 142.26 ensures that impairment tests are conducted annually, regardless of the presence of impairment indicators. The discretion inherent in the frequency provisions can mainly be exploited to accelerate goodwill impairment losses, if desired. The notable exception is the provision in SFAS 142.27, which enables management to avoid the goodwill impairment test altogether when certain criteria are met.

4.4 Level of aggregation

The level of aggregation on which goodwill impairment tests are conducted allows management to influence the likelihood that any goodwill impairment will be detected in step one of the impairment test. According to SFAS 142.18, goodwill shall be tested for impairment at a level of reporting referred to as a *reporting unit*. As shown in Figure 12 and explained in more detail below, a reporting unit is either an operating segment according to par. 10 of SFAS 131, *Disclosures about Segments of an Enterprise and Related Information*, or a component, i.e. one level below an operating segment.[970]

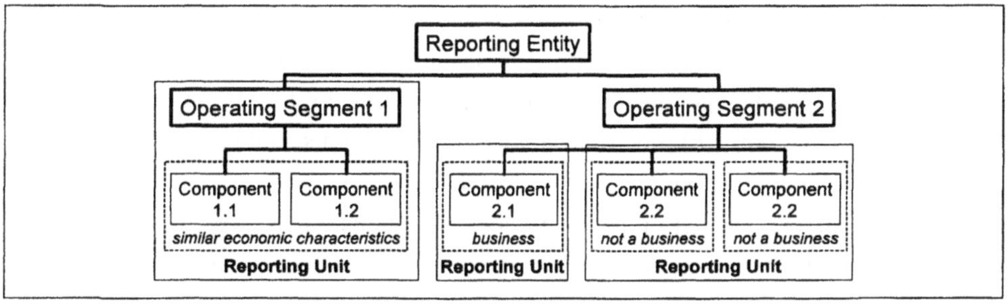

Figure 12: Defining reporting units

SFAS 131.10 defines an operating segment as a component of an enterprise that engages in business activities from which it may earn revenues and incur expenses, whose operating results are regularly reviewed by the enterprise's chief operating decision maker to decide about resource allocation and performance assessment, and for which separate financial information is available.[971] Under this so-called "management approach",[972]

[970] See SFAS 142.30. See also Hitz and Kuhner (2002, pp. 275-6), Küting, Weber and Wirth (2001, p. 186), and Lüdenbach and Frowein (2003, pp. 218-9).

[971] For an analysis of SFAS 131, refer to Williams (2002, ch. 43).

firms rely for external financial reporting purposes on data generated and used in the context of their internal control and reporting structures.[973] A firm's organizational and financial reporting decisions are likely to be jointly determined and influenced by management's incentives as well as considerations of organizational efficiency.[974] Therefore, while the management approach to defining operating segments (and, therefore, reporting units) gives management considerable discretion, it is unlikely that earnings management incentives will be the only or even the most influential determinant of a firm's organizational set-up. Stated differently, management will establish and maintain an organizational set-up that maximizes the utility derived from earnings management, efficiency, and other incentives.

Under certain circumstances, firms are required to use *components*, i.e. organizational units below the operating segment level, as reporting units. "A component of an operating segment is a reporting unit if the component constitutes a *business* for which discrete financial information is available and segment management regularly reviews the operating results of that component."[975] The definition of "business" is contained in EITF Issue 98-03, *Determining Whether a Nonmonetary Transaction Involves Receipt of Productive Assets or of a Business*: "A business is a self-sustaining integrated set of activities and assets conducted and managed for the purpose of providing a return to investors. A business consists of (a) inputs, (b) processes applied to those inputs, and (c) resulting outputs that are used to generate revenues."[976] As a result, whenever an operating segment consists of several distinct smaller units that amount to separate businesses and are reviewed on a regular basis by one or more segment managers,[977] these components are to be used as reporting units for the purpose of applying SFS 142.

---

972 This term was coined by the FASB in SFAS 131. According to par. 4, the "management approach is based on the way that management organizes the segments within the enterprise for making operating decisions and assessing performance." In contrast to prescribing the exact nature and extent of disclosures, the Board gives management what it intends to be a cost-effective and timely opportunity to disclose the "information that an enterprise's decision makers use to make decisions about the enterprise's operating matters" (SFAS 131.5).

973 For a discussion in the context of SFAS 142, see also Hitz and Kuhner (2002, p. 276), Lüdenbach and Frowein (2003, pp. 218-9), and Nestler and Thuy (2002, pp. 170-1).

974 Refer to section 3.3.2.3.6 above.

975 SFAS 142.30 (emphasis added).

976 EITF Issue 98-03.6. Further guidance is provided on the definitions of inputs, processes, and outputs.

977 According to SFAS 131.14, a *segment manager* is "directly accountable to and maintains regular contact with the chief operating decision maker to discuss operating activities, financial results, forecasts, or plans for the segment. The term segment manager identifies a function, not necessarily a manager with a specific title."

This guidance is another example of a rigorous management approach, because it implies that firms are not required to allocate goodwill to components below the operating segment level when either no discrete financial information is available for them or their operating results are not reviewed on a regular basis by senior executives who fit the definition of "segment management". In other words, the guidance suggests that firms with inappropriate internal reporting systems and/or neglectful management are spared the potentially costly requirement of breaking down their operating segments into components. They are apparently not required to generate and review component data for application of SFAS 142 unless they are already doing so for internal control purposes.

SFAS 142.30 states an exception to the above rule: Two or more components are to be aggregated to a single reporting unit if they have *similar economic characteristics*. In determining whether several components have similar economic characteristics, firms are referred to the "aggregation criteria" given in SFAS 131.17 for defining reportable segments. However, this guidance is rather unclear about what constitutes similar economic characteristics. The criteria listed in SFAS 131.17[978] cannot be meant as indicators of economic similarity since their presence is required *over and above* the similar economic characteristics of the reporting segments.[979] Also, similar performance and margin measures across segments are not necessarily indicators, but may or may not be *results* of several segments' similar economic characteristics.[980] Overall, since the guidance on similar economic characteristics provided in SFAS 142.30 and, by reference, in SFAS 131.17, is rather vague, it is at management's discretion whether components of operating segments are aggregated to form a larger reporting unit.

This subjectivity has fundamental implications for the likelihood of impairment being found. The higher the level of aggregation at which reporting units are formed, the larger is the probability that a goodwill value decrease in one sub-set of a reporting unit is com-

---

978 The list includes criteria such as the nature of the products, services, and of the production process, customer types, and distribution methods.

979 SFAS 131.17: "Two or more operating segments may be aggregated into a single operating segment if aggregation is consistent with the objective and basic principles of this Statement, if the segments have similar economic characteristics, *and* if the segments are similar in each of the following areas: [...]" (emphasis added).

980 SFAS 131.17: "For example, similar long-term average gross margins for two operating segments would be expected if their economic characteristics were similar."

pensated by an increase in the value of (internally generated) goodwill in another.[981] Therefore, the level at which an entity initially defines its reporting units determines to a large extent the likelihood of goodwill write-offs occurring in later periods.[982] This conclusion is also reached by Henning, Shaw and Stock (2002), who state that "a narrower unit of analysis is likely to reduce managerial discretion, resulting in more impairment."[983] Depending on management's financial reporting strategy, incentives might exist to avoid/delay/understate any transitional SFAS 142 goodwill write-offs. In this case, management would have incentive to argue, for example, that any components existing below the reporting segment level either do not constitute businesses or have similar economic characteristics. Overall, the guidance on defining reporting units is very discretionary, owing in part to the rigorous implementation of the management approach.

4.5 Existence

The first step of the goodwill impairment test is designed to determine whether impairment is present *at all*. According to SFAS 142.19, the fair value of a reporting unit is compared with its carrying amount, including goodwill. It is only when the carrying amount exceeds the fair value that the second test step is to be performed because, in that event, impairment is assumed to exist. Consequently, the main discretionary elements inherent in the testing procedure itself relate, first, to determining reporting unit fair value and, second, to assigning the carrying amounts of assets, liabilities, and goodwill to reporting units.[984]

---

981 SFAS 142.B86 states that "the higher the level of review, the more difficult it would be to develop a robust impairment test". Osterland (2002) points out that "large companies with multiple business units and little existing [purchased] goodwill have an advantage over smaller companies in the acquisition market." The impact of aggregation on measuring impairment is also discussed in Braun, Rohan and Yospe's (1991) article on the FASB's standard-setting process preceding SFAS 121. See also Kahle (2002b, p. 902), Küting, Weber and Wirth (2001, p. 192), Pfeil and Vater (2002c, p. 262), and Pfeil and Vater (2002a, p. 71).

982 SFAS 142.B84-7. For a numerical example, refer to Pellens and Sellhorn (2001a, pp. 1685-6). Braun, Rohan and Yospe (1991, p. 68) conclude that "the manner in which assets are grouped can have a dramatic impact on the writeoff amount of an asset impairment."

983 Henning, Shaw and Stock (2002, p. 7).

984 Special problems arise where portions of reporting units are disposed of and where reporting units include subsidiaries that are not wholly owned by the reporting entity. These latter problems of impairment testing in the presence of non-controlling (minority) interests are not discussed in detail. Instead, refer to SFAS 142.38, Pellens and Sellhorn (2003), Küting, Weber and Wirth (2001, p. 192), and Lüdenbach and Frowein (2003, pp. 221-2).

4.5.1 Reporting unit fair value

According to SFAS 142.19, the guidance in SFAS 142.23-25 is relevant in determining reporting unit fair value.[985] The concept of fair value is applied in SFAS 142.23 to reporting units using a quote from the glossary of SFAC 7, *Using Cash Flow Information and Present Value in Accounting Measurements*, which defines fair value of an asset or liability as the "amount at which that asset (or liability) could be bought (or incurred) or sold (or settled) in a current transaction between willing parties, that is, other than in a forced or liquidation sale."[986]

SFAS 142.23-25 establish a fair value hierarchy applicable to reporting units:

1. *Quoted market prices* in active markets are the best evidence of fair value and shall be used as the basis for the measurement, if available."[987]

2. "If quoted market prices are not available, the estimate of fair value shall be based on the best information available, including prices for similar assets and liabilities and the results of using other valuation techniques. A *present value technique* is often the best available technique with which to estimate the fair value of a group of net assets (such as a reporting unit)."[988]

3. "In estimating the fair value of a reporting unit, a valuation technique based on *multiples of earnings or revenue* or a similar performance measure may be used if that technique is consistent with the objective of measuring fair value."[989]

Subjective elements inherent in these fair value measurements are discussed in the following sections.

---

985 As has been discussed at length in section 4.3.1.2 above, reporting unit fair value can be carried over from the previous goodwill impairment test when certain criteria are met (SFAS 142.27).

986 Stated differently, fair value can be characterized as a present value measurement that attempts to "capture the elements that taken together would comprise a market price if one existed" (SFAC 7.25). In German terms, the concept of fair value is closest to the measurement construct of "beizulegender Zeitwert". See, for example, German Accounting Standard (GAS) 4.7: "Betrag, zu dem im Bewertungszeitpunkt zwischen geschäftsbereiten und sachverständigen Geschäftspartnern ein Vermögenswert ausgetauscht oder eine Schuld beglichen werden kann."

987 SFAS 142.23 (emphasis added).

988 SFAS 142.24 (emphasis added).

989 SFAS 142.25 (emphasis added).

4.5.1.1 Quoted market prices

Where equity securities of a reporting unit are publicly traded, quoted market prices are the preferable measure of reporting unit fair value.[990] However, since in most cases only a relatively small portion of a given reporting unit's equity is publicly traded,[991] proportionally extrapolating the reporting unit's market capitalization may not be a good indicator of the reporting unit's overall fair value.[992] The Board acknowledges that this notion seems to contradict SFAS 115, *Accounting for Certain Investments in Debt and Equity Securities*, and SFAS 133, *Accounting for Derivative Instruments and Hedging Activities*, according to which fair value is the product of the number of trading units times market price per trading unit.[993]

However, the Board argues that due to the existence of a *control premium*,[994] the quoted market price of, for example, 30% of a reporting unit's stock may be significantly less than 30% of its fair value as a whole.[995] An acquirer of a controlling 70% stake in a reporting unit may be willing to pay more than 70% of the reporting unit's overall fair value, since the ability to exercise control[996] over the operations of the reporting unit may be of substantial value to the acquirer,[997] for example because it could give rise to synergies between the acquirer's and the reporting unit's operations.[998]

By allowing firms to deviate from quoted market prices when determining reporting unit fair value even where those prices are available, the FASB prefers (allegedly) relevant measures of fair value over reliable, verifiable ones.[999] This decision results in consider-

---

990 For a discussion of the role of quoted market prices in company valuation, refer to Böcking and Nowak (2000).

991 A reporting unit, as defined in SFAS 142 (refer to section 4.4 above), does not necessarily constitute a separate legal entity.

992 See SFAS 142.23.

993 See SFAS 142.B154. Refer also to SFAS 133.540 (glossary), 534 lit j. (amendment of SFAS 115.137).

994 See, for example, Küting and Leinen (2002, p. 1203). For an empirical approach to estimating such premiums, refer to Henning, Lewis and Shaw (2000).

995 See also Hitz and Kuhner (2002, p. 278).

996 See SFAS 94, *Consolidation of All Majority-owned Subsidiaries*, par. 13.

997 See, for example, von Wysocki and Wohlgemuth (1996, p. 124).

998 See SFAS 142.23 fn. 16.

999 See SFAC 7.17, 73. Even where quoted market prices for reporting unit are available and deemed to be relevant, it is unclear whether valuation should be based on stock price at some *point* in time or on an average price measured over a certain *period*. See, for example, Nestler and Thuy (2002, p. 173) with further references.

able room for management judgment and argumentation. As will be discussed next, the following stages in the fair value hierarchy are increasingly subjective.[1000]

4.5.1.2 Present value techniques

4.5.1.2.1 Measuring fair value as the objective

Where quoted market prices are either unavailable or deemed inappropriate for measuring reporting unit fair value, SFAS 142.24 requires firms to revert to valuation methods.[1001] Preference is given to present value techniques, as long as the cash flow estimates used are consistent with the objective of measuring fair value.[1002] SFAS 142.24 includes structural guidance from SFAC 7 for measuring present values.[1003] It is required that a present value measurement consistent with determining fair value incorporates the following elements:

1. An estimate of the future cash flow, or in more complex cases, series of future cash flows at different times.
2. Expectations about possible variations in the amount or timing of those cash flows.
3. The time value of money, represented by the risk-free rate of interest.
4. The price for bearing the uncertainty inherent in the asset or liability.
5. Other, sometimes unidentifiable, factors including illiquidity and market imperfections.[1004]

In order to be consistent with the objective of measuring fair value and thereby achieve some degree of objectivity and verifiability, cash flow estimates are to include assump-

---

[1000] This circumstance was deplored by some of the respondents to the FASB's revised exposure draft *Business Combinations and Intangible Assets – Accounting for Goodwill.* See SFAS 142.B151.

[1001] The terms *measurement technique* and *valuation method* are considered to be synonymous. The application of methods of company valuation to the SFAS 142 impairment-only approach is discussed at length in AAA's Financial Accounting Standards Committee (2001), Frowein and Lüdenbach (2003), Lüdenbach and Schulz (2002), Mard et al. (2002), Mercer Capital (2001), Nestler and Thuy (2002), Richter (2004, ch. 6) and Schultze (2003).

[1002] See also SFAC 7.25.

[1003] See, for example, Hitz and Kuhner (2000) and Starbatty (2001). Also, refer to the FASB's four-article "Understanding the Issues" series on SFAC 7, available at www.fasb.org. /articles&reports.

[1004] See SFAC 7.23, 39. See also Hitz and Kuhner (2002, p. 278).

tions that *marketplace participants* would use in their estimates of fair value.[1005] This requirement to use third-party assumptions represents an attempt to limit management's financial reporting discretion by enhancing the degree of both reliability and relevance of the fair value measures generated. It has the effect that synergies among different reporting units are not part of the fair value measurements.[1006]

However, where these assumptions are not available without undue cost and effort, management may use *its own* assumptions, as long as they are "reasonable and supportable" and "all available evidence" is considered.[1007] The conditions under which costs and efforts of obtaining information on market participants' assumptions can be regarded as "undue" are somewhat vague. In effect, managers may use their own estimates, as long as there is no information indicating that marketplace participants would use different assumptions. If such information exists, management must adjust its assumptions to incorporate that market information.[1008] According to SFAC 7.38, the objective of measuring fair value is not violated under these circumstances. Interestingly, SFAC 7 24 lit. b indicates that a measurement based on management's own estimates, expectations and other assumptions, as opposed to those of market-place participants, is not strictly a fair value measurement. It is in fact referred to as a *value-in-use* or *entity-specific value*.

This discussion indicates that the borders between different types of measurements, each having different measurement objectives,[1009] are fairly indistinct. It is doubtful that the guidance given in SFAS 142.24 will ensure that market-based assumptions are consistently used in measuring reporting unit fair value and, thereby, that the resulting measures can be characterized as fair values in the sense of SFAC 7. In summary, whereas the FASB, via SFAC 7, prescribes the elements and variables to be considered when using present value techniques for measuring fair value, it is left entirely up to management

1005 SFAC 7.24 lit. a explicitly states that a fair value measurement captures all of the five elements listed in SFAC 7.23, using the estimates and expectations of marketplace participants rather than those of management.

1006 See Hitz and Kuhner (2002, pp. 280-1), Hommel (2001b, p. 1946), Kahle (2002a, p. 854), Küting, Weber and Wirth (2001, p. 189), and Nestler and Thuy (2002, p. 177).

1007 SFAS 142.24 (both quotes).

1008 See SFAS 142.B155.

1009 As noted in SFAC 7.24 lit. b fn. 4, the "entity-specific value ... can be characterized as the amount at which independent willing parties that share the same information and ability to generate the entity's estimated cash flows would agree to a transaction that exchanges the estimated future cash flows for a current amount." This definition is quite different from that of fair value, which is given in the glossary to SFAC 7 (see quote above).

exactly what parameter values it chooses to assign to those variables.[1010] Projecting uncertain future cash flows, earnings, or other input data and choosing appropriate discount rates is a difficult task even for those attempting to generate unbiased results. In effect, management is safe in using business plans based almost entirely on its own assumption regarding the five elements listed above.

4.5.1.2.2 Measurement techniques

SFAS 142.24 gives firms considerable discretion regarding their choice of valuation method, as long as the approach used is consistent with the objective of measuring fair value. Two different approaches to computing present value are explicitly referred to in SFAC 7.40: When the preferred *expected cash flow approach* is used, the discount rate is intended to capture only the time value of money. Therefore, a risk-free interest rate is applied and cash flows are included at their expected values to incorporate uncertainty and risk. Under the *traditional approach*, the discount rate captures all uncertainty surrounding future cash flows, including a risk premium, whereas cash flows are not adjusted for any of these elements.[1011] While the guidance in SFAS 142 implies that the equity variant of the discounted-cash-flow (DCF) method be used,[1012] it is argued that both the entity *and* equity approaches can accommodate the standard's requirements.[1013]

However, applicable techniques are not limited to DCF methods. During the standard-setting deliberations, the Board also considered approaches based on market capitalization, residual income, and performance measures such as cash-flow return on investment

---

[1010] See SFAS 142.B153. A different approach is pursued in the British FRS 11, *Impairment of Fixed Assets and Goodwill*, which provides concrete guidance on estimating cash flows, e.g. growth rate assumptions. The FASB decided against this approach based on the argument that such guidance could interfere with the objective of measuring fair value, since cash flows used to measure fair value should be estimated according to the management approach, i.e. based on "the most recent budgets and plans approved by management". However, the Board did indicate that "some consideration should be given to industry trends" (SFAS 142.B152 [both quotes]).

[1011] Under German terminology, the first approach is referred to as the "Sicherheitsäquivalenzmethode", whereas the second method corresponds to the German "Risikozuschlagsmethode". For an introduction to these concepts, refer to Mandl and Rabel (1997, pp. 218-22, 226-35, respectively) and the cited literature. See also Starbatty (2001, p. 545).

[1012] The equity and entity variants of the DCF method are discussed in Hachmeister (2000, pp. 118-23), Hachmeister (1996) and Mandl and Rabel (1997, pp. 37-43). For a brief overview of valuation methods that are potentially consistent with the requirements of SFAS 142, refer to Nestler and Thuy (2002, pp. 172-9).

[1013] See, for example, Lüdenbach and Frowein (2003, p. 222).

(CFROI) and economic value added (EVA),[1014] all of which were deemed to be consistent with the objective of measuring reporting unit fair value. According to the Board's credo, "entities should be permitted to use a valuation method with which they are familiar, providing that the result is consistent with the objective of fair value",[1015] and SFAS 142 was intended to "allow preparers latitude in applying that objective to their specific circumstances based on the guidance in Concepts Statement 7."[1016] It appears clear that encouraging firms to apply virtually any present value-based valuation technique imaginable to their own estimates, expectations, and assumptions, guided only by the sketchy catch-all reference in SFAC 7 to the objective of fair value measurement, is likely to make "reporting unit fair value" an extremely discretionary variable.

The AAA's Financial Accounting Standards Committee (2001) concludes that most techniques permitted under SFAS 142.24 are compromised by incorrect forecasts of future cash flows and are susceptible to other weaknesses like the inappropriate specification of discount rates and terminal values. Regardless of the concrete model used, the valuation process relies heavily on management's expectations about future developments and events. Detailed specification of acceptable methodology and abstract valuation model structure cannot constrain management from exercising substantial discretion when determining what values to assign to the prescribed parameters. Furthermore, even where management acts in all conscience, attempting to estimate reporting unit fair value to the best of its knowledge, the problems associated with estimating uncertain future cash flows and cost of capital are, in itself, severe. This abundance of subjectivity, combined with uncertainty, makes the resulting estimates open to criticism with regard to both relevance and reliability. The FASB is aware of these caveats but deliberately decided against providing more guidance.[1017]

It is doubtful that the requirement to incorporate marketplace participants' assumptions is sufficient eliminate much of the inherent judgment. For reporting unit fair value to represent "the amount at which the unit as a whole could be bought or sold in a current transaction between willing parties",[1018] the only relevant assumptions would be those of management and potential buyers. For reporting units whose disposal is not imminent,

---

1014 For a description of some of these methods and their appropriateness in the context of goodwill impairment testing, refer to AAA's Financial Accounting Standards Committee (2001) and Nestler and Thuy (2002, pp. 172-9).

1015 SFAS 142.B150.

1016 SFAS 142.B153.

1017 See SFAS 142.B151.

1018 SFAS 142.23.

only management's assumptions will be readily available. Also, in a transaction between willing parties, synergies are likely to play a major role in the purchase price negotiations. Since the amount of synergies depends heavily on the identity of the potential buyer, incorporating the assumptions of marketplace participants will only be meaningful in the rare event that the potential buyer is known.

4.5.1.3 Multiples

SFAS 142.25 permits the use of valuation techniques based on "multiples of earnings or revenue or a similar performance measure". Again, the methods applied must be consistent with the objective of measuring fair value. The FASB restricts the use of these techniques to circumstances where "the fair value of an entity that has comparable operations and economic characteristics is observable and the relevant multiples of the comparable entity are known."[1019] However, SFAS 142.24 does not indicate whether these known multiples must in all cases be derived from stock price or other market data. For example, the popular P/E multiple is the ratio of stock price divided by earnings. This would strictly imply that the P/E multiple can only be used where stock price and earnings data of publicly traded comparable firms are observable.[1020]

A wide range of these valuation models is available and used in practice.[1021] All of these methods are based on the "law of one price", an economic rule which states that in an efficient market, a security must have a single price, no matter how that security is created. Applied to firm valuation, it implies that two identical or at least closely comparable firms cannot have widely different prices, or otherwise arbitrage opportunities would arise.[1022] Based on this assumption, it is argued that comparable firms are priced at fixed multiples of their earnings, cash flows or other performance measures.[1023]

1019 SFAS 142.25.

1020 As the common term "market multiples" suggests, valuation based on these methods usually relies on data derived from stock prices or other market transactions. See, for example, Coenenberg and Schultze (2002a, p. 697) and Mandl and Rabel (1997, p. 265).

1021 See, for example, Aders, Galli and Wiedemann (2000), Bausch (2000), Böcking and Nowak (1999), Hillebrandt (2001), Mandl and Rabel (1997, pp. 265-74), and Seppelfricke (1999). Also, refer to Damodaran (1996).

1022 See Coenenberg and Schultze (2002a, p. 697).

1023 Instead of a performance measure or similar flow figure, the book value of equity or other accounting-based stock figures are sometimes used. However, since SFAS 142.25 explicitly refers to multiples based on performance measures, these variants are not discussed here.

The multiple approach comprises three basic steps:[1024] First, a comparative company or transaction[1025] is identified. Several dimensions, along which comparability can be judged, are conceivable, e.g. same industry, size, or market position. Due to the multitude of attributes by which firms and transactions can be distinguished, finding a truly comparable firm or transaction is especially problematic.[1026] Second, the relevant performance measure is ascertained and the multiple calculated. Performance measures mainly used besides earnings include income statement sub-totals such as revenues, earnings before interest, taxes, depreciation, and amortization (EBITDA), and earnings before interest and taxes (EBIT), or cash flow figures such as free cash flow (FCF) and flow to equity (FTE). Frequently, several comparable companies or transactions are considered and averaged. Finally, the value figure is computed by applying the multiple to the performance measure.[1027]

Valuation techniques based on multiples might at first sight appear to generate relatively objective and verifiable results, since they resort to market-based measures such as stock prices or prices generated in other market transactions. However, the appropriateness of multiples for valuation purposes critically hinges not only on management's ability to identify comparable companies or transactions, but also on data availability. Where no data is available for the first-best comparison firm, management might be tempted to use sub-optimal benchmarks. Also, since the reporting unit to be valued and the comparable firm from which the multiple is observed are usually not equally sized, the accurateness of the valuation depends on whether the relation between the firm value measure and the performance measure is proportional.[1028] Special problems arise when transaction prices are used. These may be distorted due to transaction-specific circumstances, such as control premiums paid in acquisitions or the value of synergies that is (partly) reimbursed in the purchase consideration,[1029] which might not be applicable to the reporting unit at is-

---

1024 See, for example, Hillebrandt (2001, p. 618).

1025 Transactions include recent mergers, acquisitions or (initial) public offerings.

1026 See Coenenberg and Schultze (2002a, p. 698). Nestler and Thuy (2002, pp. 174-5) note that unlisted reporting units should be valued at a discount compared with their publicly traded comparatives.

1027 It is important to assure that the value figure is consistent with the performance measure. For example, a performance measure to which only shareholders are entitled, e.g. net income, will generate a measure of the firm's equity value. Conversely, if a performance measure such as FCF is used, the firm value generated will represent the market values of both equity and liabilities (so-called enterprise value).

1028 See Bausch (2000, p. 451).

1029 See Coenenberg and Schultze (2002a, p. 698).

sue. For these reasons, reporting unit fair values arrived at by using multiples will have a distinct discretionary component.[1030]

4.5.1.4 Preliminary conclusion

Since the majority of reporting units of SFAS 142 adopters are not publicly traded,[1031] firms will largely apply present value methods and/or market multiples to determine reporting unit fair value in the context of step one of the impairment test. The range of available methods is depicted in Figure 13. Having extensive control over the determinants of present value as well as over the parameters used in the market multiple approach, management will be able to justify a wide range of reporting unit fair values.[1032] This is especially true since the results are very sensitive to (changes in) underlying assumptions regarding growth and other determinants of terminal value, interest rates, and inter-company comparability.[1033]

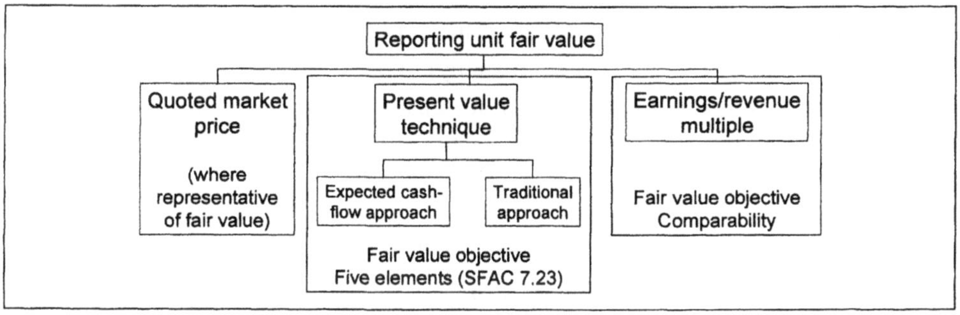

Figure 13: Hierarchy of reporting unit fair value measurements

Reporting unit fair value determines to a large extent the outcome of the first test step, i.e. whether the second test step is "triggered" because a potential goodwill impairment loss is assumed to exist. For that reason, management has a strong incentive to influence reporting unit fair value to conform to its financial reporting strategy. If management's incentive is to avoid/delay/understate a goodwill impairment loss, it will use assumptions

1030 Due to the shortcomings of this concept, the use of market multiples in practice is usually limited to providing plausibility checks for values generated using more elaborate techniques, and making quick "back-of-the-envelope" calculations. See Coenenberg and Schultze (2002b, pp. 602-3), who are therefore critical of firms using multiples as the only measure in applying SFAS 142. Also, refer to Lüdenbach and Schulz (2002, pp. 494-5) and Nestler and Thuy (2002, p. 175).

1031 Even where a reporting unit is publicly traded, stock price need not be the relevant fair value measure. Refer to section 4.5.1.1 above.

1032 See also Busse von Colbe (2001a) and Hitz and Kuhner (2002, p. 283). In a more general context, Ordelheide (1997, p. 584) and Moxter (2001) arrive at the same conclusion.

1033 See also Küting, Weber and Wirth (2001, p. 189).

and data to maximize reporting unit fair value. Conversely, management will rely on pessimistic scenarios when it intends to recognize/accelerate/overstate a goodwill impairment loss.

4.5.2 Carrying value of reporting unit net assets

The second variable required to complete the first test step is the carrying value of the reporting unit's net assets, including goodwill. This value is derived from the carrying values of the reporting entity's assets, liabilities, and goodwill as a whole. The requirement of allocating these items to the reporting unit level creates significant elbowroom for management, as will be discussed below.

4.5.2.1 Allocating assets and liabilities

The guidance provided in SFAS 142.32-3 focuses on the case of assigning the assets acquired and liabilities assumed in a recent acquisition to the firm's reporting units.[1034] Two conditions must be met for an asset (liability) to be allocated to a reporting unit:[1035] First, the asset (liability) will be employed in (relates to) the operations of a reporting unit. Second, the asset or liability will be considered in determining the fair value of the reporting unit.

In some cases, it should be relatively clear to which reporting unit the assets and liabilities from a recent acquisition relate. For example, if an acquired entity is not integrated into the acquirer's operations but operated as a stand-alone reporting unit, the assets and liabilities originally acquired will naturally be assigned to that unit. The same is true when an acquired entity is grouped with a pre-existing reporting unit to form a part of it. However, if an acquired entity is integrated across several reporting units, complex allocation problems arise that are not likely to be solved by the criteria described above. For these instances, SFAS 142.33 requires that assets (liabilities) that are employed in (relate to) the operations of multiple reporting units be assigned to those reporting units according to a methodology that is "reasonable and supportable" and consistently applied. This requirement is rather vague and gives management considerable discretion in determining a reporting unit's net asset base and, thereby, the outcome of the first test step. For example, if an acquired brand name is expected to benefit several of a firm's geographi-

---

1034 The allocation of the entity's pre-existing assets and liabilities to reporting units upon initial application of SFAS 142 is specifically governed by SFAS 142.54, which refers to the guidance in SFAS 142.32-3.

1035 See SFAS 142.32.

cally divided reporting units, allocation will be have to be based on some measure of future benefits that each of the reporting units is likely to derive from that brand name. Present value techniques are likely to be employed here, with all the discretionary components inherent in these procedures.[1036] In general, all assets that are expected to generate synergies for several reporting units are difficult to allocate.[1037] Likewise, liabilities are equally problematic to assign.[1038]

In the special case of corporate items, i.e. assets or liabilities that are used at the reporting unit's top organizational level and are not easily broken down to the reporting unit level, SFAS 142.32 requires allocation to a reporting unit if both of the above criteria are met. Examples where the criteria are considered to be met are "environmental liabilities that relate to an existing operating facility of the reporting unit and a pension obligation that would be included in the determination of the fair value of the reporting unit."[1039] However, due to the unique characteristics of corporate items, i.e. their inherent relation to the entity level and not to some lower level, it is doubtful whether the above criteria *ever* apply to true corporate times or, stated differently, whether assets and liabilities that meet the above criteria are corporate items at all.[1040] Assigning corporate items to reporting units is by definition an extremely arbitrary process.[1041]

The "management approach" plays an important role in the process of allocating assets and liabilities to reporting units. A firm's allocation decisions are likely to be in part driven by its existing internal organization and reporting structure. The manner in which a firm allocates its assets and liabilities to reporting units is likely to be in part predetermined by its decisions relating to the reporting unit definition itself.[1042]

1036 Refer to section 4.5.1.2.

1037 Another possibility suggested in SFAS 142.33 is an allocation procedure based on the relative fair values of the different reporting units.

1038 SFAS 142.33 suggests that pension liabilities be allocated *pro rata* to multiple reporting units, based on relative payroll expense. For other liabilities, allocation formulas might not be so obvious.

1039 SFAS 142.32.

1040 See also Lüdenbach and Frowein (2003, p. 218).

1041 Respondents to the FASB's 2001 exposure draft expressed the same concerns. See SFAS 142.B115. Furthermore, in some cases it can lead to results that are inconsistent with the requirements in Statement 131 since, for purposes of segment reporting, firms are required to allocate to reported segments only those assets that are included in the chief operating decision maker's measure of segment assets. Therefore, goodwill and other (corporate) assets and liabilities may not be included in reported segment assets. See SFAS 142.B121.

1042 Refer to section 4.4.

4.5.2.2 Allocating goodwill

As with other assets and liabilities, the guidance provided in SFAS 142.34-5 on allocating goodwill to reporting units focuses on the case of a recent acquisition.[1043] However, in contrast to assets and liabilities, which are only to be allocated to reporting units when certain criteria are met,[1044] all of a firm's acquired goodwill must be assigned in its entirety.[1045] The allocation procedure considers which reporting unit, or several reporting units, of the acquirer are expected to benefit from the synergies of the business combination.[1046] Here again, the allocation method is required to be "reasonable and supportable and ... applied in a consistent manner."[1047] SFAS 142.35 provides additional guidance, depending on whether a reporting unit that goodwill is going to be allocated to has also been assigned assets and liabilities from the same acquisition.

"In concept, the amount of goodwill assigned to a reporting unit would be determined in a manner similar to how the amount of goodwill recognized in a business combination is determined."[1048] For each reporting unit expected to benefit from the acquisition, a fair value as a surrogate for purchase price would be determined and allocated to the net assets of that unit as would be the case if the reporting unit had been acquired in a business combination. Consider the following simple example in which entity A is acquired and the acquirer's reporting units RU_i are expected to benefit from the synergies of the acquisition of A:[1049]

	A	**RU_1**	**RU_2**	**RU_3**
Purchase price of A; fair values of RU_i	100	200	500	50
Net assets	60	80	500	20
Acquired goodwill of A; internally generated goodwills of RU_i	40	120	0	30

These arbitrary numbers show that only by coincidence is the sum of the reporting units' internally generated goodwills (here: 150 MU) equal to the acquired goodwill of A that is to be allocated (here: 40 MU). Therefore, the guidance in SFAS 142.35 does not represent a viable method of allocating A's goodwill. A "reasonable and supportable" method

1043 The allocation of the entity's pre-existing goodwill to reporting units upon initial application of SFAS 142 is governed by SFAS 142.54.

1044 Refer to section 4.5.2.1.

1045 See SFAS 142.34, 54. See also Hitz and Kuhner (2002, p. 276).

1046 It is not necessary that goodwill be allocated solely to reporting units that have also been allocated assets and/or liabilities from the same business combination.

1047 SFAS 142.34.

1048 SFAS 142.35.

1049 All amounts are expressed in monetary units (MU). For a similar example, refer to Pellens, Crasselt and Schremper (2002).

could be to allocate A's goodwill based on the three reporting units' relative internally generated goodwills:

	A	RU_1	RU_2	RU_3	ΣRU_i
Goodwill	40	120	0	30	150
Relative proportion of RU_i goodwills		120 / 150 = 0.8	0	30 / 150 = 0.2	1.0
Portion of A's goodwill allocated to RU_i		0.8 x 40 = 32	0	0.2 x 40 = 8	40

Alternatively, another "reasonable and supportable" method could be to distribute A's goodwill in proportion to the three reporting units' relative size as measured by net assets:[1050]

	A	RU_1	RU_2	RU_3	ΣRU_i
Goodwill	40	120	0	30	150
Net assets		80	500	20	600
Relative proportion of RU_i total assets		80 / 600 = 0.13	500 / 600 = 0.83	20 / 600 = 0.03	1.0
Portion of A's goodwill allocated to RU_i		0.13 x 40 = 5.3	0.83 x 40 = 33.3	0.03 x 40 = 1.3	40

It is doubtful whether these or other, similar procedures are consistent with the objective of assigning goodwill to reporting units proportionally to the benefits expected to arise from the acquisition,[1051] since all they achieve is an allocation of acquired goodwill proportional to some arbitrarily chosen apportionment formula.

The procedure described above is deemed to be inappropriate if goodwill is to a reporting unit to which none of the assets acquired or liabilities assumed in that specific acquisition were allocated. Goodwill might be allocated to such a reporting unit based on a "with and without" computation. "That is, the difference between the fair value of that reporting unit before the acquisition and its fair value after the acquisition represents the amount of goodwill to be assigned to that reporting unit."[1052] This with and without computation is intended to capture the incremental increase, resulting from a recent business combination, in the reporting unit's internally generated goodwill.[1053] This increment will in most cases be due to synergies that are expected to arise from combining the acquired entity with the acquirer's operations, and from which benefits are expected to accrue to the reporting unit in question. For example, assume that entity A in the above example pro-

1050 A third alternative would be an allocation based on reporting unit fair value; see SFAS 142.33. Also, refer to Lüdenbach and Frowein (2003, p. 218).

1051 See SFAS 142.34.

1052 SFAS 142.35 (both quotes).

1053 See also Küting, Weber and Wirth (2001, p. 188).

vides distribution channels to all three RU_i, albeit being operated as a stand-alone reporting unit. It might be feasible to assume that the future cash flows, and therefore the fair values, of RU_i will increase to the extent that the distribution channels provided by A result in a reduction of distribution expenses and/or an increase in revenues, although no assets or liabilities are assigned to them:

	RU_1	RU_2	RU_3	ΣRU_i
Fair values of RU_i before acquisition of A	150	500	30	680
Fair values of RU_i after acquisition of A	200	500	50	750
Fair value increment due to acquisition of A	50	0	20	70

However, as the example shows, the total amount of goodwill that, according to the "with and without" computation, can be potentially assigned to RU_i (70 MU) will only by coincidence be equal to the amount that is to be distributed to these reporting units (40 MU).[1054]

While the guidance on allocating acquisition-specific goodwill, given in SFAS 142.34-5, already involves considerable discretion, this is even truer in the event that the firm's entire existing goodwill must be allocated to reporting units upon initial application of SFAS 142.[1055] As in SFAS 142.34, no more is required in SFAS 142.54 than that the method used to allocate goodwill to reporting units at transition be "reasonable and supportable". Firms are encouraged to consider the original sources of pre-existing goodwill and give special attention to those reporting units to which the related assets and liabilities were assigned. The guidance applicable to allocating acquisition-specific goodwill is also recommended for allocating pre-existing goodwill upon initial application of SFAS 142. However, for goodwill components resulting from business combinations that have been completed a relatively long time before, the allocation will tend to be even more subjective.

1054 Taken literally, the guidance in SFAS 142.35 suggests that the total amount of 70 MU ("the difference between the fair value of that reporting unit before the acquisition and its fair value after the acquisition") can be recognized in the acquirer's financial statements. This would imply that not only the purchased goodwill of 40 is recognized but, as the case might be, part of the internally generated goodwills of reporting units expected to benefit from the acquisition might end up being recognized as well. This result would be in contrast to SFAS 142.F1, which defines goodwill as the "excess of the cost of an acquired entity over the net of the amounts assigned to assets acquired and liabilities assumed." In this example, not only this excess value of 40 MU, but an additional 30 MU, would be recognized.

1055 SFAS 142.54 explicitly requires that all recognized goodwill be assigned to reporting units.

4.5.3 Disposal

When a *component* (constituting a business) of a reporting unit is to be disposed of, management must determine how much of the reporting unit's goodwill to include in the carrying value of that component, in order to determine the gain or loss on disposal.[1056] According to SFAS 142.39, the portion of reporting unit goodwill that enters into that calculation depends on whether or not the business to be disposed of was integrated into the reporting unit after its acquisition. If it was, the portion of the reporting unit's goodwill that relates to the business to be disposed of is not readily apparent. In that event, some allocation key must be devised. According to SFAS 142.39, that allocation is to be based on the relative fair values of, first, the business to be disposed of and, second, the portion of the reporting unit to be retained. The fair value of the business to be disposed of will usually be derived from the purchase price realized. The discretion inherent in determining the fair value of the retained portion is identical to that involved in valuing reporting units *per se*.[1057] Subsequent to the disposal, any goodwill remaining in the reporting unit must be tested for impairment.[1058]

The guidance in SFAS 142.30 implies that a "business" as defined in EITF Issue No. 98-03 is a separate reporting unit whenever it is situated directly below the operating segment level.[1059] In contrast, SFAS 142.39 suggests that businesses might exist even further down in the organizational hierarchy. Since reporting units are either segments or components immediately below the segment level, such businesses would not be viewed as reporting units. Conversely, if the reporting unit level is identical to the operating segment level, and no economically dissimilar businesses exist below that level, it will not be possible to allocate the goodwill portion to be disposed of in the manner required in SFAS 142.39. In that case, the disposed portion of the reporting unit would not have constituted a business, and no goodwill would have to be allocated to it. Therefore, management's argument that the disposed portion did not constitute a business would enable management to record a higher gain (or lower loss) on disposal. However, the FASB maintains that goodwill cannot relate to a group of assets that does not constitute a business.[1060]

1056 The discretion related to determining what constitutes a "business" is discussed in section 4.4.

1057 Refer to section 4.5.1 above.

1058 See SFAS 142.39.

1059 Refer to section 4.4 above.

1060 See SFAS 142.B164.

4.6 Measurement

The second test step compares the carrying value of reporting unit goodwill with its implied fair value. The implied fair value of goodwill is measured by comparing reporting unit fair value (representing a fictitious purchase price) to reporting unit net assets (without goodwill) at fair value. The FASB coined the term „implied" fair value of goodwill because, conceptually, it is difficult to measure the fair value of this residual directly.[1061]

4.6.1 Fair value of reporting unit net assets

4.6.1.1 Fictitious purchase price allocation

Determining the fair value of reporting unit net assets requires management to measure reporting unit assets and liabilities "as if" the reporting unit under scrutiny had been acquired as of the impairment test date.[1062] This fictitious "purchase price allocation" process[1063] or "fair value adjustment"[1064] is governed by the provisions in SFAS 142.21.[1065] It involves discretionary parameters similar to those encountered during actual purchase price allocations subsequent to acquisitions. While it is beyond the scope of this chapter to discuss all the details and discretionary elements of the purchase price allocation process,[1066] it appears necessary to discuss the application of the relevant guidance in SFAS 141 to the second step of the goodwill impairment test and indicate the subjectivity involved in measuring the fair value of reporting unit net assets.[1067] Assets and liabilities are to be measured at "their estimated fair values at date of acquisition".[1068] Most of the discretionary parameters involved in estimating fair value measurements for entire re-

---

1061 See SFAS 142.18 fn. 13.

1062 See SFAS 142.21.

1063 Lüdenbach and Frowein (2003, pp. 217-8) coin the term "Quasi-Kaufpreisallokation". See also Frowein and Lüdenbach (2003, p. 65).

1064 See Küting, Weber and Wirth (2001, p. 187).

1065 SFAS 142.21 refers to SFAS 141.35-8. SFAS 141.35 in turn refers to SFAS 141.26-46 for guidance on the process of purchase price allocation.

1066 For example, refer to Beams, Brozovsky and Shoulders (2000, pp. 76-82), Jeter and Chaney (2001, ch. 5), Larsen (1997, pp. 189-91), and Pellens (2001, pp. 294-5).

1067 The extent to which the methods and procedures applied in the original purchase price allocation are binding for the "fictitious" purchase price allocation is an open issue. Lüdenbach and Frowein (2003, p. 218) maintain that consistency should be applied in this process in order to avoid distortion of the implied fair value of goodwill due to measurement artifacts. The authors also argue that, in order to correctly account for deferred taxes, the "fictitious" purchase price allocation must include an assumption about the legal form, which the "fictitious" purchase has taken.

1068 SFAS 141.35.

porting units, discussed in section 4.5.1, also apply to measuring the fair values of individual assets and liabilities for which fair values are not readily observable.

The FASB attempted to limit subjectivity by requiring in SFAS 141.35 that, first, the valuation of any non-cash purchase consideration be reviewed. By analogy, this translates into a requirement to review the determination of reporting unit fair value when performing the second step of the goodwill impairment test according to SFAS 142.21. Second, all of the assets acquired and liabilities assumed must be identified. This requirement includes intangible assets that meet the recognition criteria in SFAS 141.39 (see discussion below) as well as all other assets and liabilities of the acquired entity, regardless of whether or not were previously recorded in the financial statements of the acquired entity. Applying this provision to the second step of the goodwill impairment test implies that not only must the reporting unit's assets and liabilities be measured at fair value, but any assets or liabilities that do not qualify for recognition when generated internally must be recognized if they do meet the recognition criteria when acquired. The remainder of this section first discusses recognition issues, followed by measurement issues.[1069]

4.6.1.2 Recognition

Special recognition provisions exist for previously recorded goodwill (SFAS 141.38), deferred taxes (SFAS 141.38), intangible assets (SFAS 141.39), preacquisition contingencies (SFAS 141.40-1), and research and development assets (SFAS 141.42). According to SFAS 141.38, goodwill recognized by the acquired entity from its own previous acquisitions cannot be carried over to the consolidated balance sheet of the acquirer. In the context of the goodwill impairment test, this requirement implies that, as stated in SFAS 142.21, the carrying amounts of any goodwill recognized as part of reporting unit net assets must be excluded when calculating the implied fair value of reporting unit goodwill. Furthermore, no internally generated goodwill is included in the fair value of reporting unit net assets.

Likewise, deferred income taxes recorded by the acquiree cannot be carried over into the acquirer's books but must be reassessed.[1070] Consistent with SFAS 109.30, deferred tax liabilities (assets) are recognized based on any differences between the amounts assigned to assets acquired (liabilities assumed) in a business combination and the accordant tax

---

1069 See also Lüdenbach and Frowein (2003, pp. 219-22) and Frowein and Lüdenbach (2003, pp. 67-72).

1070 See SFAS 141.38 and Lüdenbach and Frowein (DB 2003, p. 221).

bases. No deferred taxes are recorded in association with goodwill for which amortization is not tax-deductible.[1071] The general rules for recognition and measurement of deferred taxes are contained in SFAS 109.17.[1072] For the measurement of deferred tax assets, a valuation allowance must be established if "it is *more likely than not* (a likelihood of more than 50 percent) that some portion or all of the deferred tax assets will not be realized."[1073] This term requires management's estimates of the likelihood of a future event occurring. To the extent that deferred tax assets are deemed to be more likely than not to be realized, the implied fair value of goodwill is reduced, and *vice versa*.

Subjectivity plays an especially pronounced role where intangible assets generated internally by the reporting unit must be identified. According to SFAS 141.39, intangible assets must be recognized separately from goodwill if they satisfy one of two recognition criteria:[1074] The *contractual-legal criterion* requires that the intangible asset arise from contractual or other legal rights. According to the *separability criterion*, the intangible asset in question must be capable of being sold, transferred, licensed, rented, or otherwise exchanged either separately or in combination with a related contract, asset, or liability.[1075] These renewed recognition criteria for acquired intangible assets were intended by the Board to take some of the subjectivity out of the process of purchase price allocation, since it observed that many firms chose not to recognize previously unrecognized intangible assets acquired in a business combination, but to include them within goodwill.[1076] Relying on contractual/legal rights and separate usability will tend to limit management's discretion in two ways: On the one hand, it will be more difficult for firms interested in avoiding/delaying/understating goodwill impairment losses to maximize the implied fair value of goodwill by recognizing as few previously unrecognized intangible assets as possible, because relatively objective criteria now exist that, if met, require an intangible asset to be recognized as part of the fair value of reporting unit net assets. On the other hand, firms that have incentive to recognize/accelerate/overstate a goodwill impairment loss will face difficulties in minimizing the implied fair value of goodwill by recognizing

---

1071 See also Pellens (2001, pp. 261-2).

1072 Refer to Pellens (2001, pp. 260-9).

1073 SFAS 109.17 lit. e (emphasis in original).

1074 See, for example, Alvarez and Biberacher (2002, pp. 347-8).

1075 An assembled workforce cannot be recognized as a separate intangible asset. Appendix A to SFAS 141 provides additional guidance, including a list of intangible assets that meet the recognition criteria.

1076 See SFAS 141.B148. Such behavior was usually explained by management's desire to minimize annual future amortization expense, considering that goodwill was usually amortized over longer periods (or, in some jurisdictions, deducted from equity) than were separately identifiable intangible assets. Refer to section 2.3.2 above.

as many previously unrecognized intangible assets as possible, because such intangible assets cannot be recognized apart from goodwill unless relatively objective criteria are met.[1077]

Preacquisition contingencies, previously governed by SFAS 38, *Accounting for Preacquisition Contingencies of Purchased Enterprises*, are contingencies of an enterprise acquired in a purchase-method business combination that exist before the combination is consummated.[1078] Without regard to details of the sources of contingencies in general,[1079] it is important to note that preacquisition contingencies, usually measured at fair value determined during the allocation period,[1080] are recognized at reasonably estimated values when fair value cannot be determined by the end of the allocation period.[1081] Applying these provisions to the second step of the goodwill impairment test is not straightforward since preacquisition contingencies are an acquisition-specific accounting issue. In the context of SFAS 142, they would have to be recognized and measured at fair value when in existence before the impairment test date.[1082] In analogy to SFAS 142.22, it could be argued that reasonably estimated values must be used when fair value cannot be determined before the issuance of the financial statements.[1083] Under this condition, management would be able to use estimated values of preacquisition contingencies to either

1077 However, significant discretion still exists with regard to measurement issues. SFAS 141.37 lit. e requires intangible assets to be measured at estimated fair values. Where quoted market prices are unavailable or deemed inappropriate, valuation techniques will be applied. The discretion inherent in these methods is discussed extensively in section 4.5.1 above.

1078 This definition in SFAS 38.4 lit. a is carried forward unchanged in SFAS 141.F1. See SFAS 141.B175. Preacquisition contingencies can be contingent assets, contingent liabilities, or contingent impairments of assets.

1079 Refer to SFAS 5. See also Pellens (2001, pp. 227-35) and Kieso, Weygandt and Warfield (2001, pp. 670-9).

1080 According to SFAS 141.F1, the allocation period is the "period that is required to identify and measure the fair value of the assets acquired and the liabilities assumed in a business combination." It ends when the acquirer has incorporated all information known to be available or obtainable. The allocation period should usually not exceed one year from the consummation of a business combination (SFAS 38.4 lit. b).

1081 See SFAS 141.40 lit. a, b. Previous adjustments are recorded in earnings in the period in which the adjustment is determined. See SFAS 141.41.

1082 Lüdenbach and Frowein (2003, p. 220) argue that, for the sake of consistency, such contingencies would be recognized or not recognized depending on whether or not their expected impact was also factored into the fair value of the reporting unit.

1083 This would also correspond with the general rules in SFAS 5.

over- or understate the implied fair value of goodwill when conducting the initial impairment test.[1084]

Finally, in-process research and development assets that would have to be written off to earnings when acquired in a business combination[1085] are included in the allocation process for purposes of goodwill impairment testing.[1086]

4.6.1.3 Measurement

Regarding measurement issues, detailed guidance is given in SFAS 141.37 for the measurement of assets acquired and liabilities assumed, excluding goodwill. The recommendations include several variants of fair value measurements, most of which require estimates.

In a purchase price allocation that follows an actual acquisition, the sum of the amounts assigned to assets acquired and liabilities assumed is in effect limited to some extent by the cost of the acquired entity. According to SFAS 141.44, the amounts assigned to assets acquired and liabilities assumed are reduced *pro rata* when their sum exceeds the cost of the acquired entity.[1087] No such limit exists when the fair value of reporting unit net assets is determined for purposes of the second test step. If management has incentive to overstate any goodwill impairment loss, it will assess the fair value of reporting unit net assets at the highest possible amount, without being restricted by the cost of the acquired entity.

4.6.2 Inclusion of estimates

SFAS 142.22 requires that the best estimate of a goodwill impairment loss be recognized in the financial statements in those cases where the second test step is not completed before the financial statements are issued, a goodwill impairment loss is probable, and can be reasonably estimated. This implies that "slow" firms can include or exclude an esti-

---

1084 However, it is not fully clear that preacquisition contingencies in the goodwill impairment test provide discretion over and above that already involved in accounting for contingencies under SFAS 5.

1085 According to FIN 4.5, the amounts assigned to tangible and intangible assets to be used in a particular research and development project that have no alternative future use shall be charged to expense at the acquisition date. This requirement is carried over unchanged in SFAS 141.42. However, the FASB recently announced its intention to revoke FIN 4 in order to achieve convergence with IFRS.

1086 See SFAS 142.21 fn. 14.

1087 Exempt from this rule are financial assets other than equity-method investments, assets to be disposed of by sale, deferred tax assets, prepaid assets relating to pension or other postretirement benefit plans, and any other current assets.

mated goodwill impairment loss based on their financial reporting incentives. The criteria "probable" and "reasonably estimable", originally defined in SFAS 5,[1088] are sufficiently discretionary to allow management to argue either way. However, firms are required to disclose that the measurement of the impairment loss is an estimate.[1089] After completion of the second test step, any necessary adjustments to the estimated losses are recognized. This provision will not play a major role in the transition period. SFAS 142.55 specifically states that the transitional goodwill impairment test "must be completed ... no later than the end of the year of initial application." Therefore, a situation where a firm relies on estimated goodwill impairment losses because the second test step has not been completed before issuance of the financial statements is not provided for under SFAS 142.

4.7 Transition

The provisions in SFAS 142 are written from the perspective of how goodwill arising from a recent acquisition is to be accounted for. For example, SFAS 142.32 requires that assets acquired and liabilities assumed "be assigned to a reporting unit as of the acquisition date". However, special problems arise when firms are required to apply SFAS 142 for the first time in the year of transition. For purposes of initial application, transition provisions are given in SFAS 142.48-61. This section discusses transition-specific issues and the effects of these issues on the degree of discretion available to management when making the goodwill write-off decision and determining the amount, if any, to write off.[1090]

4.7.1 Effective date and initial application

SFAS 142 takes effect in fiscal years beginning after December 15, 2001, with early application permitted for firms that have fiscal years beginning after March 15, 2001.[1091] To ensure consistent application, early application is only permitted if the first interim

1088 SFAS 5.3 lit a: "*Probable*. The future event or events are likely to occur." (Emphasis in original.) See also SFAS 5.8 lit. b.

1089 See SFAS 142.22, 47 lit. c.

1090 Some of these issues have already been touched upon within the relevant sections of this chapter.

1091 See SFAS 142.48 lit. a.

statements of the fiscal year have not been issued previously.[1092] Retroactive application is not permitted.[1093]

Some of the rules in SFAS 142 become effective before initial application. Goodwill acquired in a business combination for which the acquisition date is between June 30, 2001, and the firm's initial application of SFAS 142, is no longer amortized but tested for impairment in accordance with APB Opinion 17 or SFAS 121.[1094] However, goodwill acquired in a business combination completed before July 1, 2001, continues to be amortized until initial application of SFAS 142.[1095] If firms were interested in avoiding goodwill amortization, they had incentive to consider postponing any pending acquisitions until after June 30, 2001. Conversely, had firms preferred to amortize the greatest possible amount of their existing goodwill until amortization ceased upon initial application of SFAS 142, they would have tended to accelerate any pending acquisitions in order to complete them before the cut-off date on July 1, 2001.[1096]

4.7.2 Transitional impairment test

The prescription in SFAS 142.55 was intended to ease the transition:[1097] Firms were given six months' time to complete the first step of the goodwill impairment test in each reporting unit and another six months for the second step.[1098] Initial application took place as of the beginning of the fiscal year.[1099] Therefore, a calendar-year applied SFAS 142 as of January 1, 2002, completed the first test step by June 30, 2002, and carried out

---

1092 This implies that firms with a March 31 year-end can only apply SFAS 142 in their fiscal year ending on March 31, 2002, if no first-quarter interim reports, prepared under the SFAS 142 predecessor rules, were published. Since SFAS 142 was issued on June 29, 2001, firms only had one and a half months to change their reporting to SFAS 142. SEC filing requirements allow firms 45 days to issue their quarterly reports.

1093 See SFAS 142.48 lit. a.

1094 See SFAS 142.50-1.

1095 See SFAS 142.50.

1096 Such behavior would represent earnings management by "real" decisions ("Sachverhaltsgestaltungen") as discussed in section 3.3.1.1 above.

1097 See SFAS 142.B210-1.

1098 More precisely, "the second step of the transitional goodwill impairment test *must* be completed as soon as possible, but no later than the end of the year of initial application" (SFAS 142.55 [emphasis added]).

1099 See SFAS 142.55.

the second test step by December 31, 2002.[1100] As has been discussed briefly above, SFAS 142.58 required that firms conduct the first *annual* impairment tests in the transition year also.[1101] Besides, the existence of impairment indicators at some time during the transition year would have triggered additional impairment tests.[1102] Therefore, work on up to *three* parallel goodwill impairment tests was possibly carried out within each reporting unit during the transition year.

The transition provisions gave firms considerable flexibility regarding the timing of any goodwill impairment loss, enabling management to delay or accelerate it according to their financial reporting incentives, since the impairment test could be completed any time during the first twelve months. Likewise, a firm's announcement that no goodwill impairment loss has occurred can also be delayed or accelerated almost at will. Prior research has shown that management prefers to disclose "bad news" in later, rather than earlier quarters.[1103] It must be stressed that the information used in the transitional goodwill impairment test was based on the situation at the beginning of the year of initial application. The Board intended that the initial impairment test capture any goodwill impairment losses that result from a change in methodology,[1104] rather than primarily from economic events. Consequently, these transitional goodwill impairment losses were reported as a change in accounting principle.[1105]

In conclusion, while the transition provision did allow management discretion regarding the *timing* of disclosure of goodwill write-off behavior, it should not, in theory, have enabled management to exercise discretion with regard to the *substance* of that decision. However, in practice it is doubtful that management actually did use (possibly outdated) information and assumptions based on what it knew on January 1, 2002, when conduct-

---

1100 SFAS 142.22 allowed firms to use the „best estimate" (as defined in SFAS 5) of any goodwill impairment loss when any required second test steps were not completed by fiscal year-end. As discussed briefly above, it is not entirely clear whether this rule applies to the transitional impairment test. At any rate, SFAS 142.55 does not refer to SFAS 142.22, which suggests that the twelve-month period is binding. So does the formulation in SFAS 142.55 ("must"). See fn. 1098 above.

1101 Refer to section 4.3.1.1 above.

1102 See SFAS 142.57. For a discussion of impairment indicators that induce unscheduled impairment tests, refer to section 4.3.2 above.

1103 See, for example, Elliott and Shaw (1988, p. 97) and Mendenhall and Nichols (1988).

1104 More precisely, the transitional SFAS 142 goodwill impairment test was meant to capture impairment not detected by the goodwill impairment test prescribed by the predecessor standard, SFAS 121. For a brief description of that procedure, refer to section 2.3.2.2.1 above.

1105 See SFAS 142.B209. Economic value declines that had occurred until the end of the previous year should have been captured by impairment tests carried out according to the predecessor standard(s), SFAS 121 and/or APB Opinion 17.

ing the second step of the goodwill impairment test some time during, say, the fourth quarter of 2002.

4.7.3 Transitional presentation and disclosures

Presentation issues are argued here to be especially relevant for goodwill write-off behavior in the transition year. A goodwill impairment loss resulting from the transitional goodwill impairment test is reported as the effect of a change in accounting principle.[1106] It is presented in the income statement between the subtotals "extraordinary items" and "net income", along with any related income tax effects.[1107]

Since the transitional goodwill impairment test is based on the situation as of the first of the transition year, any transitional goodwill impairment loss is recognized in the first interim period, irrespective of when the test is completed. Consistent with SFAS 3, *Reporting Accounting Changes in Interim Financial Statements*, the first-quarter report and all other quarterly reports preceding the period in which the transitional goodwill impairment loss is measured, are restated to reflect the accounting change.[1108] The effect is included in the first-quarter report as well as any cumulative year-to-date or last-twelve-months-to-date financial reports that comprise that first quarter. For example, if the transitional goodwill impairment loss in a calendar-year firm is measured in November, the resulting effect is reported by restating net income in the first-quarter report and net income figures reported in the second-quarter report ("year-to-date June 30") and third-quarter report ("year-to-date September 30"). In contrast, any "regular" goodwill impairment loss that does *not* result from the transitional test must be presented as a separate line item in the income statement, above "income from continuing operations" or a similar subtotal.[1109]

Prior research suggests that not all components of net income are viewed equally by financial statement users, since some are judged to be more relevant to forecasting future cash flows than others.[1110] Therefore, it is reasonable to expect that financial statement users' perceptions of a goodwill impairment loss differed depending on whether this loss was reported as the effect of a change in accounting principle (and disclosed as a re-

---

1106 If not stated explicitly otherwise, refer to SFAS 142.56 for the provisions discussed in this chapter.

1107 Per-share information must also be presented for the accounting change.

1108 See SFAS 142.56. Refer to SFAS 3.10.

1109 An exception applies to a goodwill impairment loss that is associated with a discontinued operation, which must be included within the results of discontinued operations. See SFAS 142.43.

1110 Refer to section 3.3.2.4.8 above.

statement of the first-quarter report) or as a component of the current period's income from continuing operations. Possibly, a transitional goodwill impairment loss was viewed as a relatively transitory and therefore less value-relevant earnings component, since it presumably reflects a change in accounting methodology rather than an economic value decline. Under that assumption, management might have had incentive to report the highest possible amount as a transitional goodwill impairment loss, thereby decreasing the likelihood of further, regular goodwill impairment losses in the near future. In order to achieve that goal, management might have chosen to diverge from the requirement to base the transitional impairment test on the first of the transition year.[1111] The date on which management based the transitional impairment test depends on whether a punishment was expected to result from deviating from the first of the fiscal year and on whether the situation that existed as of the first of the fiscal year was more or less suited to achieve management's financial reporting incentives.[1112]

Another required disclosure in the transition period relates to the results of the first test step. Upon completion of the first step of the initial goodwill impairment test, firms had to disclose in their interim financial information any reportable segment(s) in which a transitional goodwill impairment loss was expected.[1113] Depending on their financial reporting incentives, management might have used this disclosure obligation to "warn" financial statement users of an impending goodwill impairment loss in one or more of its reporting segments, before this loss was finally measured. Although not explicitly required, management might have had incentive to voluntarily disclose a numerical estimate of the anticipated loss in order to "guide" financial statement users' expectations.[1114]

4.7.4 Reclassification of goodwill and intangible assets

It has been discussed above that SFAS 141 defines new recognition criteria for intangible assets acquired in a business combination.[1115] SFAS 142.49, parallel to SFAS 141.61, requires that these criteria be applied retroactively to intangibles assets and goodwill previously recognized in a business combination for which the acquisition date was before

---

[1111] See also the preceding section 4.7.2.

[1112] For example, if management intended to record the highest possible transitional goodwill impairment loss, it would have based the transitional test on a date at which the economic situation justified an exceptionally large goodwill impairment loss.

[1113] See SFAS 142.60.

[1114] For this type of "expectations management", refer to section 3.3.2.4.5.1 above.

[1115] Refer to section 4.6.1.

July 1, 2001.[1116] Due to this requirement, the carrying amounts of previously acquired intangible assets that did not fulfill the recognition criteria now contained in SFAS 141.39 had to be reclassified as goodwill as of the date of initial application of SFAS 142.[1117] Conversely, carrying amounts of items previously recognized within goodwill (or within similar balance sheet items such as goodwill and other intangible assets) had to be reclassified and recognized as separate intangible assets if these items met the above criteria. This would presume that accounting records had been maintained for all of these items.[1118]

These reclassification provisions gave management the opportunity to use the inherent discretion to either increase or decrease the total carrying amount of goodwill, conditional on their financial reporting incentives. Reclassifying intangible assets to goodwill would have resulted in an increased carrying value of goodwill. Since intangible assets are frequently amortized under SFAS 142.12, unless they have indefinite useful lives, reducing the carrying amount of intangible assets in favor of the carrying amount of goodwill would have resulted in less amortization expense in future periods. However, the likelihood of goodwill impairment losses would have increased correspondingly. Therefore, it is not entirely clear which incentive dominated when management increased goodwill by reclassifying amounts previously recognized as separate intangible assets (or by avoiding to reclassify amounts previously recognized as goodwill in favor of separate intangible assets).[1119]

4.8 Intermediate results

In this chapter, it is demonstrated by a detailed analysis of SFAS 142 that the goodwill impairment test in most of its facets is a highly discretionary procedure that allows management to coordinate goodwill write-off behavior with their financial reporting objec-

---

1116 The acquisition date ordinarily is the date assets are received and other assets are given, liabilities are assumed or incurred, or equity interests are issued (SFAS 141.48).

1117 See SFAS 141.61 lit. a. This requirement includes any related deferred tax liabilities.

1118 See SFAS 142.49 lit b. fn. 25.

1119 Reclassifying goodwill to intangible assets would have had the reverse effect. Amortization expense was likely to increase, unless most of the reclassified intangible assets were determined to have indefinite useful lives. The likelihood of future goodwill impairment losses decreased correspondingly. Here again, a trade-off of different financial reporting incentives would have been involved.

tives. In this respect, SFAS 142 does not appear to differ to a great extent from the predecessor standard, SFAS 121.[1120]

Management estimates and other subjective elements are required at all stages.[1121] The relevant rules refer to other vague terms and subjective provisions that are scattered throughout a wide range of GAAP pronouncements. Recognition rules that invoke vague terms such as "significant", "probable", or "substantial" provide extensive elbowroom for management.[1122] So do measurement provisions that call for estimated values or fair value measurements that, in the absence of quoted market prices, rely on valuation techniques. In addition to being subjective, the difficulties associated with estimating uncertain future cash flows contributes to the fact that these procedures generate potentially unreliable results. In other words, SFAS 142 creates verifiability problems due to both measurer bias and measurement bias.[1123]

However, several factors restrict management's ability to use these discretionary elements in a short-sighted manner to influence goodwill write-off behavior in the year of transition.[1124] For example, Lüdenbach and Frowein (2003) stress that the "fictitious" purchase price allocation in step two of the impairment test is largely guided by the procedures applied to prior actual purchase price allocations in acquisitions.[1125] Further, auditors are required to review management's assumptions and expectations,[1126] and the threat of SEC enforcement and potential shareholder litigation might discipline management even further.[1127] With regard to the use of valuation techniques to measure reporting unit fair value, the use of marketplace participants' assumptions, where available, also limits subjectivity. Further, timing flexibility might be limited by the fact that annual

---

1120 See also Segal (2003, p. 29). According to Osterland (2002), "the new rules aren't likely to hold .. management any more accountable for the success or failure of [a] merger than the pooling method did."

1121 See also Hitz and Kuhner (2002, p. 283).

1122 For example, Aharony and Dotan (2001) show that different groups (financial analysts, managers, and external auditors) ascribe different interpretations to the SFAS 5 criteria "remote" and "probable". Analysts are found to be more conservative regarding numerical interpretations than are managers and auditors, who assign similar percentages to these verbal criteria. Further, they refer to earlier research that found the threshold "remote" and "reasonably possible" ranging from 15% to 25% and that between "reasonably possible" and "probable" at 67% to 70%. See Aharony and Dotan (2001, p. 5).

1123 See Holthausen and Watts (2001, p. 28).

1124 For a general discussion of constraints to earnings management, refer to section 3.3.2.5 above.

1125 See Lüdenbach and Frowein (2003, p. 220).

1126 Hitz and Kuhner (2002, p. 285) are concerned about auditors' ability to fulfill this role in the context of SFAS 142.

1127 See Kahle (2002b, p. 903) and Küting, Weber and Wirth (2001, p. 198).

tests must be conducted at fixed dates every year. The discretion related to goodwill from future acquisitions will be limited by the fact that management must document its assumptions and expectations related to these transactions and is therefore likely to be held accountable by them.[1128]

The above analysis indicates that, with the impairment-only approach set down in SFAS 142, the FASB chose to prescribe a highly discretionary method of accounting for goodwill subsequent to its initial recognition and measurement.[1129] While it is difficult to ascertain if SFAS 142 is more or less discretionary than the predecessor rules,[1130] it probably did not fundamentally change the fact that accounting for goodwill remains one of the most subjective areas in financial reporting.[1131] According to Wilson (1996), "unrelated measurement experts would have a difficult time assessing changes in the value of goodwill, even if they were fully aware of management's private information about related economic activity".[1132] Especially with respect to the transitional SFAS 142 goodwill write-off, it is argued that it is almost completely at management's discretion whether, at what amount, and when such charges are recorded.[1133]

1128 See SFAS 141.50-1. See also Hitz and Kuhner (2002, p. 276). However, this requirement does not apply to goodwill existing upon adoption.

1129 Given this result, it is somewhat surprising to learn that the Board originally discussed a different approach, which it eventually rejected because it involved "numerous subjective judgments", afforded "opportunities for manipulation of reported amounts in financial statements" and led to "concerns about its operationality". See SFAS 142.B73 (all quotes). Under this "discernible-elements approach" (SFAS 142.B71-B73), the reasons for paying a premium over the fair value of the acquired net assets would have been documented, and the recorded amount of goodwill would have been allocated to these discernible elements. All of these elements would then have been either amortized or carried forward without amortization, based on their respective useful lives. This approach would have resulted in part of goodwill being amortized over some weighted-average useful life, with the remaining portion being accounted for under an impairment-only approach. It could be argued that this accounting treatment could not logically have resulted in *more* accounting discretion than the procedure ultimately chosen: In the one extreme, all of goodwill would have been classified as indefinite-lived and not amortized. This would have corresponded with the current accounting treatment. In the other extreme, all of goodwill would have been classified as finite-lived and amortized over the weighted average of the useful lives of the discernible elements. The recorded goodwill amount would have been reduced by amortization charges annually, which tends to limit management's discretion over both the recorded goodwill amount and annual goodwill-related charges. A small annual charge can also be achieved under the current treatment, when firms use their discretion to generate moderate goodwill impairment losses each year. Possibly, reasons other than concerns over subjectivity and discretion influenced the FASB's decision in favor of the impairment-only approach ultimately codified.

1130 Segal (2003, p. 11) claims that "SFAS No. 142 may very well not enhance the reporting for goodwill impairment in either the short or the long run. The [inherent] discretion ... may lead to amounts that do not reflect the economic reality of the firm."

1131 See, for example, Dunstan (1999, p. 2). From a German perspective, see Küting (1997).

1132 See also Henning, Shaw and Stock (2002), Jennings et al. (1996, p. 530),

1133 See also Elliott and Hanna (1996, p. 150 fn. 10).

5 Empirical investigation of write-off determinants

5.1 Chapter overview

In this chapter, a cross-sectional research design is adopted to investigate the determinants of publicly listed U. S. industrial firms' decision to write off (or not write-off) goodwill upon transition to SFAS 142 and of the amount written off, if any. The term "goodwill write-off" is used to refer collectively to these aspects. A cross-sectional approach mitigates the potential effects of changing macroeconomic circumstances and financial reporting rules on write-off activity. So far, Segal's (2003) and Henning, Shaw and Stock's (2002) analyses appear to be the only empirical studies on aspects of SFAS 142 goodwill write-offs.[1134]

The analysis in this chapter proceeds as follows: In section 5.2, testable hypotheses about the determinants of management's financial reporting behavior pertaining to transitional SFAS 142 goodwill write-offs are developed. Section 5.3 contains the definition of variables derived from the hypotheses, an outline of the sample selection procedure, as well as descriptive information and frequency analyses on sample firms. In section 5.4, applicable regression methodology is discussed, followed by Probit tests of the write-off decision and Tobit tests of the write-off amount. Model specification and robustness are investigated in both cases in order to assess the validity of inferences. In section 5.5, the empirical findings are summarized and potential limitations to the conclusions are discussed.

5.2 Hypothesis development

5.2.1 Overview

In this section, explicit hypotheses about the determinants of the goodwill write-off in the year of initial application of SFAS 142 are derived.[1135] These hypotheses are based on the theory, presented in chapter 3, on possible determinants of (and market reactions to) discretionary asset write-offs in general. However, the specific motivations pertaining to the issue of goodwill accounting (discussed in section 2.4) and the unique discretionary parameters available to management upon adoption of SFAS 142 (subject of chapter 4) are

1134 However, Segal (2003) does not differentiate between transitional and regular write-offs, but focuses on a comparison of write-offs under SFAS 121 versus SFAS 142. The question addressed in Henning, Shaw and Stock's (2002) paper is whether certain valuation models can predict the amount and timing of transitional SFAS 142 goodwill write-offs.

1135 For calendar-year firms, this year was January 1 to December 31, 2002.

also considered in order to customize the predictions to the SFAS 142 setting analyzed here.[1136]

Two general types of hypotheses are considered with respect to the transitional SFAS 142 goodwill write-off: First, predictions are made regarding the outcome of a firm's *write-off decision*, i.e. the likelihood that a write-off is expected at all, regardless of any concrete amount. These hypotheses are later tested using Probit regression methodology, in an attempt to discriminate between write-off and non-write-off firms. Second, to the extent that these or other determinants are expected to additionally influence the *write-off amount*, i.e. a "the more the larger" or comparable relation is predicted, this group of hypotheses is subjected to Tobit regression analysis. Viewed in conjunction with the two general types of write-off determinants introduced in section 3.3.2.1 above, Table 4 represents a matrix of hypothesis categories, which are elaborated upon below. All hypotheses are stated in alternative form.

Determinants / *Hypothesis*	**Economic factors**	**Financial reporting incentives**
Write-off decision	H_D^{EC} Hypotheses about economic factors determining the *write-off decision*	H_D^{FR} Hypotheses about financial reporting incentives controlling the *write-off decision*
Write-off amount	H_A^{EC} Hypotheses about economic factors influencing the *write-off amount*, given the write-off decision	H_A^{FR} Hypotheses about financial reporting incentives influencing the *write-off amount*, given the write-off decision
Data	Considered up to the end of fiscal 2001	Considered up to the end of fiscal 2002

Table 4: Categories of hypotheses

SFAS 142.55 requires that the transitional impairment test be based upon the information and circumstances prevalent at the transition date. Therefore, economic developments taking place subsequent to that date cannot affect the write-off as long as goodwill impairment is measured true to the spirit of the rule. Consequently, all economic-factors variables (see Table 6) represent time periods ending on or before the end of fiscal 2001.

In contrast to this, considering management's financial reporting incentives implies that information is likely to be lost where data are restricted to the pre-fiscal 2002 period. Although strictly required to base impairment testing on the situation as of the transition date, management is given up to one year's time to complete the transitional impairment

[1136] With these hypotheses, *ex ante* motivations that predict earnings management are presented, in contrast to relying on *ex post* realizations of actual earnings that are indicative of some earnings management pattern. See Abarbanell and Lehavy (2000, p. 4).

test.[1137] Financial reporting incentives prevailing *subsequent to* the transition date, i.e. during fiscal 2002, are likely to have dominated write-off decision and amount. Consequently, incentive variables represent time periods ending on or before the end of fiscal 2002.

5.2.2 Economic factors

If, as the FASB suggests, the SFAS 142 procedure measures goodwill impairment reliably, transitional goodwill write-offs reported by the sample firms can be expected to result (in part) from economic value declines that caused (some of) firms' reporting unit fair values to fall below their respective book values, including goodwill (first test step), and, consequently, led to (some of) the book values of firms' reporting unit goodwills exceeding their respective implied fair values (second test step).[1138] These two test steps mirror the distinction made above, between the write-off decision and the write-off amount: Goodwill impairment will, first, trigger test step one and, second, determine the amount to be written off on test step two. To the extent that accurate measures for the (unobservable) goodwill impairment can be devised, these proxy variables are expected to be associated with both the write-off decision *and* the amount written off.

Ideally, the individual "true" fair values of firms' reporting units, in combination with these reporting units' respective book values, should be used to detect the existence and extent of impairment. If these values were observable, management would be required by SFAS 142.23 to use them in the actual impairment test.[1139] Based on the spirit of the standard, an ideal-type measure of goodwill impairment is a reporting unit-level "fair value-to-book ratio" or MTB ratio. Where this measure is smaller than one, the book value of any reporting unit goodwill is no longer justified by the reporting unit's fair value.[1140] Since most reporting units are not publicly traded and firms are not required to disclose reporting unit data at this fine level of detail, a second-best solution would imply using operating segment fair values in combination with operating segment book values, i.e. operating segment-level MTB ratios.[1141] However, operating segment fair values are

---

[1137] See SFAS 142.55.

[1138] Refer to sections 4.5 and 4.6 for a detailed description of the goodwill impairment testing procedure.

[1139] As discussed in section 4.5.1, SFAS 142.23-25 describes a fair value hierarchy that firms are expected to adhere to, in order to obtain the best possible estimate of the unobservable "true" reporting unit fair value. Henning, Shaw and Stock (2002) use different valuation models to estimate the write-off amount.

[1140] See SFAS 142.19.

[1141] Refer to section 4.4 for the level of aggregation at which sub-units of the firm are tested for goodwill impairment, and for the relation of reporting units and operating segments.

also not disclosed.[1142] Also, even where such sub-entity-level fair value measures were available, the extent to which such accounting numbers measure "true" fair value is open to debate.

These constraints make it necessary to use entity-level data in this study. This problem is also acknowledged by Segal (2003), who uses enterprise-level estimates of expected goodwill impairment.[1143] The entity-level MTB ratio is a crude proxy for the reporting unit-level MTB ratio because, at the entity level, goodwill impairment in one reporting unit can be offset by internally generated goodwill in another.[1144] However, whenever the entity-level MTB ratio is smaller than one at the transition date, impaired goodwill is likely to be found in at least one of the reporting units.[1145]

$\mathbf{H_D^{EC}}$ **1:**	$\mathbf{H_A^{EC}}$ **1:**
Ceteris paribus, a negative relation exists between the write-off decision and the firm's MTB ratio.	Ceteris paribus, a negative relation exists between the write-off amount and the firm's MTB ratio.

As discussed in section 3.3.2.2 above, extant literature documents that "firms write down assets during periods of poor performance."[1146] In most studies of write-off determinants, variables representing the recent developments in market-based performance measures as well as accounting-based performance measures are included to capture the extent to which goodwill write-offs are determined by economic factors.[1147] Declining stock prices and decreasing accounting-based performance measures, such as return on assets (ROA),

1142 SFAS 142 requires some segment-level disclosures. However, these do not include segment fair values.

1143 See Segal (2003, p. 23). A similar procedure is adopted by Riedl (2002, p. 3), who analyzes SFAS 121 write-offs. This approach is supported by Strong and Meyer's (1987, p. 650) finding that "[w]ritedown firms exhibit subpar performance [relative to a control group] on … market-to-book ratio".

1144 Refer to section 4.4 above. This problem will tend to occur more frequently in firms with multiple reporting units that are economically dissimilar.

1145 The only exception to this rule occurs when the fair values of all reporting units with goodwill allocated to them are higher than the respective book values. The low entity-level MTB ratio, then, is "caused" exclusively by reporting units that have no goodwill allocated to them.

1146 White, Sondhi and Fried (2003, p. 279).

1147 See Segal (2003, p. 16), Francis, Hanna and Vincent (1996, pp. 122-3), and Riedl (2002, pp. 9-10). Here again, firm-level data are used as proxy variables for reporting unit performance.

may signal that the future prospects of a firm have deteriorated.[1148] Again, (unavailable) reporting unit performance data should ideally be used because reporting unit underperformance could require a goodwill write-off even where the entity as a whole appears unaffected. The costs of procuring the second-best segment data seem to be out of proportion compared to the expected improvement in proxy variable accuracy.

H_D^{EC} 2a : Ceteris paribus, a negative relation exists between the write-off decision and the firm's stock return.	**H_A^{EC} 2a :** Ceteris paribus, a negative relation exists between the write-off amount and the firm's stock return.
H_D^{EC} 2b : Ceteris paribus, a negative relation exists between the write-off decision and the firm's change in ROA.	**H_A^{EC} 2b :** Ceteris paribus, a negative relation exists between the write-off amount and the firm's change in ROA.

The likelihood of impairment is frequently assumed to be especially high where firms operate in industries with declining performance.[1149] While the obsolescence of individual assets and technologies might affect whole industries, it seems more difficult to justify why poor industry performance as such, incremental to *individual* firm performance, should have explanatory power for goodwill impairment in individual firms. On the contrary, good performers in poorly performing industries might try to "get away" with economically unwarranted write-offs.

5.2.3 Financial reporting incentives

Economic-consequences incentives and capital market-related incentives are argued to influence goodwill write-offs. Consequently, the two groups of hypotheses developed in this section are based on different sets of assumptions: First, predictions concerning economic-consequences incentives as discussed in section 3.3.2.3 must consider how transitional SFAS 142 goodwill write-offs influence contractual outcomes and how they affect potential regulation. Second, hypotheses about capital market-related incentives as described in section 3.3.2.4 presume certain *beliefs* on the part of management regarding

---

1148 Considering changes (versus levels) in performance variables is more likely to capture economic impairments because accounting for impairment is not intended to capture low performance in absolute terms, but declines in asset value that result from decreasing performance. No explicit assumption is made here regarding the temporal relation between accounting-based and price-based performance measures, i.e. accounting-based performance measures are not expected to lead price-based performance measures and vice versa.

1149 See Francis, Hanna and Vincent (1996, p. 123), Riedl (2002, pp. 9-10), and Segal (2003, p. 17).

the way transitional SFAS 142 goodwill write-offs are perceived by capital market participants, such as (potential) shareholders, debt holders, financial analysts and rating agencies.[1150]

5.2.3.1 Economic-consequences incentives

5.2.3.1.1 Compensation

As discussed in section 3.3.2.3.3, managements' income is frequently determined by reported accounting earnings. To the extent that the present value of managers' current and future accounting earnings-based compensation is affected by transitional SFAS 142 goodwill write-offs, this decision can be expected to be influenced by compensation considerations.[1151] Ideally, compensation plan details for each of the individuals relevant to write-off behavior would be used to test this prediction. Since the cost of procuring this information is prohibitive, several simplifying assumptions are necessary.

First, the income of financial reporting decision makers is at least in part determined by the firms' accounting earnings, i.e. accounting earnings-based compensation plans exist. Previous research shows that CEO compensation is positively related to the firm's accounting performance, even where no explicit accounting earnings-based plans are in place.[1152] However, since the actual existence of accounting earnings-based compensation plans cannot be positively ascertained, it is argued, consistent with prior research, that accounting-based plans are more likely to exist in firms with a greater portion of assets-in-place, because high-growth option firms are more likely to have compensation plans based on stock price. In the latter firms, future prospects are considered more relevant to management compensation than is income generated by existing tangible assets.[1153]

1150 "Managers", "management", or "firms" in this context refers to the person or group of persons ultimately responsible for making financial reporting decisions. In most cases, this will be either the chief executive officer (CEO) or the chief financial officer (CFO).

1151 See also Francis, Hanna and Vincent (1996, p. 123).

1152 Smith and Watts (1992, p. 275) report that CEO compensation varies with a measure of accounting ROA. See also Murphy (1985).

1153 See, for example, Dunstan (1999, p. 17), Gaver and Gaver (1995), and Smith and Watts (1992, p. 264). According to Skinner (1993, p. 419), assets-in-place are "those assets whose ultimate value does not principally depend on future discretionary investment by managers", measured by the ratio of the book value of PP&E to total firm value. He documents that the investment opportunity set "affects the nature of the firms' debt and compensation contracts. Specifically, firms with relatively more assets-in-place are more likely to employ (i) accounting-based debt covenants in their public debt contracts and (ii) bonus plans that tie the bonus directly to accounting earnings" (p. 408).

Second, it is assumed that the *transitional* SFAS 142 goodwill write-off is ignored in accounting earnings-based compensation plans, i.e. the CEO's accounting earnings-based bonus is shielded from the effect of SFAS 142 adoption. It has been documented in prior research that executive income reflects positive developments, but is protected from negative accounting entries to the extent that these have an "unusual" character or result from potentially value-enhancing activities such as restructurings.[1154] Since transitional SFAS 142 goodwill write-offs can be argued to have both of these characteristics,[1155] it is assumed that SFAS 142 goodwill write-offs are unlikely to have an adverse effect on the CEO accounting earnings-based compensation *in the year of adoption.*[1156]

Third, it is expected that write-off behavior nonetheless does influence managers' *future* accounting earnings-based compensation and therefore the present value of that income component. Future goodwill write-offs, reported within income from continuing operations, are likely to be perceived as more permanent earnings components, having relevance for earnings-based bonuses awarded management.

Based on these assumptions, managers with accounting-based plans are expected to report transitional SFAS 142 goodwill write-offs in order to shield future accounting earnings and compensation from adverse effects of future write-offs.[1157]

H_D^{FR} 1:

Ceteris paribus, a positive relation exists between the write-off decision and the existence of accounting earnings-based compensation plans for top management.

5.2.3.1.2 Debt covenants

As discussed in section 3.3.2.3.4, most firms are a party to lending agreements that specify certain cutoff points in terms of accounting-based ratios. The violation of these restrictive covenants triggers default on the loan, which may result in substantial costs to

---

1154 Refer to section 3.3.2.3.3 for a review of this literature.

1155 For example, Deutsche Telekom AG justified their record-breaking write-off by arguing that it stemmed from a "strategic review". See Deutsche Telekom AG, annual report on form 20-F for the period ending on December 12, 2002.

1156 This assumption seems reasonable despite Healy, Kang and Palepu's (1987) findings that CEO compensation is affected by voluntary changes in accounting procedures, because mandated accounting changes are more easily unraveled by compensation committees. Similar results are reported by Abdel-khalik (1985).

1157 Because assets-in-place is intended to capture the probability that an accounting-based compensation plan exists *at all*, it is not expected to be linearly associated with the *amount*. Beatty and Weber (2004, p. 15) use recent bonus payments and the existence of a bonus plan based on net income as indicators that a firm is likely to delay goodwill impairment charges.

the firm. To the extent that the accounting numbers and ratios specified in debt covenants are affected by transitional SFAS 142 goodwill write-offs, it can be expected that write-off behavior is influenced by managers' desire to avoid covenant violation and the cost associated with it.[1158] In order to assess whether debt covenant motivations play a role in transitional SFAS 142 goodwill write-off behavior, the treatment of the write-off in each of the sample firms' covenants must be known. Since obtaining actual covenant data is associated with prohibitive costs,[1159] a proxy for firms' closeness to covenant restrictions and, consequently, the expected costs of covenant violation is used here.[1160]

Regardless of the accounting-based proxy used, it is necessary to assume that the transitional SFAS 142 goodwill write-off will have repercussions on the restrictiveness of sample firms' debt covenants at all. For the following reasons, it is assumed that this accounting entry is not entirely ignored in the calculations of debt covenants:[1161] First, debt covenants frequently refer to promulgated GAAP for definitions of accounting numbers.[1162] The relevant GAAP rules are mainly those in force at the date of calculation ("rolling" GAAP), not at the original date of debt issuance ("frozen" GAAP). Therefore, new accounting standards such as SFAS 142 have the potential to influence the probability of covenant default where "rolling GAAP" is used.[1163]

Second, where debt covenants do rely on "fixed GAAP", such modifications to promulgated GAAP are regularly conservative, i.e. they *decrease*, rather than *increase*, income and assets.[1164] Where no write-off is taken, the elimination of goodwill amortization, ce-

---

1158 See also Beatty and Weber (2004, p. 11).

1159 See also Beneish and Press (1995, p. 338), Moehrle (2002, p. 410), and Press and Weintrop (1990, p. 65).

1160 It is not explicitly considered how the cost of technical default is likely to vary across firms. See Beneish and Press (1993). Therefore, a firm's closeness to covenant restrictions is used as a proxy for the expected costs of covenant violation.

1161 Much of the following relies on the findings of Leftwich (1983, pp. 35-6).

1162 See, for example, Smith and Warner (1979, p. 144). Watts and Zimmerman (1986, p. 213) argue that "[t]he specification and preparation of an additional set of accounting statements solely for a debt contract is costly." By not specifying "fixed GAAP", managers accept that lenders will require favorable terms because of the risk of "covenant-relaxing" earnings management. See also El-Gazzar, Lilien and Pastena (1989).

1163 To the extent that borrowers and lenders do negotiate debt covenants that specify "tailored" accounting rules departing from promulgated GAAP ("fixed GAAP"), transitional SFAS 142 goodwill write-off are unlikely to affect the probability of default. However, recent evidence suggests that, while "fixed GAAP" covenants have been gaining importance in recent years, a large portion of extant covenants does resort to accounting numbers based on promulgated GAAP rules. See Mohrman (1996, pp. 79, 85). The author notes that failure to account for "fixed GAAP" in debt covenants impairs researchers' ability to interpret empirical results pertaining to the debt covenant hypothesis.

1164 See Leftwich (1983, p. 36).

teris paribus, makes SFAS 142 an income- and asset-increasing accounting rule. On the opposite, substantial decreases in both income and assets result where write-offs do occur.[1165] Given that the treatment of transitional SFAS 142 goodwill write-offs in actual lending agreements is unknown, the above finding suggests that write-offs do affect the probability of covenant default even where "fixed-GAAP" modifications to promulgated GAAP are in place.[1166] In a related study, Cotter (1998) finds no evidence that goodwill amortization is added back to the numerator of the interest coverage ratios in Australian private debt agreements.[1167] Leftwich's (1983) detailed analysis of "fixed GAAP" provisions suggests that goodwill is "frequently excluded from the asset base against which firms may borrow."[1168] In that sense, transitional SFAS 142 goodwill write-offs would have no potential to influence the asset base, regardless of whether a write-off is taken or not. However, he also reports that "goodwill is eliminated from balance sheet numbers but amortization is required in the income statement."[1169] To the extent that goodwill-related charges are not added back, any transitional SFAS 142 goodwill write-off has the potential to decrease income and equity, which impairs certain accounting ratios such as the DTE ratio.[1170]

Third, departures from GAAP are more common in private rather than public lending agreements.[1171] Where sample firms rely at least in part on public debt, the arguments set forth above are likely to apply to them. In conclusion, transitional SFAS 142 goodwill write-offs are likely to be influenced by debt contracting considerations with regard to both decision and amount.

Since no actual covenant data is available, a relevant proxy variable is used to capture the restrictiveness of debt covenants. As discussed in section 3.3.2.3.4, prior research frequently and justifiably relies on the DTE ratio as such a proxy, since a firm's expected cost of covenant violation is assumed to increase in its financial leverage. Even though other ratios are common in actual covenants, the DTE ratio can be considered a suitable

---

1165 Refer to White, Sondhi and Fried (2003, pp. 527-8).

1166 However, Mohrman (1996, p. 85) finds that "there is no one standard way of writing fixed GAAP provisions".

1167 While this finding alone implies nothing about the treatment of transitional SFAS 142 goodwill write-offs, it does indicate that lenders view goodwill-related charges to be relevant for assessing borrowers' creditworthiness.

1168 Leftwich (1983, p. 39). See also Foster (1986, p. 595).

1169 Leftwich (1983, p. 39).

1170 In addition, even where such write-offs do not occur, debt covenants potentially require that some form of amortization charge related to goodwill is made nonetheless.

1171 See Leftwich (1983, p. 36) and Smith and Warner (1979, p. 144).

proxy since most other leverage-related ratios are affected when the DTE ratio deteriorates.[1172] In addition, capital market participants can be assumed to use the DTE ratio as an indicator of firm risk.[1173] Interestingly, an economic standpoint would suggest that financially distressed firms (where financial distress is approximated by the extent of financial leverage) are more likely than others to have impaired goodwill.[1174] Thus, the observation that write-offs are larger and more frequent where financial leverage is comparatively low would be strong evidence that write-off behavior is at least in part determined by financial reporting incentives. Because the absolute DTE ratio in itself is not meaningful, industry-adjusted figures are used.[1175]

H_D^{FR} 2:	H_A^{FR} 2:
Ceteris paribus, a negative relation exists between the write-off decision and the firm's industry-adjusted DTE ratio.	Ceteris paribus, a negative relation exists between the write-off amount and the firm's industry-adjusted DTE ratio.

5.2.3.1.3 Political costs

As argued in section 3.3.2.3.5, adverse legislation and other regulation is frequently directed towards firms with high, allegedly monopolistic earnings. Therefore, "politically visible" firms have incentive to take write-offs in order to decrease earnings and firm size, reducing political visibility and associated costs. Political visibility is assumed to relate to firm size,[1176] market share, industry concentration, and sharp increases in ac-

1172 See Watts and Zimmerman (1986, p. 216). Dichev and Skinner (2002, pp. 1101-4) find that net worth, or equity, is also frequently used in debt covenants. In line with this finding, Beatty and Weber (2004, p. 11) predict that SFAS 142 write-off behavior is affected by the presence of net worth-based covenants. See also Mohrman (1996, p. 86). However, since this variable is highly correlated with the DTE ratio, it is not explicitly considered here.

1173 See Bernstein (1993, pp. 619-20). As discussed in sections 3.3.2.3.4 and 5.2.3.1.2 above, similar measures are used, for the same reason, in private lending agreements between a firm and its debtholders. See also White, Sondhi and Fried (2003, pp. 130-3). This assumption is supported by the common observation that managers attempt to minimize the level of debt by keeping debt off the balance sheet. S&P (2003, p. 22) reports that, for many firms, "debt leverage (calculated without any adjustments to reported figures) is the only focal point of [financial] policy considerations." Apparently, it is quite common to strive for a debt-to-capital ratio of 35%.

1174 For example, one of the components of Altman's (1968) Z score, a popular predictor of financial distress, is the DTE ratio. See also White, Sondhi and Fried (2003, pp. 652-3).

1175 See also Moehrle (2002, p. 410), who uses the difference between the sample firm's debt-to-assets ratio and its weighted average in the firm's (four-digit SIC code) industry.

1176 Since firm size potentially is a proxy for various economic and non-economic effects, it is considered as a control variable, not as a political costs proxy. Refer to section 5.2.4 below.

counting performance.[1177] However, managers might likewise assume that regulators are concerned with post-transition earnings rather than earnings "distorted" by SFAS 142 adoption, in which case there would be incentive to avoid transitional write-offs, storing up future write-off potential. Due to this uncertainty, the following open hypotheses are posited.[1178]

H_D^{FR} 3a :

Ceteris paribus, the write-off decision is associated with the firm's market share.

H_D^{FR} 3b :

Ceteris paribus, the write-off decision is associated with measures of concentration in the firm's industry.

H_D^{FR} 3c :

Ceteris paribus, the write-off decision is associated with the firm's pre-write-off increase in ROA.

5.2.3.2 Capital market-related incentives

5.2.3.2.1 Target accounting

5.2.3.2.1.1 General decision model

Based on the capital market-related considerations discussed in section 3.3.2.4 above, transitional SFAS 142 goodwill write-offs are also expected to reflect the incentive to influence stock price favorably, *inter alia* by achieving earnings targets. To be relevant in this context, these thresholds must be affected by any transitional SFAS 142 goodwill write-off.[1179] Because measures of operating earnings exclude accounting changes, bottom-line net income is presumed to be the relevant earnings number.[1180]

1177 Refer to section 3.3.2.3.5, especially Figure 8. Membership in certain industries is also argued to give rise to political exposure; however, this notion is not explored here in a regression setting. Refer instead the descriptive information presented in Table A. 2 and Table A. 4.

1178 Because these variables can be thought of as dummy variables capturing whether or not a firm is politically visible, no linear relation to the write-off *amount* is expected.

1179 Refer to section 3.3.2.4.8 for a discussion of this critical assumption.

1180 The seminal paper, Burgstahler and Dichev (1997, pp. 101-2), also adopts this approach. According to S&P (2001), COMPUSTAT Industrial Annual item DATA18 (income before extraordinary items), another target figure used by Burgstahler and Dichev (1997), excludes transitional SFAS 142 goodwill write-offs and would therefore be unaffected by them. This is because COMPUSTAT Industrial Annual item DATA192 (extraordinary items) explicitly includes the cumulative effect of accounting changes. See S&P (2001, ch. 4, p. 130).

Figure 14 contains a simple model of earnings management behavior expected to occur when management is concerned about reaching a simple earnings target, T.[1181] Following prior literature,[1182] two earnings targets are considered: First, prior-year annual earnings capture the incentive to avoid earnings declines and, second, zero earnings are relevant where management attempts to avoid losses.[1183] With respect to the first target, it is assumed that annual 2002 earnings are managed towards a target defined by annual 2001 earnings.[1184]

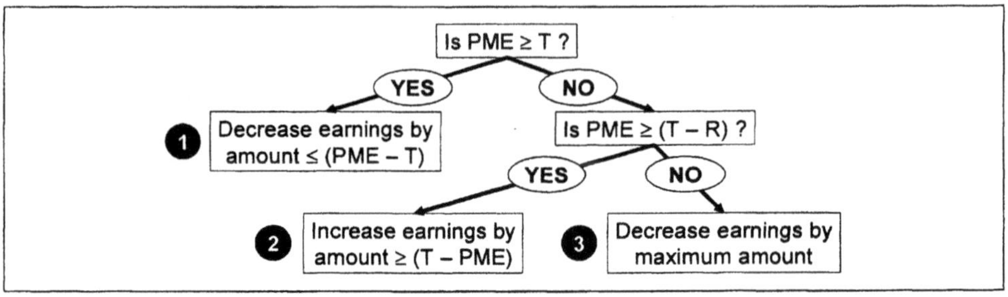

Figure 14: Earnings management relative to a simple earnings target

---

1181 Similar models have been developed by Abarbanell and Lehavy (2000, figures 1 and 2). See also Kinney and Trezevant (1997, p. 45).

1182 Again, refer to section 3.3.2.4.5 above.

1183 Below, these targets are collectively referred to as "the earnings target", T. A third target, analysts' (consensus) earnings forecasts, is not explicitly considered here due to lacking data availability as well as uncertainties regarding analysts' treatment of transitional SFAS 142 goodwill write-offs. For example, Philbrick and Ricks (1991, p. 401) state that "IBES provides no specific instructions to individual analysts about the treatment of extraordinary items. While analysts typically forecast *EPS* before extraordinary items, 'extraordinary' is undefined." They report that "*IBES* refers to extraordinary items as 'write downs which are at the discretion of management,' while according to *GAAP*, not all discretionary write-downs qualify as extraordinary items" (emphasis in original). Therefore, although transitional SFAS 142 goodwill write-offs are not extraordinary items under APB Opinion 30, they might or might not nonetheless be adjusted out of I/B/E/S forecasts. Similarly, Degeorge, Patel and Zeckhauser (1999, p. 16) state that, according to I/B/E/S, I/B/E/S forecasts exclude unusual or nonrecurring charges. For more detail on this issue, refer to section 3.3.2.4.8 above.

1184 In the special setting considered here, adoption of SFAS 142, the relevant measurement date for both actual earnings and earnings targets is not entirely self-evident. On the one hand, any goodwill impairment is to be measured as of the date of initial application (i.e. as of January 1, 2002, for calendar-year firms) and disclosed via a restatement of the first quarterly report of the fiscal year. In that respect, the relevant earnings number would be (restated) first-quarter earnings, and the relevant target would be the prior period's first-quarter earnings. However, because firms are given up to 12 months to detect and measure any goodwill impairment, more than nine months may elapse before investors would learn whether the first-quarter earnings target has been met. It is not reasonable to assume that investors attach much relevance to a restated earnings figure for a past time period. Since the year-end of fiscal 2002 is the date by which firms are required to complete their initial goodwill impairment tests, information on the outcome of the test was not available on a broad scale before the time by which annual reports for 2002 were published.

If pre-managed earnings, PME, is *above* the target, management is expected to take action ❶, i.e. engage in earnings management that decreases earnings to a level equal to or just above the target. This behavior has been referred to as "cookie jar reserving",[1185] and is based on the rationale that reserves are valuable and, by decreasing earnings, management reserves a portion of current earnings to balance potential future earnings shortfalls. Applied to the SFAS 142 setting, action ❶ would imply that management has incentive to take a goodwill write-off equal to or less than the amount by which pre-managed earnings is above the target, (PME – T). Alternatively, if managers of "target beaters" on average expect to beat targets again in future periods, these firms can be expected to avoid transitional SFAS 142 goodwill write-offs altogether, storing up write-off potential for future "cookie-jar reserving" purposes.[1186] Since the literature reviewed in section 3.3.2.4.5.1 indicates that (PME – T) is usually very small,[1187] small or no write-offs would be expected in both scenarios.

On the other hand, if PME is already *below* the target, management's expected behavior depends on the amount of earnings management reserves, R, available to offset the deficit by which PME falls short of T. If reserves are sufficient to achieve T by income-increasing earnings management, i.e. PME lies between T and (T – R), action ❷ is expected. In this case, management attempts to achieve earnings in the amount of T by income-increasing earnings management, using up all or part of R in the process. In the partial analysis focusing on SFAS 142 goodwill write-offs, R is necessarily zero, since negative write-offs (i.e. "write-ups") are not permitted under the standard.[1188] Consequently, alternative ❷ is not available to management in this setting.

Finally, if R is insufficient to balance the deficit (T – PME), managers are expected to maximize future reserves by taking action ❸. As a second-best solution when achieving T is impossible, earnings are decreased by the largest possible amount in order to anticipate future write-offs in the current period. This behavior is referred to as the "big bath"

1185 See Levitt (1998) and Abarbanell and Lehavy (2000, p. 8).

1186 Duvall et al. (1992) suggest that investors find it difficult to unravel goodwill-related financial statement effects in later periods, implying that regular goodwill write-offs are likely to be less "visible" than transitional ones.

1187 See, for example, Burgstahler and Dichev (1997), who indicate that firms frequently employ earnings management to push earnings just beyond the target. In such cases, it would be unreasonable to assume that transitional SFAS 142 write-offs would be used to manage earnings in the opposite direction.

1188 Reversals of prior impairment losses are explicitly prohibited by SFAS 142.20. If goodwill could be written up (or goodwill write-offs reversed), a more comprehensive test of the model could be conducted. For example, Moehrle (2002) analyzes whether restructuring charge reversals are used to meet or beat earnings targets.

strategy.[1189] Applied to the SFAS 142 setting, this rationale implies that managers have incentive to write off the highest possible amount of goodwill.[1190] This is especially true to the extent that managers expect transitional SFAS 142 goodwill write-offs to be ignored by investors due to their (perceived) transitory nature.[1191] Taken together, the write-off amounts are expected to be significantly different where PME ≥ T versus PME < T, with larger write-offs expected for the second group.

H_D^{FR} 4:

Ceteris paribus, a negative relation exists between the write-off decision and the firms' pre-write-off earnings meeting earnings targets.

5.2.3.2.1.2 Firms exceeding earnings targets

Consistent with the considerations above, firms that, before the transitional SFAS 142 goodwill write-off decision is made, exceed their target earnings are assumed to either avoid write-offs altogether or engage in "cookie-jar reserving", writing off no more than the amount by which pre-write-off earnings exceed the target.

H_A^{FR} 5:

Ceteris paribus, for firms with pre-write-off earnings in excess of targets, a positive relation exists between the write-off amount and the amount of the excess.

5.2.3.2.1.3 Firms falling short of earnings targets

Where the above model predicts action ❸ ("big bath"), it is not reasonable to assume that the available goodwill book value will be written off in full in all cases. Generally, management will increase the write-off amount as long as the marginal benefits of this behavior exceed the marginal costs. Certain factors are expected to limit the extent to which management's net benefits increase in the amount of goodwill written off.[1192] In general, where a firm expects that a higher write-off will cause some accounting-based heuristic used by (potential) investors to exceed (or fall short of, respectively) some cutoff point, the amount written off will be limited by the lower amount of goodwill book value and the number relevant to such cutoff point.

1189 As has been discussed in section 3.3.2.4.6 above, the capital market penalties associated with large shortfalls have been found to be proportionately less than those following relatively small shortfalls. In other words, managers might consider the benefits of "big bath" accounting to outweigh its cost.

1190 See also Hitz and Kuhner (2002, p. 285) and Küting, Weber and Wirth (2001, p. 192).

1191 See also Eberle (2002b, p. 190), Pellens, Sellhorn and Weinreis (2002), and Segal (2003, p. 21). Refer to section 3.3.2.4.8.

1192 Among these factors are the contracting considerations discussed in the previous section.

Extant empirical research surrounding the debate on goodwill accounting and the purchase/pooling decision mainly focuses on the impact of these procedures on firms' income statements and assets.[1193] It might also be important how a firm's equity and leverage are influenced by financial reporting decisions related to goodwill. In the simplest case, the write-off amount will be limited by the amount of equity on the firm's books, since managers have incentive to avoid negative equity. However, this restriction will only apply where goodwill book value is large enough to, where written off completely, jeopardize the amount of equity.

H_A^{FR} 6:

Ceteris paribus, for firms that fall short of earnings targets, a positive relation exists between the write-off amount and the smaller amount of goodwill and equity.

While firms that fall short of earnings targets are expected to practice "big bath", the observation of frequent, large write-offs in that group is not sufficient to conclude that these write-offs result from earnings management. This conclusion can be strengthened when write-offs are observed to coincide with other indicators of a "big bath" strategy. According to the considerations discussed in section 3.3.2.4.6 above, "big bath" can be expected to be most successful when the signal conveyed by management is credibly associated with good news. Such circumstances include recent changes in top management, where a new CEO re-evaluates corporate strategy and abandons unprofitable operations.[1194] In these situations, goodwill write-offs frequently coincide with other restructuring-type charges, which have found to be associated with positive stock market reactions.[1195] Likewise, the assumption that write-offs are recorded as part of a "big bath" strategy would be further supported if other income-decreasing earnings management measures were observed concurrently.[1196] The focus is placed on coinciding special items, because this specific accrual has been documented in prior research to be a low-cost instrument of earnings management that might have special relevance in a setting where management

---

1193 Refer to section 2.4.4.3 above.

1194 For a similar hypothesis, refer to Beatty and Weber (2004, p. 12).

1195 See, for example, Brickley and Van Drunen (1990). Bartov, Lindahl and Ricks (1998, p. 328) distinguish write-offs that purely reflect declines in asset values from those that result from the decision to change operations. Consistent with the notion that the latter category is assumed to convey (at least in part) good news to investors, the authors find positive, albeit insignificant, market reactions to these write-offs. For similar evidence, refer to sections 3.3.2.4.6 and 3.4.3.1 above.

1196 In contrast to this notion, Rees, Gill and Gore (1996, p. 168) argue that "documented abnormal accruals in the write-down year ... imply that managers are responding to changes in economic circumstances as opposed to acting opportunistically."

is concerned about achieving earnings targets.[1197] Overall, it must be noted that the simultaneous occurrence of goodwill write-offs, restructuring-type charges, and management changes does not necessarily imply earnings management, because it might indicate that an actual restructuring is under way.[1198]

H_D^{FR} 7a :

Ceteris paribus, for firms that fall short of earnings targets, a positive relation exists between the write-off decision and a recent CEO change.

H_D^{FR} 7b :

Ceteris paribus, for firms that fall short of earnings targets, a positive relation exists between the write-off decision and concurrent restructuring charges.

H_D^{FR} 7c :

Ceteris paribus, for firms that fall short of earnings targets, a positive relation exists between the write-off decision and concurrent special items.

5.2.3.2.2 Rating

As discussed in section 3.3.2.4.7, it is proposed that a manager's financial reporting decision is influenced by its expected repercussions on rating agencies' assessments of the firm and potentially resulting changes in the cost of capital. The discussion in that section outlines the rating process and the role of financial ratios in that process. Measures of financial leverage are crucial elements in arriving at a rating. Therefore, it is likely that managers are concerned about the effect that transitional SFAS 142 goodwill write-offs might have on measures of financial leverage.

S&P is concerned about a lack of balance sheet comparability due to internationally different accounting treatments of goodwill.[1199] With specific regard to SFAS 142, S&P recommends in its proposal of a "core earnings" measure that goodwill impairment charges be excluded from core earnings.[1200] However, no statement is made to the effect

1197 See Marquardt and Wiedman (2002, pp. 29-30). In a related study, Kinney and Trezevant (1997) report that firms incur negative special items to achieve "big bath" results. See also Pourciau (1993, p. 330). Although special items are by definition expected to average out to zero under normal circumstances, both studies report negative means for special items.

1198 It is the coincidence of all those factors combined in firms that have a powerful "big bath" incentive (i.e. falling short of a target) that provides a strong indication that earnings management is behind the write-off.

1199 See S&P (2003, p. 31).

1200 See S&P (2002). Charges due to other asset write-offs are also added back to earnings, which affects earnings-based ratios. See S&P (2003, p. 53).

that write-offs are adjusted for in the balance sheet. On the contrary, an S&P analyst states that, "in general [the way in which a firm's SFAS 142 goodwill write-off impacts its credit rating] is not a yes or no answer and the impact on rating, if any, will be assessed based on numerous qualitative as well as quantitative attributes associated with the writedown, and the reasons thereof, as well as any other potential consequences such as violation of debt covenants, minimum regulatory capital requirements, etc."[1201] This statement suggests that S&P treats SFAS 142 write-offs similar to direct deductions of goodwill from equity. Therefore, transitional SFAS 142 write-offs have the potential to alter leverage ratios via their effect on stockholders' equity. Managers, then, have incentive to limit the write-off's effect on financial leverage ratios.[1202]

Elliott and Hanna (1996) report that bond ratings, as a measure of financial risk, decline as firms record discretionary asset write-offs, especially where such write-offs occur repeatedly in consecutive years.[1203] Knowing this, managers might have incentive to avoid such write-offs.[1204] Therefore, it is assumed here that firms with low bond ratings are more reluctant than others to further jeopardize their rating by recording a write-off.[1205]

$\mathbf{H_D^{FR}\ 8:}$	$\mathbf{H_A^{FR}\ 8:}$
Ceteris paribus, a negative relation exists between the write-off decision and the bond rating.[1206]	Ceteris paribus, a negative relation exists between the write-off amount and the bond rating.

5.2.4 Control variables

Because transitional SFAS 142 goodwill write-off behavior is expected to be influenced by factors that are not explicitly modeled, the following control variables are considered:

1201 Email correspondence dated June 23, 2003, with Neri Bukspan, credit analyst with Standard & Poor's.

1202 It must be noted that other rating-relevant ratios are affected *positively* by SFAS 142: Even if write-offs are not simply backed out of earnings but replaced by some amortization charge, ratios such as "return on capital" (S&P (2003, p. 55) will increase due to lower equity. However, it is not plausible that firms are rewarded for decreased equity and impaired assets.

1203 See Elliott and Hanna (1996, p. 152).

1204 On the other hand, causality is not clear: Write-offs and rating downgrades are likely to be jointly determined by adverse changes in the firm's future prospects. To that extent, it is difficult to distinguish empirically between economic and incentive factors influencing write-off behavior. Refer to section 3.3.2.3.6.

1205 More accurately, this reluctance should increase in the probability of a downgrade and the amount of costs anticipated to follow from it. Measuring these more subtle criteria is beyond the scope of this study.

1206 As explained in Table 6 below, the bond rating is coded as an integer descending in the firm's rating. Therefore, the lower the rating, the higher the rating variable.

First, the amount, economic characteristics, and fair value of the goodwill asset are expected to vary across industries. Therefore, industry membership is expected to be an explanatory factor behind write-off behavior, although no specific relation is predicted.[1207]

Second, firm size is possibly associated with a multitude of factors, including leverage, information production costs, competitive advantage, management ability, quality of accounting advice, and risk (income variability).[1208] Further, it might be a proxy for bargaining power, implying that smaller firms are forced to pay the full net present value for their acquisitions and incur larger goodwills that tend to fall below fair value more quickly when adverse economic developments occur.[1209] Also, prior research indicates that smaller firms are to a lesser extent followed by analysts, possibly implying that capital market-related incentives are less strong for them.[1210]

Third, firms adopting SFAS 142 as of January 1, 2002, possibly face different economic and incentive environments than do early or late adopters. Therefore, a fiscal year-end indicator variable is included to capture any difference.

Finally, the write-off amount (deflated by total assets in order to eliminate size effects) might be associated with the relative significance that overall goodwill book value has for the firm. For example, firms for which goodwill represents a substantial portion of their asset base might be reluctant to record large write-offs, which would significantly diminish their earnings and size. Also, an association of the two variables is expected simply because the write-off amount is limited by the absolute amount of goodwill.[1211] For these reasons, goodwill book value, also deflated by total assets, is considered as a control variable.

1207 Industry membership is explicitly considered in the descriptive analysis below (Table A. 2 and Table A. 4). But since there is no economic reason to assume a linear relation between the write-off amount and the firm's SIC code, it is not included as an explanatory variable in the regression analysis.

1208 Refer to Moses (1987, p. 363 fn. 6). See also Ball and Foster (1982, p. 184 fn. 36). Bujaki and Richardson (1997) provide a review of the uses of firm size in accounting research.

1209 See Clinch (1997, p. 344).

1210 See Foster, Olsen and Shevlin (1984).

1211 Furthermore, firms with larger goodwill (scaled by total assets) will, ceteris paribus, record higher goodwill write-offs (scaled by total assets).

5.3 Research design and descriptive information

5.3.1 Variable definition

Since transitional SFAS 142 goodwill write-offs are presented as a first-quarter accounting change in the adoption year,[1212] COMPUSTAT quarterly item DATA117 (accounting changes – cumulative effect) is used to capture the transitional write-off amount.[1213] This variable is subject to potential measurement error because accounting changes other than the adoption of SFAS 142 might be included in COMPUSTAT quarterly item DATA117. In an attempt to minimize this potential measurement error, recent FASB statements are examined in order to ascertain the extent to which their adoption has possibly resulted in accounting changes being disclosed within COMPUSTAT quarterly item DATA117. This analysis suggests that such effects are limited at most: First, SFAS 140, *Accounting for Transfers and Servicing of Financial Assets and Extinguishments of Liabilities – A replacement of FASB Statement 125*, issued in September 2000, was to be applied to transfers and servicing of financial assets and extinguishments of liabilities occurring after March 31, 2001 (SFAS 140.19-25). Therefore, no effect on the Q1/2002 accounting change is expected.

Second, According to SFAS 141.62, any unamortized „negative goodwill" balances from pre-SFAS 141 periods were to be written off and recognized as the effect of a change in accounting principle. This accounting change was, as a rule, to be recognized at the adoption date of SFAS 142. Before SFAS 141 was issued, "negative goodwill" was accounted for under APB Opinion 16. APB Opinion 16.91 requires that "negative goodwill" first be allocated to reduce proportionately the values assigned to non-current assets, and that any remainder be classified as a deferred credit and amortized systematically to income over no more than 40 years. This implies that accounting changes disclosed in the first quarter of 2002 potentially include write-offs of such unamortized „negative goodwill" balances. However, according to economic reasoning, such remaining deferred credits should be observed only in very exceptional circumstances, because acquirers will in most cases have to pay an acquisition price that is at least equal to the book value of net assets. Therefore, it is assumed here that any measurement error in the transitional SFAS 142 goodwill write-off variable that is introduced by this SFAS 141 effect is immaterial.

[1212] Refer to section 4.7.3.

[1213] COMPUSTAT annual items DATA368 and DATA369 (goodwill impairment pre-tax and after tax, respectively) are not adequate in this respect, since they only capture write-offs taken *subsequent to* the transitional impairment test.

Third, although SFAS 143, *Accounting for Asset Retirement Obligations*, issued in June 2001, is only effective for fiscal years beginning after June 15, 2002 (SFAS 143.24), early adopters of this statement also present its adoption effect as a Q1/2002 accounting change (SFAS 143.24, 26). Therefore, firms with asset retirement obligations that also choose to adopt SFAS 143 early as of the beginning of fiscal 2002 might distort the transitional SFAS 142 goodwill write-off variable. However, due to the infrequent concurrence of these two conditions, any measurement error is assumed to be immaterial.

Finally, SFAS 144, *Accounting for the Impairment or Disposal of Long-Lived Assets*, issued in August 2001, takes effect at the same time as SFAS 142 (SFAS 144.49). However, its initial application does not result in Q1/2002 accounting changes. All other FASB statements issued subsequent to SFAS 144 were effective after the first quarter of 2002 and did, even where applied early, in most cases not involve disclosure as a first-quarter change in accounting principle. In addition, some of these statements involved only minor changes to existing GAAP. Consistent with the considerations explained above, any measurement error in the transitional SFAS 142 goodwill write-off variable potentially introduced by (early) adoption of other FASB statements is assumed to be immaterial.

Table 5 provides further reassurance on this issue; documenting that negative DATA117 entries are observed relatively frequently in goodwill firms (13.40%), whereas they hardly occur at all (0.71%) in firms having no goodwill at the end of fiscal 2001. This finding further corroborates that negative effects of accounting changes in the goodwill sample are the result of transitional SFAS 142 goodwill write-offs.

Cumulative effect of accounting change in 2001 (DATA117_Q1)	**Firms on the COMPUSTAT Industrial Annual tape**[1214]			
	Positive goodwill (DATA204_2001 > 0)		**Zero goodwill (DATA204_2001 = 0)**	
	N	%	N	%
DATA117_Q1 unavailable	182	6.02	215	5.85
DATA117_Q1 > 0	30	0.99	18	0.49
DATA117_Q1 = 0	2,406	79.59	3,418	92.96
DATA117_Q1 < 0	405	13.40	26	0.71
Total	**3,023**	**100.0**	**3,677**	**100.0**

Table 5: Potential measurement error in the dependent variable

In addition, since transitional SFAS 142 goodwill write-offs are negative items, a small number of firms that reported a positive number in the Q1/2002 COMPUSTAT quarterly

[1214] For the remaining firms, no goodwill data are available.

item DATA117 were excluded from the sample. Likewise, since the write-off cannot be higher than goodwill book value, all firms that wrote off more than that amount were also not considered.

The write-off amount is defined as a positive number.[1215] Deflators encountered in the literature include total assets,[1216] the market value of equity, and the number of shares.[1217] Another possibility would be the book value of goodwill itself; however, this deflator has the disadvantage that even enormous write-offs, relative to goodwill book value, might still be immaterial to both financial statement preparers and users where goodwill book value itself is immaterial. In contrast, measuring the goodwill write-off as a percentage of total assets ensures that the materiality of the resulting financial statement effect is adequately captured.

Table 6 describes all the variables used below.

1215 For non-write-off firms, the write-off amount is entered as zero.

1216 Francis, Hanna and Vincent (1996, p. 125) and Segal (2003, p. 17).

1217 Heflin and Warfield (1997, pp. 24, 26-8) use both of these deflators.

Variable	Hypothesis (predicted sign)	Verbal explanation	Calculation and data source[1218]
Explained variable			
TGWO_D$_i$		Dichotomous variable: 1 where firm i records a *transitional* SFAS 142 goodwill write-off; 0 otherwise.	
TGWO_A$_i$		Firm i's amount of *transitional* SFAS 142 goodwill write-off, deflated by prior-period total assets, measured at the end of the first fiscal quarter 2002.	COMPUSTAT quarterly item DATA117, as a positive number. $TGWO\_A = \frac{(-1)\cdot DATA117\_Q1}{DATA6\_2001}$.
Explanatory variables – economic factors			
MTB$_i$	H_D^{EC} 1 (–) H_A^{EC} 1 (–)	Firm i's MTB ratio, measured at the end of 2001.	$MTB = \frac{DATA25\_2001 \cdot DATA199\_2001}{DATA60\_2001}$
RET$_i$	H_D^{EC} 2a (–) H_A^{EC} 2a (–)	Firm i's cumulative stock performance, measured over the fiscal years 2000 and 2001.	$RET = \frac{DATA199\_2001}{DATA199\_1999} - 1$
ΔROA$_i$	H_D^{EC} 2b (–) H_A^{EC} 2b (–)	Firm i's percentage point change in ROA between the fiscal years 2000 and 2001.	$\Delta ROA = ROA01 - ROA00$, where $ROA01 = \frac{DATA172\_2001 + DATA15\_2001}{\frac{1}{2}[DATA6\_2000 + DATA6\_2001 - (DATA172\_2001 + DATA15\_2001)]}$ and $ROA00 = \frac{DATA172\_2000 + DATA15\_2000}{\frac{1}{2}[DATA6\_1999 + DATA6\_2000 - (DATA172\_2000 + DATA15\_2000)]}$.

Continued on next page

1218 The items listed denote COMPUSTAT Industrial Annual data items, unless otherwise stated, with suffixes representing the respective fiscal years. With the exception of stock price (DATA199; measured in dollars and cents) and common shares outstanding (DATA25; measured in millions), all data are measured in millions of dollars. Stock price data is not adjusted for dividends and stock splits.

Variable	Hypothesis (predicted sign)	Verbal explanation	Calculation and data source
Explanatory variables – economic-consequences incentives			
AIP_i	H_D^{FR} 1 (+)	Mean of firm i's assets-in-place, measured as the relation of PP&E (net of accumulated depreciation) to total market value, at the end of 2001 and 2002.	$AIP = \frac{1}{2}(AIP02 + AIP01)$, where $AIP02 = \frac{DATA8\_2002}{DATA25\_2002 \cdot DATA1999\_2002 + DATA9\_2002 + DATA34\_2002}$ and $AIP01 = \frac{DATA8\_2001}{DATA25\_2001 \cdot DATA1999\_2001 + DATA9\_2001 + DATA34\_2001}$.
DTE_i	H_D^{FR} 2 (–) H_A^{FR} 2 (–)	Mean of the differences between firm i's DTE ratio and the median DTE ratio in firm i's two-digit SIC industry, at the end of 2001 and 2002.	$DTE = \frac{(DTE02 - INDDTE02) + (DTE01 - INDDTE01)}{2}$, where $DTE02 = \frac{DATA9\_2002 + DATA34\_2002}{DATA60\_2002 - DATA117\_Q1}$, $DTE01 = \frac{DATA9\_2001 + DATA34\_2001}{DATA60\_2001}$, INDDTE02=industry median (DTE02), and INDDTE01= industry median (DTE01).
MSH_i	H_D^{FR} 3a (?)	Mean of firm i's market shares, measured as the relation of firm sales (DATA12) to two-digit SIC industry sales, at the end of 2001 and 2002; industry sales based on all available firms.	
$HERF_i$	H_D^{FR} 3b (?)	Mean of the Herfindahl indexes of firm i's two-digit SIC industry, measured as the sum of the squares of the market shares of each firm in the industry, at the end of 2001 and 2002; industry sales based on all available firms.	
$\Delta PWOROA_i$	H_D^{FR} 3c (?)	Firm i's change in ROA (before transitional SFAS 142 goodwill write-off) in 2002 over regular ROA in 2001.	$\Delta PWOROA = \frac{DATA172\_2002 + DATA15\_2002 - DATA117\_Q1}{\frac{1}{2}[DATA6\_2001 + DATA6\_2002 - (DATA172\_2002 + DATA15\_2002) - DATA117\_Q1]}$

Continued on next page

Variable	Hypothesis (predicted sign)	Verbal explanation	Calculation and data source
Explanatory variables – capital market-related incentives			
$TARGET\_PP_i$ $TARGET\_Z_i$	H_D^{FR} 4 (–)	Dichotomous variable: 1 where firm i's annual pre-write-off net income is above the prior year's level (above zero) in 2002; 0 otherwise.	TARGET_PP: (DATA172_2002 – DATA117_Q1) ≥ DATA172_2001 and TARGET_Z: (DATA172_2002 – DATA117_Q1) ≥ 0
DIF_PP_i DIF_Z_i	H_A^{FR} 5 (+)	Difference between firm i's annual pre-write-off net income and the prior year's level (and zero), deflated by prior-period total assets, in 2002.	$DIF\_PP = \frac{DATA172\_2002 - DATA117\_Q1 - DATA172\_2001}{DATA6\_2001}$ and $DIF\_Z = \frac{DATA172\_2002 - DATA117\_Q1}{DATA6\_2001}$.
EQ_i	H_A^{FR} 6 (+)	Firm i's pre-write-off common equity, deflated by pre-write-off total assets, at the end of 2002.	$EQ = \frac{DATA60\_2002 - DATA117\_Q1}{DATA6\_2002 - DATA117\_Q1}$
ΔCEO_i	H_D^{FR} 7a (+)	Dichotomous variable: 1 where firm i experienced a change in the CEO position during 2001 or 2002; 0 otherwise. ΔCEO_i is coded based on ExecuComp data items BECAMECEO and PCEO.	
$RESTR_i$	H_D^{FR} 7b (+)	Firm i's restructuring cost (pre-tax), deflated by total assets, measured at the end of 2002.	$RESTR = \frac{DATA376\_2002}{DATA6\_2002}$
$SPEC_i$	H_D^{FR} 7c (+)	Firm i's special items and write-downs (pre-tax), deflated by total assets, measured at the end of 2002.	$SPEC = \frac{DATA17\_2002 + DATA384\_2002 + DATA380\_2002}{DATA6\_2002}$
$RATING_i$	H_D^{FR} 8 (–) H_A^{FR} 8 (–)	Firm i's long-term domestic issuer credit rating in 2001.	DATA280. RATING is coded as an ascending series of integers, running from 2 for AAA through 29 for SD (selective default). Therefore, the better a firm's rating, the lower DATA280.

Continued on next page

Variable	Hypothesis (predicted sign)	Verbal explanation	Calculation and data source
Explanatory variables – control variables			
FYR_i	(?)	Dichotomous variable: 1 where firm i's fiscal year-end in 2001 is December 31; 0 otherwise. FYR is coded based on COMPUSTAT annual item FYR.	
$SIZE_i$	(?)	Firm i's size, measured by the mean of firm i's market values of equity at the end of 2001 and 2002.	$SIZE = \frac{1}{2}\left[(DATA25\_2001 \cdot DATA199\_2001) + (DATA25\_2002 \cdot DATA199\_2002)\right]$
$SIZE\_LOG_i$	(?)	Natural logarithm of SIZE.	$SIZE\_LOG = \log(SIZE)$
GW_i	(?)	Firm i's goodwill book value, deflated by total assets, measured at the end of 2001.	$GW = \frac{DATA204\_2001}{DATA6\_2001}$

Table 6: Definition and explanation of variables

5.3.2 Sample selection

Previous studies of SFAS 142 goodwill write-offs analyze firms that publicly announce their write-off decision in addition to publishing their financial statements.[1219] By announcing the write-off without being required to do so, firms self-select into a sample not strictly comprised of write-off firms but of firms that, having written off their goodwill, chose to disclose this fact. Arguably, this group is different from write-off firms that choose not to announce the write-off.[1220] To mitigate potential problems stemming from this sample selection procedure, a broad sample of publicly listed U. S. firms is used. These firms are subjected to certain requirements. Table 7 describes the sample selection procedure.

Panel A: Basic sample	**firms**	**remain**	**% of available**
Observations included on the COMPUSTAT Industrial Annual tape ("available")	22,078	22,078	100.0
Less: Observations not included on the COMPUSTAT Industrial Quarterly tape	-4,193	17,885	81.0
Less: Banking and financial institutions (SIC category 6)	-4,087	13,798	62.5
Less: Firms for which not all data items required for the full-sample regression analyses are available[1221]	-11,120	2,678	12.1
Less: Firms with negative equity	-459	2,219	10.1
Basic sample		**2,219**	**10.1**

Panel B: Goodwill and non-goodwill samples	**firms**	**% of available**	**% of basic sample**
Basic sample	2,219	10.1	100.0
Less: 16 firms excluded due to problems with the dependent variable[1222]	2,203	10.0	99.3
Goodwill sample: Firms with positive goodwill	**1,248**	**5.7**	**56.2**
Non-goodwill sample: Firms without positive goodwill	**955**	**4.3**	**43.0**

Continued on next page

1219 Refer to Henning, Shaw and Stock (2002) and Segal (2003).

1220 Francis, Hanna and Vincent (1996, p. 119) acknowledge this problem, stating that their "analyses of the causes and shareholder wealth effects of write-offs are joint tests of managements' decisions to write off assets and to disclose in press releases that they have done so." They document that a substantial portion of write-off firms do not specifically disclose the write-off. The authors also point to other studies potentially suffering from this same shortcoming.

1221 Smaller sub-samples are later formed for specific regressions. Data required for these regressions may not be available for the full sample.

1222 11 firms were excluded due to *positive* effects of a change in accounting principle (DATA117) in the first quarter of 2002. 5 more firms were excluded because DATA117 is larger in absolute value than goodwill itself.

Panel C: Write-off and non-write-off samples	**firms**	**% of available**	**% of basic sample**	**% of goodwill sample**
Goodwill sample	1,248	5.7	56.2	100.0
Non-write-off sample: Firms without transitional SFAS 142 goodwill write-off[1223]	**1,024**	**4.6**	**46.1**	**82.1**
Write-off sample: Firms with transitional SFAS 142 goodwill write-off[1224]	**224**	**1.0**	**10.1**	**17.9**

Table 7: Sample selection

The starting point is the population of the COMPUSTAT Industrial Annual tape. As of the retrieval date, 22,078 firms were included in the database.[1225] Since annual as well as quarterly data are required for my analysis, 4,193 firms are deleted that are not included on the COMPUSTAT Industrial Quarterly tape.[1226] Next, 4,087 banks and financial institutions are excluded because the financial statement structures of these firms are widely different from those of most other firms and therefore would be likely to distort results.[1227] Subsequently, it is required that firms have available the data required to calculate the variables summarized in Table 6 above.[1228] This requirement represents the most substantial cut, resulting in 11,120 observations being dropped. Finally, 459 firms with negative equity in fiscal 2001 or 2002 are excluded, because not only are these firms' financial ratios difficult to interpret, they are also likely to operate in radically different economic and incentive environments than the rest of the sample. This procedure (Panel A) results in a basic sample of 2,219 firms.

Panel B reconciles this basic sample to a sample of firms that are potential candidates for transitional SFAS 142 goodwill write-offs. These firms meet two additional data requirements: First, they are adopters of SFAS 142 in the year of transition. According to SFAS 142.48, that is the case when a firm has positive goodwill on its balance sheet as of

1223 Thereof firms with *regular* (post-transitional) SFAS 142 goodwill write-offs in 2002: 116 (11.3% of the non-write-off sample).

1224 Thereof firms with *regular* (post-transitional) SFAS 142 goodwill write-offs in 2002: 27 (12.1% of the write-off sample).

1225 Annual data was retrieved on June 4, 2003, i.e. before the annual update for 2003 was available. Repeating the analysis subsequent to the annual update would result in far fewer firms being eliminated from the sample due to missing data.

1226 Quarterly data was retrieved on July 22, 2003.

1227 Like in Riedl (2002, pp. 20, 36), firms falling within the SIC 6 category are excluded.

1228 However, since data items required for computing some of the capital market-related incentives variables (e.g. change in the CEO position for 2002) are not available for the majority of firms, the sample size would be unduly reduced if firms lacking those data were *a priori* excluded from the sample. Therefore, tests relying on these data are restricted to a smaller sample size, as will be indicated where applicable.

the beginning of the fiscal year. For 955 firms, goodwill (COMPUSTAT item DATA204) is zero. Second, only those firms are included for which a potential transitional SFAS 142 goodwill write-off can be ascertained with reasonable certainty. Therefore, 11 firms are eliminated from the sample because they report positive accounting changes (DATA117) in the first quarter of 2002, and 5 more firms are excluded because DATA117 is larger in absolute amount than goodwill itself. Consequently, the basic sample disaggregates into a non-goodwill sample of 955 and a goodwill sample of 1,248 usable observations.

Finally, Panel C distinguishes two sub-samples of the goodwill sample. The 1,024 firms in the non-write-off sample did not write off their goodwill as a result of the transitional impairment test upon adoption of SFAS 142. Conversely, the 224 firms included in the write-off sample did write off their goodwill upon adoption,[1229] which amounts to 17.9% of the whole goodwill sample.

5.3.3 Descriptive statistics and comparative analyses

In this section, descriptive statistics for the four samples are provided and preliminary comparative tests undertaken. First, the four samples are compared based on the most important variables defined in Table 6 above, and equality tests for the median and mean are provided. Second, the significance of goodwill write-offs is assessed for the firms in the goodwill sample. Third, preliminary evidence on some of the hypotheses posited in section 5.2 is presented.

Table 8 provides descriptive comparisons of the two groups comprising the basic sample: the non-goodwill firms and the goodwill firms (see Panel B of Table 7).

1229 A total of 143 regular (post-transition) SFAS 142 goodwill write-offs were reported by the firms in the goodwill sample during fiscal 2002.

Panel A: Non-goodwill sample (N = 955)

Variable	Mean	StDev	Min	1st qrt	Med	3rd qrt	Max
MTB	5.10**	23.61	0.00	0.89	1.74	3.73	547.64
RET	2.96	67.62	-1.00	-0.59	-0.16**	0.48	2,049.00
ΔROA	-0.03	0.90	-24.00	-0.08	-0.02	0.04	7.32
AIP	0.39**	0.47	0.00	0.06	0.23	0.60	5.09
DTE02	1.70	17.02	0.00	0.00	0.20***	0.78	455.39
MV°	1,075***	9,703	0	10	44***	234	250,846
TA°	863***	5,906	0	11	45***	220	147,909
SAL°	793***	6,989	0	6	32***	167	183,210
MSH	0.005***	0.026	0.000	0.000	0.000***	0.001	0.413
HERF	0.075	0.067	0.015	0.044	0.050***	0.085	0.569
ΔPWOROA	-0.03**	0.36	-7.16	-0.09	-0.01***	0.05	1.46
EQ	0.56***	0.25	0.00	0.37	0.57***	0.76	1.00

Panel B: Goodwill sample (N = 1,248)

Variable	Mean	StDev	Min	1st qrt	Med	3rd qrt	Max
MTB	3.49**	12.49	0.00	0.96	1.73	3.01	250.66
RET	0.65	16.46	-1.00	-0.45	-0.07**	0.36	576.78
ΔROA	-0.01	0.35	-0.80	-0.06	-0.02	0.01	11.05
AIP	0.34**	0.47	0.00	0.10	0.23	0.48	11.17
DTE02	1.32	3.77	0.00	0.16	0.52***	1.14	73.79
MV°	3,569***	17,173	0	42	269***	1,230	320,299
TA°	3,578***	20,175	1	84	400***	1,552	535,134
SAL°	2,803***	11,046	0	83	402***	1,551	176,470
MSH	0.017***	0.045	0.000	0.000	0.002***	0.012	0.623
HERF	0.075	0.060	0.015	0.046	0.050***	0.087	0.623
ΔPWOROA	-0.01**	0.13	-2.18	-0.04	0.00***	0.03	0.66
EQ	0.47***	0.22	0.01	0.31	0.46***	0.62	0.99

*, **, ***: Differences in mean (t-test) and median (adjusted $\chi 2$-test), respectively, significant at the 10, 5, or 1% levels. Test statistics and p-values are reported in Table A. 1 in the appendix.

° MV, TA, and SAL represent mean values (fiscal 2001 and 2002) for the market value of equity, total assets, and sales, respectively.

For other variable definitions, refer to Table 6. Monetary amounts are in million $.

Table 8: Comparison of the non-goodwill and goodwill samples

The comparative analysis suggests that the two sub-samples are significantly different in several respects, albeit widely similar in others. The median MTB ratios are roughly equal, while the mean in the non-goodwill sample is substantially larger due to outlying observations. Accounting performance measured in terms of ROA change during 2001 is also comparable, whereas goodwill firms experienced a significantly (at the 5% level) higher median stock return during 2000 and 2001. Most strikingly, goodwill firms are vastly larger and more highly in debt, whereas the respective portions of assets-in-place are similar on average. Furthermore, goodwill firms seem to have higher market shares in their industries, which are also more concentrated. Overall, the goodwill sample appears to consist of larger, more established firms than the non-goodwill sample.

Structurally equivalent to Table 8, Table 9 provides comparative evidence for the non-write-off and write-off samples. Goodwill-related information is also reported for these firms.

Panel A: Non-write-off sample (N = 1,024)

Variable	Mean	StDev	Min	1st qrt	Med	3rd qrt	Max
Goodwill 2002							
in million $	354***	1,390	0	4	29***	181	26,093
% total assets	15.17	14.61	0.00	4.07	10.63	22.14	78.19
% BV equity	58.13**	178.46	0.00	8.88	24.83*	58.43	4,102.99
% MV of equity	42.54**	133.51	0.00	4.84	15.64*	37.80	3,083.67
Goodwill 2001							
in million $	311***	1,309	0	5	27***	147	29,791
% total assets	14.76***	14.12	0.04	4.22	10.49***	21.11	80.97
% BV of equity	60.85	202.32	0.06	9.11	24.89***	52.97	3,973.02
% MV of equity	112.66	1,628.51	0.01	4.02	12.72***	32.88	39,413.53
MTB	3.84**	13.57	0.00	1.07	1.88***	3.19	250.66
RET	0.82	18.17	-1.00	-0.41	-0.04***	0.43	576.78
ΔROA	-0.01	0.38	-0.80	-0.06	-0.02	0.01	11.05
AIP	0.33**	0.47	0.00	0.09	0.21***	0.47	11.17
DTE02	1.34	4.01	0.00	0.13	0.49**	1.12	73.79
MV°	3,191*	13,922	0	40	242	1,137	170,960
TA°	2,660***	10,623	1	68	327***	1,317	190,514
SAL°	2,402***	9,819	0	70	311***	1,324	176,470
MSH	0.013***	0.037	0.000	0.000	0.002***	0.010	0.623
HERF	0.072***	0.056	0.015	0.046	0.050***	0.087	0.623
ΔPWOROA	-0.01	0.14	-2.18	-0.04	0.00	0.03	0.64
EQ	0.48***	0.22	0.01	0.31	0.47**	0.64	0.99

Continued on next page

Panel B: Write-off sample (N = 224)

Variable	Mean	StDev	Min	1st qrt	Med	3rd qrt	Max
Goodwill 2002							
in million $	722***	2,931	0	10	66***	457	39,138
% total assets	15.65	15.68	0.00	2.46	11.02	25.06	77.14
% BV of equity	4,454.71**	65,076.97	0.00	6.71	31.87*	76.62	965,312.50
% MV of equity	68.40**	162.55	0.00	4.42	22.84*	57.54	1,620.16
Goodwill 2001							
in million $	919***	2,878	1	32	139***	593	28,287
% total assets	22.46***	17.57	0.44	8.56	17.21***	34.18	81.96
% BV of equity	71.81	154.05	2.17	21.43	47.46***	85.80	2,177.68
% MV of equity	81.15	129.17	0.30	17.33	35.14***	92.78	1,100.70
MTB	1.94**	4.86	0.06	0.62	1.14***	2.01	67.87
RET	-0.12	0.67	-0.97	-0.54	-0.18***	0.17	5.57
ΔROA	-0.02	0.09	-0.43	-0.04	-0.02	0.01	0.35
AIP	0.40**	0.48	0.03	0.15	0.29***	0.57	6.03
DTE02	1.24	2.37	0.00	0.30	0.67**	1.38	25.47
MV°	5,294*	27,502	1	72	347	1,736	320,299
TA°	7,775***	41,675	6	188	813***	3,259	535,134
SAL°	4,635***	15,360	5	220	832***	2,863	162,499
MSH	0.032***	0.067	0.000	0.001	0.006***	0.024	0.501
HERF	0.088***	0.075	0.015	0.046	0.059***	0.091	0.471
ΔPWOROA	0.00	0.09	-0.42	-0.03	0.00	0.02	0.66
EQ	0.43***	0.19	0.02	0.31	0.43**	0.57	0.96

*, **, ***: Differences in mean (t-test) and median (adjusted χ2-test), respectively, significant at the 10, 5, or 1% levels. Test statistics and p-values are reported in Table A. 1 in the appendix.

° MV, TA, and SAL represent mean values (fiscal 2001 and 2002) for the market value of equity, total assets, and sales, respectively.

For other variable definitions, refer to Table 6. Monetary amounts are in million $. Goodwill figures are scaled by beginning-of-period balance sheet numbers.

Table 9: Comparison of the non-write-off and write-off samples

The two subgroups of the goodwill sample exhibit significant differences. The median goodwill book value in the pre-adoption period, expressed in absolute and relative terms, is much larger in the write-off sample. At the end of 2001, median goodwill was more than five times larger in the write-off sample ($139 million) than in the non-write-off sample ($27 million). Due to substantial goodwill write-offs in 2002, these differences tend to disappear in 2002, making the subgroups much more homogenous. Consistent with economic factors hypothesis 1, the MTB ratios of write-off firms are, on average, significantly lower. These companies also underperform non-write-off firms in terms of stock return, albeit not on change in ROA. Moreover, write-off firms have significantly higher exposure to debt and operate with a higher proportion of assets-in-place. They are also significantly larger and more dominant in their respective markets. This preliminary evidence on economic differences between the subgroups is consistent with the assumptions expressed in the economic factors hypotheses: Write-offs occur in large firms that are viewed by market participants as undergoing a phase of economic difficulty.

Table A. 2 in the Appendix contains a classification of firms by industry membership. 25 two-digit SIC categories, each with a membership of more than 1% of all 13.798 available firms, are reported explicitly, while the rest, including the category "non-classifiable establishments" (two-digit SIC category 99), is grouped into the "all other" category. The analysis suggests that industry representation differs among the sub-samples. While the majority of industries are represented almost equally in the non-goodwill and goodwill samples, goodwill firms seem to be distinctly over-represented in the industrial machinery/equipment, transportation equipment, fabricated metal products, printing/publishing, and paper industries, perhaps suggesting that these industries underwent significant consolidation in recent years. A reverse relation exists in the chemicals, oil/gas extraction, and metal mining industries, where goodwill firms are much less frequently represented than are non-goodwill firms.

A comparison of the non-write-off and write-off samples indicates that, on average, write-offs occur more frequently in the durable goods wholesale, amusement/recreation, and paper industries. Conversely, firms in the electronics, instruments, oil/gas extraction, food, and nondurable goods wholesale industries apparently are less susceptible to recording transitional SFAS 142 goodwill write-offs, given that they have any goodwill. Notably, the fact that oil/gas firms record write-offs less frequently provides preliminary corroboration to the notion brought up in section 3.3.2.3.5, according to which "politically visible" firms could expected to avoid transitional SFAS 142 goodwill write-offs.

Table 10 describes transitional SFAS 142 goodwill write-offs in the write-off sample.[1230]

TWGO_A	Mean	StDev	Min	1st qrt	Med	3rd qrt	Max
in million $	149	315	0	7	28	129	2,944
% total assets	7.4	8.8	0.0	1.6	4.7	9.3	55.8
% common equity (BV)	18.8	23.1	0.1	3.8	12.7	23.8	197.9
% goodwill	38.8	31.1	0.2	10.4	32.1	62.2	100.0
% common equity (MV)	32.2	61.3	0.0	2.4	9.4	34.6	438.6
% sales	16.1	105.4	0.0	1.3	4.0	10.6	1,560.3

Goodwill figures are scaled by beginning-of-period balance sheet numbers and end-of-period sales. These data comprise write-offs taken by the 224 firms in the write-off sample.

Table 10: Descriptive analysis of transitional write-offs

1230 It would be interesting to compare transitional SFAS 142 write-off amounts to prior-period goodwill amortization charges. However, goodwill amortization is rarely disclosed separately, so data availability on this item is insufficient. See, for example, Duvall et al. (1992), who document the problem of extracting goodwill-related information from published financial statements. Furthermore, the amounts of amortization and write-off do not necessarily compare, because the write-off may relate to only part of entity-level goodwill, whereas amortization represents an arbitrary charge based a weighted average of the individual useful lives of all the components of entity-level goodwill.

The analysis indicates that the write-offs represent substantial accounting events for the affected firms. The median amount is $28 million, whereas the considerably higher mean ($149 million) as well as the large standard deviation suggest that several much higher write-offs distort the distribution. The maximum of the distribution is at nearly $3 billion.[1231] The median firm wrote off 4.7% of total assets and almost 13% of equity upon transition, with mean amounts, again, being much higher. Transitional write-offs slashed about a third of goodwill book value and represented more than 9% of the market value of equity. Finally, the median transitional SFAS 142 goodwill write-off amounted to 4% of sales.

Further descriptive information on the SFAS 142 goodwill write-off is given in the Appendix: Table A. 3 mirrors Table 10, reporting descriptive information on *regular* SFAS 142 goodwill write-offs taken by the firms in the goodwill sample during 2002. These charges are smaller, on average (median = $7 million), than the transitional ones, and are also less significant in relative terms. The fact that they also represent, on average, about one third of goodwill book value (median = 29.1%), reflects the circumstance that these write-offs are mainly taken by firms in the transitional non-write-off sample. These firms, as shown in Table 9, have smaller goodwills than their write-off counterparts.

Furthermore, Table A. 4 in the Appendix additionally breaks down the information provided in Table 10 by industry. The analysis indicates that the most substantial write-offs (in absolute dollars) are recorded in the communications industry (median = $393 million), followed by the miscellaneous manufacturing ($246 million) and special trade contracting ($243 million) industries. Write-offs in the latter group also represented the largest percentages of total assets (23.7%) and of the book value of equity (44.1%). However, these industries represent only a small fraction of the write-off sample. Large write-offs were also taken by the 18 firms in the chemicals industry (median = $45 million) and by the 16 firms in the industrial machinery/equipment industry (median = $50 million). However, because firms in these industries are typically large, these write-offs are minor in relative terms. The highest percentages of goodwill were written off in the eating/drinking places (median = 62.6%), rubber/plastics (60.0%), and amusement/recreation (56.7%) industries.

[1231] Extreme amounts such as the one recorded by AOL Time Warner are not represented here because these firms were eliminated from the sample during the sample selection procedure.

Table 11 reports the distribution of fiscal year-ends among the firms in the four samples in order to assess whether calendar-year firm are more or less likely than other firms to record an SFAS 142 goodwill write-off upon transition.

Fiscal year-end	Total firms available		Non-goodwill sample		Goodwill sample		Non-write-off sample		Write-off sample	
	N	%	N	%	N	%	N	%	N	%
January	336	2.9	20	2.1	26	2.1	20	2.0	6	2.7
February	127	1.1	1	0.1	2	0.2	2	0.2	0	0.0
March	672	5.7	2	0.2	2	0.2	2	0.2	0	0.0
April	184	1.6	0	0.0	0	0.0	0	0.0	0	0.0
May	184	1.6	0	0.0	0	0.0	0	0.0	0	0.0
June	904	7.7	102	10.7	120	9.6	108	10.5	12	5.4
July	180	1.5	24	2.5	23	1.8	21	2.1	2	0.9
August	181	1.5	27	2.8	22	1.8	21	2.1	1	0.4
September	750	6.4	67	7.0	106	8.5	88	8.6	18	8.0
October	323	2.7	33	3.5	43	3.4	38	3.7	5	2.2
November	147	1.2	16	1.7	21	1.7	19	1.9	2	0.9
December	7,776	66.1	663	69.4	883	70.8	705	68.8	178	79.5
Total	**11,764**	**100.0**	**955**	**100.0**	**1,248**	**100.0**	**1,024**	**100.0**	**224**	**100.0**

Total firms available represent those firms for which information on the fiscal year end 2001 is observed.

Table 11: Distribution of fiscal year-ends

This table shows that a higher proportion of the write-off firms have December year ends (79.5%) than would have been expected based on the percentages of calendar-year firms in the other sub-samples. This finding might indicate that firms with deviating year ends were reluctant to record transitional write-offs because they were unsure whether investors would be aware of their transitory nature. Speculating further, management of calendar-year firms observed (neutral and or positive) market responses to early adopters' write-offs and thus might have overcome any reluctance to incur these charges.

Table 12 provides information on whether firms in the four samples differ systematically based on whether their MTB ratios at the end of 2001 are higher or lower than one. Of special interest here is a comparison of the write-off and non-write-off samples because economic factors hypothesis 1 implies that firms with MTB ratios below one are more likely than others to have impaired goodwill.

MTB	Goodwill sample		Non-goodwill sample		Non-write-off sample		Write-off sample	
	N	%	N	%	N	%	N	%
≥ 1	921	73.8	677	70.9	797	77.8	124	55.4
< 1	327	26.2	277	29.0	227	22.2	100	44.6
Total	**1,248**	**100.0**	**954**	**100.0**	**1,024**	**100.0**	**224**	**100.0**

Table 12: MTB ratios in the write-off and non-write-off samples

Consistent with what the impairment test procedure in SFAS 142 would suggest, firms in the write-off sample more frequently have MTB ratios below one than do non-write-off firms. This difference is highly significant,[1232] which further corroborates the notion that transitional SFAS 142 goodwill write-offs more clearly reflect economic developments rather than financial reporting incentives.

Table A. 5 in the Appendix explores this notion further. In addition to significant differences in MTB ratios, the MTB≤1 firms appear to be significantly smaller, on average, most notably in terms of the market value of equity. They are also more reliant on debt financing than their MTB>1 counterparts, and underperform them significantly in terms of stock return. These findings suggest that write-offs in the MTB≤1 group reflect economic problems experienced by smaller firms. As of the transition date, the MTB>1 firms, on average, had MTB ratios (median = 1.78) almost as high as those in the non-write-off sample (1.88) and outperformed them in terms of stock return. This suggests that economic causes for write-offs recorded by MTB>1 firms are not so readily apparent. Possibly, these large, successful firms, concerned about the potentially adverse effects of regular write-offs becoming necessary in future periods, take the opportunity of accelerating write-offs into the transition year. Regarding the development of the MTB ratio over time (not tabulated), the median MTB ratio for the first group declined from 1.78 in 2001 to 1.66 in 2002, while that of the second group rose from 0.57 in 2001 to 0.72 in 2002. This diametrical development suggests that write-offs in the first group were perceived negatively, possibly as indicative of future problems. Conversely, those reported by the second group might have been viewed as part of a restructuring effort, promising future improvement, or simply as reflections of past problems that had already been impounded in stock price.

Financial reporting incentives hypothesis 4 predicts that managers' desire to reach earnings targets influences firms' transitional SFAS 142 goodwill write-off behavior. In Table 13, the write-off and non-write-off samples are compared based on the frequency with which sample firms' earnings figures *before* the transitional SFAS 142 goodwill write-off are above or below different earnings targets. Two earnings targets are considered: Panel A reports on the frequency with which firms in the four samples meet prior-period net income, while Panel B contains equivalent information for an earnings target embodied by positive net income.

[1232] An ANOVA F-test on equality of means yields an F-statistic of 49.853 (p-value = 0.000).

Earnings target	Goodwill sample		Non-goodwill sample		Non-write-off sample		Write-off sample	
	N	%	N	%	N	%	N	%
Panel A: Prior-year NI								
NI 2002 ≥ NI 2001	754	60.4	498	52.1	625	61.0	129	57.6
NI 2002 < NI 2001	494	39.6	457	47.9	399	39.0	95	42.4
Total	**1,248**	**100.0**	**955**	**100.0**	**1,024**	**100.0**	**224**	**100.0**
Panel B: Zero NI								
NI 2002 ≥ 0	818	65.5	461	48.3	681	66.5	137	61.2
NI 2002 < 0	430	34.5	494	51.7	343	33.5	87	38.8
Total	**1,248**	**100.0**	**955**	**100.0**	**1,024**	**100.0**	**224**	**100.0**

Table 13: Pre-write-off earnings performance relative to earnings targets

The results provide weak evidence that write-off behavior is influenced by the desire to avoid losses (Panel B). Write-off firms avoid pre-write-off net losses less frequently than do non-write-off firms, although the difference between the two groups is not strictly significant.[1233] Significant results are also not found where prior-period net income is considered as the relevant target (p-value = 0.340).

In Table 14, further evidence is provided on financial reporting incentives hypothesis 4. The transitional write-off amounts (as a percentage of total assets) are compared between subgroups of the write-off sample that are defined based on whether a firm meets or falls short of a simple earnings target.

Earnings target	TGWO_A (N = 224)						
	Mean	**StDev**	**Min**	**1st qrt**	**Med**	**3rd qrt**	**Max**
Panel A: Prior-year NI							
NI 2002 ≥ NI 2001	7.2	9.2	0.1	1.3	4.3	9.3	55.8
NI 2002 < NI 2001	7.6	8.2	0.0	2.0	5.2	9.8	42.1
Panel B: Zero NI							
NI 2002 ≥ 0	7.4	9.7	0.1	1.3	4.1	9.3	55.8
NI 2002 < 0	7.3	7.1	0.0	2.1	5.7	9.3	32.9

Table 14: Comparison of write-off amounts depending on earnings performance

A pattern similar to that observed in Table 13 above emerges: Where firms are unsuccessful in meeting their net income-based earnings targets, they appear, on average, to record large write-offs suggestive of a "big bath" strategy. Write-offs are significantly larger for net loss firms than they are for firms that meet or beat this specific target (Panel

---

1233 An ANOVA F-test on equality of means yields an F-statistic of 2.324 (p-value = 0.128).

B).[1234] This relation, albeit insignificant, is also found where prior-period net income is used as the relevant target (p-value = 0.224).

Table 15 provides information on whether non-write-off firms and write-off firms differ systematically depending on whether they experienced CEO changes in the years 2001 or 2002 (financial reporting incentives hypothesis 7a).

CEO change	Goodwill sample		Non-goodwill sample		Non-write-off sample		Write-off sample	
	N	%	N	%	N	%	N	%
in 2001	43	3.45	14	1.47	33	3.22	10	4.46
in 2002	9	0.72	2	0.21	7	0.68	2	0.89
in either year	**52**	**4.17**	**16**	**1.68**	**40**	**3.91**	**12**	**5.36**

Table 15: Frequency of CEO changes

It appears that CEO changes, on average were more frequent in write-off firms than they were in non-write-off firms during both 2001 and 2002. Due to small sample size, these differences are not found to be statistically significant.[1235] This is also true when the occurrence of CEO changes in *either* year is considered (p-value = 0.325). The stable finding in prior literature that "big bath" behavior frequently coincides with top management turnover has mostly been documented using samples of firms where (routine or non-routine) executive changes had been observed, ensuring that sufficiently large samples of such firms were available.[1236]

Financial reporting incentives hypothesis 8 suggests that firms with low credit rating might be reluctant to record transitional SFAS 142 goodwill write-offs out of concern about the resulting financial statement effects and any negative repercussions on credit rating and the cost of capital. Therefore, it would be expected that highly rated firms are more frequent in the write-off sample, and vice versa. Table 16 reports the distribution of rating categories at the end of 2001.

1234 The adjusted χ^2-test of equality of medians generates a test statistic of 4.229 (p-value = 0.040).

1235 For 2001 (2002), an ANOVA F-test of equality of means yields an F-statistic of 0.006 (0.017). The p-values are 0.936 and 0.898, respectively.

1236 Refer to section 3.3.2.4.6 above.

RATING[1237]		Total firms available		Non-goodwill sample		Goodwill sample		Non-write-off sample		Write-off sample	
		N	%	N	%	N	%	N	%	N	%
AAA	(2)	25	1.2	1	0.9	8	1.8	5	1.5	3	2.6
AA+	(4)	17	0.8	0	0.0	2	0.4	2	0.6	0	0.0
AA	(5)	30	1.4	1	0.9	7	1.6	6	1.8	1	0.9
AA–	(6)	65	3.0	2	1.8	8	1.8	6	1.8	2	1.8
A+	(7)	127	5.9	3	2.6	21	4.7	16	4.8	5	4.4
A	(8)	155	7.2	7	6.1	28	6.3	23	6.9	5	4.4
A–	(9)	174	8.1	5	4.4	35	7.8	29	8.7	6	5.3
BBB+	(10)	195	9.1	8	7.0	40	8.9	33	9.9	7	6.1
BBB	(11)	227	10.6	8	7.0	53	11.9	37	11.1	16	14.0
BBB–	(12)	183	8.5	11	9.6	48	10.7	30	9.0	18	15.8
BB+	(13)	101	4.7	10	8.8	32	7.2	22	6.6	10	8.8
BB	(14)	147	6.9	13	11.4	53	11.9	41	12.3	12	10.5
BB–	(15)	157	7.3	11	9.6	42	9.4	30	9.0	12	10.5
B+	(16)	204	9.5	14	12.3	40	8.9	30	9.0	10	8.8
B	(17)	113	5.3	8	7.0	16	3.6	12	3.6	4	3.5
B–	(18)	73	3.4	7	6.1	7	1.6	6	1.8	1	0.9
CCC+	(19)	33	1.5	2	1.8	2	0.4	1	0.3	1	0.9
CCC	(20)	19	0.9	0	0.0	1	0.2	1	0.3	0	0.0
CCC–	(21)	11	0.5	1	0.9	1	0.2	1	0.3	0	0.0
CC	(23)	12	0.6	0	0.0	0	0.0	0	0.0	0	0.0
D	(27)	67	3.1	1	0.9	2	0.4	1	0.3	1	0.9
SD	(29)	7	0.3	1	0.9	1	0.2	1	0.3	0	0.0
Total		**2,142**	**100.0**	**114**	**100.0**	**447**	**100.0**	**333**	**100.0**	**114**	**100.0**
Median (StDev)		12.0 (4.7)		14.0 (4.0)		12.0 (3.7)		12.0 (3.7)		12.0 (3.6)	

Table 16: Distribution of rating categories

Since rating categories represents ordinal (rank) numbers, the conditions for calculating the mean and standard deviation are not given.[1238] With this caveat in mind, the standard deviation is reported as a crude proxy for the distribution of the rating categories. Based on the median and on visual inspection of the distributions, no support for financial reporting incentives hypothesis 8 is found.[1239]

[1237] Codes no. 1, 3, 22, and 25 are unassigned. Code no. 28 is labeled "not meaningful". Refer to S&P (2001). The rating categories C (24) and CI (26) are not represented in the data.

[1238] See, for example, Bamberg and Baur (2002, pp. 17, 21).

[1239] The summary figures must be interpreted with caution because of the lacking categories.

5.4 *Regression analysis*

5.4.1 Methods employed in studies of write-off determinants

Most of the studies related to the determinants of discretionary asset write-offs[1240] employ regression analysis, the specific variant of which depends on whether or not the dependent variable is observable on a continuous and unrestricted scale. While the fundamentals of regression analysis are not explicitly discussed here,[1241] specific issues frequently encountered in discretionary write-off studies and relevant to the regression analysis below are the subject of this section.

Regression analysis is appropriate when analyzing hypothesized functional relations between a dependent variable[1242] and one or several independent variables.[1243] For example, researchers interested in the causes of discretionary asset write-offs hope to find a statistically significant relation between the existence and/or amount of a write-off (the dependent variable) and certain explanatory variables that represent factors hypothesized to have caused that write-off and/or influenced its amount (independent variables).[1244] Conditional on the nature of the dependent variable, the ordinary least squares (OLS) estimator might or might not be the optimal estimator.[1245] Below, specific problems stemming from the dependent variable being, first, a dichotomous variable (i.e. the decision whether or not to write off at all) or, second, a censored variable (i.e. the amount written off) are discussed.

1240 Refer to section 3.3 above.

1241 For excellent textbook expositions of regression analysis, refer to Backhaus et al. (2003, ch. 1), Bamberg and Baur (2002, pp. 42-51), Greene (2003), Gujarati (2003), Kennedy (1998), von Auer (1999), and Winker (1997, ch. 7).

1242 Common synonyms include explained variable, predictand, regressand, response, and endogenous variable. See Gujarati (2003, p. 24). However, the term "response" is inadequate in this context because it suggests a causal relation, which cannot be readily ascertained in discretionary asset write-off studies.

1243 The terms explanatory variable, predictor, regressor, stimulus, and exogenous variable are frequently used synonyms. See Gujarati (2003, p. 24). The term "stimulus" should be avoided for the same reason given in connection with the term response.

1244 Similarly, authors analyzing the effects of discretionary asset write-offs attempt to ascertain a statistically significant relation between a market-based metric (the dependent variable) and certain explanatory variables related to write-off behavior (independent variables).

1245 For an overview, refer to Greene (2003, ch. 2), Gujarati (2003, ch. 3), and Kennedy (1998, ch. 2).

5.4.1.1 Qualitative dependent variables: The write-off decision

If the researcher intends to distinguish statistically between two separate groups, the dependent variable represents qualitative as opposed to quantitative characteristics. In discretionary asset write-off studies, for example, the data consists of firms belonging to two groups: Write-off firms and non-write-off firms. The researcher intends to relate the probability of observing a write-off, regardless of the specific amount, to potential explanatory factors. The dependent variable is a *binary* or dichotomous variable, referred to as WO_D, which assumes a value of one where a firm decides to record a write-off, and zero otherwise. This indicator variable partitions the sample into two subgroups: Write-off firms, i.e. firms that decided to record a non-zero write-off (WO_D = 1), and non-write-off firms, i.e. firms that have not recorded any write-off (WO_D = 0).

In this case, special estimating problems make applying OLS methodology inappropriate.[1246] If WO_D is regressed on the explanatory variables, the predicted values should fall within the 0–1 interval because, for each firm, the predicted value would be interpreted as the likelihood that the firm, given its characteristics represented by the explanatory variables, is a write-off firm. However, the estimated OLS line (or, in a multivariate context, the multidimensional regression hyper space) will also yield estimated probabilities that are outside the 0–1 range.[1247] Under this *linear probability model*, predicted values for WO_D that are larger than one would converted to one, and those that are smaller than zero, to zero.[1248]

However, this conversion implies that there is no difference between those firms for which the probability of them being a write-off firm was estimated at 1 and those for which the probability was estimated at, say, 2.5. Also, estimates such as zero and one suggest that outcomes, for which certainty does not exist, are predicted with certainty. To alleviate this concern, a function is required that "squeezes" the probability estimates asymptotically inside the 0–1 range, without creating estimates that are exactly zero or exactly one. In other words, the 0–1 observations on the dependent variable are interpreted as dichotomous realizations of a "true" *latent* variable. In the context of discretionary asset write-off studies, this latent variable could be interpreted as the amount that

1246 For much of the following, refer to Kennedy (1998, pp. 233-5).

1247 For a graphical depiction of this problem, see Kennedy (1998, p. 234) and Maddala (2001, p. 320).

1248 See Maddala (2001, pp. 318-20) and Maddala (1991, p. 789).

the firm would "desire" to write off, which is coded as one, if positive, and as zero, if negative.[1249]

Two methods are frequently used: In the *Probit* model, the probability of obtaining the dependent variable is written as a cumulative normal function of the explanatory variables, while in the *Logit* model, this probability is written as a logistic function of the explanatory variables. Estimation itself is undertaken using a maximum likelihood (ML) procedure.[1250] Maddala (2001) notes that the cumulative normal and the logistic distributions are so close to each other that the two methods are likely to generate similar results.[1251]

Although Probit and Logit are frequently used in classificatory accounting research,[1252] few discretionary asset write-off studies actually apply this methodology, most being interested in the write-off *amount* or other quantitative (in most cases, continuous) variables. Examples include Chen and Lee (1995), Kim and Kwon (2001), Loh and Tan (2002), and Strong and Meyer (1987).[1253] Discriminant analysis is occasionally used as an alternative methodological approach.[1254] Comparisons of the OLS and Probit/Logit approaches in accounting choice studies are provided, respectively, by Noreen (1988) and Stone and Rasp (1991).

5.4.1.2 Limited dependent variables: The write-off amount

In several of the studies presented in section 3.3 above, it is tested whether the amount written off can be statistically linked to economic factors and/or variables that stand for financial reporting incentives. In these studies, the write-off amount, commonly scaled by a size proxy such as total assets and expressed as a positive number (hereafter, WO_A), is the dependent variable in a regression on one or several explanatory variables. WO_A does not have an unlimited range. Because most of the studies analyze a

---

1249 See Maddala (2001, p. 322).

1250 See Greene (2003, p. 670). For an in-depth explanation of this topic area as well as a discussion comparing the relative merits of the Logit and Probit specifications, refer to Backhaus et al. (2003, ch. 3), Kennedy (1998, pp. 237-40), Maddala (1983, esp. pp. 22-7), and Maddala (1991, pp. 788-94).

1251 See Maddala (2001, p. 323).

1252 See Noreen (1988, p. 119 fn. 1).

1253 See Chen and Lee (1995, p. 108-9), Kim and Kwon (2001, pp. 10-3), Loh and Tan (2002, pp. 142-8), and Strong and Meyer (1987, p. 651 fn. 18).

1254 See, for example, Strong and Meyer (1987, p. 649-51). Maddala (1991, pp. 788-94) contrasts Logit and Probit analysis with discriminant analysis.

setting in which upward revaluations are prohibited,[1255] WO_A is either positive or zero. In this context, the OLS estimator is not appropriate because the dependent variable is limited in its range, causing OLS estimates to be biased as well as inconsistent, i.e. the estimates are biased even asymptotically.[1256]

A censored regression model is applicable when the data on some observations on the dependent variable is *censored* or unobserved, meaning that for some known values of the independent variable(s), the corresponding exact values of the dependent variable are not observable for some reason. It is only known whether they are above or below a certain threshold.[1257] However, these observations remain included in the sample, and the unobservable values of the dependent variable are coded to assume some limit value, frequently zero.[1258] In other words, the known observations on the dependent variable are a function of a "true" *latent* variable,[1259] which is partially unobservable. The observable dependent variable, y, assumes the value of this latent variable, y*, where the latter is above (below) the censoring limit, but is censored to assume the value of the censoring limit where the latent variable is below (above) the censoring limit.[1260] In the case of the censoring limit being zero, the probability of observing $y = 0$ is equal to the probability of observing $y^* \leq 0$.

Applied to the transitional SFAS 142 setting, the write-off amount actually observed, TGWO_A, is either zero or positive.[1261] However, TGWO_A values smaller than zero may theoretically exist in cases where the impairment testing procedure shows that not a decline, but rather an appreciation in the value of goodwill has occurred. The unob-

---

1255 Riedl (2002) analyzes write-offs under SFAS 121 and under the pre-SFAS 121 accounting regime. SFAS 121.11 explicitly prohibits "[r]estoration of previously recognized impairment losses." Previously, the general historical cost framework of GAAP also provided no basis for asset write-ups over and above historical cost.

1256 More technically, the coefficient estimates are biased because the expected value of the disturbances is not zero. See Gujarati (2003, p. 616), Kennedy (1998, p. 114), and Maddala (1991, p. 795). According to Greene (2003, p. 762), "[c]onventional regression methods fail to account for the qualitative difference between *limit* (zero) observations and *nonlimit* (continuous) observations" (emphasis in original). For much of the following, refer also to Kennedy (1998, ch. 16).

1257 Refer to Maddala (1983, pp. 3-6). The problems associated with censored data are also discussed in Greene (2003, pp. 761-80), Gujarati (2003, pp. 616-9), and Kennedy (1998, ch. 16).

1258 In the words of Greene (2003, p. 761), "values in a certain range [here: below zero] are all transformed to (or reported as) a single value [here: zero]."

1259 See Greene (2003, p. 764).

1260 Stated technically, where the censoring limit is zero, $y = y^*$ if $y^* > 0$ and $y = 0$ otherwise. See Maddala (1983, p. 149) and Greene (2003, p. 764).

1261 This implies that, as is custom in the literature and also the chosen approach in this study, write-offs are measured as positive numbers.

served, latent variable, then, is the amount of change in goodwill value. SFAS 142, prohibiting upward revaluations such as write-off reversals (i.e., negative values of TGWO_A), in effect censors TGWO_A to exclude values below zero. It is worth noting that, in this example, the threshold or cut-off point of zero for TGWO_A is known and identical for all observations.[1262] Therefore, negative values of TGWO_A cannot be observed although firms exist that would have recorded upward asset revaluations, had it not been for the restriction imposed by SFAS 142. The explanatory variables for these firms are available. The data is censored at zero.

The applicable procedure for regression analysis using censored data was developed by Tobin (1958) and is called the Tobit model.[1263] The Tobit model is a censored normal regression model.[1264] Here, estimation is undertaken employing an ML estimator.[1265] The parameter estimates generated by an ML estimator are those for which the probability of having obtained the particular sample used is greatest.[1266] Specifically, the canonical Tobit model is appropriate in this setting, since the dependent variable is a censored variable with a left limit value of zero and no right limit value.[1267]

Studies also applying this methodology include Riedl (2002), Francis, Hanna and Vincent (1996), and Loh and Tan (2002). Riedl (2002) examines the determinants of the amounts of long-lived asset write-offs.[1268] He assumes that his data is censored, arguing that "the explanatory .. variables are available for all the observations, but the explained .. variable is equivalent to 0 because it falls below some .. threshold value .. for a subset of observations".[1269] However, he documents robustness of his findings to different distribu-

---

1262 For settings in which the threshold is either unknown, different for each observation, or both, refer to Maddala (1983, pp. 3-6).

1263 See Greene (2003, pp. 764-6), Kennedy (1998, pp. 250-2, 255-6), Maddala (1983, pp. 151-162), and Maddala (1991, pp. 794-7).

1264 See Maddala (1983, p. 151).

1265 Characterizing it as "rather involved", Gujarati (2003, p. 617) considers ML estimation beyond the scope of his "Basic econometrics" textbook.

1266 See, for example, Greene (2003, ch. 17), Gujarati (2003, pp. 114-7), and Kennedy (1998, pp. 21-2). For a more technical definition, see Kennedy (1998, pp. 30-1).

1267 Regression analysis using ML estimation requires specifying the distribution of the error term. In the context of this study, no specific distribution of the errors is known. Since, according to the central limit theorem, large numbers tend to be approximately normally distributed, the normal distribution is assumed to describe the error terms. See Kennedy (1998, p. 30). This corresponds to the assumption used in the Tobit model. See Maddala (1983, p. 151).

1268 His variable $WOTA_{it}$, denoting the net of tax amount of the asset write-off recorded by firm i in period t, divided by beginning-of-period total assets, is largely equivalent to WO_A defined above.

1269 Riedl (2002, p. 8).

tional assumptions, *inter alia* an OLS model.[1270] Arguing against the applicability of the Tobit specification in his setting, he maintains that, "because GAAP during [the] sample period does not allow firms to record .. increases in asset values, the distribution is not censored",[1271] implying that the data is *truncated* instead.[1272] In the case of truncated data, calling for a truncated regression model,[1273] an observation is entirely omitted from the sample when the value of the dependent variable falls above (or below) the threshold discussed above. Applied to the write-off setting, this would be a case where only write-off firms are considered and non-write-off firms are excluded from the sample. In this context, the Tobit model is not applicable and a different ML technique should be used.[1274] Under the Tobit or censored regression model, in contrast, non-write-off firms are included in the study, but the write-off amount is censored to zero.

While researchers are prudent to conduct sensitivity analyses by using different specifications, Riedl's latter line of reasoning with respect to the non-applicability of the Tobit model does not appear to be valid. As noted above, asset write-offs are supposed to reflect economic value declines of assets. Riedl assumes that economic value increases do not occur in the sample just because the accounting regime happens to have determined an arbitrary cutoff point at zero, beyond which economic value fluctuations cannot become reflected in accounting numbers. In reality, write-offs may range above (fair value < book value) or below (fair value > book value) zero, implying that a data set that limits observations on WO_A to assume values of zero or above is censored.[1275] The fact that Francis, Hanna and Vincent (1996) also apply a Tobit procedure without explicitly expounding the problem whether or not their data is censored might be interpreted as confirming this notion.[1276] However, Maddala (1991) cautions researchers about using the Tobit model inappropriately. Because it is "tempting to use the tobit model every time

---

1270 Among the studies using an OLS specification are Cotter, Stokes and Wyatt (1998) and Segal (2003), who do not, however, explicitly discuss the relative merits of the OLS and Tobit specifications.

1271 Riedl (2002, p. 25). Results for both specifications are reported in table 3 panel A and B, respectively.

1272 The distinction between censored and truncated data is discussed in Kennedy (1998, pp. 250-1), Maddala (1983, pp. 1-3, 149-51), and Maddala (1991, pp. 794-7).

1273 Refer to Maddala (1983, pp. 1-3, 165-70).

1274 Refer to Kennedy (1998, pp. 251, 257-8).

1275 As examples of data where use of the Tobit model is inappropriate due to the data being truncated, not censored, Maddala (1991, pp. 795-6) refers to individual choices, e.g. automobile expenditures and hours worked, for which there is no way that the data can be negative. In this case, however, "negative" discretionary asset write-offs would be most likely be observed if standard setters did not arbitrarily prohibit write-ups and write-off reversals. For a slightly different take, refer to Gujarati (2003, p. 616), who interprets data on housing expenditures as censored.

1276 See also Riedl (2002, p. 25). Francis, Hanna and Vincent's (1996, p. 125) variable $WRITE\text{-}OFF_i$ denotes the write-off recorded by firm i, deflated by total assets.

one has a bunch of zero (or other limit) observations on [the dependent variable] … there are many more examples of the inappropriate use of the tobit model than of its correct use."[1277]

5.4.2 Summary of hypotheses

Table 17 provides a summary of the hypotheses developed in section 5.2 above, indicating that the majority of predictions are relevant to both the write-off decision *and* the write-off amount, while some relate to only one of those aspects.

	Hypothesis	Predicted sign	Write-off decision	Write-off amount
Economic Factors	H^{EC} 1	–	X	X
	H^{EC} 2a	–	X	X
	H^{EC} 2b	–	X	X
	Hypothesis	**Predicted sign**	**Write-off decision**	**Write-off amount**
Financial Reporting Incentives	H^{FR} 1	+	X	—
	H^{FR} 2	–	X	X
	H^{FR} 3a	?	X	—
	H^{FR} 3b	?	X	—
	H^{FR} 3c	?	X	—
	H^{FR} 4	–	X	—
	H^{FR} 5	+	—	X
	H^{FR} 6	+	—	X
	H^{FR} 7a	+	X	—
	H^{FR} 7b	+	X	—
	H^{FR} 7c	+	X	—
	H^{FR} 8	–	X	X

Table 17: Summary of hypotheses

In the following section, hypotheses pertaining to the dichotomous write-off *decision* are tested using primarily Probit regression methodology, whereas hypotheses about the write-off *amount* are subjected to Tobit regression analysis. While the economic factors hypotheses as well as the financial reporting incentives hypotheses 1-4 are tested on the whole goodwill sample, sub-groups of that sample are relevant for financial reporting incentives hypotheses 5-8.

1277 Maddala (1991, p. 795).

5.4.3 Analysis of the write-off decision

As discussed in section 5.4.1.1 above, ML estimation using the Probit model is appropriate where determinants of the write-off *decision*, expressed as the dichotomous dependent variable TGWO_D, are analyzed. Three multivariate models are considered in turn: Model D1 represents explanatory variables derived from the economic factors hypotheses as well as the financial reporting incentives hypotheses 1-4. It is tested using all firms in the goodwill sample. Model D2, considering only those firms in the goodwill sample that incur a pre-write-off loss in 2002 (TARGET_Z = 0), contains the "big bath" variables suggested by financial reporting incentives hypothesis 7. Model D3 is a variant of model D1 with RATING as an added explanatory factor. Consequently, only those (high-profile) firms for which S&P debt ratings are available are included in regression tests of model D3. The control variables defined in section 5.2.4 are included in all models.

5.4.3.1 Full-sample test

The correlation matrix for model D1 (reported in Table A. 6 in the Appendix) indicates that, on the whole, most of the variables are largely uncorrelated with each other. Notable positive correlation exists, *inter alia*, between TARGET_PP and ΔPWOROA (both reflect the change in accounting earnings over the prior year), DTE and MTB (highly leveraged firms apparently trade at a premium), HERF and MSH (market share per firm is higher, on average, in concentrated industries), and SIZE and MSH (larger firms have higher market share).

Probit regression results for model D1 are reported in Table 18 below.

$$TGWO\_D_i = \alpha + \beta_1 MTB_i + \beta_2 RET_i + \beta_3 \Delta ROA_i + \beta_4 AIP_i + \beta_5 DTE_i + \beta_6 MSH_i$$
$$+ \beta_7 HERF_i + \beta_8 \Delta PWOROA_i + \beta_9 TARGET\_PP_i + \beta_{10} TARGET\_Z_i$$
$$+ \beta_{11} SIZE_i + \beta_{12} FYR_i + \beta_{13} GW_i + \varepsilon_i$$

Variable	**Hypothesis (predicted sign)**	**Coefficient estimate**	**z-statistic**	**Significance level (p-value)**
C	(?)	-1.444665	-10.05380	0.0000
MTB	H_D^{EC} 1 (–)	-0.031350	-2.401063	0.0163
RET	H_D^{EC} 2a (–)	-0.194186	-3.116553	0.0018
ΔROA	H_D^{EC} 2b (–)	-0.041955	-0.186227	0.8523
AIP	H_D^{FR} 1 (+)	0.145979	1.796326	0.0724
DTE	H_D^{FR} 2 (–)	0.001259	0.077649	0.9381
MSH	H_D^{FR} 3a (?)	4.152666	4.089040	0.0000
HERF	H_D^{FR} 3b (?)	0.755804	1.019518	0.3080
ΔPWOROA	H_D^{FR} 3c (?)	0.704047	1.531942	0.1255
TARGET_PP	H_D^{FR} 4 (–)	-0.207617	-1.870725	0.0614
TARGET_Z		-0.015156	-0.146019	0.8839
SIZE	(?)	0.000001	0.527720	0.5977
FYR	(?)	0.281511	2.754562	0.0059
GW	(?)	0.019001	6.771698	0.0000
Likelihood ratio (p-value)			122.04 (0.000)	
McFadden R^2			0.104	
Observations	Goodwill sample	Total: 1,248	TGWO_D = 0: 1,024 (82.1%)	TGWO_D = 1: 224 (17.9%)

Variable definitions (refer to Table 6 for further details):

MTB	MTB ratio, measured at the end of 2001.
RET	Cumulative stock performance, measured over the fiscal years 2000 and 2001.
ΔROA	Percentage point change in ROA between the fiscal years 2000 and 2001.
AIP	Mean of assets-in-place, measured as the relation of PP&E (net of accumulated depreciation) to total market value, at the end of 2001 and 2002.
DTE	Mean of the differences between firm and median two-digit SIC industry DTE ratios, at the end of 2001 and 2002.
MSH	Mean of market shares, measured as the relation of firm sales (DATA12) to two-digit SIC industry sales, at the end of 2001 and 2002; industry sales based on all available firms.
HERF	Mean of the Herfindahl indexes of the two-digit SIC industry, measured as the sum of the squares of the market shares of each firm in the industry, at the end of 2001 and 2002; industry sales based on all available firms.
ΔPWOROA	Change in ROA (before transitional SFAS 142 goodwill write-off) in 2002 over regular ROA in 2001.
TARGET_PP TARGET_Z	Dichotomous variable: 1 where annual pre-write-off net income is above the prior year's level (above zero) in 2002; 0 otherwise.
SIZE	Size, measured by the mean of the market values of equity at the end of 2001 and 2002.
FYR	Dichotomous variable: 1 where fiscal year-end in 2001 is December 31; 0 otherwise. FYR is coded based on COMPUSTAT annual item FYR.
GW	Goodwill book value, deflated by total assets, measured at the end of 2001.

Table 18: Probit regression results for model D1 (full sample)

The likelihood ratio (LR) test statistic of 122.04 indicates that the overall model contributes significantly to explaining variation in the dependent variable.[1278] The McFadden R^2, an analog to the R^2 in the OLS regression context, is 10.4%.[1279] The majority of coefficient estimates carry the expected signs. Both MTB and RET have a highly significant (p-values = 0.016 and 0.002, respectively), negative association with the probability of observing a transitional SFAS 142 goodwill write-off. For the change in ROA over the pre-adoption period, however, this relation is insignificant.[1280] Also according to expectations, the proportion of assets-in-place is positively associated with write-off probability (p-value = 0.072). To the extent that high assets-in-place stand for the existence of an accounting-based compensation plan, this result suggests that management operating under such plans are more likely to record a (potentially compensation-neutral) transitional write-off, possibly to decrease the likelihood of having to record future, compensation-decreasing write-offs. On the other hand, it must be noted that a pure earnings-management explanation might be premature since assets-in-place potentially proxy for other factors, such as industry membership. The coefficient estimate on DTE neither is significant nor does it have the predicted sign, suggesting that the extent to which a firm's DTE ratio is below the industry median does not influence the likelihood of observing a write-off.[1281] All three political visibility proxies, for which no signs were predicted, are found to be positively associated with write-off probability, albeit only MSH significantly so. A possible earnings-management interpretation is that dominant, high-profile firms, ceteris paribus, accelerate write-offs in order to decrease bottom-line income and firm size, reducing potential exposure to regulatory scrutiny. However, alternative economic interpretations include the notion that such firms to a large extent had to

---

1278 In the Probit and Logit models, the LR test is used to assess whether all the slope coefficients are zero. See Greene (2003, p. 678). LR tests for all of the independent variables individually (not tabulated) produce results largely identical to those indicated by the corresponding *z*-statistics. The *z*-statistic is the equivalent to the OLS *t*-statistic in estimating situations where normality holds only asymptotically, as is the case in the Probit, Logit, and Tobit models. Z values follow a standard normal distribution. See Gujarati (2003, p. 619). They are obtained by dividing the coefficient estimate by its standard error.

1279 This measure is selected from a multitude of goodness-of-fit measures applicable in binary models. It assumes values between zero and one and increases as the fit of the model increases. See Greene (2003, pp. 683-6), Maddala (2001, pp. 327-9), and Veall and Zimmermann (1996).

1280 Substituting the change in sales from 2000 to 2001 for ΔROA as an alternative accounting-based performance measure (not tabulated) yields a significantly negative coefficient estimate (p-value = 0.008). The other coefficients are largely unchanged. However, this variable is likely to capture changes in firm size rather than firm profitability, and is therefore difficult to interpret. Another substitute, the change in income before extraordinary items from 2000 to 2001, generates results equivalent to ΔROA (not tabulated).

1281 When the pre-write-off DTE ratio at the end of 2002 is used alternatively, the coefficient estimate has the expected negative sign but remains insignificant (p-value = 0.363).

rely on external growth, forcing them to overpay in acquisitions.[1282] Regarding the target variables, both coefficient estimates carry the expected signs, which might indicate that especially prior-period net income (p-value = 0.061) is an earnings target that management deems important to obtain. The control variable FYR exhibits a significantly positive relation with the likelihood of observing a write-off. Calendar-year firms are more likely to record transitional write-offs, although the reasons for this finding can only be speculated upon.[1283] Finally, the significant positive coefficient estimate on GW indicates that a write-off is more likely to occur where goodwill is a significant portion of the firm's overall asset base. On the whole, consistent with the tenor of the descriptive evidence presented in section 5.3.3 above, this finding suggests that economic factors strongly contribute to explaining variation in write-off probability, with write-offs being more frequent in firms that are viewed unfavorably by the market. The effects of financial reporting incentives, on the other hand, are open to several explanations.

Since economic factors hypothesis 1 suggests that firms for which MTB>1 have no economic inducement to record a write-off,[1284] model D1 is re-estimated using only this sub-sample (not tabulated). The number of observations drops to 921 firms, only 124 (13.5%) of which record a transitional SFAS 142 goodwill write-off. As expected, the economic factors lose their explanatory power in this sub-sample. From among the other explanatory factors, AIP (p-value = 0.075) and TARGET_PP (0.032) yield coefficient estimates that are significant and carry the expected signs. MSH is also highly explanatory (p-value = 0.000), suggesting that dominant firms are more likely to report write-offs. Overall, these results are consistent with the notion that economically successful firms' write-offs are motivated by factors other than goodwill impairment.

1282 In any event, MSH to some extent seems to capture size effects, which is also indicated by the fact that the SIZE variable itself is insignificant. The insignificant, positive coefficient estimate on the SIZE variable is stable to alternative measures such as total assets (p-value = 0.168) and sales (0.475). However, the estimates are significantly positive when the logarithmized variants SIZE_LOG are used (not tabulated). In that event, the other inferences remain unchanged. Since the coefficient estimate on MSH also retains its significance, it can be concluded with some confidence that MSH captures earnings-management motivations.

1283 Refer to the interpretation of Table 11 above.

1284 See also the descriptive evidence presented in Table 12 and Table A. 5. Again, it must be cautioned that the entity-level MTB ratio is a potentially noisy proxy for goodwill impairment in diversified, multi-segment firms.

5.4.3.2 Tests for robustness

Applying a Logit specification to model D1 yields widely similar results (not tabulated).[1285] The only exception is that the coefficient estimate on AIP is insignificant in this setting (p-value = 0.235). These similarities are consistent with Maddala's (2001) statement that the Probit and Logit models generate comparable estimates.[1286]

In order to restrain the influence that outlying observations on the regressors have on the inferences, model D1 is re-estimated using a truncated sample (not tabulated). Truncation is achieved by excluding those firms representing the bottom 5% and the top 5% of the respective distributions. As a result of truncation, the sample size drops to 687 firms, 106 (15.4%) of which record a transitional SFAS 142 goodwill write-off. Apparently, write-off firms are overrepresented in the outlying firms (21.0%). Applying the Probit estimator to model D1 based on this truncated sample yields results that are somewhat different from the initial estimate reported in Table 18. While the coefficient estimate on MTB remains highly significant with the expected negative sign (p-value = 0.000), RET and ΔROA lose the predicted sign and are insignificant. This latter fact might indicate that economic developments resulting in the write-off had not yet been captured by previous performance measures. AIP, while retaining the predicted sign, is also no longer found to have significant explanatory power. Again, the size effect is captured by SIZE_LOG (p-value = 0.025), rendering the coefficient estimate on MSH insignificantly positive (0.537). Both target variables are insignificant with the expected sign. Overall, the write-off decision in the outlier-adjusted sample still appears to be predominantly associated with the MTB ratio, suggesting that financial reporting motivations play only a minor role in "average" firms' write-off decisions.

5.4.3.3 Sub-sample tests

Probit regression results for model D2 are reported in Table 19 below.[1287] Because SPEC is only observed for a small minority of firms, this variable is omitted from the regression equation.[1288]

1285 Despite the theoretical shortcomings of OLS regression in the context of dichotomous dependent variables, Noreen (1988) documents empirically that, for certain kinds of data and sample sizes commonly encountered in classificatory accounting studies, OLS performs as good as the theoretically superior Probit model. However, because it is not certain that the write-off decision setting at hand corresponds to those investigated by Noreen (1988), OLS methodology is not applied here.

1286 See Maddala (2001, p. 323).

1287 The correlation matrix is reported in Table A. 7 in the Appendix.

$TGWO\_D_i = \alpha + \beta_1 \Delta CEO_i + \beta_2 RESTR_i + \beta_3 SIZE_i + \beta_4 FYR_i + \beta_5 GW_i + \varepsilon_i$				
Variable	**Hypothesis (predicted sign)**	**Coefficient estimate**	**z-statistic**	**Significance level (p-value)**
C	(?)	-1.092868	-6.511958	0.0000
ΔCEO	H_D^{EC} 7a (+)	-0.034432	-0.124063	0.9013
RESTR	H_D^{FR} 7b (+)	2.389634	1.050848	0.2933
SIZE	(?)	0.000006	1.981839	0.0475
FYR	(?)	0.136248	0.804718	0.4210
GW	(?)	0.019043	4.218368	0.0000
Likelihood ratio (p-value)			26.19 (0.000)	
McFadden R^2			0.058	
Observations	Goodwill sample where TARGET_Z = 0	Total: 391	TGWO_D = 0: 288 (73.7%)	TGWO_D = 1: 103 (26.3%)

Variable definitions (refer to Table 6 for further details):

ΔCEO	Dichotomous variable: 1 where a change occurred in the CEO position during 2001 or 2002; 0 otherwise.
RESTR	Restructuring cost (pre-tax), deflated by total assets, measured at the end of 2002.
SIZE	Size, measured by the mean of the market values of equity at the end of 2001 and 2002.
FYR	Dichotomous variable: 1 where fiscal year-end in 2001 is December 31; 0 otherwise. FYR is coded based on COMPUSTAT annual item FYR.
GW	Goodwill book value, deflated by total assets, measured at the end of 2001.

Table 19: Probit regression results for model D2 (partial sample of firms missing earnings targets)

The analysis indicates that financial reporting incentives hypothesis 7 does not appear to predict the write-off decisions of firms with pre-write-off net losses. While the overall fit of the model is significant (p-value = 0.000), LR tests for the explanatory factors individually (not tabulated) yield insignificant results. These findings are stable in a Logit specification (not tabulated). The explanatory power that the model does exhibit can be traced back to the control variables SIZE and GW. This finding suggests that there is no significant association of "big bath"-type incentives and/or restructuring situations with the write-off decision in firms that fail to avoid net losses in the adoption year of SFAS 142.

Finally, the variable RATING is added to the set of explanatory variables in model D1, yielding model D3. As shown in Table A. 8 in the Appendix, this variable is highly correlated with several of the other regressors. Most notably, it is negatively associated with SIZE and MSH, suggesting that larger, more dominant firms are viewed more favorably

1288 Its inclusion truncates the sample to 51 observations (TGWO_D = 0: 32; TGWO_D = 1: 19). Probit regression analysis of this smaller sample (not tabulated) yields no significant coefficient estimates.

by S&P.[1289] Conversely, positive correlation is found between AIP and DTE. Probit regression results for model D3 are reported in Table 20.

$$TGWO\_D_i = \alpha \quad +\beta_1 MTB_i + \beta_2 RET_i + \beta_3 \Delta ROA_i + \beta_4 AIP_i + \beta_5 DTE_i + \beta_6 MSH_i + \beta_7 HERF_i + \beta_8 \Delta PWOROA_i + \beta_9 TARGET\_PP_i + \beta_{10} TARGET\_Z_i + \beta_{11} RATING_i + \beta_{12} SIZE_i + \beta_{13} FYR_i + \beta_{14} GW_i + \varepsilon_i$$

Variable	Hypothesis (predicted sign)	Coefficient estimate	z-statistic	Significance level (p-value)
C	(?)	-1.014125	-2.226267	0.0260
MTB	H_D^{EC} 1 (–)	-0.013596	-0.954416	0.3399
RET	H_D^{EC} 2a (–)	-0.144535	-1.563256	0.1180
ΔROA	H_D^{EC} 2b (–)	0.990918	0.907692	0.3640
AIP	H_D^{FR} 1 (+)	0.409366	1.907339	0.0565
DTE	H_D^{FR} 2 (–)	0.000022	0.000983	0.9992
MSH	H_D^{FR} 3a (?)	2.832140	2.291373	0.0219
HERF	H_D^{FR} 3b (?)	1.219696	1.074196	0.2827
ΔPWOROA	H_D^{FR} 3c (?)	1.546458	0.963450	0.3353
TARGET_PP	H_D^{FR} 4 (–)	0.029938	0.156842	0.8754
TARGET_Z		-0.428407	-2.158407	0.0309
RATING	H_D^{FR} 8 (–)	-0.023211	-0.854516	0.3928
SIZE	(?)	0.000001	0.276728	0.7820
FYR	(?)	0.141802	0.818594	0.4130
GW	(?)	0.028020	5.205984	0.0000
Likelihood ratio (p-value)			57.66 (0.000)	
McFadden R^2			0.114	
Observations	Goodwill sample where RATING available	Total: 447	TGWO_D = 0: 333 (74.5%)	TGWO_D = 1: 114 (25.5%)

Continued on next page

[1289] Recall that high scores on the RATING variable represent low rating categories.

Variable definitions (refer to Table 6 for further details):

MTB	MTB ratio, measured at the end of 2001.
RET	Cumulative stock performance, measured over the fiscal years 2000 and 2001.
ΔROA	Percentage point change in ROA between the fiscal years 2000 and 2001.
AIP	Mean of assets-in-place, measured as the relation of PP&E (net of accumulated depreciation) to total market value, at the end of 2001 and 2002.
DTE	Mean of the differences between firm and median two-digit SIC industry DTE ratios, at the end of 2001 and 2002.
MSH	Mean of market shares, measured as the relation of firm sales (DATA12) to two-digit SIC industry sales, at the end of 2001 and 2002; industry sales based on all available firms.
HERF	Mean of the Herfindahl indexes of the two-digit SIC industry, measured as the sum of the squares of the market shares of each firm in the industry, at the end of 2001 and 2002; industry sales based on all available firms.
ΔPWOROA	Change in ROA (before transitional SFAS 142 goodwill write-off) in 2002 over regular ROA in 2001.
TARGET_PP TARGET_Z	Dichotomous variable: 1 where annual pre-write-off net income is above the prior year's level (above zero) in 2002; 0 otherwise.
RATING	Long-term domestic issuer credit rating in 2001.
SIZE	Size, measured by the mean of the market values of equity at the end of 2001 and 2002.
FYR	Dichotomous variable: 1 where fiscal year-end in 2001 is December 31; 0 otherwise. FYR is coded based on COMPUSTAT annual item FYR.
GW	Goodwill book value, deflated by total assets, measured at the end of 2001.

Table 20: Probit regression results for model D3 (partial sample of firms rated by S&P)

Restricting the analysis to a set of goodwill firms for which S&P domestic issuer credit ratings (RATING) are available yields a completely different sample. Only the largest, most visible firms are represented, which decreases the number of observations to a total of 447.[1290] The write-off firms (114) represent a larger portion of the sample (25.5%) than is the case in the overall goodwill sample (17.9%). Interestingly, economic factors no longer significantly explain the write-off decision in these firms. The formerly significantly negative coefficient estimates on both MTB and RET are insignificant, while still negative. While most of the other coefficients are roughly unchanged, avoiding a pre-write-off net loss (TARGET_Z) appears to be a powerful incentive for these high-profile firms (p-value = 0.031).[1291] The RATING variable itself, however, does not appear to be associated with write-off probability, indicating that the costs of recording a transitional write-off are not a linear function of the rating category.[1292] Consistent with the findings

1290 For example, these firms are, on average, more than six times larger in terms of the market value of equity (median = $1,747 million) than are firms in the overall goodwill sample. They also have significantly higher market shares (median = 1.3%). Their median MTB ratio is 2.00.

1291 Recall that, in model D1, the coefficient estimate on this variable is insignificant.

1292 Possibly, downgrades are more costly for firms in the higher rating categories because such events potentially trigger large increases in financing cost. Likewise, these costs might be especially high around certain cutoff points, e.g. where a firm is in jeopardy of losing its investment grade rating.

discussed above, financial reporting incentives appear to play a more important role in large, high-profile firms than they do in the overall sample.

Re-estimating model D3 using only firms for which MTB>1 generates results similar to those discussed in the context of model D1 above (not tabulated).[1293] In this setting, economic factors largely lose their explanatory power, whereas TARGET_Z (p-value = 0.029) yields a highly significant coefficient estimate that carries the expected sign. The findings are consistent with the interpretation that these high-profile firms avoid write-offs where in perceived jeopardy of recording a net loss. The RATING variable, again insignificant, appears to proxy for the high profiles and capital market following of the firms in this sub-sample.

5.4.4 Analysis of the write-off amount

The determinants of the write-off *amount*, expressed as the left-censored dependent variable TGWO_A, are analyzed using the Tobit model.[1294] Four separate models are estimated: Model A1 contains explanatory variables derived from the economic factors hypotheses as well as financial reporting incentives hypothesis 2. It is tested using all firms in the goodwill sample. Model A2 is used to investigate financial reporting incentives hypothesis 5, considering only those firms in the goodwill sample that meet the zero pre-write-off net income target in 2002 (TARGET_Z = 1). Model A3, a test of financial reporting incentives hypothesis 6, is applied to the other half of the goodwill sample (TARGET_Z = 0) in an attempt to ascertain whether "big bath"-type write-offs are limited by the available amount of equity.[1295] Finally, model A4 is an analog to Probit model D3, where RATING is added as an explanatory factor to the initial model, A1.[1296]

1293 This sample comprises 368 observations, of which 79 firms (21.5%) record a write-off.

1294 Tobit regression coefficients must be interpreted somewhat differently from those obtained in OLS estimation. Refer to Kennedy (1998, pp. 255-6) and McDonald and Moffitt (1980, pp. 318-9). The Tobit slope coefficient indicates the degree of change in the independent variable necessary to bring about a one-unit change in the *desired* transitional SFAS 142 goodwill write-off. The expected *actual* change in write-off is comprised of two components, owing to the fact that the write-off amount is left-censored at zero. Due to the censoring limit, observing any change in write-off at all for a given firm is conditional on the probability with which that firm is a non-limit observation, i.e. a write-off firm. Consequently, the components are, first, the change in expected write-off of above-limit observations times the probability of being above the limit, plus, second, the expected write-off of above-limit observations weighted by the change in probability of being above the limit

1295 To exclude firms for which the amount of equity is not a limiting factor, this test is restricted to firms where goodwill > equity. The restriction of positive equity imposed during the sample selection procedure (see Panel A of Table 7) is removed to allow for write-offs to cause negative equity.

1296 Again, only those (large) firms for which S&P debt rating data is available are included in this model.

5.4.4.1 Full-sample test

Tobit regression results for model A1 are reported in Table 21 below.

$$TGWO\_A_i = \alpha + \beta_1 MTB_i + \beta_2 RET_i + \beta_3 \Delta ROA_i + \beta_4 DTE_i + \beta_5 SIZE_i + \beta_6 FYR_i + \beta_7 GW_i + \varepsilon_i$$

Variable	Hypothesis (predicted sign)	Coefficient estimate	z-statistic	Significance level (p-value)
C	(?)	-0.190545	-11.59715	0.0000
MTB	H_A^{EC} 1 (–)	-0.005337	-3.234351	0.0012
RET	H_A^{EC} 2a (–)	-0.030820	-4.027769	0.0001
ΔROA	H_A^{EC} 2b (–)	-0.005722	-0.214255	0.8303
DTE	H_A^{FR} 2 (–)	-0.000087	-0.042113	0.9664
SIZE	(?)	0.000000	1.467386	0.1423
FYR	(?)	0.033777	2.633068	0.0085
GW	(?)	0.003138	9.262502	0.0000
Log likelihood ratio (p-value)			139.13 (0.000)	
Adjusted R^2			0.187	
Observations	Goodwill sample	Total: 1,248	Left censored: 1,024 (81.1%)	Uncensored: 224 (17.9%)

Variable definitions (refer to Table 6 for further details):

MTB	MTB ratio, measured at the end of 2001.
RET	Cumulative stock performance, measured over the fiscal years 2000 and 2001.
ΔROA	Percentage point change in ROA between the fiscal years 2000 and 2001.
DTE	Mean of the differences between firm and median two-digit SIC industry DTE ratios, at the end of 2001 and 2002.
SIZE	Size, measured by the mean of the market values of equity at the end of 2001 and 2002.
FYR	Dichotomous variable: 1 where fiscal year-end in 2001 is December 31; 0 otherwise. FYR is coded based on COMPUSTAT annual item FYR.
GW	Goodwill book value, deflated by total assets, measured at the end of 2001.

Table 21: Tobit regression results for model A1 (full sample)

The results yielded in the Tobit specification correspond to a large extent to those found for model D1 in the dichotomous setting: The write-off amount is significantly higher when price-based performance measures such as MTB and RET are lower, whereas for ΔROA, the accounting-based performance variable, such association is not found.[1297] Also, DTE lacks explanatory power.[1298] This finding suggests that economic factors, more significantly than do variables associated with financial reporting incentives, ex-

---

1297 As in model D1 above, substituting the change in sales from 2000 to 2001 for ΔROA as an alternative accounting-based performance measure (not tabulated) yields a significantly negative coefficient estimate (p-value = 0.042), while the other coefficients remain largely unchanged. Likewise similarly, the change in income before extraordinary items from 2000 to 2001 generates results equivalent to ΔROA (not tabulated).

1298 As in model D1, when the pre-write-off DTE ratio at the end of 2002 is used alternatively, the coefficient estimate has the expected negative sign but remains insignificant (p-value = 0.304).

plain not only the write-off decision itself, but to some extent also the amount written off. Again, the control variables FYR and GW significantly account for the overall fit of model A1,[1299] which is evidenced by the high LR test statistic.[1300]

Parallel to the procedure adopted in section 5.4.3.1 above, model A1 is re-estimated including only those firms for which MTB>1 (not tabulated). In contrast to the dichotomous setting, the economic factors variables MTB (p-value = 0.064) and RET (0.063) retain significant explanatory power for the write-off *amount*. Apparently, write-offs are lower where price-based performance is higher. Furthermore, the SIZE variable exhibits a significantly positive association with the write-off amount (p-value = 0.072), especially when logarithmized (0.001), suggesting that larger firms, on average, record larger (in relative terms) write-offs.

5.4.4.2 Tests for robustness

A robustness check of the preceding findings is undertaken by re-estimating model A1 using an OLS estimator (not tabulated). With the exception of the SIZE variable, all of the coefficient estimates retain their signs from the Tobit setting.[1301] However, the coefficients on all variables but GW become insignificant, indicating that the adjusted R^2 of 11.5% is largely attributable to that variable. Considering the methodological discussion in section 5.4.1.2 above, Tobit rather than OLS estimation, is appropriate to this censored dependent variable situation. Therefore, the results presented in Table 21 are regarded as relevant.

Corresponding to the procedure used for the binary model D1 in section 5.4.3.2 above, the Tobit model A1 is re-estimated for the same truncated sample.[1302] The results are very similar to those yielded and explained above. Most notably, MTB remains highly

---

1299 Parallel to model D1, firm size only contributes significantly to explaining variation in the write-off amount when the logarithmized variant SIZE_LOG is used (p-value = 0.060).

1300 As in the binary setting, the LR test is an overall significance test for Tobit models as well. See, for example, Kennedy (1998, pp. 60-1, 67-8, 70-1). The LR test statistic has an unknown small-sample distribution, but is asymptotically distributed as a χ^2. See also Quantitative Micro Software (2002, pp. 451-2). It indicates whether specified (groups of) independent variables contribute to the fit of the model or must be classified as redundant.

1301 As a general rule, the OLS coefficient estimates are approximately obtained by multiplying the Tobit estimates with the proportion of non-limit (i.e. non-write-off) observations in the goodwill sample. See Kennedy (1998, p. 255).

1302 As indicated above, truncation is achieved by excluding those firms representing the bottom 5% and the top 5% of the respective distributions.

significant (p-value = 0.000), consistent with the fact that economic factors are highly associated with the write-off amount even after adjusting for outlying observations.

5.4.4.3 Sub-sample tests

Table 22 contains the Tobit regression results for model A2.[1303]

$$TGWO\_A_i = \alpha + \beta_1 DIF\_PP_i + \beta_2 DIF\_Z_i + \beta_3 SIZE_i + \beta_4 FYR_i + \beta_5 GW_i + \varepsilon_i$$

Variable	Hypothesis (predicted sign)	Coefficient estimate	z-statistic	Significance level (p-value)
C	(?)	-0.173484	-7.760966	0.0000
DIF_PP	H_A^{EC} 5 (+)	0.209904	2.404245	0.0162
DIF_Z		-0.778433	-4.490724	0.0000
SIZE	(?)	0.000001	2.085737	0.0370
FYR	(?)	0.015266	0.892970	0.3719
GW	(?)	0.003325	7.046530	0.0000
Log likelihood ratio (p-value)			77.79 (0.000)	
Adjusted R^2			0.165	
Observations	Goodwill sample where TARGET_Z = 1	Total: 818	Left censored: 681 (83.3%)	Uncensored: 137 (16.7%)

Variable definitions (refer to Table 6 for further details):

DIF_PP DIF_Z	Difference between annual pre-write-off net income and the prior year's level (and zero), deflated by prior-period total assets, in 2002.
SIZE	Size, measured by the mean of the market values of equity at the end of 2001 and 2002.
FYR	Dichotomous variable: 1 where fiscal year-end in 2001 is December 31; 0 otherwise. FYR is coded based on COMPUSTAT annual item FYR.
GW	Goodwill book value, deflated by total assets, measured at the end of 2001.

Table 22: Tobit regression results for model A2 (partial sample of firms meeting earnings targets)

Estimating model A2 yields mixed evidence on financial reporting incentives hypothesis 5, according to which firms that obtain net income-based earnings targets will tend to record transitional write-offs in the amount of the "slack", i.e. the difference between actual pre-write-off earnings and the relevant target. While the results shown in Table 22 suggest such behavior where prior-period earnings are the target (p-value = 0.016), the negative coefficient estimate on DIF_Z calls for a different interpretation: Apparently, the amount written off decreases in pre-write-off net income, which again indicates an economic, rather than earnings-management explanation for the write-off amount. This

[1303] The correlation matrix for this model is shown in Table A. 9 in the Appendix.

notion is further corroborated by the fact that write-off firms are underrepresented in this sub-sample (16.7%).[1304]

Results for the firms that fall short of earnings targets are presented in Table 23.[1305]

$$TGWO\_A_i = \alpha + \beta_1 EQ_i + \beta_2 SIZE_i + \beta_3 FYR_i + \beta_4 GW_i + \varepsilon_i$$

Variable	Hypothesis (predicted sign)	Coefficient estimate	z-statistic	Significance level (p-value)
C	(?)	-0.262342	-4.206014	0.0000
EQ	H_A^{FR} 6 (+)	0.058459	2.012433	0.0442
SIZE_LOG	(?)	0.005440	0.835508	0.4034
FYR	(?)	0.072110	1.720265	0.0854
GW	(?)	0.003297	3.918789	0.0001
Log likelihood ratio (p-value)			32.68 (0.000)	
Adjusted R^2			0.059	
Observations	Goodwill sample including firms with negative equity, where TARGET_Z = 0 and goodwill ≥ pre-write-off equity	Total: 180	Left censored: 130 (72.2%)	Uncensored: 50 (27.8%)

Variable definitions (refer to Table 6 for further details):

EQ	Pre-write-off common equity, deflated by pre-write-off total assets, at the end of 2002.
SIZE_LOG	Natural logarithm of size, which is measured by the mean of the market values of equity at the end of 2001 and 2002.
FYR	Dichotomous variable: 1 where fiscal year-end in 2001 is December 31; 0 otherwise. FYR is coded based on COMPUSTAT annual item FYR.
GW	Goodwill book value, deflated by total assets, measured at the end of 2001.

Table 23: Tobit regression results for model A3 (partial sample of firms missing earnings targets)

The coefficient estimate on the EQ variable has the expected sign and is significant at the 5% level. From these results, it appears that financial reporting incentives hypothesis 6 is supported by the data.[1306] Where firms record "big bath" write-offs, the amount of equity seems to represent a behavioral threshold that is difficult to explain in economic terms.

1304 Because DIF_PP and DIF_Z are highly correlated (Pearson correlation coefficient = 0.342), the regressions are repeated by including each of these regressors individually (not tabulated). This procedure yields an insignificantly positive coefficient estimate on DIF_PP (p-value = 0.523), suggesting that the amount by which prior-period net income is beaten, in itself, does not explain variation in the transitional write-off amount. However, the significantly negative coefficient estimate on DIF_Z is almost unchanged (p-value = 0.000), which validates the initial interpretation.

1305 The correlation matrix for this model is shown in Table A. 10 in the Appendix.

1306 Further analysis shows that only five firms recorded transitional SFAS 142 goodwill write-offs that caused their equity to become negative.

Finally, similar to the procedure followed in the Probit setting above, the initial model A1 is re-estimated after adding RATING as a supplementary regressor. The results are shown in Table 24.

$$TGWO\_A_i = \alpha \quad +\beta_1 MTB_i + \beta_2 RET_i + \beta_3 \Delta ROA_i + \beta_4 DTE_i + \beta_5 RATING + \beta_6 SIZE_i + \beta_7 FYR_i + \beta_8 GW_i + \varepsilon_i$$

Variable	**Hypothesis (predicted sign)**	**Coefficient estimate**	**z-statistic**	**Significance level (p-value)**
C	(?)	-0.117314	-3.855549	0.0001
MTB	H_A^{EC} 1 (–)	-0.002259	-1.641569	0.1007
RET	H_A^{EC} 2a (–)	-0.018327	-2.319798	0.0204
ΔROA	H_A^{EC} 2b (–)	0.047800	0.613279	0.5397
DTE	H_A^{FR} 2 (–)	-0.000051	-0.025661	0.9795
RATING	H_D^{FR} 8 (–)	0.001623	0.808696	0.4187
SIZE	(?)	0.000000	0.858702	0.3905
FYR	(?)	-0.002053	-0.142883	0.8864
GW	(?)	0.002403	5.755406	0.0000
Log likelihood ratio (p-value)			48.66 (0.000)	
Adjusted R^2			0.113	
Observations	Goodwill sample where RATING available	Total: 447	Left censored: 333 (74.5%)	Uncensored: 114 (25.5%)

Variable definitions (refer to Table 6 for further details):

MTB	MTB ratio, measured at the end of 2001.
RET	Cumulative stock performance, measured over the fiscal years 2000 and 2001.
ΔROA	Percentage point change in ROA between the fiscal years 2000 and 2001.
DTE	Mean of the differences between firm and median two-digit SIC industry DTE ratios, at the end of 2001 and 2002.
RATING	Long-term domestic issuer credit rating in 2001.
SIZE	Size, measured by the mean of the market values of equity at the end of 2001 and 2002.
FYR	Dichotomous variable: 1 where fiscal year-end in 2001 is December 31; 0 otherwise. FYR is coded based on COMPUSTAT annual item FYR.
GW	Goodwill book value, deflated by total assets, measured at the end of 2001.

Table 24: Tobit regression results for model A4 (partial sample of firms rated by S&P)

As in the Probit setting, the economic factors variables lose their initial explanatory power compared to the initial model, while the coefficient estimate on the RATING variable itself turns out insignificant. Again, this effect arguably relates to the dramatically altered sample composition achieved by focusing on firms rated by S&P.

5.5 *Inferences*

5.5.1 Summary of findings

Guided by the hypotheses derived in section 5.2 above, the preceding analysis of determinants of transitional SFAS 142 goodwill write-offs comprised three steps: First, descriptive evidence and comparative significance tests were presented in order to portray the sample, deriving preliminary conclusions about differences between goodwill and non-goodwill firms and, primarily, write-off and non-write-off firms. Second, multivariate Probit regression analysis was conducted to assess the aggregate explanatory power of a set of potential write-off determinants for the dichotomous write-off decision. Third, multivariate Tobit regression analysis was employed to explain the transitional SFAS 142 goodwill write-off amount. A cautious interpretation of the results follows.[1307]

Transitional SFAS 142 goodwill write-offs, on average, represent significant accounting events in terms of their effects on write-off firms' financial statements. The analysis strongly indicates that write-off behavior predominantly reflects economic circumstances. In the overall goodwill sample, Probit regressions indicate that write-offs are less likely where MTB ratios and stock performance are higher. Using Tobit regression methodology, the same relation is found for the amount written off, which decreases, on average, in firms' price-based performance. On average, write-off firms are also larger and more highly in debt than their non-write-off counterparts. The findings are further consistent with the notion that managers are concerned with avoiding losses and earnings declines. Also, calendar-year firms are more susceptible to write-offs, possibly because they used their opportunity to observe capital market reactions to early adopters' write-off announcements and judged that transitional write-offs are not penalized by investors.[1308]

These findings, especially regarding the MTB ratio, are largely stable to alternative estimation procedures, sub-sample analyses, and the truncation of outlying observations. Despite the enormous discretion that characterizes SFAS 142 especially upon adoption, the impairment-only approach is apparently successful at capturing goodwill impairment at least to some extent, inducing weak performers to record write-offs.[1309] The fact that

---

1307 Hong, Kaplan and Mandelker (1978, p. 44) accurately point out that "[n]o single study is ever completely convincing on settling a controversy. Problems in sample selection, financial and statistical models, and interpretation of results are inherent in all empirical work."

1308 A similar conclusion is reached by Henning, Shaw and Stock (2002, p. 26).

1309 Segal's (2003, p. 29) conclusion is somewhat less optimistic; his comparison of SFAS 121 and SFAS 142 "raises questions with respect to the new rule's ability to deliver."

transitional SFAS 142 goodwill write-offs apparently represent the accounting "echo" of economic declines occurring as long as two years previously is consistent with the assumption that such transitional write-offs partly "catch up" impairments that the weaker SFAS 121 trigger was unable to detect.

A prominent pattern emerging in the sub-sample analysis indicates that the transitional SFAS 142 goodwill write-off behavior of large, dominant firms is clearly different from that of smaller, less "visible" companies. Several proxies of "high profile", including size, market share, and the availability of S&P rating data, are associated with large write-offs even where goodwill impairment is not necessarily apparent *a priori*. In these firms, write-off behavior seems to reflect financial reporting incentives rather than economic developments. Apparently, the transition period is perceived to be a window of opportunity, in which goodwill, the "Sword of Damocles" hanging above many firms' financial statements, can be discarded at low cost. Write-offs are accelerated into the transition period, possibly in order to decrease political visibility, shelter future management compensation, and avoid future hits to earnings that might be viewed more negatively by capital market participants. Nevertheless, this finding is likewise open to different interpretations, including conservatism.

Most of the economic-consequences hypotheses do not appear to be descriptive, possibly due to data availability constraints and the resulting reliance on inappropriate proxy variables. In addition, among the hypothesis not corroborated by the data are those related to "cookie-jar reserving" and, in part, "big bath" behavior. There is only weak evidence that write-offs coincide with CEO changes or restructuring efforts in firms falling short of earnings targets. Likewise, firms beating earnings targets do not appear to coordinate write-off amounts with the available "slack", possibly because financial reporting decisions other than the write-off amount are made after the latter is ultimately determined. However, the data indicates that the amount of equity presents a strong limiting factor for the amount written off.

Overall, the stable core findings suggest that write-off behavior differs with the degree of firms' "visibility" in the capital markets. In smaller, less exposed firms, write-offs seem to mainly reflect difficult economic circumstances, whereas larger, more dominant firms appear to more actively coordinate their write-off behavior with management's financial reporting strategies. However, even where the findings appear to be consistent with earnings management behavior, the availability of alternative, economic explanations rules out premature conclusions. Further, while financial reporting objectives might play a significant role in explaining most firms' *overall* financial reporting behavior in the

SFAS 142 adoption period, it is not necessarily the transitional write-off that is used to achieve them. This fact might in part be explained by the notion that outstanding, non-recurring income statement items, especially those met with substantial prior attention, are too costly to be suited for certain subtle types of earnings management, such as target accounting. Possibly, other financial reporting incentives that are not captured by my hypotheses explain part of the variation in write-off behavior.

5.5.2 Limitations

A possible limitation of this study relates to potential measurement error in the dependent variable. While every attempt was made to ascertain that TGWO reflected nothing but the transitional SFAS 142 goodwill write-off, disclosed as a change in accounting principle, the discussion in section 5.3.1 above indicates that other effects might be captured by that variable. To the extent that such measurement error does not introduce systematic bias, it is incorporated in the disturbance term and the resulting coefficient estimates are unaffected.[1310]

Further, the results might, at least to some extent, be influenced by measurement error in some of the independent variables. As has been discussed at length in sections 3.3.2.3 and 5.2.3.1 above, this study, like much of the preceding earnings management literature, had to rely on potentially imprecise proxy variables, which might have decreased the power of the regression tests.[1311] For example, recent research has increasingly relied on actual contract data to circumvent these problems.[1312] However, due to restrictions in data availability, no superior surrogate variables could be devised at this point. To the extent that the proxies used measure the underlying variables with error, the resulting coefficient estimates might be biased and also inconsistent.[1313] Measurement error might also plague the economic-factors variables because these are based on firm-level as op-

---

1310 See, for example, Kennedy (1998, p. 140). However, the estimates might have larger variances than would be the case in the absence of measurement error. See Gujarati (2003, pp. 524-5).

1311 See, for example, Huijgen (1996, pp. 48-50). Watts and Zimmerman (1990, pp. 143-6) also discuss research method issues typical to empirical tests of positive accounting theory.

1312 See, for example, Dichev and Skinner (2002, p. 1101) for actual accounting-based debt covenant restrictions. Some of the most frequent ratios used (debt to cash flow, interest coverage, fixed charge coverage, tangible net worth) are not influenced by transitional SFAS 142 goodwill write-offs. Also, AOL Time Warner, in its annual report on form 10-K/A for the period ended on December 31, 2001, states that its expected $54 billion goodwill write-off "will not result in a violation of any of the Company's covenants."

1313 Refer to Gujarati (2003, pp. 526-8) and Kennedy (1998, pp. 140-3). The fact that measurement error might hamper the conclusions from goodwill write-off studies is also discussed by Wilson (1996, p. 173).

posed to reporting unit-level data. The analysis could be further refined by using segment data where more detailed information is unattainable.[1314] Overall, a possibility remains that, while the hypotheses accurately described the data, the testing methods and variables lacked the power necessary to find at least some of the expected relations. Inference problems might also stem from the fact that management expects financial statement users to respond differently to transitional SFAS 142 goodwill write-offs than what is predicted here.

In addition, it has not been explicitly tested whether all the conditions required for using limited dependent variable models are fulfilled in the data.[1315] For example, since firm size appears to be a significant explanatory factor, heteroskedasticity is a potential problem. On the other hand, autocorrelation should not be of concern because cross-sectional data is used. While these methodological concerns might preclude exact, quantitative inferences, the findings appear to be sufficiently stable to allow general, qualitative conclusions to be drawn.

Finally, caution must be exercised with regard to generalization of the results found here. First, the transition to the SFAS 142 goodwill impairment-only approach represents a unique setting in which to study write-off determinants.[1316] Future, "regular" write-offs might be associated with vastly different determinants, one possible reason being that any "catching-up" effect is likely to be out of the way. The way in which future SFAS 142 write-offs will be considered in accounting-based contracts, in the political arena, and, perhaps most importantly, by capital-market participants, is likely to be far less uncertain to management.[1317] Second, since the sample selection and truncation procedures resulted in significant trimming of the available observations, some of the findings do not necessarily generalize to the entirety to of publicly listed U. S. corporations, let alone to firms domiciled in other economies.

[1314] See also Riedl (2002, p. 3).

[1315] Refer to Greene (2003, ch. 21, 22), Maddala (2001, ch. 8), and Maddala (1983, ch. 2, 6).

[1316] For a similar "disclaimer", refer to Segal (2003, p. 30).

[1317] Henning, Shaw and Stock (2002, p. 2) provide evidence suggesting that "the market will view .. transition write-offs differently from [pre-SFAS 142] write-offs of goodwill."

6 Conclusion

Published in 2001, SFAS 142, *Goodwill and Other Intangible Assets*, preliminarily concludes decades of heated debate about the appropriate accounting procedures for acquired goodwill. The impairment-only approach, which replaced goodwill amortization, met with a largely critical echo from the financial community. While the theoretical, conceptual soundness of this method is largely acknowledged, constituents are concerned about the tremendous degree of subjectivity that the goodwill impairment test involves. The predecessor standard, SFAS 121, also relied heavily on management's judgment, but the goodwill amortization requirement assured that this dubious asset was charged to earnings over a predictable, if arbitrary, period of time. Under the new rules, however, goodwill can be carried on a firm's books indefinitely under certain circumstances.

Firms applying U. S. GAAP adopted SFAS 142 in the fiscal year 2002. Due to the standard's immense discretionary freedom and the uncertainty regarding its perception by financial statement users, firms had the opportunity to harmonize transitional goodwill write-off behavior with their financial reporting incentives and objectives. In this setting, the study at hand analyzes whether managers of a large sample of publicly traded U. S. firms took advantage of this opportunity or whether firms' economic circumstances explain transitional write-off behavior.

In order to generate hypotheses regarding managers' expected write-off behavior, two distinct areas of research are analyzed in detail. In **chapter 2**, a review of empirical evidence on the goodwill debate suggests that managers are concerned about the financial statement effects of goodwill accounting. Apparently, the assumption is widespread among managers that financial statement users take accounting information at face value, which induces them to avoid and/or delay goodwill-related charges where possible. In contrast to that, tests of investors' perceptions indicate that management's "cosmetic" earnings management is not rewarded because market participants, on average, appear to see through it to the firms' underlying economic characteristics.

In **chapter 3**, it is argued that a transitional SFAS 142 goodwill charge can be characterized as a discretionary asset write-off. These accounting events, large and growing in economic significance, are governed by accounting guidance involving a high degree of flexibility and judgment. Because they are also extremely visible due to separate disclosure, these charges have been thoroughly investigated. Based on the assumption that write-off behavior is largely at the discretion of management, empirical researchers are interested in the determinants of that decision and in its assessment by investors. This research is reviewed extensively in order to draw inferences about the extent to which management's past write-off behavior is applicable to the transitional SFAS 142 setting and to lay the theoretical groundwork for hypothesis development. Studies of write-off determinants suggest that these charges can be explained to some extent by impairment of the underlying assets, but frequently to a greater degree by managers' contract-based as well as capital market-related financial reporting incentives. Perhaps the most stable finding is that discretionary asset write-offs are taken when a new CEO adopts a "big bath" strategy, signaling to investors that past problems are being aggressively dealt with. With regard to investors' perception of write-offs, empirical findings indicate that these charges are frequently anticipated and that the market reaction depends on the kind of information conveyed.

Predicting earnings management explanations behind transitional SFAS 142 goodwill write-offs requires that the new standard actually provides sufficient subjective elements for being applied at management's discretion. Therefore, much of **chapter 4** is devoted to exposing the manifold discretionary parameters in the impairment-only approach. The analysis shows that management's subjectivity and judgment is called upon at all levels, especially during the period in which SFAS 142 is applied for the first time.

Finally, **chapter 5** contains an empirical study of transitional SFAS 142 goodwill write-off behavior exhibited by a large sample of publicly traded U. S. firms. Based on theory and empirical findings presented in chapters 2 and 3, hypotheses are derived about the determinants of write-off behavior. These predictions are grouped into three main categories: First, since the impairment-only approach is designed to detect declines in goodwill value (impairment), variables representing economic downturns affecting the sample firms are expected to be associated with write-off behavior. Second, to the extent that management expects write-offs to affect the firm's exposure to contractual consequences, write-off behavior is predicted to relate to proxies for these consequences. Third, because firms are expected to gear write-off behavior towards favorably influencing investors' perceptions, variables representing such incentives are assumed to explain write-offs.

Descriptive analyses, univariate significance tests, and multivariate Probit and Tobit regressions were used to examine these hypotheses. A persistent pattern emerging from the data suggests that write-off behavior, on average, reflects the economic situation of sample firms. In full sample tests, Probit regressions indicate that write-off probability is lower where MTB ratios and price-based performance are higher. Tobit regression tests reveal a similar relation of these variables to the write-off amount. In addition, write-off firms are larger and more highly in debt than their non-write-off counterparts. Further, sample firms are concerned about achieving simple earnings targets and maintaining positive equity. They are also more likely to record a transitional write-off when their fiscal year is the calendar year. These core results are largely stable to robustness checks and alternative specifications, suggesting that the highly discretionary impairment-only approach does capture goodwill impairment at least to some extent. Possibly, transitional SFAS 142 write-offs in part represent a "catching up" of value declines that the weaker SFAS 121 procedure was unable to reveal.

Comprehensive sub-sample analyses indicate that transitional SFAS 142 goodwill write-off behavior is not homogenous throughout the goodwill sample. Large, high-profile firms apparently record write-offs even where goodwill impairment is not apparent from observation of economic conditions. Rather, write-off behavior seems to be consistent with financial reporting incentives, suggesting that "visible" firms use the window of opportunity presented by the adoption of SFAS 142 to inexpensively discard goodwill, the "Sword of Damocles" hanging above their financial statements. Such accelerating of write-offs is consistent with political cost considerations and a desire to shelter future earnings and compensation.

Overall, the qualitatively established core findings indicate that write-off behavior differs with the degree of sample firms' "visibility" in the capital markets. On average and especially in smaller firms, write-offs appear to be economically induced, while high-profile firms apparently harmonize their write-off behavior with management's financial reporting objectives to a higher degree. However, premature conclusions about earnings management causes for the observed behavior are unwarranted due to the availability of alternative, economic explanations.

The impairment-only approach is likely to remain a fruitful area of research for some time to come, and the research approach chosen here can be extended into several promising directions. Perhaps the most natural complementary approach to this study would be an investigation of market reactions to transitional SFAS 142 goodwill write-offs in order to ascertain investors' perception of the "quality" of these charges. However, researchers must be mindful of several methodological problems associated with this approach. For example, market reactions can only be studied where write-offs are voluntarily announced in a timely manner. The fact that not all write-offs fulfill this criterion is likely to introduce selection bias into the sample. Further, an analysis of market responses usually takes the form of an event study. This research design involves specific difficulties, which include determining the exact event date, modeling the expected market development absent the write-off, estimating the amount of write-off expected by investors at the write-off date, and taking into account the effects of any concurrent events affecting the write-off firm. These problems invariably imply that two or more joint hypotheses are tested, which enormously complicates the drawing of inferences.

Another viable avenue would be to compare goodwill write-off determinants and/or market responses between SFAS 142 and its predecessor regimes. However, due to changed economic and institutional circumstances, such comparison might be hard to interpret and conclusions regarding the superiority of one set of rules over the other difficult to justify. In order to keep as many factors as possible constant, it might be rewarding to analyze management's goodwill-related write-off behavior post-adoption, where financial statement users' interpretation of these "regular" write-offs is likely to be much more predictable to management.

Finally, future research could investigate what other concurrent indicators of earnings management, e.g. aggregate discretionary accruals or individual discretionary accounts, suggest about management's financial reporting strategy. As noted above, the highly visible transitional SFAS 142 goodwill write-off might not have been the earnings management instrument of choice for some firms, and the extent to which firms preferred other instruments might vary cross-sectionally. A small-sample or case study approach might be a worthwhile methodological alternative to using large samples and relying on crude proxy variables construed from commercially available data. Further progress could also result from studies of auditors' role in the context of discretionary financial reporting decisions.

Currently, the FASB and the IASB are contemplating another radical change in the accounting procedures for business combinations: In acquisitions of less than 100% of the acquiree's equity, any resulting goodwill will be grossed up to reflect the entire difference between the acquiree's overall fair value and the fair value of its net assets. The resulting goodwill, to be allocated in part to non-controlling shareholders' remaining interest in the acquiree's equity, can no longer be termed "purchased" goodwill in its entirety. This "full goodwill method" introduces new discretionary elements into the accounting for goodwill.[1318] Exploring management's use of this flexibility will be another interesting research opportunity.

[1318] See, for example, Pellens, Basche and Sellhorn (2003).

Appendix

Variable	Non-goodwill / goodwill samples				Non-write-off / write-off samples			
	Equality of medians (Adj. median χ^2- test)		Equality of means (t-test)		Equality of medians (Adj. median χ^2- test)		Equality of means (t-test)	
	χ^2	*p-value*	*t-statistic*	*p-value*	χ^2	*p-value*	*t-statistic*	*p-value*
Goodwill 2002								
In million $	NA	NA	NA	NA	14.51783	0.0001	2.796869	0.0052
% total assets	NA	NA	NA	NA	0.056044	0.8129	0.433348	0.6648
% BV of equity	NA	NA	NA	NA	2.978007	0.0844	2.142716	0.0323
% MV of equity	NA	NA	NA	NA	3.514072	0.0608	2.495752	0.0127
Goodwill 2001								
In million $	NA	NA	NA	NA	53.32575	0.0000	4.849931	0.0000
% total assets	NA	NA	NA	NA	21.59473	0.0000	7.053583	0.0000
% BV of equity	NA	NA	NA	NA	27.42732	0.0000	0.763602	0.4452
% MV of equity	NA	NA	NA	NA	74.47977	0.0000	0.289259	0.7724
MTB	0.016646	0.8973	2.059759	0.0395	45.05566	0.0000	2.060898	0.0395
RET	4.182144	0.0409	1.162877	0.2450	8.275530	0.0040	0.777743	0.4369
ΔROA	0.090626	0.7634	0.718982	0.4722	0.266602	0.6056	0.491423	0.6232
AIP	0.010946	0.9167	2.444166	0.0146	11.01772	0.0009	2.115625	0.0346
DTE02	76.21605	0.0000	0.746498	0.4554	5.228655	0.0222	0.359825	0.7190
MV°	165.8758	0.0000	4.023226	0.0001	2.399414	0.1214	1.661461	0.0969
TA°	269.1145	0.0000	4.028126	0.0001	27.42732	0.0000	3.452232	0.0006
SAL°	331.6193	0.0000	4.918754	0.0000	24.42397	0.0000	2.747248	0.0061
MSH	244.3230	0.0000	7.004372	0.0000	35.69741	0.0000	5.795052	0.0000
HERF	18.77189	0.0000	0.163767	0.8699	8.463352	0.0036	3.538952	0.0004
ΔPWOROA	19.06767	0.0000	2.126163	0.0336	0.005441	0.9412	0.858409	0.3908
EQ	39.63488	0.0000	8.926660	0.0000	3.966378	0.0464	2.723789	0.0065

° MV, TA, and SAL represent mean values (fiscal 2001 and 2002) for the market value of equity, total assets, and sales, respectively.

For other variable definitions, refer to Table 6. Monetary amounts are in million $.

Table A. 1: Univariate comparisons of the non-goodwill/goodwill and non-write-off/write-off samples

Industry	2-digit SIC category	Total firms		Non-goodwill sample		Goodwill sample		Non-write-off sample		Write-off sample	
		N	%	N	%	N	%	N	%	N	%
Business services	73	2,155	15.6	101	10.6	133	10.7	111	10.8	22	9.8
Electronic, electric equipment	36	990	7.2	66	6.9	91	7.3	83	8.1	8	3.6
Chemicals, allied products	28	983	7.1	133	13.9	86	6.9	68	6.6	18	8.0
Industrial machinery, equipment	35	879	6.4	52	5.4	108	8.7	92	9.0	16	7.1
Instruments, related products	38	853	6.2	74	7.7	88	7.1	79	7.7	9	4.0
Communication	48	739	5.4	17	1.8	32	2.6	26	2.5	6	2.7
Electric, gas, sanitary services	49	567	4.1	18	1.9	18	1.4	15	1.5	3	1.3
Oil, gas extraction	13	543	3.9	89	9.3	32	2.6	29	2.8	3	1.3
Engineering, management services	87	407	2.3	26	2.6	25	1.9	21	2.0	4	1.6
Wholesale trade: Durable goods	50	367	2.7	21	2.2	46	3.7	30	2.9	16	7.1
Health services	80	328	2.4	24	2.5	24	1.9	21	2.1	3	1.3
Food, kindred products	20	316	2.3	28	2.9	22	1.8	21	2.1	1	0.4
Miscellaneous retail	59	313	2.3	17	1.8	26	2.1	22	2.1	4	1.8
Transportation equipment	37	276	2.0	13	1.4	37	3.0	30	2.9	7	3.1
Wholesale trade: Nondurable goods	51	245	1.8	11	1.2	24	1.9	22	2.1	2	0.9
Eating, drinking places	58	219	1.6	14	1.5	30	2.4	26	2.5	4	1.8
Metal mining	10	200	1.4	28	2.9	0	0.0	0	0.0	0	0.0
Fabricated metal products	34	195	1.4	11	1.2	34	2.7	25	2.4	9	4.0
Printing, publishing	27	188	1.4	3	0.3	22	1.8	17	1.7	5	2.2
Amusement, recreation services	79	188	1.4	19	2.0	16	1.3	11	1.1	5	2.2
Primary metal industries	33	184	1.3	16	1.7	32	2.6	24	2.3	8	3.6
Rubber and misc. plastics products	30	166	1.2	11	1.2	27	2.2	20	2.0	7	3.1
Misc. manufacturing industries	39	166	1.2	10	1.0	17	1.4	14	1.4	3	1.3
Motion pictures	78	152	1.1	4	0.4	7	0.6	6	0.6	1	0.4
Paper, allied products	26	135	1.0	10	1.0	25	2.0	17	1.7	8	3.6
All other°		2,044	15.3	139	14.7	246	19.4	194	19.1	52	23.7
Total		**13,798**	**100.0**	**955**	**100.0**	**1,248**	**100.0**	**1,024**	**100.0**	**224**	**100.0**

The following 2-digit SIC categories are not represented (reasons given in parentheses): 3-6, 11, 18, 19, 66, 68, 69, 71, 74, 77, 85, 90-98 (unassigned), 43 (U. S. Postal Service), 60-65 and 67 (depository institutions, eliminated during sample selection), 84 (cultural institutions), and 88 (private households).

° Includes category 99 (non-classifiable establishments, 1.4% of "total firms available") and all other categories representing less than 1% of "total firms available".

Table A. 2: Industry breakdown of the four samples

RWGO_A	Mean	StDev	Min	1st qrt	Med	3rd qrt	Max
in million $	94	356	0	2	7	43	2,876.0
% total assets	6.9	9.5	0.0	0.7	3.4	8.7	54.9
% common equity (BV)	19.1	44.0	0.0	1.6	7.3	22.3	442.3
% goodwill	54.8	87.9	0.0	7.3	29.1	85.3	660.2
% common equity (MV)	134.0	1,395.2	0.0	0.7	5.1	17.8	16,870.8
% sales	31.2	119.8	0.0	0.6	4.2	13.8	992.8

RGWO_A is the regular SFAS 142 goodwill write-off. Goodwill figures are scaled by beginning-of-period balance sheet numbers and end-of-period sales. These data comprise write-offs taken during fiscal 2002 by 143 firms in the goodwill sample.

Table A. 3: Descriptive analysis of regular SFAS 142 goodwill write-offs taken during fiscal 2002 by firms in the goodwill sample

Transitional write-off	2-digit SIC	N	in million $		% total assets		% BV of equity		% goodwill		% MV of equity		% sales	
Industry	category		Md	Mn	Md	Mn	Md	Mn	Md	Mn	Md	Mn	Md	Mn
Agricultural production – crops	1	3	55	60	4.37	4.64	16.29	26.51	45.44	33.40	8.00	25.42	2.73	6.47
Oil and gas extraction	13	3	73	499	6.61	5.84	12.50	12.85	38.57	32.78	12.65	13.61	15.34	25.22
Special trade contractors	17	4	243	244	23.71	24.16	44.07	44.66	52.44	55.50	100.51	98.61	25.08	25.95
Textile mill products	22	3	12	26	5.80	5.09	18.31	25.48	16.57	13.16	19.43	33.60	5.99	6.27
Apparel and other textile products	23	6	15	97	4.82	5.40	7.84	12.81	45.21	37.28	9.68	21.19	3.17	4.65
Lumber and wood products	24	3	14	19	8.13	9.45	17.66	15.34	34.02	42.56	27.65	20.65	3.66	8.73
Paper and allied products	26	8	42	149	1.42	3.17	4.63	10.36	10.22	17.62	2.44	18.10	2.08	3.66
Printing and publishing	27	5	24	60	4.99	5.31	10.86	10.38	13.53	19.49	11.03	9.34	6.15	6.38
Chemicals and allied products	28	18	45	304	2.43	6.63	6.57	16.83	39.97	42.94	6.13	18.06	2.83	8.41
Rubber and miscellaneous plastics products	30	7	8	33	6.58	12.94	10.12	26.01	59.95	63.67	34.97	85.12	5.25	11.20
Stone, clay, glass, and concrete products	32	4	95	168	5.10	11.61	23.31	29.82	41.45	44.92	35.03	42.07	6.49	15.16
Primary metal industries	33	8	24	37	5.11	5.25	17.42	15.74	42.48	43.13	25.52	64.07	4.17	5.39
Fabricated metal products	34	9	30	49	4.45	7.63	19.70	22.60	19.89	31.03	25.97	35.13	4.09	6.79
Industrial machinery and equipment	35	16	50	123	4.70	4.83	10.82	14.91	23.72	34.91	4.80	8.93	3.56	4.47
Electronic and other electric equipment	36	8	16	27	7.34	7.41	12.72	17.58	32.20	38.07	16.29	20.67	6.38	7.44
Transportation equipment	37	7	5	214	3.60	4.48	10.99	11.06	26.16	51.88	10.67	18.57	2.29	3.63
Instruments and related products	38	9	14	94	3.60	5.09	7.80	9.65	11.39	31.74	2.71	10.66	3.86	6.21
Miscellaneous manufacturing industries	39	3	246	167	7.29	8.92	18.16	19.54	32.27	30.77	8.75	18.76	8.73	9.60
Motor freight transportation and warehousing	42	5	17	25	0.77	2.36	7.09	10.40	6.47	20.69	3.39	14.16	0.49	1.79
Communications	48	6	393	581	2.77	3.91	7.30	16.50	26.27	25.82	4.41	11.22	7.70	11.32
Electric, gas, and sanitary services	49	3	2	6	0.47	1.14	1.42	2.30	13.43	10.91	1.38	1.56	1.89	1.97
Wholesale trade – durable goods	50	16	12	130	5.35	5.75	17.49	28.26	54.03	53.97	15.81	42.23	1.82	3.06
Food stores	54	3	28	248	0.97	1.69	11.89	10.27	13.80	37.00	2.29	1.94	0.32	0.84
Eating and drinking places	58	4	52	71	2.95	6.30	6.69	20.40	62.58	56.54	13.27	15.48	1.92	4.34
Miscellaneous retail	59	4	38	137	2.84	4.57	7.55	9.56	13.27	26.85	3.69	17.74	2.01	3.64
Personal services	72	3	30	61	1.96	6.37	9.46	13.96	43.24	38.26	8.85	6.65	5.97	7.05
Business services	73	22	14	121	10.81	15.66	18.95	31.51	53.21	46.05	29.73	58.82	9.48	95.28
Automotive repair, services, and parking	75	3	9	9	0.38	0.46	1.54	1.35	3.73	5.11	1.40	1.16	0.40	0.60
Amusement and recreational services	79	5	91	335	6.85	10.79	17.75	22.40	56.66	55.87	24.50	20.80	21.04	31.75
Educational services	82	3	48	47	11.11	11.40	17.82	18.12	19.71	21.77	15.16	48.67	12.70	18.34
Engineering and management services	87	3	17	33	5.04	7.53	10.24	11.70	10.74	16.71	4.33	14.91	4.84	8.10
Non-classifiable establishments	99	3	126	395	3.13	2.38	8.10	12.84	13.31	15.72	3.91	9.77	2.22	3.16

The table is sorted by two-digit SIC category. Industries containing < 3 write-off firms are dropped. Overall, 179 out of 224 write-off firms are included.

Table A. 4: Industry breakdown of transitional write-offs

Panel A: WO sample with MTB>1 (N = 124)

Variable	Mean	StDev	Min	1st qrt	Med	3rd qrt	Max
Goodwill 2002							
In million $	1,149**	3,842	0	43	234***	865	39,138
% total assets	16.19	14.99	0.00	4.77	13.31	24.19	77.14
% BV of equity	8,048.82	87,749.30	0.00	13.14	39.91*	76.65	965,312.50
% MV of equity	41.32***	70.00	0.00	7.69	20.29	40.44	523.17
Goodwill 2001							
In million $	1,378***	3,705	1	65	308***	1,101	28,287
% total assets	20.59***	15.45	1.00	8.28	16.67***	29.17	74.60
% BV of equity	78.74	198.19	3.20	22.03	48.55	82.08	2,177.68
% MV of equity	33.47***	33.59	0.30	11.21	23.00***	37.86	152.79
MTB	3.03***	6.33	1.02	1.38	1.78***	2.84	67.87
RET	0.10***	0.73	-0.97	-0.29	0.03***	0.31	5.57
ΔROA	-0.03	0.08	-0.43	-0.04	-0.02	0.01	0.22
AIP	0.30***	0.23	0.03	0.11	0.25***	0.42	1.05
DTE02	1.32	2.67	0.00	0.30	0.61	1.34	25.47
MV°	9,262**	36,535	3	379	972***	4,161	320,299
TA°	12,831**	55,480	6	557	1,738***	5,118	535,134
SAL°	7,527**	20,121	5	546	1,630***	5,134	162,499
MSH	0.046***	0.084	0.000	0.002	0.008***	0.044	0.501
HERF	0.086	0.080	0.015	0.042	0.052	0.091	0.465
ΔPWOROA	0.00	0.09	-0.26	-0.03	0.00	0.02	0.66
EQ	0.41**	0.17	0.02	0.29	0.42	0.54	0.92

Panel B: WO sample with MTB≤1 (N = 100)

Variable	Mean	StDev	Min	1st qrt	Med	3rd qrt	Max
Goodwill 2002							
In million $	200**	790	0	0	24***	102	7,090
% total assets	14.99	16.54	0.00	0.00	10.09	26.88	70.03
% BV of equity	61.92	120.99	0.00	0.01	27.50*	74.68	826.46
% MV of equity	101.50***	225.91	0.00	0.13	33.03	88.34	1,620.16
Goodwill 2001							
In million $	350***	1004	1	15	59***	250	6,875
% total assets	24.78***	19.73	0.44	8.83	18.82***	37.84	81.96
% BV of equity	63.21	67.24	2.17	20.96	44.95	86.15	501.36
% MV of equity	140.28***	172.64	3.67	39.53	79.32***	193.63	1,100.70
MTB	0.58***	0.25	0.06	0.40	0.57***	0.81	0.99
RET	-0.39***	0.47	-0.95	-0.73	-0.48***	-0.13	2.19
ΔROA	-0.01	0.10	-0.31	-0.04	-0.02	0.01	0.35
AIP	0.53***	0.66	0.03	0.19	0.37***	0.74	6.03
DTE02	1.14	1.94	0.00	0.26	0.74	1.42	17.25
MV°	375**	1094	1	20	77***	221	9094
TA°	1,506**	4036	7	102	283***	946	31,554
SAL°	1,048**	2,224	7	125	362***	1,026	18,131
MSH	0.015***	0.032	0.000	0.001	0.003***	0.009	0.148
HERF	0.090	0.069	0.015	0.050	0.069	0.100	0.471
ΔPWOROA	0.00	0.10	-0.42	-0.03	0.00	0.03	0.33
EQ	0.46**	0.20	0.03	0.32	0.44	0.60	0.96

*, **, ***: Differences in mean (t-test) and median (adjusted $\chi 2$-test) significant at 10, 5, or 1%.

° MV, TA, and SAL represent mean values (fiscal 2001 and 2002) for the market value of equity, total assets, and sales, respectively. For other variable definitions, refer to Table 6.

Monetary amounts in million $. Goodwill figures scaled by beginning-of-period balance sheet numbers.

Table A. 5: Comparison of write-off firms with MTB>1 versus MTB≤1

Variable	TGWO_D	MTB	RET	DROA	AIP	DTE	MSH	HERF	DPWOROA	TARGET_PP	TARGET_Z	SIZE	FYR	GW
TGWO_D		-0.058	-0.022	-0.014	0.060	-0.019	0.162	0.100	0.024	-0.027	-0.043	0.047	0.090	0.196
MTB			-0.003	0.003	-0.066	0.496	-0.002	-0.047	0.131	0.055	0.023	0.046	0.043	-0.039
RET				0.047	0.013	-0.008	0.010	-0.001	-0.107	-0.031	0.035	-0.009	0.021	-0.019
DROA					-0.029	-0.022	-0.004	0.004	-0.186	-0.029	0.010	-0.010	0.027	0.006
AIP						0.058	0.047	0.143	0.039	-0.024	-0.050	-0.061	0.051	-0.187
DTE							-0.009	-0.014	0.097	0.044	-0.045	-0.010	0.038	-0.009
MSH								0.406	0.001	0.062	0.110	0.369	0.045	-0.037
HERF									0.060	0.067	0.044	0.035	-0.004	-0.029
DPWOROA										0.508	0.223	-0.006	0.044	0.014
TARGET_PP											0.354	0.014	0.023	0.056
TARGET_Z												0.098	0.012	-0.023
SIZE													0.069	-0.068
FYR														0.076

Table A. 6: Correlation matrix for model D1

Variable	TGWO_D	CH_200X	RESTR	SIZE	FYR	GW
TGWO_D		0.000	0.150	0.007	0.154	0.338
CH_200X			-0.067	-0.062	-0.118	-0.012
RESTR				0.061	0.137	0.159
SIZE					-0.050	-0.007
FYR						0.211

Table A. 7: Correlation matrix for model D2

Variable	MTB	RET	DROA	AIP	DTE	MSH	HERF	DPWOROA	TARGET_PP	TARGET_Z	RATING	SIZE	FYR	GW
TGWO_D	-0.075	-0.090	-0.016	0.075	-0.007	0.157	0.127	0.032	0.014	-0.107	0.031	0.019	0.058	0.211
MTB		0.014	0.068	-0.134	0.386	-0.001	-0.054	0.073	0.117	0.145	-0.157	0.115	0.088	-0.041
RET			0.430	-0.100	-0.038	-0.028	0.010	-0.399	0.054	0.097	0.034	-0.073	0.002	0.044
DROA				-0.008	0.010	0.019	-0.010	-0.772	-0.123	0.061	0.003	-0.025	-0.066	-0.007
AIP					0.114	0.039	0.128	0.036	-0.080	-0.187	0.339	-0.146	0.052	-0.287
DTE						-0.053	0.042	0.073	0.057	-0.078	0.283	-0.050	0.080	0.018
MSH							0.536	0.027	0.089	0.095	-0.254	0.326	-0.002	-0.151
HERF								0.043	0.080	0.028	0.010	0.037	-0.092	-0.097
DPWOROA									0.394	0.252	0.025	0.000	0.080	0.055
TARGET_PP										0.372	0.057	0.010	0.029	0.076
TARGET_Z											-0.314	0.112	-0.030	0.016
RATING												-0.491	-0.070	0.129
SIZE													0.074	-0.144
FYR														0.094

Table A. 8: Correlation matrix for model D3

Variable	TGWO_A	DIF_PP	DIF_Z	SIZE	FYR	GW
TGWO_A		0.066	-0.088	-0.039	0.027	0.340
DIF_PP			0.342	-0.050	-0.005	0.063
DIF_Z				0.109	-0.012	-0.050
SIZE					0.084	-0.087
FYR						0.068

Table A. 9: Correlation matrix for model A2

Variable	TGWO_A	EQ	SIZE	FYR	GW
TGWO_A		0.039	-0.037	0.096	0.348
EQ			-0.064	-0.090	-0.066
SIZE				0.014	0.014
FYR					0.096

Table A. 10: Correlation matrix for model A3

List of references

AAA Financial Accounting Standards Committee (2004), Commentary on the IASB's Exposure Draft on Business Combinations, in: *Accounting Horizons*, Vol. 18 (2004), No. 1 (March), pp. 55-64.

AAA's Financial Accounting Standards Committee (2001), Commentary: Equity valuation models and measuring goodwill impairment, in: *Accounting Horizons*, Vol. 15 (2001), No. 2 (June), pp. 161-170.

Abarbanell, Jeffery and Lehavy, Reuven (2003), Can stock recommendations predict earnings management and analysts' earnings forecast errors?, in: *Journal of Accounting Research*, Vol. 41 (2003), No. 1 (March), pp. 1-31.

Abarbanell, Jeffery and Lehavy, Reuven (2000), Differences in commercial database reported earnings: Implications for inferences concerning analyst forecast rationality, the association between prices and earnings, and firm reporting discretion, Chapel Hill: University of North Carolina, 2000.

Abdel-khalik, A. Rashad (1985), The effect of LIFO-switching and firm ownership on executives' pay, in: *Journal of Accounting Research*, Vol. 23 (1985), No. 2 (Autumn), pp. 427-447.

Aboody, David, Kasznik, Ron and Williams, Michael (2000), Purchase versus pooling in stock-for-stock acquisitions: Why do firms care?, in: *Journal of Accounting and Economics*, Vol. 29 (2000), No. 2 (June), pp. 261-286.

Aders, Christian, Galli, Albert and Wiedemann, Florian (2000), Unternehmenswerte auf Basis der Multiplikatormethode? – Eine Überprüfung mit dem Netto-Ansatz der DCF-Methode, in: *Finanz-Betrieb*, Vol. 2 (2000), No. 4, pp. 197-203.

Adler, Hans, Düring, Walther and Schmaltz, Kurt (1995/2000), Rechnungslegung und Prüfung der Unternehmen, edited by Karl-Heinz Forster, Reinhard Goerdeler, Josef Lanfermann, Hans-Peter Müller, Günter Siepe, Klaus Stolberg, Stuttgart: Schäffer-Poeschel, 6th ed. 1995/2000.

Aharony, Joseph and Dotan, Amihud (2001), A comparative analysis of auditor, manager and financial analyst interpretations of SFAS 5 disclosure guidelines, Tel Aviv: Tel Aviv University, 2001.

Alciatore, Mimi, Dee, Carol Callaway, Easton, Peter and Spear, Nasser (1998), Asset write-downs: A decade of research, in: *Journal of Accounting Literature*, Vol. 17 (1998), No. 1, pp. 1-39.

Alciatore, Mimi, Easton, Peter and Spear, Nasser (2000), Accounting for the impairment of long-lived assets: Evidence from the petroleum industry, in: *Journal of Accounting and Economics*, Vol. 29 (2000), No. 2 (April), pp. 151-172.

Ali, Ashiq and Kumar, Krishna R. (1993), Earnings management under pension accounting standards: SFAS 87 versus APB 8, in: *Journal of Accounting, Auditing and Finance*, Vol. 8 (1993), No. 4, pp. 427-446.

Alich, Holger (2001), Neue Bilanzregeln verwirren Anleger, in: *Handelsblatt* 2001, No. 161, p. 31.

Altenburger, Otto A. (2002), Erlaubt die Bilanzrichtlinie einen Verzicht auf die planmäßige Abschreibung des Goodwill?, in: *Die Wirtschaftsprüfung*, Vol. 55 (2002), No. 15, pp. 806-809.

Altman, Edward I. (1968), Financial ratios, discriminant analysis and the prediction of corporate bankruptcy, in: *Journal of Finance*, Vol. 23 (1968), No. 4 (September), pp. 589-609.

Alvarez, Manuel and Biberacher, Johannes (2002), Goodwill-Bilanzierung nach US-GAAP – Anforderungen an Unternehmenssteuerung und -berichterstattung, in: *Betriebs-Berater*, Vol. 57 (2002), No. 7, pp. 346-353.

Amir, Eli, Harris, Trevor S. and Venuti, Elizabeth K. (1993), A comparison of the value-relevance of U.S. versus non-U.S. GAAP accounting measures using form 20-F reconciliations, in: *Journal of Accounting Research*, Vol. 31 (1993), Supplement, pp. 230-264.

Anderson, John C. and Louderback, Joseph G. (1975), Income manipulation and purchase-pooling: Some additional results, in: *Journal of Accounting Research*, Vol. 13 (1975), No. 2 (Autumn), pp. 338-343.

Arbeitsgruppe "Normierung der Rechnungslegung" der Wissenschaftlichen Kommission Rechnungswesen im Verband der Hochschullehrer für Betriebswirtschaft e.V. (2002), Stellungnahme Nr. 1: Bilanzierung des Goodwill nach DRS 1a, in: *Betriebs-Berater*, Vol. 57 (2002), No. 17, pp. 880-881.

Archibald, T. Ross (1972), Stock market reaction to the depreciation switch-back, in: *The Accounting Review*, Vol. 47 (1972), No. 1 (January), pp. 22-30.

Arnold, Hans-Joachim (1997), Die Bilanzierung des Geschäfts- oder Firmenwertes in der Handels-, Steuer- und Ergänzungsbilanz, Frankfurt am Main et al.: Peter Lang, 1997.

Atiase, Rowland K. and Tse, Senyo (1986), Stock valuation models and accounting information: A review and synthesis, in: *Journal of Accounting Literature*, Vol. 5 (1986), pp. 1-33.

Auer, Ludwig von (1999), Ökonometrie – Eine Einführung, Berlin et al.: Springer, 1999.

Ayers, Benjamin C., Lefanowicz, Craig E. and Robinson, John R. (2000a), Do firms purchase the pooling method?, The University of Georgia/Michigan State University/The University of Texas at Austin, 2000.

Ayers, Benjamin C., Lefanowicz, Craig E. and Robinson, John R. (2000b), The financial statement effects of eliminating the pooling-of-interests method of acquisition accounting, in: *Accounting Horizons*, Vol. 14 (2000), No. 1 (March), pp. 1-19.

Backhaus, Klaus et al. (2003), Multivariate Analysemethoden – Eine anwendungsorientierte Einführung, Berlin et al.: Springer, 10th ed. 2003.

Baetge, Jörg and Ballwieser, Wolfgang (1977), Zum bilanzpolitischen Spielraum der Unternehmensleitung, in: *Betriebswirtschaftliche Forschung und Praxis*, Vol. 29 (1977), pp. 199-215.

Baetge, Jörg, Kirsch, Hans-Jürgen and Thiele, Stefan (2002a), Bilanzen, Düsseldorf: IDW-Verlag, 6th ed. 2002.

Baetge, Jörg, Kirsch, Hans-Jürgen and Thiele, Stefan (2002b), Konzernbilanzen, Düsseldorf: IDW-Verlag, 6th ed. 2002.

Baker, Richard E., Lembke, Valdean C. and King, Thomas E. (1996), Advanced financial accounting, New York et al.: McGraw-Hill, 3rd ed. 1996.

Ball, Ray and Brown, Philip (1968), An empirical evaluation of accounting income numbers, in: *Journal of Accounting Research*, Vol. 6 (1968), No. 2, pp. 159-178.

Ball, Ray and Foster, George (1982), Corporate financial reporting: A methodological review of empirical research, in: *Journal of Accounting Research*, Vol. 20 (1982), Supplement, pp. 161-234.

Ballwieser, Wolfgang (1998), Geschäftswert, in: Busse von Colbe, Walther and Pellens, Bernhard (ed.), Lexikon des Rechnungswesens – Handbuch der Bilanzierung und Prüfung, der Erlös-, Finanz-, Investitions- und Kostenrechnung, München and Wien: R. Oldenbourg, 1998, pp. 283-286.

Ballwieser, Wolfgang (1993), Die Entwicklung der Theorie der Rechnungslegung in den USA, in: *Zeitschrift für betriebswirtschaftliche Forschung*, Supplement 32 (1993), pp. 107-138.

Bamberg, Günter and Baur, Franz (2002), Statistik, München/Wien: Oldenbourg, 12th ed. 2002.

Barker, Richard G. (1999), The role of dividends in valuation models used by analysts and fund managers, in: *The European Accounting Review*, Vol. 8 (1999), No. 2, pp. 195-218.

Barnea, A., Ronen, Joshua and Sadan, Simcha (1976), Classificatory smoothing of income with extraordinary items, in: *The Accounting Review*, Vol. 51 (1976), No. 1, pp. 110-122.

Barnea, A., Ronen, Joshua and Sadan, Simcha (1975), The implementation of accounting objectives: An application to extraordinary items, in: *The Accounting Review*, Vol. 50 (1975), No. 1 (January), pp. 58-68.

Barth, Mary E., Beaver, William H. and Landsman, Wayne R. (2001), The relevance of the value relevance literature for financial accounting standard setting: Another view, in: *Journal of Accounting and Economics*, Vol. 31 (2001), No. 1-3 (September), pp. 77-104.

Barth, Mary E. and Clinch, Greg (1996), International accounting differences and their relation to share prices: Evidence from U.K., Australian, and Canadian firms, in: *Contemporary Accounting Research*, Vol. 13 (1996), No. 1 (Spring), pp. 135-170.

Barth, Mary E., Elliott, John A. and Finn, Mark W. (1999), Market rewards associated with patterns of increasing earnings, in: *Journal of Accounting Research*, Vol. 37 (1999), No. 2 (Autumn), pp. 387-413.

Bartov, Eli (1993), The timing of asset sales and earnings manipulation, in: *The Accounting Review*, Vol. 68 (1993), No. 4 (October), pp. 840-855.

Bartov, Eli, Lindahl, Frederick W. and Ricks, William E. (1998), Stock price behavior around announcements of write-offs, in: *Review of Accounting Studies*, Vol. 3 (1998), No. 4, pp. 327-346.

Bausch, Andreas (2000), Die Multiplikator-Methode – Ein betriebswirtschaftlich sinnvolles Instrument zur Unternehmenswert- und Kaufpreisfindung in Akquisitionsprozessen?, in: *Finanz-Betrieb*, Vol. 2 (2000), No. 7/8, pp. 448-459.

Beams, Floyd A., Brozovsky, John A. and Shoulders, Craig A. (2000), Advanced accounting, Upper Saddle River: Prentice Hall, 7th ed. 2000.

Beatty, Anne L., Ke, Bin and Petroni, Kathy R. (2002), Earnings management to avoid earnings declines across publicly and privately held banks, in: *The Accounting Review*, Vol. 77 (2002), No. 3 (July), pp. 547-570.

Beatty, Anne L., Ramesh, K. and Weber, Joseph (2002), The importance of accounting changes in debt contracts: The cost of flexibility in covenant calculations, in: *Journal of Accounting and Economics*, Vol. 33 (2002), No. 2 (June), pp. 205-227.

Beatty, Anne and Weber, Joseph (2004), The importance of mandatory accounting changes in accounting choice: An examination of the adoption of SFAS 142, University Park: Pennsylvania State University, 2004.

Beatty, Anne L. and Weber, Joseph (2003), The effects of debt contracting on voluntary accounting method changes, in: *The Accounting Review*, Vol. 78 (2003), No. 1 (January), pp. 119-142.

Beatty, Randolph P. and Verrecchia, Robert E. (1989), The effect of a mandated accounting change on the capitalization process, in: *Contemporary Accounting Research*, Vol. 5 (1989), No. 2, pp. 472-493.

Beaver, William H. (2002), Perspectives on recent capital market research, in: *The Accounting Review*, Vol. 77 (2002), No. 2 (April), pp. 453-474.

Beaver, William H. (1998), Financial Reporting – An accounting revolution, Upper Saddle River, New Jersey: Prentice Hall, 3rd ed. 1998.

Beaver, William H. (1996), Commentary on Directions in accounting research: NEAR and FAR, in: *Accounting Horizons*, Vol. 10 (1996), No. 2 (June), pp. 113-124.

Beaver, William H. (1981), Market efficiency, in: *The Accounting Review*, Vol. 56 (1981), No. 1 (January).

Beaver, William H. (1968), The information content of annual earnings announcements, in: *Journal of Accounting Research*, Vol. 6 (1968), Supplement, pp. 67-92.

Beaver, William H. and Dukes, Roland E. (1973), Interperiod tax allocation and δ-depreciation methods: Some empirical results, in: *The Accounting Review*, Vol. 48 (1973), No. 3 (July), pp. 549-559.

Beaver, William and Morse, Dale (1978), What determines price-earnings ratios?, in: *Financial Analysts Journal*, Vol. 34 (1978), No. 4 (July/August), pp. 65-76.

Beidleman, Carl R. (1975), Income smoothing: The role of management: A reply, in: *The Accounting Review*, Vol. 50 (1975), No. 1, pp. 122-126.

Beidleman, Carl R. (1973), Income smoothing: The role of management, in: *The Accounting Review*, Vol. 48 (1973), No. 4 (October), pp. 653-667.

Beneish, Messod D. (2001), Earnings management: A perspective, Bloomington: Indiana University, 2001.

Beneish, Messod D. (1999), The detection of earnings manipulation, in: *Financial Analysts Journal*, Vol. 55 (1999), No. 5 (September/October), pp. 24-36.

Beneish, Messod D. (1998), A call for papers: Earnings management, in: *Journal of Accounting and Public Policy*, Vol. 17 (1998), No. 1 (Spring), pp. 85-88.

Beneish, Messod D. (1997), Detecting GAAP violation: Implications for assessing earnings management among firms with extreme financial performance, in: *Journal of Accounting and Public Policy*, Vol. 16 (1997), No. 3 (Fall), pp. 271-309.

Beneish, Messod D. and Press, Eric G. (1995), The resolution of technical default, in: *The Accounting Review*, Vol. 70 (1995), No. 2 (April), pp. 337-353.

Beneish, Messod D. and Press, Eric (1993), Costs of technical violation of accounting-based debt covenants, in: *The Accounting Review*, Vol. 68 (1993), No. 2 (April), pp. 233-257.

Beresford, Dennis R. (2001), Commentary: Congress looks at accounting for business combinations, in: *Accounting Horizons*, Vol. 15 (2001), No. 1 (March), pp. 73-86.

Bernard, Victor L. (1989), Capital markets research in accounting during the 1980's: A critical review, in: Frecka, Thomas J. (ed.), The state of accounting research as we enter the 1990's: Illinois PhD Jubilee 1939-1989, University of Illinois at Urbana-Champaign: 1989, pp. 72-120.

Bernard, Victor L. and Skinner, Douglas J. (1996), What motivates managers' choice of discretionary accruals?, in: *Journal of Accounting and Economics*, Vol. 22 (1996), pp. 313-325.

Bernstein, Leopold A. (1993), Financial statement analysis: Theory, application, and interpretation, Chicago et al.: Irwin, 5th ed. 1993.

Bieker, Marcus and Esser, Maik (2004), Der Impairment-Only-Ansatz des IASB: Goodwillbilanzierung nach IFRS 3 "Business Combinations", in: *Kapitalmarktorientierte Rechnungslegung*, Vol. 6 (2004), No. 10, pp. 449-458.

Bieker, Marcus and Esser, Maik (2003), Goodwill-Bilanzierung nach ED 3 "Business Combinations" – Darstellung des vom IASB geplanten Impairment-Only-Ansatzes, in: *Kapitalmarktorientierte Rechnungslegung*, Vol. 5 (2003), No. 2, pp. 75-84.

Binder, John J. (1998), The event study methodology since 1969, in: *Review of Quantitative Finance and Accounting*, Vol. 11 (1998), No. 2 (September), pp. 111-137.

Black, Ervin L., Sellers, Keith F. and Manly, Tracy S. (1998), Earnings management using asset sales: An international study of countries allowing noncurrent asset revaluation, in: *Journal of Business Finance and Accounting*, Vol. 25 (1998), No. 9/10 (November/December), pp. 1287-1317.

Blackburn Norris, Kathleen and Ayres, Frances L. (2000), Security market reaction to purchase business combinations at the first earnings announcement date, in: *Journal of Business Research*, Vol. 49 (2000), No. 1 (July), pp. 79-88.

Block, Stanley B. (1999), A study of financial analysts: Practice and theory, in: *Financial Analysts Journal*, Vol. 55 (1999), No. 4 (July/August), pp. 86-95.

Böcking, Hans-Joachim, Klein, Gabriele and Lopatta, Kerstin (2001), Internationale Entwicklungen bei der Bilanzierung von Unternehmenszusammenschlüssen – Die Abschaffung der Pooling of Interests-Methode als Hinwendung zu einer kapitalmarktorientierten Rechnungslegung?, in: *Kapitalmarktorientierte Rechnungslegung*, Vol. 1 (2001), No. 1, pp. 17-25.

Böcking, Hans-Joachim, Klein, Gabriele and Lopatta, Kerstin (2000), Darstellung des E-DRS 4: Unternehmenserwerbe im Konzernabschluß, in: *Finanz-Betrieb*, Vol. 2 (2000), No. 7/8, pp. 433-440.

Böcking, Hans-Joachim and Nowak, Karsten (2000), Die Bedeutung des Börsenkurses bei Unternehmensbewertungen, in: *Finanz-Betrieb*, Vol. 2 (2000), No. 1, pp. 17-24.

Böcking, Hans-Joachim and Nowak, Karsten (1999), Marktorientierte Unternehmensbewertung – Darstellung und Würdigung der marktorientierten Vergleichsverfahren vor dem Hintergrund der deutschen Kapitalmarktverhältnisse, in: *Finanz-Betrieb*, Vol. 1 (1999), No. 8, pp. 169-176.

Bonse, Andreas (2004), Informationsgehalt von Konzernabschlüssen nach HGB, IAS und US-GAAP – Eine empirische Analyse aus Sicht der Eigenkapitalgeber, Frankfurt am Main et al.: Peter Lang, 2004.

Boschen, John F., Duru, Augustine, Gordon, Lawrence A., Smith, Kimberly (2003), Accounting and stock price performance in dynamic CEO compensation arrangements, in: *The Accounting Review*, Vol. 78 (2003), No. 1 (January), pp. 143-168.

Bowman, Robert G. (1983), Understanding and conducting event studies, in: *Journal of Business Finance and Accounting*, Vol. 10 (1983), No. 4, pp. 561-584.

Bradbury, Michael, Godfrey, Jayne M. and Koh, Ping-Sheng (2003), Investment opportunity set influence on goodwill amortisation, in: *Asia-Pacific Journal of Accounting and Economics*, Vol. 10 (2003), pp. 57-79.

Bradley, Michael, Desai, Anand and Kim, E. Han (1988), Synergistic gains from corporate acquisitions and their division between the stockholders of target and acquiring firms, in: *Journal of Financial Economics*, Vol. 21 (1988), No. 1, pp. 3-40.

Braun, Stephen, Rohan, Paul and Yospe, Joseph F. (1991), Asset write-offs: A matter of grouping?, in: *Journal of Accountancy*, Vol. 171 (1991), No. 4 (April), pp. 63-68.

Brecht, Angelika (2002), Die erfolgswirtschaftliche Analyse von US-GAAP-Abschlüssen, Hamburg: Dr. Kovac, 2002.

Breidert, Ulrike (1994), Grundsätze ordnungsmäßiger Abschreibung auf abnutzbare Anlagegegenstände, Düsseldorf: IDW-Verlag, 1994.

Brickley, J. A. and Van Drunen, L. D. (1990), Internal corporate restructuring: An empirical analysis, in: *Journal of Accounting and Economics*, Vol. 12 (1990), No. 1-3, pp. 251-280.

Brown, Lawrence D. (2001), A temporal analysis of earnings surprises: Profits versus losses, in: *Journal of Accounting Research*, Vol. 39 (2001), No. 2 (September), pp. 221-241.

Brown, Lawrence D. (1998), Managerial behavior and the bias in analysts' earnings forecasts, Georgia State University, 1998.

Brown, Philip (2001), Capital markets-based research in accounting, electronic edition, 2001.

Brown, Philip (1995), A note on the reverse (inverse) sum-of-the-years'-digits method and other ways to amortize goodwill, in: *Australian Accounting Review*, Vol. 5 (1995), pp. 17-21.

Brown, Stephen, Finn, Mark and Hope, Ole-Kristian (2000), Acquisition-related provision-taking and post-acquisition performance in the UK prior to FRS 7, in: *Journal of Business Finance and Accounting*, Vol. 27 (2000), No. 9/10 (November/December), pp. 1233-1265.

Brown, William D., Tucker, Karen J. and Pfeiffer, Ray J. (1999), A prospective look at the usefulness of separately reporting goodwill charges: An evaluation of 'cash earnings', Amherst: University of Massachusetts, 1999.

Brücks, Michael and Wiederhold, Philipp (2004), IFRS 3 Business Combinations - Darstellung der neuen Regelungen des IASB und Vergleich mit SFAS 141 und SFAS 142, in: *Kapitalmarktorientierte Rechnungslegung*, Vol. 4 (2004), No. 5, pp. 177-185.

Brücks, Michael and Wiederhold, Philipp (2003), Exposure Draft 3 "Business Combinations" des IASB – Darstellung der wesentlichen Unterschiede zu den bestehenden Regelungen, in: *Kapitalmarktorientierte Rechnungslegung*, Vol. 3 (2003), No. 1, pp. 21-29.

Brunovs, Rudolf and Kirsch, Robert J. (1991), Goodwill accounting in selected countries and the harmonization of international accounting standards, in: *Abacus*, Vol. 27 (1991), No. 2 (September), pp. 135-161.

Bujaki, Merridee L. and Richardson, Alan J. (1997), A citation trail review of the uses of firm size in accounting research, in: *Journal of Accounting Literature*, Vol. 16 (1997), No. 1, pp. 1-27.

Bunsis, Howard (1997), A description and market analysis of write-off announcements, in: *Journal of Business Finance and Accounting*, Vol. 24 (1997), No. 9/10 (October/December), pp. 1385-1400.

Burgstahler, David C. (1997), Incentives to manage earnings to avoid earnings decreases and losses: Evidence from quarterly earnings, University of Washington, 1997.

Burgstahler, David C. and Dichev, Ilia D. (1997), Earnings management to avoid earnings decreases and losses, in: *Journal of Accounting and Economics*, Vol. 24 (1997), No. 1, pp. 99-126.

Burgstahler, David C. and Eames, Michael (2001), Management of earnings and analyst forecasts to achieve zero earnings surprise, University of Washington; Santa Clara University, 2001.

Burgstahler, David C., Elliott, W. Brooke and Hanlon, Michelle (2002), How firms avoid losses: Evidence of use of the net deferred tax asset account, Seattle: University of Washington, 2002.

Burgstahler, David C., Jiambalvo, James J. and Shevlin, Terry J. (2002), Do stock prices fully reflect the implications of special items for future earnings?, in: *Journal of Accounting Research*, Vol. 40 (2002), No. 3, pp. 585-612.

Bushman, Robert M. and Smith, Abbie J. (2001), Financial accounting information and corporate governance, in: *Journal of Accounting and Economics*, Vol. 32 (2001), No. 1-3 (December), pp. 237-333.

Busse von Colbe, Walther (2001a), Bilanzierung des Goodwill – FASB bläst zum Rückzug, in: *Betriebs-Berater*, Vol. 56 (2001), No. 9, Die erste Seite (editorial).

Busse von Colbe, Walther (2001b), Commentary on section 309 HGB, in: Schmidt, Karsten (ed.), Münchner Kommentar zum Handelsgesetzbuch, München: C. H. Beck/Vahlen, 2001.

Busse von Colbe, Walther (2001c), Ist die Bilanzierung des Firmenwerts nach dem Nonamortization-Impairment-Ansatz des SFAS-Entwurfs von 2001 mit § 292a HGB vereinbar?, in: *Der Betrieb*, Vol. 54 (2001), No. 17, pp. 877-879.

Busse von Colbe, Walther and Ordelheide, Dieter (1993), Konzernabschlüsse, Heidelberg: Gabler, 6th ed. 1993.

Busse von Colbe, Walther, Ordelheide, Dieter, Gebhardt, Günther and Pellens, Bernhard (2003), Konzernabschlüsse, Heidelberg: Gabler, 7th ed. 2003.

Cahan, Steven F. (1993), Electric utility income in response to the breakdown at the Three Mile Island nuclear power plant und subsequent political events, in: *Journal of Accounting and Public Policy*, Vol. 12 (1993), No. 1, pp. 37-63.

Cahan, Steven F. (1992), The effect of antitrust investigations on discretionary accruals: A refined test of the political-cost hypothesis, in: *The Accounting Review*, Vol. 67 (1992), No. 1 (January), pp. 77-95.

Cameron, Alex B. (1986), A review of management's earnings forecast research, in: *Journal of Accounting Literature*, Vol. 5 (1986), pp. 57-83.

Carslaw, Charles A. P. N. (1988), Anomalies in income numbers: Evidence of goal oriented behavior, in: *The Accounting Review*, Vol. 63 (1988), No. 2 (April), pp. 321-327.

Catlett, George R. and Olson, Norman O. (1968), Accounting for goodwill, New York: American Institute of Certified Public Accountants, 1968.

Chaney, Paul K., Hogan, Chris E. and Jeter, Debra C. (2000), The information content of restructuring charges: A contextual analysis, Vanderbilt University, 2000.

Chauvin, Keith W. and Hirschey, Mark (1994), Goodwill, profitability, and the market value of the firm, in: *Journal of Accounting and Public Policy*, Vol. 13 (1994), No. 2, pp. 159-180.

Chen, Kevin C. W., Danielson, Morris G. and Schoderbek, Michael P. (2003), Analysts' interpretation of transitory earnings components: Evidence from forecast revisions after disclosure of the 1993 deferred tax adjustment, in: *Journal of Accounting, Auditing and Finance*, Vol. 18 (2003), No. 3 (Summer), pp. 333-353.

Chen, Kevin C. W. and Lee, Chi-Wen Jevons (1995), Executive bonus plans and accounting trade-offs: The case of the oil and gas industry, 1985-86, in: *The Accounting Review*, Vol. 70 (1995), No. 1 (January), pp. 91-111.

Choi, Frederick D. S. and Lee, Changwoo (1991), Merger premia and national differences in accounting for goodwill, in: *Journal of International Financial Management and Accounting*, Vol. 3 (1991), No. 3, pp. 219-240.

Christensen, John A. and Demski, Joel S. (2003), Accounting theory – an information content perspective, New York et al.: McGraw-Hill, 2003.

Christie, Andrew A. (1990), Aggregation of test statistics – An evaluation of the evidence on contracting and size hypotheses, in: *Journal of Accounting and Economics*, Vol. 12 (1990), No. 1-3, pp. 15-36.

Christie, Andrew A. and Zimmerman, Jerold L. (1994), Efficient and opportunistic choices of accounting procedures: Corporate control contests, in: *The Accounting Review*, Vol. 69 (1994), No. 4, pp. 539-566.

Clinch, Greg (1997), Capital markets research and the goodwill debate, in: Zeff, Stephen A. and Dharan, Bala G. (ed.), Readings and notes on financial accounting, New York et al.: McGraw-Hill, 1997, pp. 340-350.

Coenenberg, Adolf Gerhard (2003), Jahresabschluss und Jahresabschlussanalyse: Betriebswirtschaftliche, handelsrechtliche, steuerrechtliche und internationale Grundsätze – HGB, IAS/IFRS, US-GAAP, DRS, Stuttgart: Schäffer-Poeschel, 19th ed. 2003.

Coenenberg, Adolf G. (1974), Jahresabschlußinformation und Kapitalmarkt: Zur Diskussion empirischer Forschungsansätze und -ergebnisse zum Informationsgehalt von Jahresabschlüssen für Aktionäre, in: *Zeitschrift für betriebswirtschaftliche Forschung*, Vol. 26 (1974), pp. 647-657.

Coenenberg, Adolf G. and Schultze, Wolfgang (2002a), Das Multiplikator-Verfahren in der Unternehmensbewertung: Konzeption und Kritik, in: *Finanz-Betrieb*, Vol. 4 (2002), No. 12, pp. 697-703.

Coenenberg, Adolf G. and Schultze, Wolfgang (2002b), Unternehmensbewertung: Konzeptionen und Perspektiven, in: *Die Betriebswirtschaft*, Vol. 62 (2002), No. 6, pp. 597-621.

Coenenberg, Adolf G., Berndsen, Hans-Peter, Möller, Peter, Schmidt, Franz and Schönbrodt, Bernd (1978), Empirische Bilanzforschung in Deutschland – Eine Bestandsaufnahme, in: *Die Betriebswirtschaft*, Vol. 38 (1978), No. 4, pp. 495-507.

Colley, Ron J. and Volkan, Ara G. (1988), Accounting for goodwill, in: *Accounting Horizons*, Vol. 2 (1988), No. 1 (March), pp. 35-41.

Collins, Daniel W., Rozeff, Michael S. and Dhaliwal, Dan S. (1981), The economic determinants of the market reaction to proposed mandatory accounting changes in the oil and gas industry – A cross-sectional analysis, in: *Journal of Accounting and Economics*, Vol. 3 (1981), No. 1, pp. 37-71.

Comprix, Joe (2000), The valuation of impaired assets surrounding write-off announcements, Champaign: University of Illinois, 2000.

Copeland, Ronald M. (1968), Income smoothing, in: *Journal of Accounting Research*, Vol. 6 (1968), Supplement, pp. 101-116.

Copeland, Ronald M. and Licastro, Ralph D. (1968), A note on income smoothing, in: *The Accounting Review*, Vol. 43 (1968), No. 3, pp. 540-545.

Copeland, Ronald M. and Wojdak, Joseph F. (1969), Income manipulation and the purchase-pooling choice, in: *Journal of Accounting Research*, Vol. 7 (1969), No. 2, pp. 188-195.

Cotter, Julie (1998), Utilisation and restrictiveness of covenants in Australian private debt contracts, in: *Accounting and Finance*, Vol. 38 (1998), No. 2, pp. 181-196.

Cotter, Julie, Stokes, D. and Wyatt, A. (1998), An analysis of factors influencing asset writedowns, in: *Accounting and Finance*, Vol. 38 (1998), No. 2 (November), pp. 157-179.

Crawford, Dean (1987), The structure of corporate mergers – accounting, tax, and form-of-payment choices, Rochester: University of Rochester, 1987.

Crouhy, Michel, Galai, Dan and Mark, Robert (2001), Prototype risk rating system, in: *Journal of Banking and Finance*, Vol. 25 (2001), No. 1 (January), pp. 47-95.

Daley, Lane A. and Vigeland, Robert L. (1983), The effects of debt covenants and political costs on the choice of accounting methods: The case of accounting for R&D costs, in: *Journal of Accounting and Economics*, Vol. 5 (1983), No. 3, pp. 195-211.

Damodaran, Aswath (1996), Investment valuation – Tools and techniques for determining the value of any asset, New York et al.: John Wiley & Sons, Inc., 1996.

Das, Somnath and Zhang, Huai (2003), Rounding-up in reported EPS, behavioral thresholds, and earnings management, in: *Journal of Accounting and Economics*, Vol. 35 (2003), No. 1 (April), pp. 31-50.

Davis, Michael L. (1997), Goodwill accounting: Time for an overhaul, in: Zeff, Stephen A. and Dharan, Bala G. (ed.), Readings and notes on financial accounting, New York et al.: McGraw-Hill, 1997, pp. 332-339.

Davis, Michael L. (1996), The purchase vs. pooling controversy: How the stock market responds to goodwill, in: *Journal of Applied Corporate Finance*, Vol. 9 (1996), No. 1 (Spring), pp. 50-59.

Davis, Michael L. (1992), Goodwill accounting: Time for an overhaul, in: *Journal of Accountancy*, Vol. 173 (1992), No. 6 (June), pp. 75-83.

Davis, Michael L. (1990), Differential market reaction to pooling and purchase methods, in: *The Accounting Review*, Vol. 65 (1990), No. 3 (July), pp. 696-709.

Day, Ron and Hartnett, Neil (1999/2000), An investigation of the significance of mandated changes in goodwill amortisation policy in Australia, in: *Pacific Accounting Review*, Vol. 11 (1999/2000), No. 2 (December/January), pp. 193-218.

DeAngelo, Harry, DeAngelo, Linda Elizabeth and Skinner, Douglas J. (1996), Reversal of fortune: Dividend signaling and the disappearance of sustained earnings growth, in: *Journal of Financial Economics*, Vol. 40 (1996), No. 3 (March), pp. 341-371.

DeAngelo, Linda Elizabeth (1988), Managerial competition, information costs, and corporate governance – the use of accounting performance measures in proxy contests, in: *Journal of Accounting and Economics*, Vol. 10 (1988), No. 1, pp. 3-36.

DeAngelo, Linda Elizabeth (1986), Accounting numbers as market valuation substitutes: A study of management buyouts of public stockholders, in: *The Accounting Review*, Vol. 61 (1986), No. 3 (July), pp. 400-420.

Dechow, Patricia M., Huson, Marc R. and Sloan, Richard G. (1994), The effect of restructuring charges on executives' cash compensation, in: *The Accounting Review*, Vol. 69 (1994), No. 1 (January), pp. 138-156.

Dechow, Patricia M. and Skinner, Douglas J. (2000), Earnings management: Reconciling the views of accounting academics, practitioners, and regulators, in: *Accounting Horizons*, Vol. 14 (2000), No. 2 (June), pp. 235-250.

Dechow, Patricia M., Sloan, Richard G. and Sweeney, Amy P. (1995), Detecting earnings management, in: *The Accounting Review*, Vol. 70 (1995), No. 2 (April), pp. 193-225.

DeFond, Mark L. and Park, Chul W. (1997), Smoothing income in anticipation of future earnings, in: *Journal of Accounting and Economics*, Vol. 23 (1997), No. 2 (July), pp. 115-139.

DeFond, Mark L. and Subramanyam, K.R. (1998), Auditor changes and discretionary accruals, in: *Journal of Accounting and Economics*, Vol. 25 (1998), No. 1 (February), pp. 35-67.

Degeorge, Francois, Patel, Jayendu and Zeckhauser, Richard (1999), Earnings management to exceed thresholds, in: *Journal of Business*, Vol. 72 (1999), No. 1, pp. 1-33.

Deng, Zhen and Lev, Baruch (1998), The valuation of acquired R&D, New York University, 1998.

Desai, Hemang et al. (2001), Does the choice of accounting method matter in mergers?, Dallas: Southern Methodist University, 2001.

Dichev, Ilia D. (2002), The role and characteristics of accounting-based performance pricing in private debt contracts, Ann Arbor: University of Michigan, 2002.

Dichev, Ilia D. and Skinner, Douglas J. (2002), Large-sample evidence on the debt covenant hypothesis, in: *Journal of Accounting Research*, Vol. 40 (2002), No. 4 (September), pp. 1091-1123.

Döring, Ulrich (1993), Goodwill, in: Chmielewicz, Klaus and Schweitzer, Marcell (ed.), Handwörterbuch des Rechnungswesens, Stuttgart: Schäffer-Poeschel, 1993, columns 810-818.

Dörschell, Andreas and Schulte, Jörn (2002), Bewertung von Beteiligungen für bilanzielle Zwecke, in: *Der Betrieb*, Vol. 55 (2002), No. 33, pp. 1669-1675.

Doralt, Werner (1976), Der Firmenwert in der Handels- und Steuerbilanz, Berlin: Duncker und Humblot, 1976.

Duke, Joanne C. and Hunt, Herbert G. (1990), An empirical examination of debt covenant restrictions and accounting-related debt proxies, in: *Journal of Accounting and Economics*, Vol. 12 (1990), No. 1-3, pp. 45-63.

Dunne, Kathleen M. (1990), An empirical analysis of management's choice of accounting treatment for business combinations, in: *Journal of Accounting and Public Policy*, Vol. 9 (1990), No. 2, pp. 111-133.

Dunne, Kathleen M. and Ndubizu, Gordian A. (1995), International acquisition accounting method and corporate multinationalism: Evidence from foreign acquisitions, in: *Journal of International Business Studies*, Vol. 26 (1995), No. 2nd Quarter, pp. 361-377.

Dunstan, Keitha (1999), Accounting for goodwill on the acquisition of corporate subsidiaries, Brisbane: Queensland University of Technology, 1999.

Dutta, Sunil and Gigler, Frank (2002), The effect of earnings forecasts on earnings management, in: *Journal of Accounting Research*, Vol. 40 (2002), No. 3 (June), pp. 631-655.

Duvall, Linda et al. (1992), Can investors unravel the effects of goodwill accounting?, in: *Accounting Horizons*, Vol. 6 (1992), No. 2 (June), pp. 1-14.

Easton, Peter D., Eddey, Peter H. and Harris, Trevor S. (1993), An investigation of revaluations of tangible long-lived assets, in: *Journal of Accounting Research*, Vol. 31 (1993), Supplement, pp. 1-38.

Eberle, Reto (2002), Neue Standards zur Bilanzierung von Goodwill – Konzeptionelle Analyse von FAS No. 141 und FAS No. 142 und Vergleich mit IAS 22 und IAS 38 (Teil 1), in: *Der Schweizer Treuhänder*, Vol. 76 (2002), No. 3, pp. 184-190.

Ederington, Louis H. and Yawitz, Jess B. (1987), The bond rating process, in: Altman, Edward I. (ed.), New York et al.: John Wiley & Sons, Inc., 1987, pp. 23.1-23.57.

Elder, Randy and Zhou, Jian (2003), Audit quality and earnings management by seasoned equity offering firms, Syracuse: Syracuse University, 2003.

Elder, Randy and Zhou, Jian (2002), Audit firm size, industry specialization and earnings management by initial public offering firms, Syracuse: Syracuse University, 2002.

El-Gazzar, Samir M. (1993), Stock market effects of the closeness to debt covenant restrictions resulting from capitalization of leases, in: *The Accounting Review*, Vol. 68 (1993), No. 2 (April), pp. 258-272.

El-Gazzar, Samir, Lilien, Steven B. and Pastena, Victor (1989), The use of off-balance sheet financing to circumvent financial covenant restrictions, in: *Journal of Accounting, Auditing and Finance*, Vol. 4 (1989), No. 2 (Spring), pp. 217-235.

El-Gazzar, Samir, Lilien, Steven B. and Pastena, V. (1986), Accounting for leases by lessees, in: *Journal of Accounting and Economics*, Vol. 8 (1986), No. 3, pp. 217-237.

El-Gazzar, Samir and Pastena, Victor (1990), Negotiated accounting rules in private financial contracts, in: *Journal of Accounting and Economics*, Vol. 12 (1990), No. 4, pp. 381-396.

Elgers, Pieter T., Pfeiffer Jr, Ray J. and Porter, Susan L. (2003), Anticipatory income smoothing: a re-examination, in: *Journal of Accounting and Economics*, Vol. 35 (2003), pp. 405-422.

Elliott, John A. and Hanna, Douglas J. (1996), Repeated accounting write-offs and the information content of earnings, in: *Journal of Accounting Research*, Vol. 34 (1996), Supplement, pp. 135-155.

Elliott, John A. and Philbrick, Donna R. (1990), Accounting changes and earnings predictability, in: *The Accounting Review*, Vol. 65 (1990), No. 1 (January), pp. 157-174.

Elliott, John A. and Shaw, Wayne H. (1988), Write-offs as accounting procedures to manage perceptions, in: *Journal of Accounting Research*, Vol. 26 (1988), Supplement, pp. 91-119.

Ellis, Martin (2001), Goodwill accounting: Everything has changed and nothing has changed, in: *Journal of Applied Corporate Finance*, Vol. 14 (2001), No. 3 (Fall), pp. 103-112.

Erickson, Merle and Wang, Shiing-wu (1999), Earnings management by acquiring firms in stock for stock mergers, in: *Journal of Accounting and Economics*, Vol. 27 (1999), No. 2 (April), pp. 149-176.

Espahbodi, Hassan, Espahbodi, Pouran and Tehranian, Hassan (1995), Equity price reaction to the pronouncements related to accounting for income taxes, in: *The Accounting Review*, Vol. 70 (1995), No. 4 (October), pp. 655-668.

Espahbodi, Hassan, Strock, E. and Tehranian, Hassan (1991), Impact on equity prices of pronouncements related to nonpension postretirement benefits, in: *Journal of Accounting and Economics*, Vol. 14 (1991), No. 4 (December), pp. 323-346.

Evans, John H. III et al. (2001), Honesty in managerial reporting, in: *The Accounting Review*, Vol. 76 (2001), No. 4 (October), pp. 537-559.

Falk, Haim and Gordon, L. A. (1977), Imperfect markets and the nature of goodwill, in: *Journal of Business Finance and Accounting*, Vol. 44 (1977), No. 4 (April), pp. 443-463.

Fama, Eugene F. (1970), Efficient capital markets: A review of theory and empirical work, in: *Journal of Finance*, Vol. 25 (1970), No. 2, pp. 383-417.

Fama, Eugene F., Fisher, Lawrence, Jensen, Michael C. and Roll, Richard W. (1969), The adjustment of stock prices to new information, in: *International Economic Review*, Vol. 10 (1969), No. 1, pp. 1-21.

FASB (1976), FASB discussion memorandum "An analysis of issues relating to accounting for business combinations and purchased intangibles", Norwalk, Connecticut: Financial Accounting Standards Board, 1976.

Fields, Thomas D., Lys, Thomas Z. and Vincent, Linda (2001), Empirical research on accounting choice, in: *Journal of Accounting and Economics*, Vol. 31 (2001), No. 1-3 (September), pp. 255-307.

Fischer, Andrea and Haller, Axel (1993), Bilanzpolitik zum Zwecke der Gewinnglättung – Empirische Erkenntnisse, in: *Zeitschrift für Betriebswirtschaft (ZfB)*, Vol. 63 (1993), No. 1, pp. 35-59.

Fladt, Guido and Feige, Peter (2003), Der Exposure Draft 3 "Business Combinations" des IASB – Konvergenz mit den US-GAAP?, in: *Die Wirtschaftsprüfung*, Vol. 56 (2003), No. 6, pp. 249-262.

Förschle, Gerhart and Hoffmann, Karl (2003), Commentary on section 309 HGB, in: Berger, Axel et al. (ed.), Beck'scher Bilanz-Kommentar: Handels- und Steuerrecht – §§ 238 bis 339 HGB, München: C. H. Beck, 2003.

Foster, George (1986), Financial statement analysis, Englewood Cliffs: Prentice-Hall, 2nd ed. 1986.

Foster, George, Olsen, Chris and Shevlin, Terry J. (1984), Earnings releases, anomalies, and the behavior of security returns, in: *The Accounting Review*, Vol. 59 (1984), No. 4 (October), pp. 574-603.

Francis, Jennifer (2001), Discussion of Empirical research on accounting choice, in: *Journal of Accounting and Economics*, Vol. 31 (2001), No. 1-3 (September), pp. 309-319.

Francis, Jennifer, Hanna, Douglas J. and Vincent, Linda (1996), Causes and effects of discretionary asset write-offs, in: *Journal of Accounting Research*, Vol. 34 (1996), Supplement, pp. 117-134.

Francis, Jennifer and Schipper, Katherine (1999), Have financial statements lost their relevance?, in: *Journal of Accounting Research*, Vol. 37 (1999), No. 2 (Autumn), pp. 319-352.

Francis, Jere R., Maydew, Edward L. and Sparks, H. Charles (1999), The role of Big 6 auditors in the credible reporting of accruals, in: *Auditing – A Journal of Practice and Theory*, Vol. 18 (1999), No. 2 (Fall), pp. 17-34.

Fried, Dov, Schiff, Michael and Sondhi, Ashwinpaul C. (1989), Impairments and writeoffs of long-lived assets, Montvale, NJ: 1989.

Frost, Carol A. and Bernard, Victor L. (1989), The role of debt covenants in assessing the economic consequences of limiting capitalization of exploration costs, in: *The Accounting Review*, Vol. 64 (1989), No. 4 (October), pp. 788-808.

Frowein, Nils and Lüdenbach, Norbert (2003), Der Goodwill-Impairment-Test aus Sicht der Bewertungspraxis, in: *Finanz-Betrieb*, Vol. 5 (2003), No. 2, pp. 65-72.

Fudenberg, Drew and Tirole, Jean (1995), A theory of income and dividend smoothing based on incumbency rents, in: *Journal of Political Economy*, Vol. 103 (1995), No. 1 (February), pp. 75-93.

Fülbier, Rolf Uwe (2000), Entwurf eines DRS 4 zur Bilanzierung von Unternehmenserwerben im Konzernabschluss, in: *Der Betrieb*, Vol. 53 (2000), No. 28, pp. 1341-1346.

Fülbier, Rolf Uwe (1999), Regulierung – Ökonomische Betrachtung eines allgegenwärtigen Phänomens, in: *Wirtschaftswissenschaftliches Studium*, Vol. 28 (1999), No. 9 (September), pp. 468-473.

Fülbier, Rolf Uwe (1998), Regulierung der Ad-hoc-Publizität – Ein Beitrag zur ökonomischen Analyse des Rechts, Heidelberg: Gabler, 1998.

Furubotn, Eirik G. and Richter, Rudolf (2000), Institutions and economic theory – The contribution of the new institutional economics, Ann Arbor: The University of Michigan Press, 1. paperback ed. 2000.

Gagnon, Jean-Marie (1971), The purchase-pooling choice: Some empirical evidence, in: *Journal of Accounting Research*, Vol. 9 (1971), No. 1 (Spring), pp. 52-72.

Gagnon, Jean-Marie (1967), Purchase versus pooling of interests: The search for a predictor, in: *Journal of Accounting Research*, Vol. 5 (1967), Supplement, pp. 187-204.

Gaver, Jennifer J. and Gaver, Kenneth M. (1998), The relation between nonrecurring accounting transactions and CEO cash compensation, in: *The Accounting Review*, Vol. 73 (1998), No. 2 (April), pp. 235-253.

Gaver, Jennifer J. and Gaver, Kenneth M. (1995), Compensation policy and the investment opportunity set, in: *Financial Management*, Vol. 24 (1995), No. 1 (Spring), pp. 19-32.

Gaver, Jennifer J. and Gaver, Kenneth M. (1993), Additional evidence on the association between the investment opportunity set and corporate financing, dividend, and compensation policies, in: *Journal of Accounting and Economics*, Vol. 16 (1993), No. 1-3, pp. 125-160.

Gaver, Jennifer J., Gaver, Kenneth M. and Austin, Jeffrey R. (1995), Additional evidence on bonus plans and income management, in: *Journal of Accounting and Economics*, Vol. 19 (1995), No. 1, pp. 3-28.

Gentz, Manfred and Kauffmann, Herbert (2003), Impairment-Only-Approach – Die neuen Rechnungslegungsstandards zur Bewertung von Firmenwerten, in: von Werder, Axel and Wiedmann, Harald (ed.), Internationalisierung der Rechnungslegung und Corporate Governance - Festschrift für Prof. Dr. Klaus Pohle, Schäffer-Poeschel: Stuttgart 2003, pp. 61-102.

Godfrey, Jayne M., Mather, Paul R. and Ramsay, Alan (2003), Earnings and impression management in financial reports: The case of CEO changes, in: *Abacus*, Vol. 39 (2003), No. 1, pp. 95-123.

Gomes, Glenn M. (1988), Excess earnings, competitive advantage, and goodwill value, in: *Journal of Small Business Management*, July 1988, pp. 22-31.

Gonedes, Nicholas J. (1978), Corporate signaling, external accounting, and capital market equilibrium: Evidence on dividends, income, and extraordinary items, in: *Journal of Accounting Research*, Vol. 16 (1978), No. 1 (Spring), pp. 26-79.

Gonedes, Nicholas J. and Dopuch, Nicholas (1974), Capital market equilibrium, information production, and selecting accounting techniques: Theoretical framework and review of empirical work, in: *Journal of Accounting Research*, Vol. 12 (1974), Supplement, pp. 48-129.

Gordon, Myron J. (1964), Postulates, principles and research in accounting, in: *The Accounting Review*, Vol. 39 (1964), No. 2 (April), pp. 251-263.

Gore, Pelham, Taib, Fauziah M. and Taylor, Paul A. (2000), Accounting for goodwill: An examination of factors influencing management preferences, in: *Accounting and Business Research*, Vol. 30 (2000), No. 3 (Summer), pp. 213-225.

Gowland, David (1990), The regulation of financial markets in the 1990s, Aldershot et al.: Edward Elgar, 1990.

Gräber, Hermann (1981), Die handelsrechtliche Geschäftswertbilanzierung im Blickfeld des Abschlussprüfers, Würzburg: Universität Würzburg, 1981.

Gregory, Alan (2000), Motives underlying the method of payment by UK acquirers: The influence of goodwill, in: *Accounting and Business Research*, Vol. 30 (2000), No. 3 (Summer), pp. 227-240.

Greene, William H. (2003), Econometric analysis, Upper Saddle River: Prentice Hall, 5th ed. 2003.

Grinyer, John R., Russell, Alex and Walker, Martin (1991), Managerial choices in the valuation of acquired goodwill in the UK, in: *Accounting and Business Research*, Vol. 22 (1991), No. 85 (Winter), pp. 51-55.

Grünberger, David and Grünberger, Herbert (2003), Business Combinations (Phase II): Richtungsweisende Beschlüsse des IASB, in: *Steuern und Bilanzen*, Vol. 6 (2003), No. 5, pp. 218-220.

Grünberger, David and Grünberger, Herbert (2002), Business Combinations: IFRS-Entwürfe zur Kapitalkonsolidierung und Firmenwertbilanzierung, in: *Steuern und Bilanzen*, Vol. 5 (2002), No. 3, pp. 118-122.

Guidry, Flora, Leone, Andrew J. and Rock, Steve (1999), Earnings-based bonus plans and earnings management by business-unit managers, in: *Journal of Accounting and Economics*, Vol. 26 (1999), No. 1-3 (January), pp. 113-142.

Gujarati, Damodar N. (2003), Basic econometrics, New York et al.: McGraw-Hill, 4th ed. 2003.

Gupta, Sanjay (1995), Determinants of the choice between partial and comprehensive income tax allocation: The case of the Domestic International Sales Corporation, in: *The Accounting Review*, Vol. 70 (1995), No. 3 (July), pp. 489-511.

Gynther, Reg S. (1969), Some "conceptualizing" on goodwill, in: *The Accounting Review*, Vol. 44 (1969), No. 2, pp. 247-255.

Hachmeister, Dirk (2000), Der Discounted Cash Flow als Maß der Unternehmenswertsteigerung, Frankfurt am Main et al.: Peter Lang, 4th ed. 2000.

Hachmeister, Dirk (1996), Der Discounted Cash Flow als Unternehmenswert, in: *Wirtschaft und Studium*, Vol. 25 (1996), No. 4, pp. 357-366.

Hall, Steven C. (1993a), Determinants of goodwill amortization period, in: *Journal of Business Finance and Accounting*, Vol. 20 (1993), No. 4 (June), pp. 613-621.

Hall, Steven C. (1993b), Political scrutiny and earnings management in the oil refining industry, in: *Journal of Accounting and Public Policy*, Vol. 12 (1993), No. 4 (Winter), pp. 325-351.

Haller, Axel (1994), Positive Accounting Theory – Die Erforschung der Beweggründe bilanzpolitischen Verhaltens, in: *Die Betriebswirtschaft*, Vol. 54 (1994), No. 5, pp. 597-612.

Han, Jerry C. Y./Wang, Shiing-wu (1998), Political costs and earnings management of oil companies during the 1990 Persion Gulf crisis, in: *The Accounting Review*, Vol. 73 (1998), No. 1 (January), pp. 103-117.

Hand, John R. M. (1990), A test of the extended functional fixation hypothesis, in: *The Accounting Review*, Vol. 65 (1990), No. 4 (October), pp. 740-763.

Haring, Nikolai (2002), Analyse bilanzpolitischer Spielräume des Impairment-only-Approach der Goodwill-Bilanzierung gemäß SFAS 142 unter Beachtung empirischer Ergebnisse, in: *Österreichische Zeitschrift für Recht und Rechnungswesen* 2002, No. 2, pp. 55-60.

Harris, Robert S. and Ravenscraft, David (1991), The role of acquisitions in foreign direct investment: Evidence from the U.S. stock market, in: *Journal of Finance*, Vol. 156 (1991), No. 3 (July), pp. 825-844.

Hayn, Carla (1995), The information content of losses, in: *Journal of Accounting and Economics*, Vol. 20 (1995), No. 2, pp. 125-153.

Healy, Paul M. (1985), The effect of bonus schemes on accounting decisions, in: *Journal of Accounting and Economics*, Vol. 7 (1985), pp. 85-107.

Healy, Paul M., Kang, Sok-Hyon and Palepu, Krishna G. (1987), The effect of accounting procedure changes on CEOs' cash salary and bonus compensation, in: *Journal of Accounting and Economics*, Vol. 9 (1987), No. 1, pp. 7-34.

Healy, Paul M. and Palepu, Krishna G. (2001), Information asymmetry, corporate disclosure, and the capital markets: A review of the empirical disclosure literature, in: *Journal of Accounting and Economics*, Vol. 31 (2001), No. 1-3 (September), pp. 405-440.

Healy, Paul M. and Palepu, Krishna G. (1993), The effect of firms' financial disclosure strategies on stock prices, in: *Accounting Horizons*, Vol. 7 (1993), No. 1 (March), pp. 1-11.

Healy, Paul M. and Palepu, Krishna G. (1990), The effectiveness of accounting-based dividend covenants, in: *Journal of Accounting and Economics*, Vol. 12 (1990), No. 1-3, pp. 97-123.

Healy, Paul M. and Wahlen, James M. (1999), Commentary: A review of the earnings management literature and its implications for standard setting, in: *Accounting Horizons*, Vol. 13 (1999), No. 4 (December), pp. 365-383.

Heflin, F. and Warfield, Terry D. (1997), Managerial discretion in accounting for asset write-offs, Madison: University of Wisconsin, 1997.

Heintges, Sebastian (1997), Bilanzkultur und Bilanzpolitik in den USA und in Deutschland – Einflüsse auf die Bilanzpolitik börsennotierter Unternehmen, Sternenfels: Verlag Wissenschaft & Praxis, 2nd ed. 1997.

Hendriksen, Eldon S. and van Breda, Michael F. (1992), Accounting theory, Chicago et al.: Irwin, 5th ed. 1992.

Heninger, William G. (2001), The association between auditor litigation and abnormal accruals, in: *The Accounting Review*, Vol. 76 (2001), No. 1 (January), pp. 111-126.

Hennes, Markus (2003), Thyssen-Krupp will sich wehren, in: *Handelsblatt*, 6 March 2003, p. 2.

Henning, Steven L., Lewis, Barry L. and Shaw, Wayne H. (2000), Valuation of the components of purchased goodwill, in: *Journal of Accounting Research*, Vol. 38 (2000), No. 2 (Autumn), pp. 375-386.

Henning, Steven L. and Shaw, Wayne H. (2003), Is the selection of the amortization period for goodwill a strategic choice?, in: *Review of Quantitative Finance and Accounting*, Vol. 20 (2003), pp. 315-333.

Henning, Steven L., Shaw, Wayne H. and Stock, Toby (2002), The amount and timing of goodwill write-offs and revaluations: Evidence from U.S. and U.K. firms, Dallas: Southern Methodist University, 2002.

Henning, Steven L. and Stock, Toby (1998), The value-relevance of goodwill write-offs, Dallas: Southern Methodist University, 1998.

Hepworth, Samuel R. (1953), Smoothing periodic income, in: *The Accounting Review*, Vol. 28 (1953), No. 1, pp. 32-39.

Higson, Chris (1998), Goodwill, in: *British Accounting Review*, Vol. 30 (1998), No. 2 (June), pp. 141-158.

Hillebrandt, Franca (2001), Multiplikatorverfahren, in: *Die Betriebswirtschaft*, Vol. 61 (2001), No. 5, pp. 618-621.

Hirschey, Mark and Richardson, Vernon J. (2003), Investor underreaction to goodwill write-offs, in: *Financial Analysts Journal*, Vol. 59 (2003), No. 6 (November/December), pp. 75-84.

Hirschey, Mark and Richardson, Vernon J. (2002), Information content of accounting goodwill numbers, in: *Journal of Accounting and Public Policy*, Vol. 21 (2002), pp. 173-191.

Hirst, D. Eric and Hopkins, Patrick E. (1998), Comprehensive income reporting and analysts' valuation judgments, in: *Journal of Accounting Research*, Vol. 36 (1998), Supplement, pp. 47-75.

Hitz, Markus and Kuhner, Christoph (2002), Die Neuregelung zur Bilanzierung des derivativen Goodwill nach SFAS 141 und 142 auf dem Prüfstand, in: *Die Wirtschaftsprüfung*, Vol. 55 (2002), No. 6, pp. 273-287.

Hitz, Markus and Kuhner, Christoph (2000), Erweiterung des US-amerikanischen conceptual framework um Grundsätze der Barwertermittlung – Inhalt und Bedeutung des Statement of Financial Accounting Concepts No. 7, in: *Die Wirtschaftsprüfung*, Vol. 53 (2000), No. 18, pp. 889-902.

Hodgson, Allan, Okunev, John and Willett, Roger (1993), Accounting for intangibles: A theoretical perspective, in: *Accounting and Business Research*, Vol. 23 (1993), No. 90, pp. 138-150.

Holthausen, Robert W. (1990), Accounting method choice – opportunistic behavior, efficient contracting, and information perspectives, in: *Journal of Accounting and Economics*, Vol. 12 (1990), No. 1-3, pp. 207-218.

Holthausen, Robert W. and Leftwich, Richard W. (1983), The economic consequences of accounting choice – implications of costly contracting and monitoring, in: *Journal of Accounting and Economics*, Vol. 5 (1983), No. 2, pp. 77-117.

Holthausen, Robert W., Watts, Ross L. (2001), The relevance of the value-relevance literature for financial accounting standard setting, in: *Journal of Accounting and Economics*, Vol. 31 (2001), No. 1-3 (September), pp. 3-75.

Hommel, Michael (2001a), Bilanzierung von Goodwill und Badwill im internationalen Vergleich, in: *Recht der Internationalen Wirtschaft*, Vol. 47 (2001), No. 11, pp. 801-809.

Hommel, Michael (2001b), Neue Goodwillbilanzierung – das FASB auf dem Weg zur entobjektivierten Bilanz?, in: *Betriebs-Berater*, Vol. 56 (2001), No. 38, pp. 1943-1949.

Hong, Hai, Kaplan, Robert S. and Mandelker, Gershon (1978), Pooling vs. purchase: The effects of accounting for mergers on stock prices, in: *The Accounting Review*, Vol. 53 (1978), No. 1 (January), pp. 31-47.

Hopkins, Patrick E., Houston, Richard W. and Peters, Michael F. (2000), Purchase, pooling, and equity analysts' valuation judgments, in: *The Accounting Review*, Vol. 75 (2000), No. 3 (July), pp. 257-281.

Hoyle, Joe B., Schaefer, Thomas F. and Doupnik, Timothy S. (1998), Advanced accounting, Boston et al.: Irwin/McGraw-Hill, 5th ed. 1998.

Hütten, Christoph and Lorson, Peter (2002), Überlegungen zur neuen Goodwillbilanzierung nach SFAS 142 aus Controlling-Perspektive – Eine Ergänzung zu Küting/Weber/Wirth: Die neue Goodwillbilanzierung nach SFAS 142, in: *Kapitalmarktorientierte Rechnungslegung*, Vol. 2 (2002), No. 1, pp. 25-33.

Huijgen, Carel Adriaan (1996), Valuation of purchased goodwill – Economic and accounting approaches, Groningen, NL: Rijksuniversiteit Groningen, 1996.

IDW (2003), IDW-Stellungnahme zum Exposure Draft ED 3 "Business Combinations", in: *IDW-Fachnachrichten* 2003, No. 5, pp. 202-211.

IDW (2001), IDW Stellungnahme: Revised Exposure Draft des FASB "Business Combinations and Intangible Assets – Accounting for Goodwill", in: *Die Wirtschaftsprüfung*, Vol. 54 (2001), No. 8, pp. 464-467.

IDW (2000), IDW Standard: Grundsätze zur Durchführung von Unternehmensbewertungen (IDW S1) (Stand: 28.6.2000), in: *Die Wirtschaftsprüfung*, Vol. 53 (2000), pp. 825-842.

Imhoff, Eugene A. (1975), Income smoothing: The role of management: A comment, in: *The Accounting Review*, Vol. 50 (1975), No. 1, pp. 118-121.

Jaggi, Bikki and Sannella, Alexander (1995), The association between the accuracy of management earnings forecasts and discretionary accounting changes, in: *Journal of Accounting, Auditing and Finance*, Vol. 10 (1995), No. 1 (Winter), pp. 1-21.

Janschek, Otto (2002), Die Firmenwertabschreibung nach SFAS 141/142, in: *Österreichische Zeitschrift für Recht und Rechnungswesen* 2002, No. 2, pp. 48-54.

Jenkins, H. W. (1999), Mean old FASB: Forcing us to think, in: *The Wall Street Journal*, (1999), p. A27.

Jennings, Ross, LeClere, Marc and Thompson, Robert B. (2001), Goodwill amortization and the usefulness of earnings, in: *Financial Analysts Journal*, Vol. 57 (2001), No. 5 (September/October), pp. 20-28.

Jennings, Ross, Robinson, John R., Thompson, Robert B. and Duvall, Linda (1996), The relation between accounting goodwill numbers and equity values, in: *Journal of Business Finance and Accounting*, Vol. 23 (1996), No. 4 (June), pp. 513-533.

Jensen, Daniel L., Coffman, Edward N., Stephens, Ray G., Burns, Thomas J. (1994), Advanced accounting, New York et al.: McGraw-Hill, 3rd ed. 1994.

Jeter, Debra C. and Chaney, Paul K. (2001), Advanced accounting, New York et al.: John Wiley & Sons, Inc., 2001.

John, Kose, Lang, Larry H. and Netter, Jeffry (1992), The voluntary restructuring of large firms in response to performance decline, in: *Journal of Finance*, Vol. 47 (1992), No. 3, pp. 891-917.

Johnson, L. Todd and Petrone, Kimberley R. (1998), Commentary: Is goodwill an asset?, in: *Accounting Horizons*, Vol. 12 (1998), No. 3 (September), pp. 293-303.

Jones, Jennifer J. (1991), Earnings management during import relief investigations, in: *Journal of Accounting Research*, Vol. 29 (1991), No. 2 (Autumn), pp. 193-228.

Kahle, Holger (2003), Zur Zukunft der Rechnungslegung in Deutschland: IAS im Einzel- und Konzernabschluss?, in: *Die Wirtschaftsprüfung*, Vol. 56 (2003), No. 6, pp. 262-275.

Kahle, Holger (2002a), Die neue Goodwill-Bilanzierung nach US-GAAP – Bilanzierung nach Belieben? (Teil A), in: *Steuern und Bilanzen*, Vol. 2 (2002), No. 17, pp. 849-858.

Kahle, Holger (2002b), Die neue Goodwill-Bilanzierung nach US-GAAP – Bilanzierung nach Belieben? (Teil B), in: *Steuern und Bilanzen*, Vol. 2 (2002), No. 18, pp. 900-905.

Kamin, J. Y. and Ronen, Joshua (1978), The smoothing of income numbers: Some empirical evidence on systematic differences among management-controlled and owner-controlled firms, in: *Accounting, Organizations and Society*, Vol. 3 (1978), No. 2 (September), pp. 141-157.

Kaplan, Robert S. and Roll, Richard (1972), Investor evaluation of accounting information: Some empirical evidence, in: *Journal of Business*, Vol. 45 (1972), No. 2 (April), pp. 225-257.

Kasanen, Eero, Kinnunen, Juha and Niskanen, Jyrki (1996), Dividend-based earnings management: Empirical evidence from Finland, in: *Journal of Accounting and Economics*, Vol. 22 (1996), No. 1-3 (August-December), pp. 283-312.

Kasznik, Ron (1999), On the association between voluntary disclosure and earnings management, in: *Journal of Accounting Research*, Vol. 37 (1999), No. 1 (Spring), pp. 57-81.

Kasznik, Ron and Lev, Baruch (1995), To warn or not to warn: Management disclosures in the face of an earnings surprise, in: *The Accounting Review*, Vol. 70 (1995), No. 1 (January), pp. 113-134.

Kasznik, Ron and McNichols, Maureen F. (2002), Does meeting earnings expectations matter? Evidence from analyst forecast revisions and share prices, in: *Journal of Accounting Research*, Vol. 40 (2002), No. 3, pp. 727-759.

Kelly, Lauren (1983), The development of a positive theory of corporate management's role in external financial reporting, in: *Journal of Accounting Literature*, Vol. 2 (1983), pp. 111-150.

Kennedy, Peter (1998), A guide to econometrics, Cambridge, MA: MIT Press, 4th ed. 1998.

Key, Kimberly Galligan (1997), Political cost incentives for earnings management in the cable television industry, in: *Journal of Accounting and Economics*, Vol. 23 (1997), No. 3 (November), pp. 309-337.

Khurana, Inder K. and Loudder, Martha L. (1994), The economic consequences of SFAS 106 in rate-regulated enterprises, in: *The Accounting Review*, Vol. 69 (1994), No. 2 (April), pp. 364-380.

Kieso, Donald E., Weygandt, Jerry J. and Warfield, Terry D. (2001), Intermediate Accounting, New York et al.: John Wiley & Sons, Inc., 10th ed. 2001.

Kim, Sungsoo and Kwon, Sung S. (2001), SFAS 121 asset write-down: early vs. late firms, Camden: Rutgers University, 2001.

Kinne, Stephan (1989), Der konzernbilanzielle Firmenwert von Tochterunternehmen – Eine Analyse und Weiterführung nach neuem Recht, Frankfurt am Main et al.: Peter Lang, 1989.

Kinney, Michael and Trezevant, Robert (1997), The use of special items to manage earnings and perceptions, in: *Journal of Financial Statement Analysis*, Vol. 3 (1997), No. 1 (Fall), pp. 45-53.

Kinney, William R., Burgstahler, David C. and Martin, Roger (2002), Earnings surprise "materiality" as measured by stock returns, in: *Journal of Accounting Research*, Vol. 40 (2002), No. 5 (December), pp. 1297-1329.

Kirsch, Hans-Jürgen (2003), Zur Frage der Umsetzung der Mitgliedstaatenwahlrechte der EU-Verordnung zur Anwendung der IAS/IFRS, in: *Die Wirtschaftsprüfung*, Vol. 56 (2003), No. 6, pp. 275-278.

Kirschenheiter, Michael and Melumad, Nahum D. (2002), Can "big bath" and earnings smoothing co-exist as equilibrium financial reporting strategies?, in: *Journal of Accounting Research*, Vol. 40 (2002), No. 3 (June), pp. 761-796.

Klein, Gabriele (2000), Die Erfassung des Goodwill in unterschiedlichen Rechnungslegungssystemen unter Berücksichtigung grenzüberschreitender Fusionen, in: *Deutsches Steuerrecht*, Vol. 38 (2000), No. 18, pp. 788-796.

Kleindiek, Detlef (2001), Neue Goodwill-Bilanzierung nach US-GAAP und europäisches Bilanzrecht – Stellungnahme zu E-DRS 1 a, in: *Betriebs-Berater*, Vol. 56 (2001), No. 50, pp. 2572-2577.

Kommission Rechnungswesen im Verband der Hochschullehrer für Betriebswirtschaft e. V. (1985), Stellungnahme zur Umsetzung der 7. EG-Richtlinie (Konzernabschluß-Richtlinie), in: *Die Betriebswirtschaft*, Vol. 45 (1985), No. 3, pp. 267-277.

Kort, Katharina (2003), AOL Time Warner: 99 Milliarden Miese, in: *Handelsblatt* 2003, No. 22, p. 11.

Kothari, Sriprakash P. (2001), Capital markets research in accounting, in: *Journal of Accounting and Economics*, Vol. 31 (2001), No. 1-3 (September), pp. 105-231.

Krämling, Markus (1998), Der Goodwill aus der Kapitalkonsolidierung – Bestandsaufnahme der Bilanzierungspraxis und deren Relevanz für die Aktienbewertung, Frankfurt am Main et al.: Peter Lang, 1998.

Kraft, Ernst-Thomas (2002), Commentary on section 309 HGB, in: Ulmer, Peter (ed.), HGB-Bilanzrecht: Rechnungslegung, Abschlußprüfung, Publizität – Großkommentar, Berlin/New York: Walter de Gruyter, 2002, pp. 1427-1451.

Krishnan, Gopal V. (2003), Does Big 6 auditor industry expertise constrain earnings management?, in: *Accounting Horizons*, Vol. 17 (2003), Supplement, pp. 1-16.

Krolak, Thomas (2000), Die bilanzielle Behandlung des aus der Kapitalkonsolidierung resultierenden Geschäfts- oder Firmenwertes nach HGB, U.S. GAAP und IAS, Düsseldorf: IDW-Verlag, 2000.

Kross, W. J., Park, T. and Ro, B. T. (1996), The impact of operational restructuring announcements on stock price, risk and trading volume, Purdue University, 1996.

Küting, Karlheinz (2000), Der Geschäfts- oder Firmenwert – ein Spielball der Bilanzpolitik in deutschen Konzernen, in: *Die Aktiengesellschaft*, Vol. 45 (2000), No. 3, pp. 97-106.

Küting, Karlheinz (1997), Der Geschäfts- oder Firmenwert aus der Kapitalkonsolidierung – Eine Bestandsaufnahme in Theorie und Praxis, in: Forster, Karl-Heinz et al. (ed.), Aktien- und Bilanzrecht – Festschrift für Bruno Kropff, Düsseldorf: IDW-Verlag, 1997, pp. 454-471.

Küting, Karlheinz (1995a), Aktuelle Fragen der Kapitalkonsolidierung (Teil I), in: *Deutsches Steuerrecht*, Vol. 33 (1995), No. 5, pp. 192-196.

Küting, Karlheinz (1995b), Aktuelle Fragen der Kapitalkonsolidierung (Teil II), in: *Deutsches Steuerrecht*, Vol. 33 (1995), No. 6, pp. 229-235.

Küting, Karlheinz, Brakensiek, Sonja and Wirth, Johannes (2000), Außerplanmäßige Abschreibung: Neue Tendenzen in der US-amerikanischen Rechnungslegung, in: *Betriebs-Berater*, Vol. 55 (2000), No. 48, pp. 2459-2465.

Küting, Karlheinz and Dawo, Sascha (2002), Bilanzpolitische Gestaltungspotenziale im Rahmen der International Financial Reporting Standards (IFRS) – Ansatzfragen am Beispiel der Abbildung immaterieller Werte, in: *Steuern und Bilanzen*, Vol. 4 (2002), No. 23, pp. 1157-1163.

Küting, Karlheinz, Dawo, Sascha and Wirth, Johannes (2003), Konzeption der außerplanmäßigen Abschreibung im Reformprojekt des IASB, in: *Kapitalmarktorientierte Rechnungslegung*, Vol. 3 (2003), No. 4, pp. 177-190.

Küting, Karlheinz, Dusemond, Michael and Nardmann, Benita (1994), Ausgewählte Probleme der Kapitalkonsolidierung in Theorie und Praxis – Ergebnisse einer empirischen Erhebung des Instituts für Wirtschaftsprüfung an der Universität des Saarlandes, in: *Betriebs-Berater*, Vol. 49 (1994), Supplement No. 8, pp. 1-18.

Küting, Karlheinz and Harth, Hans-Jörg (1999a), Vergleich der Kapitalkonsolidierung nach HGB, US-GAAP und IAS (Teil I), in: *Betriebs-Berater*, Vol. 54 (1999), No. 26, pp. 1370-1377.

Küting, Karlheinz and Harth, Hans-Jörg (1999b), Vergleich der Kapitalkonsolidierung nach HGB, US-GAAP und IAS (Teil II), in: *Betriebs-Berater*, Vol. 54 (1999), No. 27, pp. 1424-1429.

Küting, Karlheinz and Koch, Christian (2003), Der Goodwill in der deutschen Bilanzierungspraxis, in: *Steuern und Bilanzen*, Vol. 5 (2003), No. 2, pp. 49-54.

Küting, Karlheinz and Leinen, Markus (2002), Die Kapitalkonsolidierung bei Erwerb eines Teilkonzerns, in: *Die Wirtschaftsprüfung*, Vol. 55 (2002), No. 22, pp. 1201-1216.

Küting, Karlheinz, Weber, Claus-Peter and Wirth, Johannes (2002), Goodwill und immaterielle Vermögenswerte im Übergang auf die Anwendung des SFAS 142, in: *Kapitalmarktorientierte Rechnungslegung*, Vol. 2 (2002), No. 2, pp. 57-66.

Küting, Karlheinz, Weber, Claus-Peter and Wirth, Johannes (2001), Die neue Goodwillbilanzierung nach SFAS 142 – Ist der Weg frei für eine neue Akquisitionswelle?, in: *Kapitalmarktorientierte Rechnungslegung*, Vol. 1 (2001), No. 5 (September/Oktober), pp. 185-198.

Küting, Karlheinz and Wirth, Johannes (2004), Bilanzierung von Unternehmenszusammenschlüssen nach IFRS 3, in: *Kapitalmarktorientierte Rechnungslegung*, Vol. 4 (2004), No. 5, pp. 167-177.

Küting, Karlheinz and Wirth, Johannes (2003), Die Kapitalkonsolidierung im Spiegel der Bilanzwelten HGB – IAS/IFRS – US-GAAP (Teil I), in: *Deutsches Steuerrecht*, Vol. 41 (2003), No. 12, pp. 475-484.

Kuhn, Thomas S. (1970), The structure of scientific revolutions, Chicago: Chicago University Press, 1970.

Lachnit, Laurenz, Ammann, Helmut, Müller, Stefan, Wulf, Inge (1999), Geschäfts- oder Firmenwert als Problem der Konzernabschlußanalyse, in: Die Wirtschaftsprüfung, Vol. 52 (1999), No. 17, pp. 677-688.

Lakonishok, J., Shleifer, Andrei and Vishny, Robert W. (1994), Contrarian investment, extrapolation and risk, in: *Journal of Finance*, Vol. 49 (1994), No. 5, pp. 1541-1578.

Lambert, Richard A. (2001), Contracting theory and accounting, in: *Journal of Accounting and Economics*, Vol. 32 (2001), No. 1-3, pp. 3-87.

Lambert, Richard A. (1984), Income smoothing as rational equilibrium behavior, in: *The Accounting Review*, Vol. 59 (1984), No. 4 (October), pp. 604-618.

Langer, Russell and Lev, Baruch (1993), The FASB's policy of extended adoption for new standards: An examination of FAS No. 87, in: *The Accounting Review*, Vol. 68 (1993), No. 3 (July), pp. 515-533.

Larsen, E. John (1997), Modern advanced accounting, New York et al.: McGraw-Hill, 7th ed. 1997.

Lee, Changwoo and Choi, Frederick D. S. (1992), Effects of alternative goodwill treatments on merger premia: Further empirical evidence, in: *Journal of International Financial Management and Accounting*, Vol. 4 (1992), No. 3, pp. 220-236.

Lee, T. A. (1974), Accounting for and disclosure of business combinations – An empirical study of company practices in the United Kingdom in the period 1969-1971, in: *Journal of Business Finance and Accounting*, Vol. 1 (1974), No. 1 (Spring), pp. 1-33.

Lee, T. A. (1973), Accounting for goodwill – An empirical study of company practices in the United Kingdom – 1962 to 1971, in: *Accounting and Business Research*, Vol. none (1973), No. Summer, pp. 175-196.

Lee, T. A. (1971), Goodwill. An example of will-o'-the-wisp accounting, in: *Accounting and Business Research*, Vol. none (1971), No. Autumn, pp. 318-328.

Leftwich, Richard W. (1990), Aggregation of test statistics – Statistics vs. economics, in: *Journal of Accounting and Economics*, Vol. 12 (1990), No. 1-3, pp. 37-44.

Leftwich, Richard W. (1983), Accounting information in private markets: Evidence from private lending agreements, in: *The Accounting Review*, Vol. 58 (1983), No. 1, pp. 23-42.

Leftwich, Richard W. (1981), Evidence of the impact of mandatory changes in accounting principles on corporate loan agreements, in: *Journal of Accounting and Economics*, Vol. 3 (1981), No. 1, pp. 3-36.

Lev, Baruch (1989), On the usefulness of earnings and earnings research: Lessons and directions from two decades of empirical research, in: *Journal of Accounting Research*, Vol. 27 (1989), Supplement, pp. 153-192.

Lev, Baruch and Ohlson, James A. (1982), Market-based empirical research in accounting: A review, interpretation, and extension, in: *Journal of Accounting Research*, Vol. 20 (1982), Supplement, pp. 249-322.

Levitt, Arthur (1998), The "numbers game", http://www.sec.gov/news/speech/speecharchive/ 1998/ spch220.txt: 1998.

Libby, Robert and Kinney, William R. (2000), Does mandated audit communication reduce opportunistic corrections to manage earnings to forecasts?, in: *The Accounting Review*, Vol. 75 (2000), No. 4 (October), pp. 383-404.

Lindahl, Frederick W., Emby, Craig and Ashton, Robert H. (1988), Empirical research on LIFO: A review and analysis, in: *Journal of Accounting Literature*, Vol. 7 (1988), pp. 310-333.

Lindenberg, Eric and Ross, Michael P. (1999), To purchase or to pool: Does it matter?, in: *Journal of Applied Corporate Finance*, Vol. 12 (1999), No. 2, pp. 32-47.

Loh, Alfred Lye Chye and Tan, Tin Hoe (2002), Asset write-offs – Managerial incentives and macroeconomic factors, in: *Abacus*, Vol. 38 (2002), No. 1, pp. 134-151.

Lopatta, Kerstin (2000), Erfassung des Goodwill in unterschiedlichen Rechnungslegungssystemen unter Berücksichtigung grenzüberschreitender Fusionen, in: *Recht der Internationalen Wirtschaft*, Vol. 46 (2000), No. 5, pp. 354-363.

Lopez, Thomas J. and Rees, Lynn (2002), The effect of beating and missing analysts' forecasts on the information content of unexpected earnings, in: *Journal of Accounting, Auditing and Finance*, Vol. 17 (2002), No. 2, pp. 155-184.

Ludz, Christoph (1997), Der neue Firmenwert des Bilanzrichtlinien-Gesetzes, Frankfurt am Main et al.: Peter Lang, 1997.

Lückmann, Reinhard (2001), Bilanzexperten kritisieren neue US-Goodwill-Regeln, in: *Handelsblatt* 2001, No. 125, p. 16.

Lüdenbach, Norbert and Frowein, Nils (2003), Der Goodwill-Impairment-Test aus Sicht der Rechnungslegungspraxis, in: *Der Betrieb*, Vol. 56 (2003), No. 5, pp. 217-223.

Lüdenbach, Norbert and Hoffmann, Wolf-Dieter (2003), Imparitätische Wahrscheinlichkeit – Zukunftswerte im IAS-Regelwerk, in: *Kapitalmarktorientierte Rechnungslegung*, Vol. 3 (2003), No. 1, pp. 5-14.

Lüdenbach, Norbert and Schulz, Roland (2002), Unternehmensbewertung für Bilanzierungszwecke – Neue Herausforderungen für den Berufsstand durch den impairment-Ansatz von FAS 142?, in: *Die Wirtschaftsprüfung*, Vol. 55 (2002), No. 10, pp. 489-499.

Lys, Thomas Z. (1984), Mandated accounting changes and debt covenants: The case of oil and gas accounting, in: *Journal of Accounting and Economics*, Vol. 6 (1984), No. 1, pp. 39-65.

Lys, Thomas Z. and Vincent, Linda (1995), An analysis of value destruction in AT&T's acquisition of NCR, in: *Journal of Financial Economics*, Vol. 39 (1995), No. 2/3, pp. 353-378.

Ma, Ronald and Hopkins, Roger (1988), Goodwill – An example of puzzle-solving in accounting, in: *Abacus*, Vol. 24 (1988), No. 1, pp. 75-85.

MacKinlay, A. Craig (1997), Event studies in economics and finance, in: *Journal of Economic Literature*, Vol. 35 (1997), No. March, pp. 13-39.

Maddala, G. S. (2001), Introduction to econometrics, New York et al.: John Wiley & Sons, Inc., 3rd ed. 2001.

Maddala, G. S. (1991), A perspective on the use of limited-dependent and qualitative variables models in accounting research, in: *The Accounting Review*, Vol. 66 (1991), No. 4 (October), pp. 788-807.

Maddala, G. S. (1983), Limited-dependent and qualitative variables in econometrics, Cambridge, UK: Cambridge University Press, 1983.

Mandl, Gerwald and Rabel, Klaus (1997), Unternehmensbewertung – Eine praxisorientierte Einführung, Wien: Ueberreuter, 1997.

Mandler, Udo (2003), IASCF/IASB: Organisation, Entstehung und aktuelle Bedeutung, in: *Wirtschaft und Studium*, Vol. 32 (2003), No. 4, pp. 476-484.

Mard, Michael J. et al. (2002), Valuation for financial reporting: Intangible assets, goodwill, and impairment analysis, SFAS 141 and 142, New York et al.: John Wiley & Sons, Inc., 2002.

Marquardt, Carol A. and Wiedman, Christine I. (2002), How are earnings managed? An examination of specific accruals, New York University, 2002.

Martínez-Jerez, Francisco Asís (2001), Capital markets assessment of accounting for business combinations, Harvard University, 2001.

Matsumoto, Dawn A. (2002), Management's incentives to avoid negative earnings surprises, in: *The Accounting Review*, Vol. 77 (2002), No. 3 (July), pp. 483-514.

Matsunaga, Steven R. and Park, Chul W. (2001), The effect of missing a quartely earnings benchmark on the CEO's annual bonus, in: *The Accounting Review*, Vol. 76 (2001), No. 3 (July), pp. 313-332.

Mayer-Sommer, Alan P. (1979), Understanding and acceptance of the efficient markets hypothesis and its accounting implications, in: *The Accounting Review*, Vol. 54 (1979), No. 1 (January), pp. 88-106.

McCarthy, Mark G. and Schneider, Douglas K. (1995), Market perception of goodwill: Some empirical evidence, in: *Accounting and Business Research*, Vol. 26 (1995), No. 1, pp. 69-81.

McDonald, John F. and Moffitt, Robert A. (1980), The uses of Tobit analysis, in: *Review of Economics and Statistics*, Vol. 62 (1980), No. 2, pp. 318-321.

McLeay, Stuart, Ordelheide, Dieter and Young, Steven (2000), Constituent lobbying and its impact on the development of financial reporting regulations: Evidence from Germany, in: *Accounting, Organizations and Society*, Vol. 25 (2000), No. 1, pp. 79-98.

McNichols, Maureen (2000), Research design issues in earnings management studies, in: *Journal of Accounting and Public Policy*, Vol. 19 (2000), pp. 313-345.

Mendenhall, Richard R. and Nichols, William D. (1988), Bad news and differential market reactions to announcements of earlier-quarters versus fourth-quarter earnings, in: *Journal of Accounting Research*, Vol. 26 (1988), Supplement, pp. 63-86.

Mercer Capital (ed.) (2001), Valuation for impairment testing – The finance and accounting professional's guide to valuing reporting units for compliance with SFAS 142, Memphis, Tennessee: Peabody Publishing, LP, 2001.

Merchant, Kenneth A. and Rockness, Joanne (1994), The ethics of managing earnings: An empirical investigation, in: *Journal of Accounting and Public Policy*, Vol. 13 (1994), No. 1 (Spring), pp. 79-94.

Miller, Malcolm C. (1973), Goodwill – An aggregation issue, in: *The Accounting Review*, Vol. 48 (1973), No. 2, pp. 280-291.

Miller, Paul B. W., Redding, Rodney J. and Bahnson, Paul R. (1998), The FASB: The people, the process and the politics, Boston et al.: Irwin/McGraw-Hill, 4th ed. 1998.

Möhrle, Martin (1999), Bilanzierung des derivativen Geschäftswertes im Lichte der Investitionstheorie, Hamburg: Verlag Dr. Kovac, 1999.

Moehrle, Stephen R. (2002), Do firms use restructuring charge reversals to meet earnings targets?, in: *The Accounting Review*, Vol. 77 (2002), No. 2 (April), pp. 397-413.

Moehrle, Stephen R., Reynolds-Moehrle, Jennifer A. and Wallace, James S. (2001), How informative are earnings numbers that exclude goodwill amortization?, in: *Accounting Horizons*, Vol. 15 (2001), No. 3 (September), pp. 243-255.

Möller, Hans Peter and Hüfner, Bernd (2002), Empirische Forschung, in: Küpper, Hans-Ulrich and Wagenhofer, Alfred (ed.), Handwörterbuch Unternehmensrechnung und Controlling, Stuttgart: Schäffer-Poeschel, 2002, pp. 351-359.

Moffitt, Jacquelyn Sue and Rai, Atul (2002), Information content of earnings and special items: A re-examination, Louisiana State University, 2002.

Mohrman, Mary Beth (1996), The use of fixed GAAP provisions in debt contracts, in: *Accounting Horizons*, Vol. 10 (1996), No. 3 (September), pp. 78-91.

Mohrman, Mary Beth (1993), Debt contracts and FAS No. 19 – A test of the debt covenant hypothesis, in: *The Accounting Review*, Vol. 68 (1993), No. 2 (April), pp. 273-288.

Monsen, R. Joseph and Downs, Anthony (1965), A theory of large managerial firms, in: *Journal of Political Economy*, Vol. 73 (1965), No. 3, pp. 221-236.

Moore, Michael L. (1973), Management changes and discretionary accounting decisions, in: *Journal of Accounting Research*, Vol. 11 (1973), No. 1 (Spring), pp. 100-107.

Moses, O. Douglas (1987), Income smoothing and incentives: Empirical tests using accounting changes, in: *The Accounting Review*, Vol. 62 (1987), No. 2 (April), pp. 358-377.

Moxter, Adolf (2001), Deutscher Standardisierungsrat auf Irrwegen, in: *Betriebs-Berater*, Vol. 56 (2001), No. 50, Die erste Seite (editorial).

Moxter, Adolf (1993), Bilanzrechtliche Probleme beim Geschäfts- oder Firmenwert, in: Bierich, Marcus, Hommelhoff, Peter and Kropff, Bruno (ed.), Unternehmen und Unternehmensführung im Recht – Festschrift für Johannes Semler zum 70. Geburtstag am 28. April 1993, Berlin/New York: Walter de Gruyter, 1993, pp. 853-861.

Müller-Dahl, Frank P. (1981), Die Bilanzierung des Goodwill – betriebswirtschaftlich sowie handels- und steuerrechtlich unter Berücksichtigung des Vorentwurfs eines Bilanzrichtlinie-Gesetzes, in: *Betriebs-Berater*, Vol. 36 (1981), No. 5, pp. 274-284.

Mujkanovic, Robin (2001), Der Geschäftswert im Abschluß nach International Accounting Standards, in: *Zeitschrift für Betriebswirtschaft*, Vol. 71 (2001), No. 7, pp. 807-826.

Mujkanovic, Robin (1999), Die Zukunft der Kapitalkonsolidierung – Das Ende der Pooling-of-Interests Method?, in: *Die Wirtschaftsprüfung*, Vol. 52 (1999), No. 14, pp. 533-540.

Murphy, Kevin J. (1985), Corporate performance and managerial remuneration, in: *Journal of Accounting and Economics*, Vol. 7 (1985), No. 1-3, pp. 11-42.

Murphy, Kevin J. and Zimmerman, Jerold L. (1993), Financial performance surrounding CEO turnover, in: *Journal of Accounting and Economics*, Vol. 16 (1993), No. 1-3, pp. 273-315.

Nathan, Kevin (1988), Do firms pay to pool?: Some empirical evidence, in: *Journal of Accounting and Public Policy*, Vol. 7 (1988), No. 3 (Fall), pp. 185-200.

Nelson, Mark W., Elliott, John A. and Tarpley, Robin L. (2002), Evidence from auditors about managers' and auditors' earnings management decisions, in: *The Accounting Review*, Vol. 77 (2002), Supplement, pp. 175-202.

Nestler, Anke and Thuy, Michael (2002), Verfahren zur Bewertung von Reporting Units im Rahmen des Goodwill-Impairmenttests nach SFAS 142, in: *Kapitalmarktorientierte Rechnungslegung*, Vol. 2 (2002), No. 4, pp. 169-179.

Nobes, Christopher W. (1996), The effects of international differences in the tax treatment of goodwill: A comment, in: *Journal of International Business Studies*, Vol. 27 (1996), No. 3rd Quarter, pp. 589-592.

Nobes, Christopher W. (1992), A political history of goodwill in the U.K.: An illustration of cyclical standard setting, in: *Abacus*, Vol. 28 (1992), No. 2, pp. 142-167.

Nobes, Christopher W. and Norton, Julie (1996), International variations in the accounting and tax treatments of goodwill and the implications for research, in: *Journal of International Accounting, Auditing and Taxation*, Vol. 5 (1996), No. 2, pp. 179-196.

Noreen, Eric (1988), An empirical comparison of Probit and OLS regression hypothesis tests, in: *Journal of Accounting Research*, Vol. 26 (1988), No. 1, pp. 119-133.

o.V. (2003), S&P-Rückstufung empört Thyssen Krupp-Aktionäre, in: *Frankfurter Allgemeine Zeitung* 2003, No. 45, p. 14.

Ordelheide, Dieter (1998), Wettbewerb der Rechnungslegungssysteme IAS, US-GAAP und HGB – Plädoyer für eine Reform des deutschen Bilanzrechts, Stuttgart: Schäffer-Poeschel, 1998.

Ordelheide, Dieter (1997), Kapitalmarktorientierte Bilanzierungsregeln für den Geschäftswert – HGB, IAS und US-GAAP, in: Forster, Karl-Heinz et al. (ed.), Aktien- und Bilanzrecht – Festschrift für Bruno Kropff, Düsseldorf: IDW-Verlag, 1997, pp. 571-589.

Osterland, Andrew (2002), M&A: Back to basics? – If you think new accounting rules will make acquisitions more transparent, think again, http://www.cfo.com/article/1,5309,7771%7C%7CM%7C386,00.html, 2002.

Payne, Jeff L. and Robb, Sean W. G. (2000), Earnings management: The effect of ex ante earnings expectations, in: *Journal of Accounting, Auditing and Finance*, Vol. 15 (2000), No. 4 (Fall), pp. 371-392.

Pejic, Philip and Buschhüter, Michael (2001), Ende der planmäßigen Goodwill-Abschreibung? – Überblick über den Standardentwurf des FASB: Business Combinations and Intangible Assets – Accounting for Goodwill, in: *Kapitalmarktorientierte Rechnungslegung*, Vol. 1 (2001), No. 3 (Mai/Juni), pp. 107-112.

Pellens, Bernhard (2001), Internationale Rechnungslegung, Stuttgart: Schäffer-Poeschel, 4th ed. 2001.

Pellens, Bernhard, Basche, Kerstin and Sellhorn, Thorsten (2003), Full Goodwill Method – Renaissance der reinen Einheitstheorie in der Konzernbilanzierung, in: *Kapitalmarktorientierte Rechnungslegung*, Vol. 3 (2003), No. 1, pp. 1-4.

Pellens, Bernhard, Bonse, Andreas and Fülbier, Rolf Uwe (1996), Organisatorischer und konzeptioneller Rahmen des IASC, in: *Wirtschaftsprüferkammer-Mitteilungen*, Vol. 35 (1996), pp. 264-278.

Pellens, Bernhard, Crasselt, Nils and Schremper, Ralf (2002), Berücksichtigung von Geschäftsbereichs-Goodwills bei der wertorientierten Unternehmensführung, in: Böhler, Heymo (ed.), Marketing-Management und Unternehmensführung – Festschrift für Professor Dr. Richard Köhler zum 65. Geburtstag, Stuttgart: Schäffer-Poeschel, 2002, pp. 121-135.

Pellens, Bernhard and Sellhorn, Thorsten (2003), Minderheitenproblematik beim Goodwill Impairment Test nach geplanten IFRS und geltenden US-GAAP, in: *Der Betrieb*, Vol. 56 (2003), No. 8, pp. 401-408.

Pellens, Bernhard and Sellhorn, Thorsten (2002a), Neue US-Goodwillbilanzierung steht deutschen Unternehmen nun offen – DRS 1a vom Bundesministerium der Justiz bekannt gemacht, in: *Kapitalmarktorientierte Rechnungslegung*, Vol. 2 (2002), No. 3, pp. 113-114.

Pellens, Bernhard and Sellhorn, Thorsten (2002b), Paradigmenwechsel in der Firmenwert-Bilanzierung – IASB folgt den amerikanischen Vorschriften – Neue Herausforderungen auch für deutsche Unternehmen, in: *Frankfurter Allgemeine Zeitung* 2002, No. 150, p. 22.

Pellens, Bernhard and Sellhorn, Thorsten (2001a), Goodwill-Bilanzierung nach SFAS 141 und 142 für deutsche Unternehmen, in: *Der Betrieb*, Vol. 54 (2001), No. 32, pp. 1681-1689.

Pellens, Bernhard and Sellhorn, Thorsten (2001b), Neue Goodwill-Bilanzierung nach US-GAAP – Der Impairment-Only Approach des FASB, in: *Der Betrieb*, Vol. 54 (2001), No. 14, pp. 713-720.

Pellens, Bernhard and Sellhorn, Thorsten (1999), Kapitalkonsolidierung nach der Fresh-Start-Methode, in: *Betriebs-Berater*, Vol. 54 (1999), No. 41, pp. 2125-2132.

Pellens, Bernhard, Sellhorn, Thorsten and Weinreis, Markus (2002), Verwirrung beim Anleger wegen der neuen Firmenwertbilanzierung – Ruhr-Universität Bochum befragt deutsche Unternehmen zu neuen Bilanzierungsregeln, in: *Frankfurter Allgemeine Zeitung* 2002, No. 93, p. 25.

Perry, Susan E. and Williams, Thomas H. (1994), Earnings management preceding management buyout offers, in: *Journal of Accounting and Economics*, Vol. 18 (1994), No. 2 (September), pp. 157-179.

Petersen, Christian (2002), Is goodwill value relevant – A Danish perspective, Frederiksberg: Copenhagen Business School, 2002.

Peterson, Pamela P. (1998), Event studies and their role in financial research, Florida State University, 1998.

Peterson, Pamela P. (1989), Event studies: A review of issues and methodology, in: *Quarterly Journal of Business and Economics*, Vol. 28 (1989), No. 3, pp. 36-66.

Pfeil, Oliver P. and Vater, Hendrik J. (2002a), "Die kleine Unternehmensbewertung" oder die neuen Vorschriften zur Goodwill- und Intangible-Bilanzierung nach SFAS No. 141 und SFAS No. 142 – Eine Analyse unter bilanziellen und finanzwirtschaftlichen Gesichtspunkten, in: *Kapitalmarktorientierte Rechnungslegung*, Vol. 2 (2002), No. 2, pp. 66-81.

Pfeil, Oliver P. and Vater, Hendrik J. (2002b), Neues über Goodwill und immaterielle Werte – Analyse der SFAS No. 141/142 Teil 1: Die Auswirkungen auf die Rechnungslegung nach US GAAP bilanzierender Unternehmen, in: *Der Schweizer Treuhänder*, Vol. 76 (2002), No. 6-7, pp. 585-589.

Pfeil, Oliver P. and Vater, Hendrik J. (2002c), SFAS No. 142: "Schlaraffenland" bilanzpolitischer Möglichkeiten? – Eine Analyse aus der Sicht eines Finanzanalysten, in: *Mergers and Acquisitions* 2002, No. 5, pp. 261-265.

Philbrick, Donna R. and Ricks, William E. (1991), Using Value Line and IBES analyst forecasts in accounting research, in: *Journal of Accounting Research*, Vol. 29 (1991), No. 2 (Autumn), pp. 397-417.

Pourciau, Susan (1993), Earnings management and nonroutine executive changes, in: *Journal of Accounting and Economics*, Vol. 16 (1993), No. 1-3, pp. 317-336.

Preinreich, Gabriel A. D. (1936), The law of goodwill, in: *The Accounting Review*, Vol. 11 (1936), No. 4 (December), pp. 317-329.

Press, Eric G. and Weintrop, Joseph B. (1990), Accounting-based constraints in public and private debt agreements – Their association with leverage and impact on accounting choice, in: *Journal of Accounting and Economics*, Vol. 12 (1990), No. 1-3, pp. 65-95.

Quantitative Micro Software, LLC (2002), EViews 4 User's Guide, Irvine: 2002.

Rammert, Stefan (1999), Pooling of interests – die Entdeckung eines Auslaufmodells durch deutsche Konzerne?, in: *Die Betriebswirtschaft*, Vol. 59 (1999), No. 5, pp. 620-632.

Rammert, Stefan and Wilhelm, Harald (1991a), Die Kapitalkonsolidierung in der Bilanzierungspraxis deutscher Konzerne (Teil I), in: *Die Wirtschaftsprüfung*, Vol. 44 (1991), No. 4, pp. 98-104.

Rammert, Stefan and Wilhelm, Harald (1991b), Die Kapitalkonsolidierung in der Bilanzierungspraxis deutscher Konzerne (Teil II), in: *Die Wirtschaftsprüfung*, Vol. 44 (1991), No. 5, pp. 131-136.

Rees, Lynn, Gill, Susan and Gore, Richard (1996), An investigation of asset write-downs and concurrent abnormal accruals, in: *Journal of Accounting Research*, Vol. 34 (1996), Supplement, pp. 157-169.

Richardson, Scott A., Teoh, Siew Hong and Wysocki, Peter D. (1999), Tracking analysts' forecasts over the annual earnings horizon: Are analysts' forecasts optimistic or pessimistic?, Ann Arbor: University of Michigan, 1999.

Richter, Michael (2004), Die Bewertung des Goodwill nach SFAS No. 141 und SFAS No. 142 – Eine kritische Würdigung des impairment only-Ansatzes, Düsseldorf: IDW-Verlag, 2004.

Riedl, Edward J. (2002), An examination of long-lived asset impairments, Pennsylvania State University: 2002.

Robinson, John R. and Shane, Philip B. (1990), Acquisition accounting method and bid premia for target firms, in: *The Accounting Review*, Vol. 65 (1990), No. 1 (January), pp. 25-48.

Ronen, Joshua and Sadan, Simcha (1981), Smoothing income numbers: Objectives, means, and implications, Reading, Massachusetts et al.: Addison-Wesley Publishing Company, 1981.

Ronen, Joshua and Sadan, Simcha (1975a), Classificatory smoothing: Alternative income models, in: *Journal of Accounting Research*, Vol. 13 (1975), Supplement, pp. 133-149.

Ronen, Joshua and Sadan, Simcha (1975b), Do corporations use their discretion in classifying accounting items to smooth reported income?, in: *Financial Analysts Journal*, Vol. 31 (1975), No. 5 (September/October), pp. 62-68.

Ruhnke, Klaus (2003), Neue Bilanzregeln stellen Prüfer vor kaum lösbare Aufgaben – Impairment-only-Approach zur Behandlung des Firmenwerts führt in Vertrauenskrise, in: *Frankfurter Allgemeine Zeitung* 2003, No. 31, p. 21.

S&P (2003), Corporate ratings criteria, New York: 2003.

S&P (2002), Standard & Poor's core earnings technical bulletin, New York: 2002.

S&P (2001), Standard & Poor's COMPUSTAT (North America) User's Guide, New York: 2001.

Sapienza, Samuel R. (1967), Discussion of Purchase versus pooling of interests: The search for a predictor, in: *Journal of Accounting Research*, Vol. 5 (1967), Supplement, pp. 205-209.

Sauthoff, Jan-Philipp (1996), Der Firmenwert im Konzernabschluß – Probleme der Bilanzierung und Aussagefähigkeit, Wiesbaden: Deutscher Universitäts Verlag, 1996.

Schildbach, Thomas (2001), Der Konzernabschluß nach HGB, IAS und US-GAAP, München/Wien: Oldenbourg, 6th ed. 2001.

Schildbach, Thomas (2000), Der handelsrechtliche Jahresabschluß, Herne/Berlin: Verlag Neue Wirtschaftsbriefe, 6th ed. 2000.

Schildbach, Thomas (1999), Pensionsverpflichtungen nach US-GAAP/IAS versus HGB/GoB und die Informationsfunktion des Jahresabschlusses, in: *Zeitschrift für Betriebswirtschaft (ZfB)*, Vol. 69 (1999), No. 9, pp. 957-977.

Schipper, Katherine (1991), Commentary on Analysts' Forecasts, in: *Accounting Horizons*, Vol. 5 (1991), No. 4 (December), pp. 105-121.

Schipper, Katherine (1989), Commentary on Earnings management, in: *Accounting Horizons*, Vol. 3 (1989), No. December, pp. 91-102.

Schmidt, Franz (1977), Die empirische Analyse bilanzpolitischer Entscheidungen unter besonderer Berücksichtigung der Gewinnglättung, Augsburg: Universität Augsburg, 1977.

Schneider, Dieter (1997), Betriebswirtschaftslehre, Band 2: Rechnungswesen, München/Wien: Oldenbourg, 2nd ed. 1997.

Schoderbek, Michael P. and Slaubaugh, Michael D. (2001), The FASB exposure draft on accounting for business combinations and intangible assets: an instructional assignment, in: *Journal of Accounting Education*, Vol. 19 (2001), pp. 265-281.

Schrand, Catherine M. and Walther, Beverly R. (2000), Strategic benchmarks in earnings announcements: The selective disclosure of prior-period earnings components, in: *The Accounting Review*, Vol. 75 (2000), No. 2 (April), pp. 151-177.

Schremper, Ralf (2002), Aktienrückkauf und Kapitalmarkt – Eine theoretische und empirische Analyse deutscher Aktienrückkaufprogramme, Frankfurt am Main et al.: Peter Lang, 2002.

Schultze, Wolfgang (2003), Interpretation des Goodwill-Impairments nach FAS 142 für Zwecke der Unternehmensanalyse und -steuerung, Augsburg: Universität Augsburg, 2003.

Schurbohm, Anne and Ganssauge, Karsten (2003), Erwartungslücke bei der Prüfung von Firmenwerten - IAS sind Herausforderung für Unternehmen und Prüfer, in: *Frankfurter Allgemeine Zeitung*, 27 January 2003, pp. 23.

Segal, Benjamin (2003), Goodwill write-downs and the adoption of SFAS No. 142, New York: New York University, 2003.

Sellhorn, Thorsten (2000), Ansätze zur bilanziellen Behandlung des Goodwill im Rahmen einer kapitalmarktorientierten Rechnungslegung, in: *Der Betrieb*, Vol. 53 (2000), No. 18, pp. 885-892.

Seppelfricke, Peter (1999), Moderne Multiplikatorverfahren bei der Aktien- und Unternehmensbewertung, in: *Finanz-Betrieb*, Vol. 1 (1999), No. 10, pp. 300-307.

Shank, John K. and Burnell, A. Michael (1974), Smooth your earnings growth rate, in: *Harvard Business Review*, Vol. 52 (1974), No. 1 (January/February), pp. 136-141.

Sieben, Günter and Coenenberg, Marc (1997), Grundlagen der Bilanzpolitik (I und II), in: *Das Wirtschaftsstudium*, Vol. 26 (1997), No. 11, pp. 1043-1047, 1143-1147.

Skinner, Douglas J. (1993), The investment opportunity set and accounting procedure choice – Preliminary evidence, in: *Journal of Accounting and Economics*, Vol. 16 (1993), No. 4, pp. 407-445.

Skinner, Douglas J. and Myers, Linda A. (1999), Earnings momentum and earnings management, Ann Arbor: University of Michigan, 1999.

Skinner, Douglas J. and Sloan, Richard G. (2001), Earnings surprises, growth expectations, and stock returns or Don't let an earnings torpedo sink your portfolio, Ann Arbor: University of Michigan, 2001.

Smith, Clifford W. (1993), A perspective on accounting-based debt covenant violations, in: *The Accounting Review*, Vol. 68 (1993), No. 2 (April), pp. 289-303.

Smith, Clifford W. and Warner, Jerold B. (1979), On financial contracting – An analysis of bond covenants, in: *Journal of Accounting and Economics*, Vol. 1 (1979), No. 2, pp. 117-161.

Smith, Clifford W. and Watts, Ross L. (1992), The investment opportunity set and corporate financing, dividend, and compensation policies, in: *Journal of Financial Economics*, Vol. 32 (1992), No. 3, pp. 263-292.

Smith, E. (1976), The effect of the separation of ownership from control on accounting policy decisions, in: *The Accounting Review*, Vol. 51 (1976), No. 4 (October), pp. 707-723.

Söffing, Günter (1988), Der Geschäfts- oder Firmenwert, in: Knobbe-Keuk, Brigitte, Klein, Franz and Moxter, Adolf (ed.), Handelsrecht und Steuerrecht – Festschrift für Dr. Dr. h. c. Georg Döllerer, Düsseldorf: IDW-Verlag, 1988, pp. 593-614.

Starbatty, Nikolaus (2001), Fair Value Accounting gemäß Statement of Financial Accounting Concept No. 7, in: *Die Wirtschaftsprüfung*, Vol. 54 (2001), No. 10, pp. 543-558.

Stauber, Jürgen and Ketterle, Tobias (2001), Goodwill-Bilanzierung nach US-GAAP – Die neuen Vorschriften des FASB im Vergleich – Auswirkungen für börsennotierte Schweizer Unternehmen, in: *Der Schweizer Treuhänder*, Vol. 75 (2001), No. 10, pp. 955-966.

Stone, Mary and Rasp, John (1991), Tradeoffs in the choice between logit and OLS for accounting choice studies, in: *The Accounting Review*, Vol. 66 (1991), No. 1 (January), pp. 170-187.

Streim, Hannes (1988), Grundzüge der handels- und steuerrechtlichen Bilanzierung, Stuttgart: Kohlhammer, 1988.

Streim, Hannes, Bieker, Marcus and Esser, Maik (2003), Vermittlung entscheidungsnützlicher Informationen durch Fair Values – Sackgasse oder Licht am Horizont?, in: *Betriebswirtschaftliche Forschung und Praxis*, Vol. 105 (2003), No. 4, pp. 457-479.

Strong, John S. and Meyer, John R. (1987), Asset writedowns: Managerial incentives and security returns, in: *Journal of Finance*, Vol. 42 (1987), No. 3 (July), pp. 643-663.

Subramanyam, K.R. (1996), The pricing of discretionary accruals, in: *Journal of Accounting and Economics*, Vol. 22 (1996), No. 1-3 (August-December), pp. 249-281.

Süchting, Joachim (1995), Finanzmanagement – Theorie und Politik der Unternehmensfinanzierung, Heidelberg: Gabler, 6th ed. 1995.

Sweeney, Amy P. (1994), Debt-covenant violations and managers' accounting responses, in: *Journal of Accounting and Economics*, Vol. 17 (1994), No. 3 (May), pp. 281-308.

Taub, Stephen (2003), AOL Time Warner reports $100 billion loss, www.cfo.com: 2003.

Teitler-Feinberg, Evelyn (2001), Neue Bewertung von Goodwill und anderen immateriellen Aktiven – Neue Bewertung nach US GAAP – Stand des Projektes des FASB, in: *Der Schweizer Treuhänder*, Vol. 75 (2001), No. 4, pp. 331-338.

Telkamp, Heinz-Jürgen and Bruns, Carsten (2000), Pooling-of-interests-Methode versus Fresh-Start-Methode – ein Vergleich, in: *Die Wirtschaftsprüfung*, Vol. 53 (2000), No. 16, pp. 744-749.

Tergesen, Anne (2002), How much is the goodwill worth?, in: Business Week, September 16, 2002.

Thomas, Jacob K. (1989), Unusual patterns in reported earnings, in: *The Accounting Review*, Vol. 64 (1989), No. 4 (October), pp. 773-787.

Thompson, Rex (1995), Empirical methods of event studies in corporate finance, in: Jarrow, R.A., Maksimovic, V. and Ziemba, W.T. (ed.), Finance, Amsterdam et al.: Elsevier, 1995, pp. 963-992.

Tinker, Tony and Puxty, Tony (1994), Policing accounting knowledge: The market for excuses affair, Princeton/London: Markus Wiener Publishers/Paul Chapman Publishing Ltd., 1994.

Tobin, James (1958), Estimation of relationships for limited dependent variables, in: *Econometrica*, Vol. 26 (1958), No. 1, pp. 24-36.

Trueman, Brett and Titman, Sheridan (1988), An explanation for accounting income smoothing, in: *Journal of Accounting Research*, Vol. 26 (1988), Supplement, pp. 127-139.

Vater, Hendrik J. (2001), M&A Accounting: Abschaffung des Pooling of Interests?, in: *Der Betrieb*, Vol. 54 (2001), No. 35, pp. 1841-1848.

Veall, Michael R. and Zimmermann, Klaus F. (1996), Pseudo-R^2 measures for some common limited dependent variable models, in: *Journal of Economic Surveys*, Vol. 10 (1996), No. 3, pp. 241-259.

Veit, Klaus-Rüdiger (2002), Bilanzpolitik, München: Vahlen, 2002.

Vincent, Linda (1997), Equity valuation implications of purchase versus pooling accounting, in: *Journal of Financial Statement Analysis*, Vol. 2 (1997), No. 4 (Summer), pp. 5-19.

Wagenhofer, Alfred (1988), Positive Theorie im Rechnungswesen – Zugleich Besprechungsaufsatz zu Watts und Zimmerman: Positive Accounting Theory, in: *Journal für Betriebswirtschaft* 1988, pp. 87-94.

Walkling, Ralph A. and Edmister, Robert O. (1985), Determinants of tender offer premiums, in: *Financial Analysts Journal*, Vol. 41 (1985), No. 1 (January/February), pp. 27-37.

Wang, Zhemin (1995), An empirical assessment of IASC's proposed goodwill amortization requirement, in: *International Journal of Accounting*, Vol. 30 (1995), No. 1, pp. 37-47.

Wang, Zhemin (1993), An empirical evaluation of goodwill accounting, in: *Journal of Applied Business Research*, Vol. 9 (1993), No. 4, pp. 127-133.

Warnock, Keith (1999), Approaches to persuasion: The submissions of major accounting firms on the goodwill debate in the United Kingdom and Ireland, http://panopticon.csustan.edu/cpa99/html/warnock.html: 1999.

Watts, Ross L. (1992), Accounting choice theory and market-based research in accounting, in: *British Accounting Review*, Vol. 24 (1992), pp. 235-267.

Watts, Ross L. (1977), Corporate financial statements, a product of the market and political processes, in: *Australian Journal of Management*, Vol. 2 (1977), pp. 53-78.

Watts, Ross L. and Zimmerman, Jerold L. (1990), Positive accounting theory: A ten year perspective, in: *The Accounting Review*, Vol. 65 (1990), No. 1 (January), pp. 131-156.

Watts, Ross L. and Zimmerman, Jerold L. (1986), Positive accounting theory, Englewood Cliffs, New Jersey: Prentice-Hall, 1986.

Watts, Ross L. and Zimmerman, Jerold L. (1979), The demand for and supply of accounting theories: The market for excuses, in: *The Accounting Review*, Vol. 54 (1979), No. 2 (April), pp. 273-305.

Watts, Ross L. and Zimmerman, Jerold L. (1978), Towards a positive theory of the determination of accounting standards, in: *The Accounting Review*, Vol. 53 (1978), No. 1 (January), pp. 112-134.

Waymire, Gregory (1988), Discussion of Write-offs as accounting procedures to manage perceptions, in: *Journal of Accounting Research*, Vol. 26 (1988), Supplement, pp. 120-126.

Weber, Claus-Peter and Zündorf, Horst (1998), Commentary on section 309 HGB, in: Schmidt, Karsten (ed.), Handbuch der Konzernrechnungslegung – Kommentar zur Bilanzierung und Prüfung, Volume II, München: C. H. Beck, 1998, pp. 1641-1664.

Weber, Claus-Peter and Zündorf, Horst (1989), Der Posten "Geschäfts- oder Firmenwert" im Konzernabschluß, in: *Der Betrieb*, Vol. 42 (1989), No. 7, pp. 333-340.

Weber, Joseph P. (2000), Share wealth effects of pooling-of-interests accounting: Evidence from the SEC's restriction on share repurchases following pooling transactions, Cambridge, MA: Massachusetts Institute of Technology, 2000.

Weisbach, Michael S. (1988), Outside directors and CEO turnover, in: *Journal of Financial Economics*, Vol. 20 (1988), No. 1/2 (January-March), pp. 431-460.

White, Gerald I., Sondhi, Ashwinpaul C. and Fried, Dov (2003), The analysis and use of financial statements, New York et al.: John Wiley & Sons, Inc., 3rd ed. 2003.

White, Gerald I., Sondhi, Ashwinpaul C. and Fried, Dov (1997), The analysis and use of financial statements, New York et al.: John Wiley & Sons, Inc., 2nd ed. 1997.

Wilkins, Michael S., Swanson, Edward P. and Loudder, Martha L. (1998), Market valuation of goodwill and other intangible assets: The United States as a laboratory market for IASC E60 and E61, in: *Advances in International Accounting*, Vol. 11 (1998), No. 1, pp. 117-132.

Williams, Jan R. (2002), 2002 Miller GAAP Guide – Restatement and analysis of current FASB standards, New York/Gaithersburg: Aspen Publishers, 2002.

Williamson, Oliver E. (1975), Markets and hierarchies: Analysis and antitrust implications – a study in the economics of internal organization, New York: Free Press, 1975.

Wilson, G. Peter (1996), Discussion of Write-offs: Manipulation or impairment, in: *Journal of Accounting Research*, Vol. 34 (1996), Supplement, pp. 171-177.

Wines, Graeme and Ferguson, Colin (1993), An empirical investigation of accounting methods for goodwill and identifiable intangible assets: 1985 to 1989, in: *Abacus*, Vol. 29 (1993), No. 1, pp. 90-105.

Winker, Peter (1997), Empirische Wirtschaftsforschung, Berlin et al.: Springer, 1997.

Wöhe, Günter (1980), Zur Bilanzierung und Bewertung des Firmenwertes, in: *Steuer und Wirtschaft* 1980, No. 2, pp. 89-108.

Wong, Jilnaught and Wong, Norman (2001), The investment opportunity set and acquired goodwill, in: *Contemporary Accounting Research*, Vol. 18 (2001), No. 1 (Spring), pp. 173-196.

Wu, Y. Woody (1997), Management buyouts and earnings management, in: *Journal of Accounting, Auditing and Finance*, Vol. 12 (1997), No. 2 (Spring), pp. 373-389.

Wüstemann, Jens and Duhr, Andreas (2003), Geschäftswertbilanzierung nach dem Exposure Draft ED 3 des IASB – Entobjektivierung auf den Spuren des FASB?, in: *Betriebs-Berater*, Vol. 58 (2003), No. 5, pp. 247-253.

Wyatt, Arthur Ramer (1983), Efficient market theory: Its impact on accounting, in: *Journal of Accountancy*, Vol. 155 (1983), No. 2 (February), pp. 56-65.

Wyatt, Arthur Ramer (1967), Discussion of Purchase versus pooling of interests: The search for a predictor, in: *Journal of Accounting Research*, Vol. 5 (1967), Supplement, pp. 210-212.

Wyatt, Arthur Ramer (1963), A critical study of accounting for business combinations, New York: American Institute of Certified Public Accountants, 1963.

Wyrwich, Philip H. (2002), Goodwill-Wertberichtigung nach US-GAAP – Eine Analyse aus dem Blickwinkel der positiven Regulierungstheorie, Bochum: Ruhr-Universität Bochum, 2002.

Zarowin, Paul (2002), Does smoothing make stock prices more informative?, New York: New York University, 2002.

Zeff, Stephen A. (2002), "Political" lobbying on proposed standards: A challenge to the IASB, in: *Accounting Horizons*, Vol. 16 (2002), No. 1 (March), pp. 43-54.

Zielke, Wolfgang (1995), Zur Behandlung des Goodwill im Konzernabschluß, in: Lanfermann, Josef (ed.), Internationale Wirtschaftsprüfung – Festschrift zum 65. Geburtstag von Prof. Dr. Dr. h.c. Hans Havermann, Düsseldorf: IDW-Verlag, 1995, pp. 829-843.

Zimmerman, Jerold L. (1983), Taxes and firm size, in: *Journal of Accounting and Economics*, Vol. 5 (1983), No. 2 (August), pp. 119-149.

Zmijewski, M. and Hagerman, R. (1981), An income strategy approach to the positive theory of accounting standard setting/choice, in: *Journal of Accounting and Economics*, Vol. 3 (1981), No. 2 (August), pp. 129-149.

Zucca, Linda J. and Campbell, David R. (1992), A closer look at discretionary writedowns of impaired assets, in: *Accounting Horizons*, Vol. 6 (1992), No. 3 (September), pp. 30-41.

List of accounting pronouncements and legal provisions

APB Opinions

(Printed in: FASB, Original pronouncements, 2002/2003 edition – Accounting Standards as of June 1, 2002, Vol. III, New York et al.: John Wiley & Sons, Inc., 2002.)

APB Opinion 16, Business Combinations, August 1970.

APB Opinion 17, Intangible Assets, August 1970.

APB Opinion 18, The Equity Method of Accounting for Investments in Common Stock, March 1971.

APB Opinion 20, Accounting Changes, July 1971.

APB Opinion 30, Reporting the Results of Operations--Reporting the Effects of Disposal of a Segment of a Business, and Extraordinary, Unusual and Infrequently Occurring Events and Transactions, June 1973.

IAS

(Printed in: IASB, International Financial Reporting Standards 2003 incorporating International Accounting Standards and Interpretations – The full text of all International Financial Reporting Standards extant at 1 January 2003, London: International Accounting Standards Committee Foundation, 2003.)

IAS 22, Business Combinations, July 1998.

IAS 36, Impairment of Assets, January 2001.

IAS 38, Intangible Assets, July 1998.

SFAC

(Printed in: FASB, Original pronouncements, 2002/2003 edition – Accounting Standards as of June 1, 2002, Vol. III, New York et al.: John Wiley & Sons, Inc., 2002.)

SFAC 1, Objectives of Financial Reporting by Business Enterprises, November 1978.

SFAC 2, Qualitative Characteristics of Accounting Information, May 1980.

SFAC 7, Using Cash Flow Information and Present Value in Accounting Measurements, February 2000.

SFAS

(Printed in: FASB, Original pronouncements, 2002/2003 edition – Accounting Standards as of June 1, 2002, Vol. I and II, New York et al.: John Wiley & Sons, Inc., 2002. Available for download at http://www.fasb.org/st/.)

SFAS 3, Reporting Accounting Changes in Interim Financial Statements—an amendment of APB Opinion No. 28, December 1974.

SFAS 5, Accounting for Contingencies, March 1975.

SFAS 38, Accounting for Preacquisition Contingencies of Purchased Enterprises—an amendment of APB Opinion No. 16, September 1980.

SFAS 71, Accounting for the Effects of Certain Types of Regulation, December 1982.

SFAS 87, Employers' Accounting for Pensions, December 1985.

SFAS 90, Regulated Enterprises-Accounting for Abandonments and Disallowances of Plant Costs—an amendment of FASB Statement No. 71, December 1986.

SFAS 94, Consolidation of All Majority-owned Subsidiaries—an amendment of ARB No. 51, with related amendments of APB Opinion No. 18 and ARB No. 43, Chapter 12, October 1987.

SFAS 95, Statement of Cash Flows, November 1987.

SFAS 106, Employers' Accounting for Postretirement Benefits Other Than Pensions, December 1990.

SFAS 109, Accounting for Income Taxes, February 1992.

SFAS 114, Accounting by Creditors for Impairment of a Loan—an amendment of FASB Statements No. 5 and 15, May 1993.

SFAS 115, Accounting for Certain Investments in Debt and Equity Securities, May 1993.

SFAS 121, Accounting for the Impairment of Long-Lived Assets and for Long-Lived Assets to Be Disposed Of, March 1995.

SFAS 123, Accounting for Stock-Based Compensation, October 1995.

SFAS 131, Disclosures about Segments of an Enterprise and Related Information, June 1997.

SFAS 133, Accounting for Derivative Instruments and Hedging Activities, June 1998.

SFAS 140, Accounting for Transfers and Servicing of Financial Assets and Extinguishments of Liabilities-a replacement of FASB Statement No. 125, September 2000.

SFAS 141, Business Combinations, June 2001.

SFAS 142, Goodwill and Other Intangible Assets, June 2001.

SFAS 143, Accounting for Asset Retirement Obligations, June 2001.

SFAS 144, Accounting for the Impairment or Disposal of Long-Lived Assets, August 2001.

Other regulation

Aktiengesetz (German Stock Corporation Act) of 6 September 1965. (Status: 1 October, 2002.)

EITF Issue 98-03, Determining Whether a Nonmonetary Transaction Involves Receipt of Productive Assets or of a Business. (Printed in: FASB, EITF Abstracts – A Summary of Proceedings of the FASB Emerging Issues Task Force as of September 20 and 28, 2001, Norwalk, CT: Financial Accounting Standards Board, 2001.)

European "Consolidated accounts" directive. (Seventh Council Directive 83/349/EEC of 13.6.1983 based on the Article 54 (3) (g) of the Treaty.)

FASB Exposure Draft, Business Combinations and Intangible Assets – Accounting for Goodwill, February 2001.

FIN 4, Applicability of FASB Statement No. 2 to Business Combinations Accounted for by the Purchase Method, an Interpretation of FASB Statement No. 2, February 1975. (Printed in: FASB, Original pronouncements, 2002/2003 edition – Accounting Standards as of June 1, 2002, Vol. III, New York et al.: John Wiley & Sons, Inc., 2002.)

GAS 1a, Exempting Consolidated Financial Statements in accordance with § 292a of the Commercial Code, January 2002. (Printed in: DRSC, Deutsche Rechnungslegungs Standards (DRS) – German Accounting Standards (GAS), Stand: September 2002, Stuttgart: Schäffer-Poeschel, 2002.)

GAS 4, Acquisition Accounting in Consolidated Financial Statements, August 2000. (Printed in: DRSC, Deutsche Rechnungslegungs Standards (DRS) – German Accounting Standards (GAS), Stand: September 2002, Stuttgart: Schäffer-Poeschel, 2002.)

Handelsgesetzbuch (German Commercial Code) of 10 May, 1897. (Status: 1 October, 2002.)

IASB ED 3, Business Combinations, December 2002.

IASB ED-IAS 36, Impairment of Assets, December 2002.

IASB IAS 36, Impairment of Assets, March 2004.

IASB IFRS 3, Business Combinations, March 2004.

SEC Concept Release, Rating Agencies and the Use of Credit Ratings under the Federal Securities Laws. (Available for download at http://www.sec.gov/rules/ concept/33-8236.htm.)

Bochumer Beiträge zur Unternehmungsführung und Unternehmensforschung

Herausgegeben vom Direktorium des Instituts
für Unternehmungsführung und Unternehmensforschung
der Ruhr-Universität Bochum

Band 1 Busse von Colbe, Walther/Mattessich, Richard (Hrsg.): Der Computer im Dienste der Unternehmungsführung (1968)

Band 2 Busse von Colbe, Walther/Meyer-Dohm, Peter (Hrsg.): Unternehmerische Planung und Entscheidung (1969)

Band 3 Anthony, Robert N.: Harvard-Fälle aus der Praxis des betrieblichen Rechnungswesens. Herausgegeben von Richard V. Mattessich unter Mitarbeit von Klaus Herrnberger und Wolf Lange (1969)

Band 4 Mattessich, Richard: Die wissenschaftlichen Grundlagen des Rechnungswesens (1970)

Band 5 Schweim, Joachim: Integrierte Unternehmungsplanung (1969)

Band 6 Busse von Colbe, Walther (Hrsg.): Das Rechnungswesen als Instrument der Unternehmungsführung (1969)

Band 7 Domsch, Michel: Simultane Personal- und Investitionsplanung im Produktionsbereich (1970)

Band 8 Leunig, Manfred: Die Bilanzierung von Beteiligungen. Eine bilanztheoretische Untersuchung (1970)

Band 9 Franke, Reimund: Betriebsmodelle. Rechensystem für Zwecke der kurzfristigen Planung, Kontrolle und Kalkulation (1972)

Band 10 Wittenbrink, Hartwig: Kurzfristige Erfolgsplanung und Erfolgskontrolle mit Betriebsmodellen (1975)

Band 11 Lutter, Marcus (Hrsg.): Recht und Steuer der internationalen Unternehmensverbindungen (1972)

Band 12 Niebling, Helmut: Kurzfristige Finanzrechnung auf der Grundlage von Kosten- und Erlösmodellen (1973)

Band 13 Perlitz, Manfred: Die Prognose des Unternehmenswachstums aus Jahresabschlüssen deutscher Aktiengesellschaften (1973)

Band 14 Niggemann, Walter: Optimale Informationsprozesse in betriebswirtschaftlichen Entscheidungssituationen (1973)

Band 15 Richardt, Harald: Der aktienrechtliche Abhängigkeitsbericht unter ökonomischen Aspekten (1974)

Band 16 Backhaus, Klaus: Direktvertrieb in der Investitionsgüterindustrie – Eine Marketing-Entscheidung (1974)

Band 17 Plinke, Wulff: Kapitalsteuerung in Filialbanken (1975)

Band 18 Steffen, Rainer: Produktionsplanung bei Fließbandfertigung (1977)

Band 19 Kolb, Jürgen: Industrielle Erlösrechnung – Grundlagen und Anwendungen (1978)

Band 20 Busse von Colbe, Walther/Lutter, Marcus (Hrsg.): Wirtschaftsprüfung heute: Entwicklung oder Reform? (1977)

Band 21 Uphues, Peter: Unternehmerische Anpassung in der Rezession (1979)

Band 22 Gebhardt, Günther: Insolvenzprognosen aus aktienrechtlichen Jahresabschlüssen (1980)

Band 23 Domsch, Michel: Systemgestützte Personalarbeit (1980)

Band 24 Schmied, Volker: Alternativen der Arbeitsgestaltung und ihre Bewertung (1982)

Band 25 Wäscher, Gerhard: Innerbetriebliche Standortplanung bei einfacher und mehrfacher Zielsetzung (1982)

Band 26 Weber, Martin: Entscheidungen bei Mehrfachzielen – Verfahren zur Unterstützung von Individual- und Gruppenentscheidungen (1983)

Band 27 Kroesen, Alfred: Instandhaltungsplanung und Betriebsplankostenrechnung (1983)

Band 28 Plinke, Wulf: Erlösplanung im industriellen Anlagengeschäft (1985)

Band 29 Chamoni, Peter: Simulation störanfälliger Systeme (1986)

Band 30 Arning, Andreas: Die wirtschaftliche Bewertung der Zentrenfertigung – Dargestellt am Beispiel einer Fertigungsinsel (1987)

Band 31 Gebhardt, Günther: Finanzielle Planung und Kontrolle bei internationaler Unternehmenstätigkeit

Band 32 Markiewicz, Michael: Ersatzteildisposition im Maschinenbau – Betriebswirtschaftliche Methoden der Planung und Überwachung (1988)

Band 33 Pellens, Bernd: Der Informationswert von Konzernabschlüssen – Eine empirische Untersuchung deutscher Börsengesellschaften (1989)

Band 34 Mrotzek, Rüdiger: Bewertung direkter Auslandsinvestitionen mit Hilfe betrieblicher Investitionskalküle (1989)

Band 35 Deppe, Joachim: Quality Circle und Lernstatt – Ein integrativer Ansatz (1989, 3. Auflage 1993)

Band 36 Rademacher, Michael: Arbeitszeitverkürzung und -flexibilisierung – Formen und betriebliche Auswirkungen (1990)

Band 37 Kaiser, Klaus: Kosten- und Leistungsrechung bei automatisierter Produktion (1991, 2. Auflage 1993)

Band 38 Müller, Hermann: Industrielle Abfallbewältigung – Entscheidungsprobleme aus betriebswirtschaftlicher Sicht (1991)

Band 39 Schörner, Peter: Gesetzliches Insiderhandelsverbot – Eine ordnungspolitische Analyse (1991)

Band 40 Bentler, Martin: Grundsätze ordnungsmäßiger Bilanzierung für die Equitymethode (1991)

Band 41 Brüggerhoff, Jürgen: Management von Desinvestitionen (1992)

Band 42 Bröker, Erich W.: Erfolgsrechnung im industriellen Anlagengeschäft – Ein dynamischer Ansatz auf Zahlungsbasis – (1993)

Band 43 Frankenberg, Peter: Transnationale Analyse US-amerikanischer und deutscher Jahresabschlüsse – Eine theoretische und empirische Untersuchung (1993)

Band 44 Kleinaltenkamp, Michael: Standardisierung und Marktprozeß – Entwicklungen und Auswirkungen im CIM-Bereich (1993)

Band 45 Pellens, Bernhard: Aktionärsschutz im Konzern – Empirische und theoretische Analyse der Reformvorschläge der Konzernverfassung (1994)

Band 46 Reckenfelderbäumer, Martin: Marketing-Accounting im Dienstleistungsbereich – Konzeption eines prozeßkostengestützten Instrumentariums (1995)

Band 47 Knittel, Friedrich: Technikgestützte Kommunikation und Kooperation im Büro. Entwicklungshindernisse – Einsatzstrategien – Gestaltungskonzepte (1995)

Band 48 Riezler, Stephan: Lebenszyklusrechnung – Instrument des Controlling strategischer Projekte (1996)

Band 49 Schulte, Jörn: Rechnungslegung und Aktienkursentwicklung – Erklärung und Prognose von Aktienrenditen durch Einzel- und Konzernabschlußdaten (1996)

Band 50 Muhr, Martin: Zeitsparmodelle in der Industrie – Grundlagen und betriebswirtschaftliche Bedeutung mehrjähriger Arbeitszeitkonten (1996)

Band 51 Brotte, Jörg: US-amerikanische und deutsche Geschäftsberichte. Notwendigkeit, Regulierung und Praxis jahresabschlußergänzender Informationen (1997)

Band 52 Gersch, Martin: Vernetzte Geschäftsbeziehungen. Die Nutzung von EDI als Instrument des Geschäftsbeziehungsmanagement (1998)

Band 53 Währisch, Michael: Kostenrechnungspraxis in der deutschen Industrie. Eine empirische Studie (1998)

Band 54 Völkner, Peer: Modellbasierte Planung von Geschäftsprozeßabläufen (1998)

Band 55 Fülbier, Rolf Uwe: Regulierung der Ad-hoc-Publizität. Ein Beitrag zur ökonomischen Analyse des Rechts (1998)

Band 1 - 55 erschienen beim Gabler Verlag Wiesbaden

Band 56 Ane-Kristin Reif-Mosel: Computergestützte Kooperation im Büro. Gestaltung unter Berücksichtigung der Elemente *Aufgabe, Struktur, Technik* und *Personal* (2000)

Band 57 Claude Tomaszewski: Bewertung strategischer Flexibilität beim Unternehmenserwerb. Der Wertbeitrag von Realoptionen (2000)

Band 58 Thomas Erler: Business Objects als Gestaltungskonzept strategischer Informationssystemplanung (2000)

Band 59 Joachim Gassen: Datenbankgestützte Rechnungslegungspublizität. Ein Beitrag zur Evolution der Rechnungslegung (2000)

Band 60 Frauke Streubel: Organisatorische Gestaltung und Informationsmanagement in der lernenden Unternehmung. Bausteine eines Managementkonzeptes organisationalen Lernens (2000)

Band 61 Andreas von der Gathen: Marken in Jahresabschluß und Lagebericht (2001)

Band 62 Lars Otterpohl: Koordination in nichtlinearen dynamischen Systemen (2002)

Band 63 Ralf Schremper: Aktienrückkauf und Kapitalmarkt. Eine theoretische und empirische Analyse deutscher Aktienrückkaufprogramme (2002)

Band 64 Peter Ruhwedel: Aufsichtsratsplanungssysteme. Theoretische Grundlagen und praktische Ausgestaltung in Publikumsaktiengesellschaften (2002)

Band 65 Jens Thorn: Taktisches Supply Chain Planning. Planungsunterstützung durch deterministische und stochastische Optimierungsmodelle (2002)

Band 66 Dirk Beier: Informationsmanagement aus Sicht der Betriebswirtschaftslehre. Theoretische Ansätze und das Beispiel Mobile Business. (2002)

Band 67 Nils Crasselt: Wertorientierte Managemententlohnung, Unternehmensrechnung und Investitionssteuerung. Analyse unter Berücksichtigung von Realoptionen. (2003)

Band 68 Franca Ruhwedel: Eigentümerstruktur und Unternehmenserfolg. Eine theoretische und empirische Analyse deutscher börsennotierter Unternehmen. (2003)

Band 69 Andreas Bonse: Informationsgehalt von Konzernabschlüssen nach HGB, IAS und US-GAAP. Eine empirische Analyse aus Sicht der Eigenkapitalgeber. (2004)

Band 70 Thorsten Sellhorn: Goodwill Impairment. An Empirical Investigation of Write-Offs under SFAS 142. (2004)

Peter Lang · Europäischer Verlag der Wissenschaften

Ingo Tschach

The Theory of Development Finance

How Microcredit Programmes Alleviate Credit and Labour Market Segmentation

Frankfurt am Main, Berlin, Bern, Bruxelles, New York, Oxford, Wien, 2002.
XIII, 160 pp., 64 fig., 3 tab.
Development and Finance.
Edited by Manfred Nitsch, Reinhard H. Schmidt and Claus Peter Zeitinger. Vol. 11
ISBN 3-631-39203-6 / US-ISBN 0-8204-5493-1 · pb. € 39.00*

The book explores the problem of credit market segmentation, a widespread phenomenon in developing countries, within a theoretical framework based on graphical analysis. It investigates the causes and effects of this problem, and the impact of possible solutions. Credit market segmentation is an outgrowth of information-related problems and high transaction costs in lending. It leads to segmentation in labour markets and also results in inefficient factor allocation and highly skewed income distribution patterns. A theoretical impact analysis shows that microcredit programmes can eliminate the causes and effects of credit market segmentation and that their impact is much broader than is usually assumed. This book should be required reading for everyone who is interested in microcredit.

Contents: The Theoretical Derivation of Credit Market Segmentation · The Impacts of Credit Market Segmentation · Approaches Taken by Successful Small Loan Programmes · Impact Analysis of Small Loan Programmes: How They Affect Financial Markets, Labour Markets, Factor Allocation, Income Distribution and Growth